Migration Law in Canada

Migration Law in Canada

Second Edition

Sharryn J. Aiken
Donald Galloway
Colin Grey
Audrey Macklin

This book was originally published as a monograph in the International Encyclopaedia of Laws/Migration Law.

General Editors: Roger Blanpain, Frank Hendrickx
Volume Editor: Dirk Vanheule

Wolters Kluwer
Law & Business

Published by:
Kluwer Law International
PO Box 316
2400 AH Alphen aan den Rijn
The Netherlands
Website: www.kluwerlaw.com

Sold and distributed in North, Central and South America by:
Aspen Publishers, Inc.
7201 McKinney Circle
Frederick, MD 21704
United States of America
Email: customer.service@aspenpublishers.com

Sold and distributed in all other countries by:
Turpin Distribution Services Ltd.
Stratton Business Park
Pegasus Drive, Biggleswade
Bedfordshire SG18 8TQ
United Kingdom
Email: kluwerlaw@turpin-distribution.com

ISBN 978-90-411-6013-3

This title is available on www.kluwerlawonline.com

The Authors

Sharryn J. Aiken is an Associate Professor and Associate Dean in the faculty of law at Queen's University where she teaches international refugee law, immigration law and administrative law. Prior to her current academic appointment, Sharry practiced immigration and refugee law with legal aid clinics in Toronto and in private practice. A past President of the Canadian Council for Refugees and former editor-in-chief of *Refuge* (2001–2011), Sharry continues to be actively engaged in scholarship and advocacy on migration related issues.

Donald Galloway specializes in immigration law, refugee law and citizenship law. He is a former member of the Immigration and Refugee Board of Canada and is currently the President of the Canadian Association for Refugee and Forced Migration Studies. As well as authoring two texts on immigration and refugee law, he has published several articles in the fields of criminal law, tort law and legal theory. Professor Galloway is co-chair of the Legal Research Committee of the Canadian Association of Refugee Lawyers (CARL).

The Authors

Colin Grey holds a doctorate in juridical science and a master of laws from New York University, and a bachelor of laws from the University of Toronto. He is a member of the Ontario bar, and is presently legal advisor to the Immigration and Refugee Board of Canada. He has worked in Bangkok, Thailand for the UNHCR, and clerked for the Ontario Court of Appeal. His has presented and published scholarly work on justice and authority in immigration. The views expressed in this entry are those of the authors and do not reflect, nor should they be attributed to, the Immigration and Refugee Board.

Audrey Macklin is Professor of Law at the University of Toronto and Chair in Human Rights Law. She teaches, researches and writes in the fields of administrative law, migration, multiculturalism, gender and culture, and business and human rights. From 1994–1996, she adjudicated asylum claims as a Member of Canada's Immigration and Refugee Board. She has co-authored a text on Canadian immigration and refugee law, and has published in legal and inter-disciplinary academic journals and edited volumes. She is a founding member of the Canadian Association of Refugee Lawyers. Many of Prof Macklin's publications are listed and available at http://www.law.utoronto.ca/faculty-staff/full-time-faculty/audrey-macklin.

Table of Contents

List of Abbreviations

BOC	Basis of Claim
BRRA	Balanced Refugee Reform Act
BSO	Border Services Officer
CAD	Canadian Dollars
CAQ	Québec Certificate of Acceptance
CAT	Convention against Torture
CBSA	Canada Border Services Agency
CEC	Canadian Experience Class
Charter	Canadian Charter of Rights and Freedoms
CIC	Ministry of Citizenship and Immigration Canada
CSQ	Quebec Selection Certificate
DCO	Designated Countries of Origin
FCA	Federal Courts Act
FSW	Foreign Skilled Worker
GATS	General Agreement on Trade in Services
Gender Guidelines	Guideline 4: Women Refugee Claimants Fearing Gender-Related Persecution
H&C	Humanitarian and compassionate discretion
ESDC/HRSDC	Employment and Social Development Canada (2014 +)/ Human Resources and Skills Development Canada (pre-2014)
IAD	Immigration Appeal Division
IBET	Integrated Border Enforcement Teams
ICCPR	International Covenant on Civil and Political Rights
ICCRC	Immigration Consultants of Canada Regulatory Council
ID	Immigration Division
IJMT	International Joint Management Team
IRB	Immigration and Refugee Board
IRPA/Act	Immigration and Refugee Protection Act
IRPR/Regulations	Immigration and Refugee Protection Regulations

List of Abbreviations

IT	Information Technology
LMIA/LMO	Labour Market Impact Assessment (July 2014 +)/ Labour-Market Opinion (pre-July 2014)
Ministry	Ministry of Citizenship and Immigration
NAFTA	North American Free Trade Agreement
NOC	National Occupational Classification
PIL	Primary Inspection Line
POE	Port of Entry
PRRA	Pre-removal Risk Assessment
PRV	Permanent Resident Visa
QSC	Québec Selection Certificate
RAD	Refugee Appeal Division
RCMP	Royal Canadian Mounted Police
Refugee Convention	Convention Relating to the Status of Refugees
RIAS	Regulatory Impact Analysis Statement
RPD	Refugee Protection Division
SAWP	Seasonal Agricultural Worker Programme
TFW	Temporary Foreign Worker
TRP	Temporary Resident Permit
TRV	Temporary Resident Visa
UNHCR	United Nations High Commissioner for Refugees

Online Sources (as of 31 July 2014)

The Immigration and Refugee Protection Act, SC 2001, c27, available online at http://laws-lois.justice.gc.ca/eng/acts/I-2.5/index.html

Immigration and Refugee Protection Regulations, SOR/2002-227, available online at http://laws-lois.justice.gc.ca/eng/regulations/SOR-2002-227/index.html

Operational Manual and Bulletins http://www.cic.gc.ca/english/resources/manuals

Note that as of August 2014, several parts of the Operational Manual appear to be undergoing revision and withdrawal from public access. Readers are advised that the authors cannot assure the availability or URL location for individual chapters.

Preface

Canada is a paradigmatic settler society. One effect of this path to statehood is that Canada is not merely a country of immigration in the *descriptive* sense. Canada is a *normative* country of immigration insofar as the dominant national narrative accepts and even celebrates immigration (though not necessarily all immigrants) as constitutive of the state and the nation. Canada was and continues to be built by immigrants. This helps explains certain fundamental features of Canadian immigration law that distinguish it from countries that receive large numbers of migrants but resist identifying themselves as normative countries of immigration. One of the most significant implications of Canada's position as settler society is that permanent immigration and relatively easy access to citizenship have, until very recently, been the foundation of Canada's migration regime.

This monograph provides a survey of Canadian migration law, which comprehends both immigration and refugee law. We do not address citizenship law except as a means of explaining who is *not* a migrant. Our account describes the constitutional framework, the legislative sources, as well as the regulations and other subordinate legal instruments enacted by the executive under delegated statutory authority. Much of the practical guidance to front-line decision-makers is contained in the vast compendium known as the Operational Manual, which is issued by Citizenship and Immigration Canada (CIC). While technically non-binding 'soft law', it is relied upon extensively by CIC decision-makers. We reference case law from the Immigration and Refugee Board (IRB) (an administrative tribunal), the Federal Court and Federal Court of Appeal, and the Supreme Court of Canada.

Canadian immigration and refugee law has been undergoing rapid, ceaseless and profound change since 2007, coinciding with the election of a politically conservative government. More than other areas of Canadian law, immigration and refugee legislation is skeletal legislation. It is minimal in content, and delegates to the executive broad authority to govern through subordinate regulation. It also grants the Minister of Citizenship and Immigration wide discretion in the execution of his or her statutory functions. These traits mean that major alterations to immigration and refugee law may be accomplished without formal legislative amendment, and may also be insulated from effective judicial scrutiny. This monograph situates Canadian immigration and refugee policy in the context of a reasonably stable framework over the last forty years, but the reader should be alert to the fact of its recent, ongoing, and dramatic evolution.

General Introduction[1]

§1. Immigration History and Statistical Information

1. The territory now known as Canada was already populated by indigenous people when European settlers arrived in the sixteenth century. But the Canadian state, its institutions and its policies were devised by and for settlers. The French established the first permanent settlements in New France (now Québec) in the early seventeenth century. The British soon followed, and ultimately wrested control from France in 1763. French migration to North America more or less ceased thereafter. Great Britain then moved to consolidate control over British North America. Populating the sparsely inhabited and vast territory became a chronic pre-occupation. About 50,000 Loyalists fled north to Canada in the wake of the British defeat in the US War of Independence. This number included around 3,000 Black Loyalists, former slaves who had been promised freedom by the British in exchange for military service. Emigration from Britain, especially Ireland, constituted the main source of Canada's population growth prior to Confederation in 1867. Upon Confederation, the newly self-governing Dominion of Canada had a non-indigenous population of about 3.5 million. It devoted considerable effort to attracting immigrant settlers. Under section 91(25) of the British North America Act, the federal government exercised exclusive jurisdiction over 'aliens and naturalization', but shared concurrent jurisdiction over immigration with the provinces (section 95). In practice, however, the provincial governments ceded responsibility entirely to the federal government.

2. Canada promoted immigration for political, military, economic and social reasons. First, consolidating governance over the vast territory of Canada required a population base capable of linking the territories and provinces. Second, a well-populated Canada would provide a bulwark against the expansionist ambitions of the United States to the south. Third, developing a viable economy across the vast

1. Unless otherwise noted, the material in the historical survey is drawn from the following publications and the sources cited therein: Sharryn Aiken, '*From Slavery to Expulsion: Racism, Immigration Law and the Unfulfilled Promise of Modern Constitutionalism*' in *Interrogating Race and Racism,* Ch. 2 (Vijay Agnew, ed., U of Toronto Press, 2007); Donald Galloway, *Immigration Law* (Irwin Law, 1997); Ninette Kelley and Michael Trebilcock, *The Making of the Mosaic: A History of Canadian Immigration Policy* (2d ed., U of Toronto Press, 2010); Valerie Knowles, *Strangers at our Gates: Canadian Immigration and Immigration Policy* 1540–1990 (Dundurn Press, 1992).

expanse of British North America demanded a population of producers and consumers capable of supporting agricultural and industrial growth. Finally, the production and articulation of a (non-indigenous) Canadian national identity literally required more people, not just as workers, but as 'nation builders' in a demographic and social sense.

3. Many of the structural features of contemporary immigration law were set in two periods: the early twentieth century, and the 1960s and 1970s. The earliest immigration legislation did not focus on regulating admission. Rather, it mainly addressed the conditions aboard ships transporting immigrants on their transatlantic voyage to Canada, with a view to preventing the arrival of sick paupers. From the beginning, the Canadian government expended significant resources on attracting 'desirable' immigrants to Canada. Its ambitions strained against various persistent impediments. First, immigration policy was marked by chronic disjuncture: between the type of people that Canada sought to attract and those who actually wished to immigrate; between the occupational shortfalls that the government believed to exist, and the actual demands and opportunities in the existing labour market; and between where the government wanted people to settle and where immigrants would and did settle. Second, other settler societies, most importantly the United States, exerted a more powerful pull on emigrants than Canada. More emigrants chose the more prosperous United States than Canada, and secondary migration from Canada to the United States indicated that retention was also a problem. Virtually identical challenges characterize Canadian immigration law and policy in the twenty-first century: policy objectives and instruments align imperfectly with actual preferences, motivations, demand and supply of immigrants and labour markets. Canada still competes for immigrants against the United States and other states. And the conventional fiscal, economic and cultural objections to immigration remain virtually unchanged, even though main source countries of immigration have shifted.

4. By the early twentieth century, Canada had expanded its definition of preferred source countries from Northern Europe (UK, Germany, Scandinavia, Netherlands, etc.) to Central and Eastern Europe (Hungary, Ukraine, Russia, etc.). Eventually, the ambit widened to include Southern Europe (Italy, Greece, etc.). Nineteenth and early twentieth century strategies for recruiting and retaining immigrants from preferred regions included advertising in multiple languages, free or subsidized passage and land grants, the use of 'return men' to promote emigration by co-nationals, payment of commission to recruiters/travel agents, and the facilitation of group resettlement under special terms. In exchange for commitments to settle and farm, German Hutterites, German-speaking Russian Mennonites, and Russian Doukhobor communities variously secured respect for communal land holding practices and exemption from conscription. The idea that immigrants were crucial to the nation-building project in both economic and demographic terms was most famously captured in a quotation from Clifford Sifton, Canada's Minister of the Interior, from 1896–1905. Speaking years later in defence of Central and East European settlers, Sifton declared that the ideal immigrant was a 'stalwart peasant in a sheepskin coat, born on the soil, whose forefathers have been farmers for generations, with a stout wife and a half dozen children'.

5. Yet, even as Canada expanded the potential European source regions of immigration, immigration law and policy also enlarged and refined its categories and mechanisms of exclusion. Successive immigration laws prohibited the entry of individual immigrants determined to be sick, destitute, physically or mentally disabled, criminal, immoral or otherwise undesirable. For example, minimum landing-money requirements were imposed to ensure that immigrants would not become public charges, and certain low-skill occupations were selectively prohibited. The 1910 Immigration Act created administrative tribunals that would determine admissibility of prospective immigrants as they arrived in Canada, thereby deploying the nascent administrative state apparatus onto the field of migration.

6. Racist exclusion was a prominent feature of immigration regulation from Confederation onwards, and several legal instruments to deter non-white, non-Christian immigrants were devised between 1867 and World War II. They included the following: explicit legislated exclusion; a racially specific 'head tax'; discretionary executive authority to exclude 'immigrants belonging to any race deemed unsuitable to the climate or requirements of Canada'; selective and discriminatory application of general rules of inadmissibility. In the 1880s, the Canadian Pacific Railway and the west coast mining industry relied extensively on indentured Chinese labour. These male migrant workers (known as 'bachelor husbands' because they could not bring their families) provided cheaper, more exploitable labour than local workers, and generated significant local opposition and conflict in British Columbia. The federal government responded by enacting the Chinese Immigration Act, which imposed a 'head tax' of CAD 50 in each Chinese worker in 1885. The tax was gradually increased the tax to CAD 100 and then CAD 500 by 1903. The main effect was not to decrease Chinese immigration, but to increase both indentured workers' debt and federal revenue. By 1923, Chinese labour was no longer in demand by major industrial employers and the government passed legislation that effectively prohibited entry of Chinese immigrants. Japanese immigration to British Columbia also elicited racist opposition, and the federal government responded by entering into a 'Gentleman's Agreement' with Japan whereby Japan would voluntarily restrict emigration to a fixed annual quota. The Canadian government adopted other techniques to prevent immigration by Indians from 1908 onwards. Since India was part of the British Empire and all British subjects were putatively equal, Canada was pressured by the Colonial Office in London to eschew explicitly racist exclusion. Instead, the Canadian government selectively enforced general rules that excluded labourers and imposed a minimum landing-money requirement. The government also invented the so-called continuous journey provision. This regulation permitted the government to deny entry to anyone who arrived from their country of nationality other than by continuous journey. It was enforced almost exclusively against Indians, who were unable to make a continuous journey from India to Canada. In the famous Komagata Maru incident of 1914, the continuous journey provision withstood a legal challenge by 374 Sikhs who arrived by boat in Vancouver Harbour and were denied disembarkation.

7. The immigration of Blacks from the Caribbean and the United States during this period was also discouraged by various direct and indirect means. Although thousands of African American slaves took the 'underground railroad' to find refuge in Canada in the mid-nineteenth century, the Canadian government of the twentieth century was committed to excluding Blacks. However, because Canada expended considerable effort in making the Canada-US border porous to prospective white immigrants from the US, it was difficult to simultaneously devise explicit legal mechanisms for preventing the entry of African Americans. Nevertheless, the racist objective was achieved through informal, bureaucratic means, combined with strict and discriminatory application of general inadmissibility provisions.

8. Immigration to Canada dropped precipitously during World War I. In the 1920s, the government attempted to boost immigration by introducing immigration programmes that delegated to Canadian railways and to Canada employers authority to select immigrants. Though not without controversy, the Railway Agreement and the permit system respectively facilitated the admission of tens of thousands of Central, Eastern and Southern European immigrants. Under the permit scheme, employers applied to the government for permits authorizing them to recruit immigrants 'whose labour or service was required in Canada'. Ethnic and immigrant aid organizations assisted in locating and recruiting eligible workers from Hungary, Poland, Ukraine and Russia. Bureaucrats manipulated admissibility criteria to restrict the entry of Jewish immigrants from those regions. During this same period, the government confronted a rise in political mobilization among workers and general labour unrest. Grounds of inadmissibility were expanded, and immigration authorities were able to selectively deploy their discretion to round up and deport immigrant workers labelled as enemy aliens, labour agitators, political dissidents or socialists.

9. Immigration virtually ceased during the Depression and deportation for becoming a public charge was also widely used to reduce claims on social assistance by non-citizens. Despite economic recovery and the approach of World War II, Canadian immigration authorities resolutely refused to admit Jews fleeing the Nazis. Between 1939 and 1945, approximately 100,000 immigrants were admitted to Canada; less than 5,000 were Jews. When asked how many Jewish refugees Canada ought to admit, the Director of Canada's Immigration Branch famously replied 'none is too many'.

10. In the aftermath of World War II, Canada resettled hundreds of thousands of displaced and devastated Europeans, though it maintained restrictive practices toward Jewish refugees. Inadmissibility on grounds of national security was used to screen out suspected communists, though less rigorously applied to possible Nazis or Fascists. Canada did not sign the 1951 United Nations Convention Relating to the Status of Refugees. It did resettle groups of refugees on an ad hoc basis, including thousands of Hungarian dissidents fleeing the 1956 uprising. It did the same again in 1968 for Czechs in the wake of Prague Spring.

11. The 1910 immigration law was finally replaced by the Immigration Act, 1952. In the forty-year interval between statutes, immigration law had been managed via executive regulation, thereby circumventing Parliamentary debate and public accountability. The 1952 Immigration Act incorporated many of the practices already authorized by regulation, and preserved the wide ambit of delegated authority conferred on the executive to make, interpret and apply immigration law through regulation. Immigrant eligibility was organized according to a hierarchy based on country of origin, and reflected racial preferences for white Europeans over non-white and/or non-European immigrants. Immigration from least preferred regions was effectively limited to nuclear family reunification.

12. By the early 1960s, the system of restrictive racialized preferences relented in the face of several post-war trends: the public endorsement of principles of human rights and equality; labour market and demographic demand that far outstripped the supply available from preferred source countries; and increasing legal constraints on procedures around administrative decisions regarding exclusion and removal of immigrants from Canada. In 1967, Canada abandoned explicitly discriminatory selection criteria and adopted the formally neutral points system for the selection of independent (non-family) immigrants. The points system has evolved since its introduction, but its essential format remains the same: applicants for skills-based permanent resident status earn points according to several criteria. Eligibility depends on meeting or exceeding a 'pass mark' set by regulation. The points system factors broadly measure human capital, employability and adaptability. Virtually all iterations have included assessment of the following criteria: formal education, occupational training, work experience, English/French language skills, arranged employment and age.

13. Country of origin is not a factor under the points system, although the risk of discriminatory implementation remains possible at the level of implementation via the inclusion of vague criteria such as 'adaptability'. Access is also limited by the fact that Canada immigration visa offices continue to be concentrated in certain regions. (E.g., today there are ten visa offices in Europe that accept immigrant applications and four serving the entire continent of Africa). The point system favours individuals with high levels of education and professional or high-skill occupations, and so tends to tilt in favour of middle- or upper-class applicants.

14. In 1969, Canada signed and ratified the Protocol to the UN Convention Relating to the Status of Refugees. The 1976 Immigration Act replaced the 1952 Immigration Act, and consolidated in statute and regulation the three pillars of permanent immigration to Canada: the economic class (selected under the points system), the family class (selected on the basis of kinship), and the refugee/humanitarian class (admitted in fulfilment of Canada's international obligations and humanitarian commitments). Up until the last decade, entries under the family class predominated over the economic class. Today, greater numbers of people are admitted under the economic class, although statistics for this category include accompanying spouses and children of principal applicants in the economic class. These family members are not subjected to the points system. Ultimately, more immigrants still enter Canada on the basis of kinship than under the points system.

15. The 2001 Immigration and Refugee Protection Act (IRPA) was drafted prior to the events of 11 September 2001, but enacted in the immediate aftermath of the attacks. Even more than its predecessors, the IRPA is framework legislation. It elaborates few substantive rules, does so at a high level of generality, and delegates wide authority to the executive to govern through subordinate legislation, especially regulations. One of IRPA's notable features, however, is that it declares in section 3 that the statute shall be 'construed and applied in a manner that complies with international instruments to which Canada is a signatory'. IRPA effectively delegates wide authority to the executive to govern selection, admission, exclusion and removals through the subordinate Regulations created by the executive. The IRB, an independent administrative tribunal, makes refugee determinations and hears appeals against refusal of family sponsorship applications as well as appeals against deportation. Consistent with the pattern of Canadian immigration law since its inception, IRPA also grants to the Minister of Citizenship and Immigration, and his or her delegates, wide discretion in the interpretation, application and enforcement of the statute and the regulations. The exercise of discretion is meant to be constrained by principles of procedural fairness, legality, and Canada's domestic and international human rights obligations. Access to judicial review by non-citizens is limited by statute.

16. The entrenchment of the 1982 Canadian Charter of Rights and Freedoms subjected immigration law to constitutional review for compliance with fundamental rights and freedoms. The most relevant Charter provision is section 7, which guarantees that 'everyone has the right to life, liberty and security of the person, and the right not to be deprived thereof, except in accordance with fundamental justice'. This provision was successfully invoked in *Singh* to strike down the pre-1985 refugee determination system because it denied asylum seekers procedural fairness, and in particular, did not entitle them to an oral hearing before a decision-maker. Subsequent cases have not extended constitutional protection to non-citizens facing removal unless they also face the risk of persecution, torture or death as a result of deportation. In the 2002 *Suresh* decision, the Supreme Court of Canada departed from international human rights law and European jurisprudence when it left open the possibility of deportation of a non-citizen to face a substantial risk of torture 'in exceptional circumstances'. The equality provision of the Charter (section 15) prohibits discrimination on grounds of citizenship. Nevertheless, Canadian courts have generally resisted using it to protect non-citizens from discrimination, whether in public employment, or from anti-terrorism procedures under immigration law that are inferior to parallel processes under criminal law.

17. The last decade has witnessed a dramatic shift in the Canadian migration regime. The federal government has actively promoted the decentralization of immigration regulation, and has granted provincial governments beyond Québec an increasingly large role in the selection of permanent economic class immigrants.

The government has also accelerated and intensified the privatization of immigration. With the exception of seasonable agricultural workers and live-in caregivers, Canada historically avoided entrenching sectoral temporary migration schemes. The current federal government has conferred on employer's greater access to temporary migrant workers. It also appears poised to decentre (if not dismantle) the points system for selection of economic immigrants, and to give employers greater power to select future immigrants. For the first time in its history, Canada admitted more temporary migrant workers in 2008 than permanent immigrants, and this pattern continues up to the present. Many sponsored family members (spouses, parents/grandparents), who once entered as permanent residents, will now enter on more precarious, temporary or conditional status. Whether this trend toward temporary, precarious status instead of secure status represents an aberration or a transformation remains to be seen.

Figure 1 Canada: Permanent Residents, 1860–2013

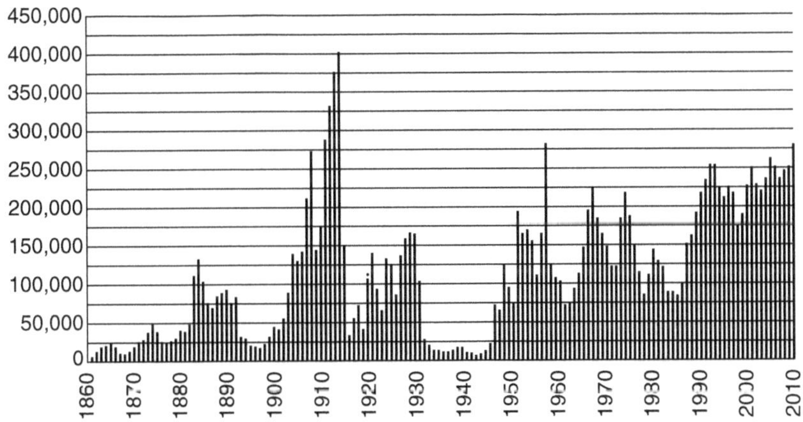

Source: 'Facts and figures 2013 – Immigration overview: Permanent and temporary residents', http://www.cic.gc.ca/english/resources/statistics/facts2013/permanent/index.asp.

Figure 2 Foreign-born Population, Canada, Selected Years, 1871–2006 (Per cent)

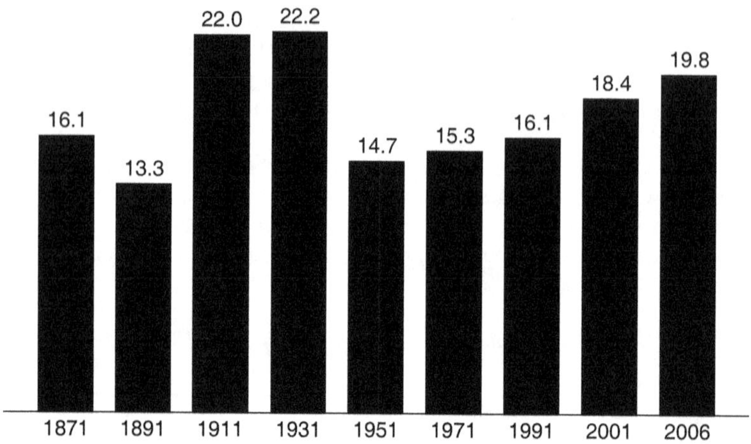

Source: Citizenship and Immigration Canada, 'Facts and figures 2009 – Immigration overview: Permanent and temporary residents', http://www.cic.gc.ca/english/resources/statistics/facts2009/index.asp, http://www4.hrsdc.gc.ca/.3ndic.1t.4r@-eng.jsp?bw=1&iid=38.

Figure 3 Region of Birth of Recent Immigrants to Canada, 1971–2006

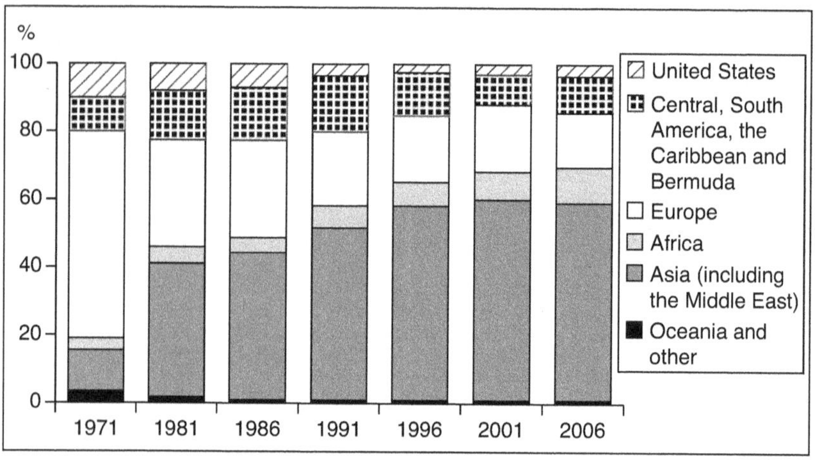

Notes:
1. 'Recent immigrants' refers to permanent (landed) immigrants who arrived in Canada within five years prior to a given census.
2. 'Other' includes Greenland, St Pierre and Miquelon, the category 'other country' as well as a small number of immigrants born in Canada.

Sources: Statistics Canada, censuses of population, 1971 to 2006. http://www12.statcan.ca/census-recensement/2006/as-sa/97-557/figures/c2-eng.cfm.

Figure 4 Canada: Permanent Residents by Top 10 Source Countries, 2010–2013

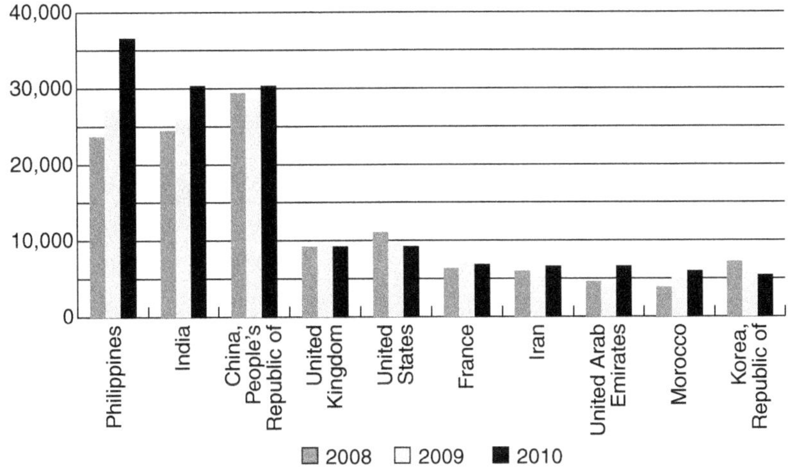

Source: 'Facts and figures 2012 – Immigration overview: Permanent and temporary residents', http://www.cic.gc.ca/english/resources/statistics/facts2013/index.asp.
Graph: http://www.cic.gc.ca/english/resources/statistics/facts2013/permanent/10.asp.

Figure 5 Canada: Permanent Residents by Category, 1988–2013

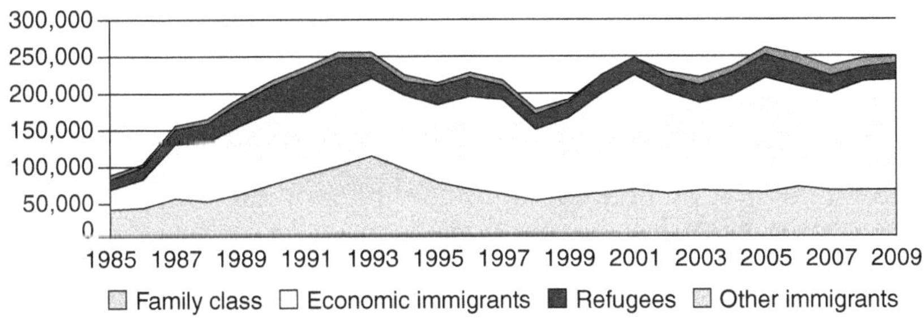

Source: 'Facts and figures 2012 – Immigration overview: Permanent and temporary residents', http://www.cic.gc.ca/english/resources/statistics/facts2012/index.asp.
Graph: http://www.cic.gc.ca/english/resources/statistics/facts2013/permanent/01.asp.

Figure 6 Canada: Total Entries of Temporary Residents by Yearly Status, 1988–2013

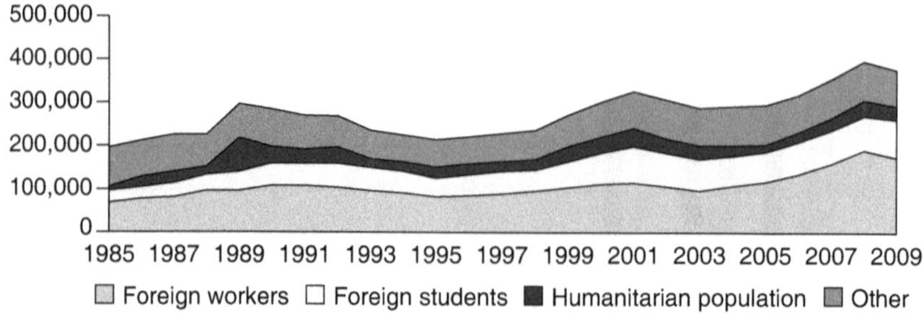

Source: Citizenship and Immigration Canada, 'Facts and figures 2013 – Immigration overview': Permanent and temporary residents', http://www.cic.gc.ca/english/resources/statistics/facts2013/index.asp. Graph: http://www.cic.gc.ca/english/resources/statistics/facts2013/temporary/01.asp.

§2. Overview of National Legal Instruments

I. Historical Overview

17.1. See section §1 Immigration History and Statistical Information, *supra.*

II. Current Applicable Legislation

18. CIC also issues an Operational Manual that consists of detailed guidelines concerning the interpretation and application of the IRPA and the Immigration and Refugee Protection Regulations (IRPR). The Manual does not have the status of binding law.[2]

IRPA, SC 2001, c. 27, as amended.[3]

IRPR, SOR/2002-227, as amended.[4]

III. Federal-Provincial Agreements

18.1. See Part I, Chapter 1, 'Organization of Border Control'.

2. The content of Operational Manuals is updated regularly and available online at http://www.cic.gc.ca/english/resources/manuals.
3. Available for download http://laws-lois.justice.gc.ca/eng/acts/I%2D2.5/.
4. Available for download http://laws-lois.justice.gc.ca/eng/regulations/SOR-2002-227/index.html.

IV. Social and Economic Rights

19. Only Canadian citizens have the constitutional right under Canada's Charter of Rights and Freedoms[5] to enter and remain in Canada, and to vote and stand for public office (section 6(1)). Only Canadian citizens may be required to serve on juries. The denial of admission by a permanent resident to practice law was declared a violation of the Charter's equality provision (section 15) in 1989.[6] Citizenship was recognized as a ground of prohibited discrimination. However, preferential access for citizens to certain federal public service positions is considered a justifiable limit on permanent residents' equality rights.[7]

20. Citizens and permanent residents of Canada enjoy constitutionally protected mobility rights within Canada under section 6(2) of the Charter. Other than as noted above, permanent residents enjoy the same social and economic rights as citizens. Children are entitled to primary and secondary school education regardless of legal status. The social and economic entitlements to employment, income support, social assistance and health care vary for other classes of non-citizens. These include temporary foreign workers, asylum seekers and non-status migrants (people with no legal status). These are described *infra*. Although the provinces typically operate the public healthcare system within their jurisdiction, the federal government assumed responsibility in the 1950s for financing health care for asylum seekers and refugees. In 2012, the federal government reduced or eliminated healthcare funding for this group.[8]

V. Citizenship[9]

21. Canadian citizenship is transmitted by *jus soli* (birth on Canadian territory), by *jus sanguinis* (descent from a Canadian citizen), or by naturalization. Under IRPA, Aboriginal people who are recognized by the federal government as 'Status Indians' possess the rights of citizenship even if they did not acquire it by birth or descent. The number of 'Status Indians' who actually lack birthright citizenship is unknown and probably very small.

5. Enacted as Schedule B to the *Canada Act 1982*, (UK) 1982, c 11, which came into force on 17 Apr. 1982.
6. *Andrews v. Law Society of British Columbia*, [1989] 1 SCR 143.
7. *Lavoie v. Canada*, [2002] 1 SCR 769.
8. Order Amending the Order Respecting the Interim Federal Health Program, 2012, PC 2012-945 28 Jun. 2012.
9. See Citizenship Act, RSC, 1985, c C-29, as amended, available for download at http://laws-lois.justice.gc.ca/eng/acts/C%2D29/; Citizenship Regulations (SOR/93-246), as amended, available for download at http://laws-lois.justice.gc.ca/eng/regulations/SOR-93-246/. In 2014, major amendments to the Citizenship Act were effected through the Strengthening Canadian Citizenship Act, SC 2014, c-22, available for download at http://www.parl.gc.ca/HousePublications/Publication.aspx?doc=C-24&pub=bill. Not all provisions have been declared in force yet.

22. Any person born on Canadian soil (other than a child of diplomats) acquires Canadian citizenship. A person born abroad to a Canadian citizen is a Canadian citizen, but since 2009, this does not extend to a second generation: if a person who acquired citizenship solely by descent subsequently gives birth to a child outside Canada, that child is not a Canadian citizen.

23. Following passage of the Strengthening Canadian Citizenship Act in 2014 (not all of which is in force), the following criteria must be met by permanent residents seeking to naturalize as citizens: The applicant must have physically resided in Canada for at least six months per year for the four out of the six years preceding the application for citizenship. Applicants between 16–64 years must pass a citizenship exam that tests knowledge of Canadian history, politics, and society, must demonstrate a minimum competence in English or French, and must intend to continue residing in Canada after naturalization. An applicant may be ineligible on the basis of criminality. Citizenship is revocable if the applicant obtained it by fraud or misrepresentation. Provisions permit revocation of citizenship of dual nationals upon conviction for designated offences against 'national security'.

24. The citizenship ceremony requires a candidate to swear an oath of citizenship, after which they receive a certificate of citizenship that enables the citizen to apply for a Canadian passport. In 2011, the Minister of Citizenship and Immigration declared that people whose faces are covered (e.g., women wearing a niqab) will be prohibited from swearing the oath of citizenship. The Federal Court found the government ban to be unlawful, but the government has announced its intention to appeal the decision.[10]

§3. Overview of International Legal Instruments Applicable in Canada, with Date of Entry into Force in Canada

Convention on the Prevention and Punishment of the Crime of Genocide, UNTS, Vol. 78, p. 277 CTS 1949/27, entered into force 2 December 1952.
Slavery Convention signed at Geneva on 25 September 1926 and amended by the Protocol of 7 December 1953, entered into force 7 July 1955
Convention on the Nationality of Married Women, UNTS, Vol. 309, p. 65, CTS 1960/2, entered into force 11 August 1958. Supplementary Convention on the Abolition of Slavery, the Slave Trade, and Institutions and Practices Similar to Slavery, UNTS, Vol. 266, p. 3, CTS 1963/7, entered into force 10 January 1963.
Optional Protocol to the International Covenant on Civil and Political Rights, UNTS, Vol. 999, p. 171, CTS 1976/47, entered into force 23 March 1966.

10. *Ishaq v. Canada (Minister of Citizenship and Immigration)*, 2015 FC 156, 6 Feb. 2015.

International Covenant on Civil and Political Rights, UNTS, Vol. 999, p. 171, CTS 1976/47, entered into force 16 December 1966.
Convention relating to the Status of Refugees, UNTS, Vol. 189, p. 137 CTS 1969/6, entered into force 2 September 1969.[11]
Convention on the Reduction of Statelessness, UNTS, Vol. 989, p. 175 CTS 1978/32, entered into force 13 December 1975.
Charter of the Organization of American States, OAS, Treaty Series, Nos. 1-C AND 61, UN Reg. 01/16/52 No. 1609 Vol. 119, ratified by Canada 20 December 1989.
General Agreement on Trade in Services (GATS), 15 April 1994, Marrakesh Agreement Establishing the World Trade Organization, Annex 1B, The Legal Texts: The Results of the Uruguay Round of Multilateral Trade Negotiations 284 (1999), 1869 UNTS. 183, 33 ILM. 1167, 15 April 1994
Convention on the Rights of the Child, A/RES/44/25, CTS 1992/3, entered into force 2 September 1990.
Optional Protocol to the Convention on the Elimination of All Forms of Discrimination against Women, A/RES/54/4, entered into force 22 December 2000.
North American Free Trade Agreement, 32 ILM 289 and 605 (1993), 1 January 1994.
Optional Protocol to the Convention on the Rights of the Child on the Sale of Children, Child Pornography and Child Prostitution, A/RES/54/263, entered into force 18 January 2002
Convention on the Rights of Persons with Disabilities, A/RES/61/106, entered into force 3 May 2008
United Nations Convention against Transnational Organized Crime, A/55/383 Appendix I, entered into force 29 October 2003.

11. Canada entered the following reservations to the Refugee Convention/1969 Protocol:

    1. 'Canada interprets the phrase "lawfully staying" as referring only to refugees admitted for permanent residence: refugees admitted for temporary residence will be accorded the same treatment with respect to the matters dealt with in Articles 23 and 24 as is accorded visitors generally.'
       In a communication received by the Secretary-General on 23 October 1970, Canada made the following declaration:
       'The Government of Canada declares that for the purposes of its obligations under the Convention relating to the Status of Refugees done at Geneva on July 28, 1951, the words "events occurring before 1 January 1951" in article 1, Section B(1) of the said Convention shall be understood as meaning "events occurring in Europe or elsewhere before 1 January 1951".'
    2. 'Inasmuch as under the Canadian constitutional system legislative jurisdiction in respect of political rights is divided between the provinces and the Federal Government, the Government of Canada is obliged, in acceding to this Convention, to make a reservation in respect of rights within the legislative jurisdiction of the provinces.'

Protocol to prevent, suppress and punish trafficking in persons, especially women and children, supplementing the United Nations Convention against Transnational Organized Crime, A/55/383 Appendix II, entered into force 24 January 2004
Protocol against the smuggling of migrants by land, sea and air, supplementing the United Nations Convention against Transnational Organized Crime, A/55/383 Appendix III, entered into force 27 February 2004.

Part I. Border Control and Entry

Chapter 1. Organization of Border Control

§1. The Constitutional Framework

25. Canada is a federal state in which legislative, regulatory and administrative powers are divided between federal and provincial institutions. Regulation of the entry of people into Canada and of their departure from the country is primarily the responsibility of the Federal Parliament, and administration of the field falls generally within the authority of branches of the Federal Government. The Constitution Act, 1867,[12] which identifies the various fields over which the Federal Parliament and the legislatures of the provinces have jurisdiction, sets out the constitutional framework that governs the ambit of this authority, but the primacy of federal law has been established only through the development of legal doctrine by the Supreme Court of Canada.

26. Two sections of the Constitution Act, 1867 are particularly relevant. Section 91(25) grants exclusive authority to the Canadian Parliament to enact laws in relation to 'Aliens and Naturalization'. In a number of important cases from the turn of the twentieth century, the Supreme Court of Canada and in earlier days, the Privy Council, were asked to determine whether provincial statutes that restrict employment and voting rights on the foreign born fall under this head of legislative power and are thereby unconstitutional. In some circumstances, such legislation has been found 'in pith and substance' to fall under the federal head of power.[13] In other cases, a narrow interpretation of the federal power over aliens and naturalization had the effect of upholding provincial laws that denied the vote to citizens on racial grounds.[14]

27. The Supreme Court of Canada developed a doctrine of 'federal paramountcy' to resolve cases where a provincial law falls within a provincial head of power, but is also inconsistent with a valid federal law. For example, in *Law Society of British Columbia v. Mangat*,[15] *the* Supreme Court of Canada considered the validity of a provision of the Immigration Act (the federal legislation then in force)

12. *Constitution Act,* 1867 (UK), 30 &31 Vict, c3 reprinted in RSC 1985, app II, no 5.
13. See especially *Union Colliery v. Bryden* [1899] AC 580 (PC).
14. See especially *Cunningham v. Tomey Homma* [1903] AC 151 (PC).
15. [2001] 3 S.C.R. 113.

that permitted non-lawyers to represent individuals before the IRB. The Court found that the subject matter of the legislation fell within both provincial and federal jurisdiction. It then recognized the inconsistency between this law and the provincial Legal Profession Act which restricted the practice of law to members of the provincial law society. The Court determined that where there is 'operational conflict' between a provincial law and a federal law, the latter should prevail. There is no requirement that there be an actual textual contradiction between federal law and provincial law. Instead, the idea of operational conflict is explained to mean that 'the provincial law may not be contrary to any *purpose* underlying the federal legislation'.[16] The consequences of a finding of operational conflict are severe: In the face of operational conflict, the paramountcy doctrine requires that the federal law prevail and the provincial law be found inoperative.

28. The doctrine of federal paramountcy is of particular importance in relation to section 95 of the Constitution Act 1867 which grants law-making authority over 'Immigration' to both Parliament and to the legislatures of the provinces. It reads as follows:

> In each Province, the Legislature may make Laws in relation to … Immigration into the Province; and it is hereby declared that the Parliament of Canada may from Time to Time make Laws, in relation to … Immigration into all or any of the Provinces; and any Law of the Legislature of a Province relative to … Immigration shall have effect in and for the Province as long and as far only as it is not repugnant to any Act of the Parliament of Canada.[17]

29. The reference to 'repugnancy' in this section reflects the understanding that federal immigration laws should be paramount where an inconsistency with provincial law exists. As a result of the Supreme Court's broad conception of repugnancy and 'operational conflict', control over immigration and the Canadian border is dominated by federal laws

30. Nevertheless, limited authority has devolved to the provinces through the development of Federal-Provincial agreements on immigration, which offer limited decision-making power to the provinces to select individuals who may enter the country and reside either temporarily or permanently. The most wide-ranging of these is the Canada-Québec Accord Relating to Immigration and Temporary Admission of Aliens,[18] first negotiated in 1978. Under the current terms of this agreement, Québec is granted 'sole responsibility for the selection of immigrants destined to that province'.[19] However, Canada retains sole authority over family class immigration, asylum seekers, and over the criteria of inadmissibility that apply to foreign nationals and permanent residents. Moreover, Québec's consent is required to admit,

---

16. *Ibid.* at 154 (emphasis added).
17. Constitution Act 1867 s. 95.
18. The text of the Accord is available at: http://www.micc.gouv.qc.ca/publications/pdf/Accord_canada_quebec_immigration_anglais.pdf.
19. *Canada-Québec Accord Relating to Immigration and Temporary Admission of Aliens*, s. 12.

on a temporary basis, foreign students, temporary foreign workers and foreign visitors seeking medical treatment. The devolution of authority has necessitated the creation of a provincial infrastructure located in other countries to deal with the selection and admission of individuals to Québec.

31. Other Federal-Provincial Agreements have created Provincial Nominee Programmes which allow provincial governments to nominate immigrants who wish to settle in the province in question. The criteria for nomination are determined by the provinces and thus reflect provincial rather than federal priorities. Some programmes offer permanent resident status immediately, while others impose a minimum period of employment on a temporary work permit prior to eligibility for permanent resident status. An individual nominated by a province must still make an application to CIC, and be determined not to be inadmissible according to federal criteria relating to (amongst other things) health, criminality and security. Section 8 of the IRPA[20] specifically recognizes the binding nature of Federal-Provincial agreements. It provides that:

> the selection and sponsorship of, and the acquisition of status by foreign nationals under this Act must be consistent with federal-provincial agreements.

32. Section 87 of the Immigrations and Refugee Protection Regulations[21] (Regulations) places restrictions on a province's ability to nominate individuals. In particular, it specifies that neither the provision of capital, nor participation in an investment scheme may by themselves lead to a provincial nomination.

§2. Departmental Authority

33. Authority over the movement of people at the border or through internal and maritime ports of entry vests in two distinct departments of the Federal Government: CIC headed by the Minister of Citizenship and Immigration, and the Canadian Border Services Agency (CBSA), a branch of the Department of Public Safety Canada, headed by the Minister of Public Safety and Emergency Preparedness.

34. Until 2003, CIC administered all aspects of federal immigration legislation, from selection to admission to enforcement, with the exception of matters delegated to the IRB.

35. The CBSA was created in 2003 to perform intelligence, interdiction and enforcement tasks formerly performed by CIC, as well as certain port of entry inspections formerly conducted by Canada Customs and Revenue Agency, and Canadian Food Inspection Agency. Although CBSA would be responsible for immigration operations at ports of entry, CIC retained a guidance and policy making role.

---

20. *Immigration and Refugee Protection Act* 2001 S.C. c. 27.
21. *Immigration and Refugee Protection Regulations*, SOR/ 2002-227 (as amended).

At the time, the transfer of powers was defended by the Government on the ground that it would:

> allow CIC to focus on citizenship, selection, settlement and integration of immigrants while also offering Canada's protection to those in need. CIC will continue to issue visas and develop admissibility policies for immigrants, refugees and temporary residents.[22]

36. The IRPA offers a general description of the responsibilities of the Department Heads. Section 4 provides:

> 4(1) Except as otherwise provided in this section, the Minister of Citizenship and Immigration is responsible for the administration of this Act … .
>
> (a) The Minister of Public Safety and Emergency Preparedness is responsible for the administration of this Act as it relates to
> (i) examinations at ports of entry;
> (ii) the enforcement of this Act, including arrest, detention and removal;
> (iii) the establishment of policies respecting the enforcement of this Act and admissibility on the grounds of security, organized criminality or violating human or international rights; or
> (iv) determinations under any of subsections 34(2), 35(2) and 37(2) [permission for inadmissible individuals to enter or remain in Canada where it is determined that it would not be detrimental to the national interest. The practical consequence of this section is that it is CBSA Officers who have operational control at ports of entry and are able to grant or deny access of individuals into Canada].

§3. The Immigration and Refugee Board (IRB)

37. A third body, the IRB, also plays a role in relation to the admission of individuals into Canada and their legal entitlement to remain. The IRB is an independent, quasi-judicial federal tribunal composed of four divisions. The Immigration Division (ID) makes decisions on inadmissibility and removal in cases that have been referred to it by CBSA officials. It also reviews detention decisions made by CBSA officials. The Immigration Appeal Division (IAD) has jurisdiction to hear appeals in a limited set of cases, most notably where a permanent resident has been denied entry or ordered removed or where an application to sponsor a family member has been denied. The Refugee Protection Division (RPD) hears and determines

22. CBSA News Release, 'Archived – Government of Canada Announces Transfer of Certain Functions Between Citizenship and Immigration Canada and the Canada Border Services Agency', http://news.gc.ca/web/article-en.do?crtr.sj1D=&mthd=advSrch&crtr.mnthndVl=&nid=103359&crtr.dpt1D=&crtr.tp1D=&crtr.lc1D=&crtr.yrStrtVl=&crtr.kw=citizenship&crtr.dyStrtVl=&crtr.aud1D=&crtr.mnthStrtVl=&crtr.yrndVl=&crtr.dyndVl=, 12 Oct. 2004 (archived).

the claims of asylum seekers in Canada and who seek Canada's protection as Convention Refugees[23] or as persons in need of protection.[24] The Refugee Appeal Division (RAD) has jurisdiction to conduct appeals from a subset of refugee decisions rendered by the RPD.

§4. Policing the Border

38. While the CBSA enjoys a monopoly of administrative control over the entry of individuals into Canada at ports of entry (legally defined to refer to locations where people must present themselves for examination), the Royal Canadian Mounted Police (RCMP) has the authority to take actions against individuals who attempt to enter Canada at other locations. The principal strategy developed by the RCMP to control such illicit cross-border movement is to coordinate joint efforts at border control with other organizations through the creation of Integrated Border Enforcement Teams (IBET):

> IBET is an integrated multi-agency law enforcement initiative that facilitates intelligence sharing and enhanced cooperative efforts among core partners: RCMP, CBSA, US Customs and Border Protection/Office of Border Patrol, US Immigration and Customs Enforcement and US Coast Guard. IBET also encourages the involvement of municipal, provincial, state, federal and First Nations law enforcement agencies, stakeholder agencies and related government departments.
>
> The enforcement teams are managed by an International Joint Management Team (IJMT) consisting of one representative from Canada Border Services Agency, the RCMP, US Immigration and Customs Enforcement, US Customs and Border Protection/ Office of the Border Patrol, and the US Coast Guard. The IJMT is responsible for providing guidance and direction to the IBET program and for ensuring coordination training and best practices.[25]

In 2013, the government implemented the *Beyond the Border Action Plan*. The initiative aims to increase border security and enhance the integrity of the immigration system by partnering with the United States.[26] As a part of the plan, Canada signed the *Immigration Information Sharing Treaty* with the United States. The treaty is an agreement to share both biographical and systematic information on third country nationals applying for visas and permits.[27] Another aspect of the action plan is the *Entry/Exit Initiative,* which allows the US and Canada to exchange data on the

23. IRPA ss 96 and 98.
24. *Ibid.* ss 97 and 98.
25. Treasury Board of Canada Secretariat, Development Performance Reports 2007–8, *Royal Canadian Mounted Police: Horizontal Initiatives,* available online at http://www.tbs-sct.gc.ca/dpr-rmr/2007-2008/inst/rcm/st-ts06-eng.asp.
26. Government of Canada, *Beyond the Border Action Plan Implementation Report,* online at: http://actionplan.gc.ca/en/page/bbg-tpf/beyond-border-implementation-report-december-2013.
27. Citizenship and Immigration Canada, *Canada/US Information Sharing Treaty Summary*, online: http://www.cic.gc.ca/english/department/atip/pia/ist.asp.

movement of third-country nationals, permanent residents of Canada who are not US citizens, and lawful permanent residents of the US who are not Canadian citizens through shared land borders.[28] The effect is to supplement each country's records of entry with exit data for non-citizens. The NEXUS programme, through which 'trusted travellers' are given expedited access across shared borders, saw more than a 50% increase in membership under *Beyond the Border*.[29]

§5. Other Agencies

39. Other departments of government are involved in various aspects of immigration. Most notable is the Ministry of Human Resources and Skills Development which is responsible for making decisions about labour market conditions in Canada on the basis of which work permits and certain permanent resident visas (PRVs) are issued. The Ministry maintains a National Occupational Classification List that is used to determine whether applicants should be selected for permanent residency as skilled workers. Service Canada, a branch of the Ministry is responsible for issuing Labour-Market Opinions (LMO), which are used to determine whether an employer should be permitted to hire temporarily a foreign national rather than a Canadian citizen or permanent resident.

---

28. Canada Border Services Agency, *Entry/Exit Initiative: Enhancing border security and the integrity of immigration programs,* online: http://www.cbsa-asfc.gc.ca/btb-pdf/ebsiip-asfipi-eng.html.
29. Government of Canada, *supra* n. 26

Chapter 2. The Right to Enter the Country

§1. Conditions for the Right to Enter

I. Status and the Right to Enter Canada

40. Entry into Canada at a port of entry depends on one's immigration status. The Canadian immigration regime recognizes three principal categories of status, each of which is founded on a different level of connection to Canada and each of which carries different criteria for legal entry into the country. They are: Citizen, Permanent Resident and Foreign National. A fourth category – that of persons registered under the Indian Act[30] – reflects the unique position of Aboriginal People. The IRPA contains specific provisions granting (or recognizing) the right of entry of persons so registered,[31] equating their position to that of citizens.

A. The Right of Entry of Citizens

41. Canadian citizens are the only individuals who have a constitutional right to enter and remain in the country. The right, entrenched in section 6(1) of the Canadian Charter of Rights and Freedoms, is not absolute but is subject to section 1 of the Charter, which identifies that guaranteed rights are 'subject only to such reasonable limits prescribed by law as can be demonstrably justified in a free and democratic society'.[32] The citizen's right to enter the country is also acknowledged in the IRPA. Section 19(1) provides:

> Every Canadian citizen within the meaning of the Citizenship Act …. has the right to enter and remain in Canada in accordance with this Act, and an officer shall allow the person to enter Canada if satisfied following an examination on their entry that the person is a citizen.

However, the Supreme Court of Canada has determined that a decision to withhold consent to the transfer of a Canadian offender from a foreign prison to a Canadian prisoner does not violate section 6(1) of the Charter.[33]

B. The Right of Entry of Individuals Registered as Indians under the Indian Act

42. Section 19(1) of the IRPA equates the position of those with Indian status to that of citizens: they have a right to enter and remain in Canada. In most circumstances a registered Indian will also be a Canadian citizen. The term 'Indian' is

30. Indian Act RSC, 1985, c. I-5.
31. IRPA, s. 19.
32. *Canadian Charter of Rights and Freedoms*, Part I of the *Constitution Act*, 1982, being Sch. B to the *Canada Act 1982*, (U.K.) 1982, c. 11.
33. *Divito v. Canada (Minister of Public Safety and Emergency Preparedness)*, 2013 SCC 47.

defined under the Indian Act as a person who is registered as an Indian or is entitled to be registered as an Indian. Section 6 of the Indian Act defines identifies the criteria of entitlement. The primary criterion is found in section 6(1)(b) which provides:

> A person is entitled to be registered if
>
> (b) that person is a member of a body of persons that has been declared by the Governor in Council on or after April 17, 1985 to be a band for the purposes of this Act;

43. Band membership may entitle some citizens of the United States who are foreign nationals to enter Canada. The Operational Manual lays out the general position of Indians:

> Under Canadian immigration law, North American Indians are only accorded the right to enter Canada if they are registered on the Canadian Band Lists. An American Indian can only obtain registered band status if they can establish that their mother or father was a member of a Canadian band. … Virtually all members of the Indian nations whose traditional lands straddle the border are entitled to be registered under the *Indian Act*, and once they have exercised this option, they may enter Canada by right under A19(1).[34]

C. The Right of Entry of Permanent Residents

44. A 'permanent resident' is defined in the IRPA as 'a person who has acquired permanent resident status and has not subsequently lost that status … '.[35] The *Canadian Charter of Rights and Freedoms* explicitly grants some rights to permanent residents, including interprovincial mobility and residence, but it does not afford them the right to enter Canada. However, the IRPA accords permanent residents a conditional right to enter Canada.[36] Three types of conditions apply. First, permanent residents must maintain residence in Canada by being physically present in the country for a required number of days for each five-year period.[37] Failure to maintain residence may lead to loss of status which would disentitle the individual from entry. Second, permanent residents may lose their status (and hence their right to enter and remain the country) should they be determined to be inadmissible according to criteria found in sections 34–40 of the IRPA. Third, in some narrowly defined circumstances, permanent residents are granted status only on provision that they meet specified criteria. The cost of failure to do so within a specified period of time

34. Citizenship and Immigration Canada, Operational Manual ENF4, *Port of Entry Examinations*, s. 10.3.
35. IRPA, s. 2(1).
36. IRPA, s. 27.
37. IRPA, s. 28. The requirement is to be physically present in Canada for 730 days for each five-year period.

is loss of status.[38] The Supreme Court of Canada has emphasized the conditional nature of the permanent residence by describing it as a 'privilege rather than an entitlement'.

45. Section 19(2) of the IRPA provides that an officer shall allow a permanent resident to enter Canada if satisfied following a port of entry examination that they have that status. A CBSA officer at a port of entry may issue a removal order against a permanent resident only on the ground that the individual has not met the residence requirement. However, the resident has the right to appeal that decision to the IAD of the IRB and the removal order does not come into force until the appeal is determined. The resident will be permitted to enter the country until that time.

46. A permanent resident loses status (and becomes a foreign national) when a removal order made against them comes into force or when it is finally determined that they have failed to comply with the residency requirement.[39]

D. The Right of Entry of Foreign Nationals

47. The general, catch-all category of *foreign national* is defined under section 2(1) of the IRPA as follows:

> 'foreign national' means a person who is not a Canadian citizen or a permanent resident and includes a stateless person.

48. Foreign nationals do not have the right to enter Canada. However, they may be authorized to do so should they apply for and be granted the status of temporary resident.

49. Four classes of foreign national may be granted the status of temporary resident. First, those who apply to come to Canada as visitors, a category that embraces both tourists and those who enter for a temporary business purpose. Second, those who apply to come as temporary workers. Third, those who apply to come to Canada to study. These three classes are identified in sections 191, 194 and 210 of the Regulations.

50. A fourth, exceptional class – that of *temporary resident permit (TRP) holder* – exists to cover those who are inadmissible to enter the country, for reasons such as ill-health or criminality, Section 24 of the IRPA grants officers broad discretion to grant temporary resident status to such individuals where 'it is justified in the circumstances'.

51. Moreover, foreign nationals may be permitted to enter and remain in Canada while their status is being determined. For example, a person who arrives at a port

38. See discussion of conditional status for sponsored spouses, Part III, Ch. 3, para. 327.
39. IRPA, s. 46(1).

of entry and who is found to be eligible to make a refugee claim will be permitted entry until the claim is determined. If their claim is successful, they are granted protected person status which carries a package of entitlements, including the right to be issued a status document.[40] Persons with protected person status may obtain refugee travel documents and, should they leave Canada, are permitted to return.

52. Barring exceptional circumstances, a foreign national without temporary resident status who is determined not to be eligible to make a claim for protection will not be permitted to enter the country.

53. Exceptions are defined in the Regulations. For example, under section 39, an officer is required to permit entry to persons who have been removed from Canada but who have been returned because of the refusal of another country to receive them.

54. It is significant that the IRPA does not use the language of rights or entitlements when providing for the entry of foreign nationals and temporary residents. Instead, it refers to permission and 'authorization'. The choice of language indicates the contingent nature of their presence in Canada. The general rule, articulated in section 11.1 of the IRPA, is that foreign nationals must apply for and obtain a visa from a visa office located outside Canada whether they seek to enter Canada temporarily or permanently. Except in specified situations, foreign nationals seeking entry as visitors, temporary workers or students, must apply for a Temporary Resident Visa (TRV).

The Minister of Immigration has a broad discretionary power to deny entry to a foreign national who otherwise meets all of the criteria for a Temporary Resident Visa. Section 22(1) of the IRPA states:

> The Minister may, on the Minister's own initiative, declare that a foreign national … may not become a temporary resident if the Minister is of the opinion that it is justified by public policy considerations.

II. The Visa Requirement

55. The general rule, which is subject to many important qualifications, is that foreign nationals who seek to enter Canada and to remain on either a temporary or permanent basis must first obtain a visa. The rule is found in section 11(1) of the IRPA which provides:

> 11(1) A foreign national must, before entering Canada, apply to an officer for a visa or for any other document required by the regulations. The visa or document may be issued if, following an examination, the officer is satisfied that the foreign national is not inadmissible and meets the requirements of this Act.

40. IRPA, s. 31(1).

A. Humanitarian and Compassionate Exemption from Visa Requirement

56. Before outlining the details of the requirement to obtain a visa, it is important to note the most important qualification. Like all requirements of Canadian immigration law, the requirement of obtaining a visa is subject to an overriding exemption based on humanitarian and compassionate or public policy considerations. The exemption is found in section 25 of the IRPA which provides:

> 25(1) Subject & subsection (1.2), the Minister must, on request of a foreign national in Canada who is inadmissible or who does not meet the requirements of this Act, and may, on request of a foreign national outside Canada, examine the circumstances concerning the foreign national and may grant the foreign national permanent resident status or an exemption from any applicable criteria or obligations of this Act if the Minister is of the opinion that it is justified by humanitarian and compassionate considerations relating to the foreign national, taking into account the best interests of a child directly affected.

It should be noted that when the applicant is outside Canada, the exemption operates differently from when the applicant is in Canada. In the former situation, the Minister (or his or her delegate) has discretion to hear the application for an exemption, while in the latter case the Minister (or his or her delegate) is *required* to consider the application.

57. Despite the breadth of section 25(1), its application by visa officers has, in practice, been limited. The Operational Manual when specifying those who are eligible for the exemption, identifies that only those who have made an application for a PRV qualify, thereby implying that those applying to come to Canada on a temporary basis are ineligible.[41]

B. Obtaining a Temporary Resident Visa

58. The Operational Manual defines a TRV in the following terms:

> A visa is a document issued or a stamped impression made on a document by an officer .... The purpose of the [temporary resident] visa is to identify the holder as a person who may become a temporary resident upon admission to Canada. The holder is a person who, in an officer's opinion, meets the requirements of the Act and Regulations.[42]

59. The requirements for obtaining a TRV are found in section 179 of the Regulations, which specifies that an officer shall issue a visa where satisfied that the

41. Citizenship and Immigration Canada, Operational Manual, Overseas Processing, OP4, *Processing of Applications under Section 25 of IRPA*, s. 1.
42. Citizenship and Immigration Canada, Operational Manual, Overseas Processing OP11, *Temporary Residents*, at s. 6.

applicant: (i) has applied as a visitor, worker or student; (ii) will leave Canada by the end of the authorized period; (iii) holds a valid passport or similar document; (iv) meets the requirements for admission as a visitor, worker or student; (v) is not inadmissible; and (vi) has submitted to a medical examination where needed.[43]

60. The onus is on applicants to satisfy the officer that these criteria are or will be met. The primary consideration will be whether the applicant is likely to depart from Canada at the end of the authorized period. Thus, applicants will have to convince the visa officer that their connection to their country of origin is sufficiently strong to motivate them to return there. They will also be required to show that they have sufficient funding either personally or from someone who is willing to support them while they are in Canada.

61. Under legislation that was in force until 2002,[44] persons who made an application for a TRV were required to satisfy the visa officer that they were not an immigrant.[45]

62. The current legislation specifies that a person who intends to become a permanent resident of Canada is not thereby disqualified as a prospective temporary resident Under section 22(2), which is entitled 'Dual Intent', the IRPA provides:

> An intention by a foreign national to become a permanent resident does not preclude them from becoming a temporary resident if the officer is satisfied that they will leave Canada by the end of the period authorized for their stay.

63. This provision has created some interpretive challenges since some programmes, (such as the Live-in Caregiver Programme) allow individuals to apply for permanent residence after having spent some time as a temporary resident in Canada. Such individuals will have no intention to leave Canada at the end of the authorized period. However, the proper focus of the inquiry should not be on whether the applicant *desires* to remain in Canada as a permanent resident, but rather on whether the applicant would depart upon expiry of temporary status should the application for permanent resident status fail. This is confirmed in a 2009 Operational Bulletin, in which it is directed that:

---

43. Regulations, s. 179.
44. *Immigration Act* s. 9(1.2).
45. While this provision is no longer found in current legislation, it has been read in by the Federal Court. In *Obeng v. Canada (Minister of Citizenship and Immigration)* 2008 FCJ No 957 Lagacé J. acknowledges that:

> A foreign national seeking to enter Canada is presumed to be an immigrant, and it is up to him to rebut this presumption. It was therefore up to the applicant, in the present instance, to prove to the visa officer that he is not an immigrant and that he would leave Canada at the end of the authorized period that he requested.

An officer should distinguish between an applicant whose intentions are *bona fide* and an applicant who has no intention of leaving Canada at the end of their authorized stay if the application for permanent residence is refused.[46]

64. A visa will not be issued where the visa officer has reasonable grounds for believing that the foreign national is inadmissible. Inadmissibility is determined on grounds of security (IRPA, section 34), human or international rights violations (section 35), criminality (including serious criminality) (section 36), organized criminality (section 37), health grounds (section 38), financial reasons (section 39), misrepresentation (section 40), non-compliance with the *Act* (section 41) and inadmissibility of an accompanying (or in very limited circumstances, a non-accompanying) family member.

65. An applicant for a TRV is not entitled to an interview before a determination is made. However, visa officers are legally obligated to provide reasons for denying a TRV.

66. Applicants who are denied a TRV may apply to the Federal Court of Canada for leave to seek judicial review of the decision. Where leave is granted, the visa officer's decision may be quashed on a number of grounds, including failure to provide adequate reasons, which is regarded as a breach of procedural fairness. As a practical matter, foreign nationals outside Canada who have been denied a TRV have limited access to Canadian courts.

1. Documentation Required for Obtaining a TRV

67. The applicant for a TRV is required to submit a package of documentation, including a travel document, an application form, two photographs and various other documents, as required in the particular circumstances.

68. A TRV will be issued only if the applicant is in possession of a passport or similar document as listed in section 52(1) of the Regulations.[47]

---

46. Citizenship and Immigration Canada, Operational Bulletin 131, 'Application of Dual Intent', at: http://www.cic.gc.ca/english/resources/manuals/bulletins/2009/ob131.asp.
47. Section 52(1) of the Regulations requires:
    - (a) … a passport that was issued by the country of which the foreign national is a citizen or national, that does not prohibit travel to Canada and that the foreign national may use to enter the country of issue;
    - (b) a travel document that was issued by the country of which the foreign national is a citizen or national, that does not prohibit travel to Canada and that the foreign national may use to enter the country of issue;
    - (c) an identity or travel document that was issued by a country, that does not prohibit travel to Canada, that the foreign national may use to enter the country of issue and that is of the type issued by that country to non-national residents, refugees or stateless persons who are unable to obtain a passport or other travel document from their country of citizenship or nationality or who have no country of citizenship or nationality;
    - (d) a laissez-passer that was issued by the United Nations;

The document must be valid for the period authorized for the stay in Canada. Citizens of the United States are amongst those exempt from this provision.[48]

69. Section 10(2) of the Regulations imposes specific content requirements on visa applications:

> The application shall, unless otherwise provided by these Regulations,
>
> (a) contain the name, birth date, address, nationality and immigration status of the applicant and of all family members of the applicant, whether accompanying or not, and a statement whether the applicant or any of the family members is the spouse, common-law partner or conjugal partner of another person;
> (b) indicate whether they are applying for a visa, permit or authorization;
> (c) indicate the class prescribed by these Regulations for which the application is made; and
> (c.1) include the name, postal address and telephone number of any person who represents the applicant, and the person's fax number and electronic mail address, if any;
> (c.2) if the person who represents the applicant is charging a fee for representation, include:
> (i) the name of the organization referred to in the definition 'authorized representative' of which the person is a member, and
> (ii) the membership identification number issued by that organization to the person; and
> (d) include a declaration that the information provided is complete and accurate.

70. In addition, the actual Application Form contains a number of questions that go beyond the stipulations in the Regulations. These questions focus on the purpose and length of the applicant's trip, the funds available for the trip, the applicant's immigration status in the country of residence, present employment, names and address of employer or school, the name, address and relationship of person or institution to be visited.

(e) a passport or travel document that was issued by the Palestinian Authority;
(f) a document that was issued by the Organization of American States and is entitled 'Official Travel Document';
(g) a passport that was issued by the Government of the United Kingdom to a British Overseas Citizen;
(h) a British National (Overseas) passport that was issued by the Government of the United Kingdom to persons born, naturalized or registered in Hong Kong; and
(i) a passport that was issued by the Government of Hong Kong Special Administrative Region of the People's Republic of China.

48. See Regulations, s. 52(2). An exemption is also granted to (among others) residents of Greenland seeking to enter from Greenland and to citizens of France who are residents of the islands of St Pierre and Miquelon, which are located to the south of Newfoundland.

71. The form also focuses on the inadmissibility of the applicant and family members and in particular on the ability of the applicant and accompanying family members to maintain themselves while in Canada, and on the reliability of the claim that they will depart from Canada after the authorized time has expired.

72. It asks specific questions about health,[49] prior arrests and prior denials of applications for a visa, refusals to enter Canada or removals from Canada, participation in war crimes or crimes against humanity. The form also requires the applicant to list all countries visited for more than six months during the past five years by all of the accompanying family members. The application form requires applicants to identify whether they are seeking a single entry visa, a multiple entry visa or a transit visa. Whereas a single entry visa permits entry into Canada only once during the term of its validity, a multiple entry visa, as its name suggests, permits re-entry on different occasions. The classification 'single entry visa' is somewhat misleading since individuals who have been issued a single-entry visa may travel to and from the United States without being required to obtain a second TRV.

73. Applicants may be represented by qualified third parties in their dealings with visa officers. Where applicants wish to be represented by another person, they must submit a separate form (IMM 5476) identifying the individual and specifying whether or not the representation is for payment. Section 91 of the IRPA specifies that only a lawyer, notary, other member in good standing of a law society or a member of a body designated by the Minister may represent or advise a person for a fee. In 2011, the Minister designated the Immigration Consultants of Canada Regulatory Council (ICCRC) as the exclusive regulator of immigration consultants.[50]

74. Visa officers focus their attention on ensuring that the applicant will leave Canada at the expiration of the TRV. Factors include the applicant's employment, familial, financial and property ties in the country of origin and whether travel is 'consistent with local customs or practices' of the applicant.[51] The following internal memorandum, obtained through Access to Information, provides candid guidance to visa officers about the assessment of applications for Temporary Resident Permits:

REFERENCE GUIDE FOR ASSESSING AN APPLICATION FOR A VISITOR VISA

(1) POSITIVE FACTORS: The following factors are positive aspects in assessing an application:
   - citizen in his/her country of usual residence

49. Focusing specifically on tuberculosis, and generally on any physical or mental disorder requiring health or social services.
50. For more information about the policy and rules related to 'authorized representatives', see Citizenship and Immigration Canada, Operational Manual IP9, *Use of Representatives*.
51. Citizenship and Immigration Canada, *Temporary Residents: Admissibility Considerations*, available online at http://www.cic.gc.ca/english/resources/tools/temp/visa/processing/admissibility.asp.

- country of usual residence is politically stable
- stable, well-paid employment (proof is required in the form of a letter from the employer stating salary, position, date when employment commenced and vacation granted)
- spouse and/or children not accompanying applicant
- owner of a substantial business (registration of business and, if necessary, financial statements)
- good financial situation (as proved by bank statements)
- previous trips to Canada
- previous trips to countries as attractive to illegal's as Canada (United States, France, United Kingdom, etc.)
- property in country of usual residence
- host (particularly in family visit cases) with legal status in Canada (citizen, permanent resident, student with student authorization, etc.)

(2) NEGATIVE FACTORS: The following factors are negative aspects in assessing an application:

- host remained in Canada with visitor visa or student authorization or entered illegally (based on record of landing or our previous files) – experience shows that where the host has already abused the system, it is highly likely that his/her guests will do the same.
- unmarried (particularly if young and chances of successful establishment in country of usual residence are poor)
- poor financial situation
- poorly-paid employment or unemployed
- host is a friend or distant family member with whom the applicant has had little contact
- no previous travel abroad
- has previously been denied a visitor visa (or student or employment authorization)
- has been denied a visa by another country
- owns no property
- wants to visit his/her fiancé(e) or spouse who is residing in Canada
- listed in FOSS (national immigration database containing entries on all applicants who have violated the Act or regarding whom a report has been written)

Naturally, no factor taken in isolation (unless it establishes inadmissibility) should result in approval or rejection of a visa application; the decision should be based on the overall assessment of all the factors.

(3) DOCUMENTS THAT MAY FACILITATE ASSESSMENT OF THE APPLICATION: The following list is not exhaustive; it provides examples of documents that may be required to assist in assessing a visitor visa application:

- property deeds
- old passports (visas issued to the applicant in the past)
- employment letter
- confirmation of vacation
- travel order

- status of host
- financial statements of applicant's business
- bank letters
- invitation letter (from family or business contacts)
- other files on the applicant (where applicable)[52]
- Family Members and Temporary Resident Visas.

75. An application for a TRV may include accompanying family members – defined to include spouse, common law partner,[53] dependent children and dependent children of dependent children – who may travel with the principal applicant or arrive later. The issue of whether the required relationship amongst the applicants exists may need to be resolved by additional documentation. Where a common law partner is included in the application, a statutory declaration of the relationship in the prescribed form (IMM5409) is required. Dependent children are defined in section 2 of the Regulations.

2. Place of Application

76. Section 11(2) of the Regulations, which came into effect in April 2005, requires that an application for a TRV must be made to an immigration office that serves:

(a) the country in which the applicant is present and has been lawfully admitted; or
(b) the applicant's country of nationality, or if the applicant is stateless, their country of habitual residence other than a country in which they are residing without having been lawfully admitted.[54]

77. The Operational Manual emphasizes that this section will be applied 'flexibly' allowing, for example, a business person from India who is spending a few days in London to make an application there as long as they were lawfully admitted to the United Kingdom.[55] However, the Operational Manual exhibits a strict approach in relation to TRV applicants who are refugee claimants in another country:

> In Canada and the United States, during the processing of a refugee/asylum claim, the individual does not have lawful status. Therefore, a person would not be considered to be lawfully admitted until a positive decision has been

52. Lexbase, Vol. 25(4), April 2014, at 2–3.
53. Defined in s. 1 of the Regulations, as meaning, 'in relation to a person, an individual who is cohabiting with the person in a conjugal relationship, having so cohabited for a period of at least one year'.
54. IRPA, s. 11(2).
55. Citizenship and Immigration Canada, Operational Manual OP1, *Procedures*, at s. 5.21.

received on the claim. However, other countries vary in their interpretation of what type of status an individual may have while awaiting a decision on a refugee claim. Therefore, officers should require applicants to provide documentary evidence of their lawful status. In all instances, a positive decision on a claim would certainly provide the individual with lawful status.

It is the opinion of Legal Services that the making of a refugee claim alone does not regularize a person's immigration status for the purpose of making an application for a visa (either permanent or temporary) to Canada. The granting of the asylum decision is the determinative date of a person's immigration status. The date the decision is rendered on the asylum claim becomes the date the individual is considered to be 'lawfully admitted'.[56]

78. The Operational Manual also makes clear that family members who are included in an application do not need to be lawfully admitted to the country in which the application is submitted. It notes that such a rule would prevent some families from making an application.[57]

3. Exemptions from the Requirement to Obtain a Temporary Resident Visa

79. Section 190 of the Regulations lists those citizens who are exempt from the requirement to obtain a TRV before seeking to enter Canada:

> A foreign national does not require a temporary resident visa if they
>
> (a) are a citizen of Andorra, Antigua and Barbuda, Australia, Austria, Bahamas, Barbados, Belgium, Brunei Darussalam, Croatia, Cyprus, Czech Republic, Denmark, Estonia, Finland, France, Federal Republic of Germany, Greece, Hungary, Iceland, Ireland, Italy, Japan, Republic of Korea, Latvia, Liechtenstein, Luxembourg, Malta, Monaco, Namibia, Netherlands, New Zealand, Norway, Papua New Guinea, Portugal, St. Kitts and Nevis, Samoa, San Marino, Singapore, Slovakia, Slovenia, Solomon Islands, Spain, Sweden or Switzerland.

British citizens, American citizens and permanent residents as well as a number of other foreign nationals holding specified passports are also exempt from the requirement to obtain a TRV before seeking to enter Canada.[58] Over the years, countries have been added or removed from this list depending on an assessment whether citizens of that country are likely to remain in Canada after authorization to do so

56. *Ibid.* Section 5.17. A Canadian Bar Association submission made shortly before this section came into force stressed the need to interpret generously the phrase 'present and has been lawfully admitted' and recommended that it include individuals whose original admission was legal but who have subsequently lost their status and also refugee claimants. Canadian Bar Association, *RE: Designation of Overseas Offices for Processing Temporary Applications,* available online at www.cba.org/CBA/submissions/pdf/04-33-eng.pdf.
57. Citizenship and Immigration Canada, Operational Manual OP1, *Procedures*, s. 5.17.
58. For details, see s. 190 (1) and (2) of the Regulations.

has expired. There is a correlation between the wealth and political stability of the state and its inclusion on the visa-exempt list. More controversially, countries have been removed from the list when there has been an increase in refugee claims from that country. For instance, the Czech Republic and Mexico were removed from the list in 2009 for this reason.[59]

80. Those who are exempted from the requirement of obtaining a TRV must still present themselves for examination at a port of entry in order to get status.

4. Issuance of Temporary Resident Visa and Grant of Status

81. The issuance of a TRV by an officer outside Canada does *not* grant temporary resident status to the visa holder or TRP holder. To acquire status, the visa holder or permit holder must be examined by an officer on arrival in Canada. The officer at the port of entry aims to determine whether the person seeking status meets the requirements of sections 20(1)(b), and section 22(1) of the IRPA which state:

> 20(1). Every foreign national … [other than registered Indians] who seeks to enter or remain in Canada must establish, …
> (*b*) to become a temporary resident, that they hold the visa or other document required under the regulations and will leave Canada by the end of the period authorized for their stay.
>
> 22(1) A foreign national becomes a temporary resident if an officer is satisfied that the foreign national has applied for that status, has met the obligations set out in paragraph 20(1)(*b*) and is not inadmissible.
>
> 24(2) A foreign national … to whom an officer issues a temporary resident permit outside Canada does not become a temporary resident until they have been examined upon arrival in Canada.

82. Thus, the acquisition of a TRV outside Canada is but a preliminary step in the process of gaining temporary resident status. It is only after the officer at the port of entry is satisfied of the matters identified that status will be acquired. Not only may the applicant's circumstances have changed since the visa was granted, the officer at the port of entry may form a different opinion about the admissibility of the applicant or about his or her intention to leave. Section 180 of the Regulations, which appears under the heading 'Holders of Temporary Resident Visas' provides:

> 180. A foreign national is not authorized to enter and remain in Canada as a temporary resident unless, following an examination, it is established that the foreign national and their accompanying family members

59. 267 Czechs applied for refugee status between 1 Nov. 2007 and 31 Mar. 2008. Between 2001 and 2007, during which time there was no visa exemption, only 123 refugee claims were filed by Czech citizens. The Czech Republic was re-added to the visa exemption list on 11 Nov 2013.

(a) met the requirements for issuance of their temporary resident visa at the time it was issued; and
(b) continue to meet these requirements at the time of the examination on entry into Canada.

83. It is important to note that the criteria of inadmissibility used by a visa officer abroad are the same as those used by an officer at a port of entry to determine whether temporary resident status should be granted and also to those used in Canada to determine whether temporary resident status should be revoked. The temporary resident in Canada does not have a stronger claim to be in Canada than the person seeking admission. While the length of time spent in Canada may be a factor to be considered when a request is made to be allowed to remain in Canada on humanitarian and compassionate grounds, such requests are determined on a purely discretionary basis.

84. Whether a temporary resident is able to re-enter Canada during the period of authorization will depend on the nature of the visa issued. Where the individual has been issued a single entry visa, their departure from Canada will terminate their status.[60]

85. Like the decision of a visa officer, the denial of status by an official at a port of entry may be reviewed by the Federal Court of Canada. The applicant must first seek leave from the Court.

C. Temporary Resident Permits

86. As noted above, it is possible for an individual who is found to fall within the criteria of inadmissibility, and who, as a result, will not be issued a visa, to be approved for a TRP instead. Section 24 of the IRPA provides:

> A foreign national who, in the opinion of an officer, is inadmissible or does not meet the requirements of this Act becomes a temporary resident if an officer is of the opinion that it is justified in the circumstances and issues a temporary resident permit, which may be cancelled at any time.

87. A TRP may be approved by a visa officer outside Canada, but will not be issued by him or her. Instead, the approval will be computerized so that it may be retrieved when the individual arrives at a port of entry. At secondary examination, described below, the Officer will issue the permit if satisfied that its issuance is still justifiable, and will then permit entry. Section 63 of the Regulations specifies the period of a permit's validity:

60. However, a person who has been issued a single entry visa may visit the United States without losing their status. See, Citizenship and Immigration Canada, Operational Manual OP-11, *Temporary Residents*, s. 12.

A temporary resident permit is valid until any one of the following events occurs:

(a) the permit is cancelled under subsection 24(1) of the Act;
(b) the permit holder leaves Canada without obtaining prior authorization to re-enter Canada;
(c) the period of validity specified on the permit expires; or
(d) a period of three years elapses from its date of validity.

88. A permit holder may seek an extension of the validity of their permit.

89. To be eligible for a TRP, a foreign national must be: (1) inadmissible and seeking to come to Canada; (2) in Canada and inadmissible, subject to a section 44(1) inadmissibility report, reportable for a violation of the Act, or otherwise in breach of the Act; or (3) not eligible for restoration of a legal status that has been lost.[61] Interviews may or may not be conducted. In general they will not be held if the grounds of inadmissibility are relatively minor and if credibility or merit is not an issue.[62]

90. The TRP is sometimes used as a device to admit a person who wishes to stay in Canada permanently but who is inadmissible. A TRP holder is permitted to apply for permanent residence from within Canada after either three or five years depending on the ground of inadmissibility, but only if they have not become inadmissible on another ground since the permit was issued.[63]

91. TRPs have been described by the courts as a 'highly discretionary' tool,[64] to be used only in compelling cases. In Nasso, the Federal Court said:

> It seems to me that an applicant who cannot satisfy an officer that he has a requirement or, to use the words of the decision under review, a compelling need to enter Canada, cannot establish that a permit is justified in the circumstances. In other words, to be granted a TRP in these exceptional circumstances requires more than showing that one has a wish or desire to enter Canada—it requires much more—otherwise, it is not an exceptional circumstance.[65]

92. The Operational Manual also stresses the exceptional nature of TRPs. It states that section 24(1) is intended for cases where there are:

---

61. Citizenship and Immigration Canada, Operational Manual IP1, *Temporary Resident Permits,* s. 5.5.
62. *Ibid.* at s. 5.9.
63. See also Part III, Ch. 2, s. 3 (Temporary Resident Permit Holders).
64. See *Farhat v. Canada (Minister of Citizenship and Immigration)* (2006) FCJ No. 1593.
65. *Nasso v. Canada (Minister of Citizenship and Immigration)*, 2008 FC 1003 at para. 15.

> compelling reasons for an officer to issue a temporary resident permit to allow a person who does not meet the requirements of the Act to enter or remain in Canada.[66]

Elsewhere, it states:

> Officers should issue permits with caution and only in special circumstances.[67]

93. Special provision is made for Protected Temporary Residents who are given a TRP for protection reasons after making a claim for refugee protection from outside Canada.[68] According to the Regulatory Impact Analysis Statement,[69] the purpose of the creation of this special status was to 'ensure that refugees resettled from outside Canada on TRPs are able to apply for permanent residence from within Canada, at no cost and without a waiting period'.

D. Obtaining a Permanent Resident Visa

94. In most circumstances, foreign nationals seeking to enter and remain permanently in Canada must first apply for a PRV. Only in exceptional cases may foreign nationals who are already in Canada apply for permanent status. Like the TRV holder, the PRV holder must present her or himself for examination at a port of entry to gain permanent resident status. Section 20(1) of the IRPA identifies their obligations at the port of entry. It provides:

> Every foreign national … who seeks to enter or remain in Canada must establish, to become a permanent resident, that they hold the visa or other document required under the regulations and have come to Canada in order to establish permanent residence.

95. Section 6 of the Regulations underlines this requirement by stating the default rule that a foreign national may not enter Canada to remain on a permanent basis without first obtaining a PRV.

1. Family Members and Permanent Resident Visas

96. An application for a PRV may be made on behalf of the principal applicant and his or her accompanying family members. For this purpose, a family member

---

66. Citizenship and Immigration Canada, Operational Manual IP1, *Temporary Resident Permits,* at s. 5.1.
67. *Ibid.* at s. 5.7.
68. Regulations, s. 151.1.
69. *Regulations Amending the Immigration and Refugee Protection Regulations,* SOR/2014-25, available online at: http://www.gazette.gc.ca/rp-pr/p1/2014/2014-06-21/html/reg1-eng.php.

is defined to include a spouse, common law partner, dependent child and dependent child of a dependent child.

97. A definition of a dependent child is precise. Section 2 of the Regulations provides:

> 'dependent child', in respect of a parent, means a child who
>
> (a) has one of the following relationships with the parent, namely,
> (i) is the biological child of the parent, if the child has not been adopted by a person other than the spouse or common-law partner of the parent, or
> (ii) is the adopted child of the parent; and
>
> (b) is in one of the following situations of dependency, namely,
> (i) is less than 19 years of age and not a spouse or common-law partner, or
> (ii) is 19 years of age or older and has depended substantially on the financial support of the parent since before the age of 19 and is unable to be financially self-supporting due to a physical or mental condition.

2. Place of Application

98. The applicant for a PRV may not select the office to which the application is submitted. An application for a PRV must be made either to the immigration office that serves the country in which the applicant is residing if the applicant has been lawfully admitted to that country for at least a year; or to the office serving the applicant's country of nationality. A stateless individual may apply to the office that serves their country of habitual residence.[70]

3. Classes of Application

99. The applicant is required to indicate the class under which they are applying. Section 12 of the IRPA outlines that an application for a PRV shall be considered under one of three general headings. It reads:

> Family reunification
>
> (1) A foreign national may be selected as a member of the family class on the basis of their relationship as the spouse, common-law partner, child, parent or other prescribed family member of a Canadian citizen or permanent resident.
>
> Economic immigration

70. Regulations, s. 11(1).

(2) A foreign national may be selected as a member of the economic class on the basis of their ability to become economically established in Canada.

Refugees

(3) A foreign national, inside or outside Canada, may be selected as a person who under this Act is a Convention refugee or as a person in similar circumstances, taking into account Canada's humanitarian tradition with respect to the displaced and the persecuted.

The Regulations specify a more detailed list of classes: The economic classes include the federal skilled worker class, the Québec skilled worker class, the provincial nominee class, the investor class, the entrepreneur class, the self-employed person's class and the Canadian experience class. The refugee classes include the Convention refugees abroad class, and the humanitarian-protected persons abroad class.

100. Section 70 of the Regulations specifies the conditions for issuance of a PRV:

> 70.(1) An officer shall issue a permanent resident visa to a foreign national if, following an examination, it is established that
>
> (a) the foreign national has applied in accordance with these Regulations for a permanent resident visa as a member of a class referred to in subsection (2);
> (b) the foreign national is coming to Canada to establish permanent residence;
> (c) the foreign national is a member of that class;
> (d) the foreign national meets the selection criteria and other requirements applicable to that class; and
> (e) the foreign national and their family members, whether accompanying or not, are not inadmissible.

101. Applicants applying for a visa under the family class category must satisfy the visa officer that they are in the identified relationship with the person seeking to sponsor them. Simultaneously, sponsors must submit an application showing that they both meet the definition of a sponsor and also meet additional criteria related to their ability to support the applicant. Applicants under the economic class must satisfy the officer that they meet requirements that relate to past experience and in addition must meet criteria that relate to age, education, skills, linguistic ability, past experience and adaptability. Those applying under the government-sponsored refugee class will be required to show that their situation meets the legal requirements. Where the refugee applicant is being privately sponsored, the sponsoring organization must submit an application that shows that the sponsor meet the definitional requirements and support criteria.

102. The criteria of inadmissibility for applicants for permanent residence, to which reference is made in section 70 of the Regulations, overlap with those that are used to determine the inadmissibility of foreign nationals applying for temporary residence. However, the financial considerations that are used to determine whether the person will be able to support himself or herself (plus accompanying family members) differ in substance.

103. The criteria of inadmissibility for foreign nationals seeking temporary or permanent resident status are the same, and they will be applied by the visa officer abroad and again at the port of entry when the foreign national arrives. However, these criteria are broader than those used in Canada to determine whether permanent resident status should be revoked. That is to say, where the status has already been granted, more stringent criteria of inadmissibility are used to revoke it. For example, a person who has already been granted permanent resident status cannot be found inadmissible on grounds of health, while foreign nationals applying for permanent resident status will be examined thoroughly and rejected if they pose a danger to public health or public safety, or if they might be expected to cause an excessive demand on health or social services.

104. Where an application for a PRV by a member of the family class has been refused, the sponsor may appeal the decision to the IAD of the IRB. Applicants from other immigrant classes who have been denied a PRV may seek leave from the Federal Court to apply for judicial review of the decision.

4. Exemptions for Foreign Nationals Already in Canada

105. Applicants who belong to five classes may apply for permanent resident status from within Canada without applying for a PRV. The five classes are the Live-in Caregiver Class, the Spouse or Common Law Partner in Canada Class, the Permit Holder Class, the Protected Temporary Residents Class and the Canadian Experience Class. Live-in caregivers are admitted to Canada as temporary residents, and after a specified period of work, they are permitted to apply for permanent resident status from within the country. Spouses and common law partners are foreign nationals who are already in Canada and who subsequently establish a relationship with a permanent resident or citizen. They may also apply for permanent resident status from within the country. Permit holders are individuals who have been granted entry as TRP holders. Protected temporary residents are individuals who have been granted a TRP for protection reasons after making a claim for refugee protection outside Canada. Temporary foreign workers or foreign graduates from a Canadian post-secondary institution, with at least one year of full-time (or equivalent) skilled work experience in Canada within the past three years, are also permitted to apply for permanent resident status from within the country.

106. Section 72(1) of the Regulations outlines the factors that determine whether permanent resident status should be granted in Canada. It provides:

> 72(1) A foreign national in Canada becomes a permanent resident if, following an examination, it is established that

(a) they have applied to remain in Canada as a permanent resident as a member of a class referred to in subsection (2);
(b) they are in Canada to establish permanent residence;
(c) they are a member of that class;
(d) they meet the selection criteria and other requirements applicable to that class;
(e) except in the case of a foreign national who has submitted a document accepted under subsection 178(2) or of a member of the protected temporary residents class,
  (i) they and their family members, whether accompanying or not, are not inadmissible,
  (ii) they hold a document described in any of paragraphs 50(1)(*a*) to (*h*), and
  (iii) they hold a medical certificate, based on the most recent medical examination to which they were required to submit under these Regulations within the previous 12 months, that indicates that their health condition is not likely to be a danger to public health or public safety and, unless subsection 38(2) of the Act applies, is not reasonably expected to cause excessive demand; and
(f) in the case of a member of the protected temporary residents class, they are not inadmissible.

107. The requirement that the foreign national be 'in Canada to establish permanent residence' prevents individuals from applying on behalf of themselves and their family members with the intent that only their family members remain in Canada. This concern arises because parents of sponsors are members of the family class, but siblings of sponsors are not. The government wishes to deter what it views as circumvention of family reunification policy whereby parents immigrate in order to bring their children (siblings of the sponsor) as accompanying family members, without actually intending to reside in Canada permanently, themselves.

108. In addition, section 25 of the IRPA grants the Minister (or a delegate) the discretion to exempt a non-citizen from any of the provisions of the IRPA on humanitarian or compassionate grounds or on the basis of public policy considerations. This discretion may be exercised to grant applications for permanent resident status from within Canada that would otherwise be contrary to the IRPA or the Regulations.

5. Documents Required by those Applying for a PRV

109. Initially, those applying for a PRV must submit a copy of the generic application form that requires them to identify the class under which they are applying. They must also submit a photocopy of the personal data pages of their passport, a background form identifying their education, military service, convictions and the names of organizations of which they have been members. They must also make a declaration that the information provided is complete and true.

110. Applicants may be represented by qualified third parties in their dealings with visa officers. Where applicants wish to be represented by another person, they must submit a separate form identifying the individual and specifying whether or not the representation is for payment.[71]

111. In addition, each visa office around the world uses different application forms, and the forms differ for each of the three different classes of applicant. At different stages of the process, applicants are required to submit their passport, a police certificate and a medical report completed by a recognized medical officer.

112. Applicants for a PRV must submit a medical report completed by a doctor authorized by CIC to examine applicants for Canadian immigration purposes. More relaxed medical criteria apply to members of the family class who are the spouse, common law partner or child of a sponsor, and to Convention refugees and protected persons – they are not required to show that they will not likely cause excessive demand on health or social services.

6. Obtaining Permanent Resident Status at a Port of Entry

113. Holders of a PRV may obtain status only after examination at a port of entry. Sections 20 and 21 of the IRPA identify the requirements that must be met:

> 20(1) Every foreign national, other than a foreign national referred to in section 19, who seeks to enter or remain in Canada must establish,
>
> (a) to become a permanent resident, that they hold the visa or other document required under the regulations and have come to Canada in order to establish permanent residence;
>
> Provincial criteria
>
> (2) A foreign national referred to in subsection 9(1) must also establish, to become a permanent resident, that they hold a document issued by the province indicating that the competent authority of the province is of the opinion that the foreign national complies with the province's selection criteria.
>
> Permanent resident
>
> 21(1) A foreign national becomes a permanent resident if an officer is satisfied that the foreign national has applied for that status, has met the obligations set out in paragraph 20(1)(a) and subsection 20(2) and is not inadmissible.

114. As noted above, the requirement that the foreign national has come 'to Canada in order to establish permanent residence' prevents individuals from applying on behalf of themselves and their family members with the intent that only their family members remain in Canada. This could happen where a person applies for

71. As noted above, only a lawyer, notary, other member in good standing of a law society, or a member of Immigration Consultants of Canada Regulatory Council may represent or advise a person for a fee.

permanent residence as a member of the Family Class, under the sponsorship of their adult child who is already a resident. While sponsors are not entitled to sponsor their siblings, they may sponsor their parents who may include dependent children within their application. The rule against sponsoring siblings could be circumvented should the parent be permitted to seek permanent residence without the intent to remain in Canada.

§2. Administrative Procedures and Documents Required at Port of Entry

I. Examinations at Port of Entry

115. In most circumstances, individuals who seek to enter Canada at a port of entry will initiate the process by joining a primary inspection line (PIL), to which all arrivals are steered. However, the Act also allows officers to initiate the process. Section 15(3) of the Act provides:

> An officer may board and inspect any means of transportation bringing persons to Canada, examine any person carried by that means of transportation and any record or document respecting that person, seize and remove the record or document to obtain copies or extracts and hold the means of transportation until the inspection and examination are completed.[72]

116. In all circumstances, the CBSA officer will ask those seeking to enter Canada questions concerning their identity, citizenship, and residency. They may be asked about the purpose of their trip, the amount of funds they have available, the presence of family in Canada, and whether they have health problems or a criminal record. The officer will also examine documents carried by the individual. If the officer is not satisfied with the responses to his or her questions, the individual will be referred to secondary examination for a more probing examination. The Operational Manual states that the responsibilities of the officer at the secondary examination include the following:

- examining persons seeking entry to Canada to determine admissibility;
- facilitating the entry of Canadians, permanent residents, and registered Indians;
- authorizing foreign nationals to enter Canada as temporary or permanent residents and issuing documents where appropriate;
- receiving refugee claims and determining eligibility to make such claims;
- reporting persons who are inadmissible;
- reviewing inadmissibility reports;
- issuing removal orders, where appropriate, to inadmissible persons;
- referring cases to the ID, where appropriate, for an admissibility hearing;
- authorizing an inadmissible person to enter Canada on a permit;

72. IRPA, s. 15(3).

- denying entry to inadmissible persons, arranging for their removal, and confirming their departure;
- allowing persons who are inadmissible to voluntarily withdraw their application; and
- arresting persons who have committed a serious infraction of the law.[73]

117. In some circumstances, an examination may not be possible. Section 40(1) of the Regulations provides:

> Except in the case of protected persons ... and refugee protection claimants, an officer who is unable to examine a person who is seeking to enter Canada at a port of entry shall, in writing, direct the person to leave Canada.[74]

II. Permission to Withdraw

118. Persons who indicate that they wish to withdraw their application to enter Canada are entitled to withdraw, unless the process of preparing an inadmissibility report has already begun. In this latter case, the entitlement to withdraw exists only where the officer decides not to issue a removal order against the individual or not to refer the report to the ID of the IRB.[75]

III. Right to an Interpreter

119. Border Service Officers (BSOs) at a port of entry are required to ensure that the person seeking entry understands the process and the questions asked during the examination. The Operational Manual notes:

> In appropriate circumstances, the BSO can ask accompanying friends or family members to assist in translation. At times a BSO may also solicit help from staff or other persons who are familiar with the language. This is a pragmatic practice that allows a BSO to facilitate the entry of travellers in cases where an official interpreter is not readily available.
>
> A BSO who is using a non-accredited interpreter to conduct an examination should suspend the examination if it becomes apparent that the person may be inadmissible. The examination can be continued once a competent interpreter is available.[76]

---

73. Citizenship and Immigration Canada, Operational Manual ENF4, *Port of Entry Examinations* (17 Jun. 2013) at s. 8.3.
74. Regulations, s. 40(1).
75. Regulations, s. 42.
76. Citizenship and Immigration Canada, Operational Manual ENF4, *Port of Entry Examinations* (17 Jun. 2013) at s. 8.5.

IV. Right to Counsel

120. In *Dehghani,*[77] the Supreme Court of Canada determined that a refugee claimant does not have a constitutional right to counsel at a secondary examination. Two reasons are offered. First, because the examination does not amount to arrest or detention and second, because:

> [t]he purpose of the port of entry interview [is] … to aid in the processing of the appellant's application for entry and to determine the appropriate procedures which should be invoked in order to deal with his application for Convention refugee status. The principles of fundamental justice do not include a right to counsel in these circumstances of routine information gathering.[78]

The Operational Manual states, 'Generally, CBSA's policy is not to permit counsel at examination if detention has not occurred.'[79]

V. Examination of Citizens at Port of Entry

121. According to the Operational Manual, the following documents are acceptable proof of Canadian citizenship:

- Canadian passport;
- Certificate of Canadian Citizenship;
- Canadian Emergency Passport (an officer at the primary inspection line will automatically refer for secondary examination a person in possession of a Canadian Emergency Passport. Once they have verified the person's identity, the officer at the secondary examination retains the passport and forwards it to the Passport Office, Foreign Affairs Canada, Ottawa);
- Certificate of Naturalization;
- Certificate of Registration of Birth Abroad; and
- Certificate of Retention of Canadian Citizenship.[80]

The Operational Manual also notes:

---

77. *Dehghani v. Canada (Minister of Employment and Immigration)*, [1993] 1 S.C.R. 1053.
78. *Ibid.* at 1078.
79. Citizenship and Immigration Canada, Operational Manual ENF4, *Port of Entry Examinations* (17 Jun. 2013) at s. 8.4. Note that the Federal Court of Appeal and the Federal Court have generally been unsympathetic to arguments that there is an automatic right to counsel before immigration officers (as opposed to members of the IRB) making decisions under the IRPA, other than in cases where a person is detained: see, e.g., *Jekula v. Canada (Minister of Citizenship and Immigration)*, [1999] 1 FCR 266 (no automatic right to counsel during determination of eligibility to claim refugee protection).
80. Citizenship and Immigration Canada, Operational Manual ENF4, *Port of Entry Examinations* (17 Jun. 2013) at s. 9.3.

> A Canadian provincial birth certificate is a good indicator of Canadian citizenship, but does not contain a photograph. The CBSA officer must therefore be satisfied that the person is the rightful holder.[81]

122. It is also possible for an individual to satisfy an officer of their Canadian citizenship without official documentation. The Manual notes:

> Canadians returning to Canada by air usually have to provide proof of identity and citizenship to get on the flight. Canadians arriving at land borders, however, will frequently be without satisfactory documentary proof of Canadian citizenship. In these cases, a BSO should question the person until they are satisfied of the person's Canadian citizenship. Once satisfied that the person is a Canadian, the person must be allowed to enter Canada without further delay.[82]

VI. Examination of Individuals Registered under the *Indian Act*

123. Individuals registered as Indians under the Indian Act may use a Certificate of Indian Status issued by the Department of Indian and Northern Affairs as proof of status at the port of entry. As with citizens, it is possible for a registered Indian to satisfy an officer of their status without documentation.[83]

VII. Examination of Permanent Residents

124. The Act provides that permanent residents shall be provided with a document (a Permanent Resident Card) indicating their status. It also provides that a person who is in possession of such document is presumed to have the status and that a person outside Canada who does not present such document is presumed not to be a permanent resident.[84] In most cases the Permanent Resident Card is valid for five years.[85]

125. A permanent resident must be physically present in Canada for 730 days during every five-year period in order to retain permanent resident status.[86] Officers outside Canada and those stationed at the port of entry have the authority to determine that a person has lost their status because of not meeting this requirement.

126. Where there are concerns about the admissibility of a permanent resident (or foreign national), the officer may take intrusive measures. Section 16(3) of the Act provides that:

---

81. *Ibid.*
82. *Ibid.* at s. 9.4.
83. *Ibid.* at s. 10.1 and 10.2.
84. IRPA, s. 31.
85. Regulations, s. 54.
86. IRPA, s. 28(1) and (2).

An officer may require or obtain from a permanent resident or a foreign national who is arrested, detained or subject to a removal order, any evidence – photographic, fingerprint or otherwise – that may be used to establish their identity or compliance with this Act.[87]

VIII. Examination of Foreign Nationals Seeking Permanent Resident Status

127. Section 16(1) of the Act provides that:

A person who makes an application must answer truthfully all questions put to them for the purpose of the examination and must produce a visa and all relevant evidence and documents that the officer reasonably requires.[88]

128. Section 16(2) adds more details specific to foreign nationals:

In the case of a foreign national,

(a) the relevant evidence referred to in subsection (1) includes photographic and fingerprint evidence; and
(b) subject to the regulations, the foreign national must submit to a medical examination.[89]

129. A person who has been issued a PRV must submit it to an officer at the port of entry along with a Confirmation of Permanent Residence Document (IMM 5292B) to show that a visa officer was satisfied that the applicant met the selection criteria and was not inadmissible.[90]

130. Under section 51 of the Regulations, a foreign national seeking to become a permanent resident is also under an obligation to inform the officer at the port of entry if he or she 'has become a spouse or common-law partner or has ceased to be a spouse, common-law partner or conjugal partner after the visa was issued' or if 'material facts relevant to the issuance of the visa have changed since the visa was issued or were not divulged when it was issued … '.[91] The same section requires applicants to establish at the time of examination that 'they and their family members, whether accompanying or not, meet the requirements of the Act and Regulations'.

87. IRPA, s. 16(3).
88. IRPA, s. 16(1).
89. IRPA, s. 16(2).
90. Citizenship and Immigration Canada, Operational Manual ENF4, *Port of Entry Examinations* (17 Jun. 2013) at s. 12.1.
91. Regulations, s. 51.

131. Section 50 of the Regulations requires applicants for permanent resident status to hold a passport or equivalent travel document, unless they are applying as protected persons and are unable to obtain such a document.[92]

132. An officer at the port of entry may and sometimes must impose conditions on the grant of permanent resident status. Failure to meet these conditions may lead to revocation of status for the applicant and their family members. The officer may also require that the permanent resident report for a medical examination, surveillance or treatment, and provide proof of compliance.

IX. Examination of Foreign Nationals Seeking Temporary Resident Status

133. A foreign national seeking temporary status must hold a passport or equivalent, unless exempted.[93] Exceptions to this requirement, among others, include citizens and lawful permanent residents of the United States[94] and crew members of ships and planes.[95]

134. Where a visa is required, a foreign national must satisfy the officer at the port of entry that they and accompanying family members met the requirements for a visa at the time it was issued and that they continue to do so.[96] All temporary residents are subject to the mandatory conditions that they leave Canada at the end of the authorized period and that they do not work or study unless authorized to do so.[97] The officer will need to determine whether visa holders have the financial means to be self-sufficient without working, and whether they have sufficiently strong connections to their country of origin to motivate them to return. The Regulations specifically bar foreign nationals from entering into or extending employment agreements with employers who offer stripteases, erotic dance, escort services, or erotic massages or with employers who have violated the terms of Canada's temporary foreign worker programme.[98]

135. Generally a foreign national will be authorized to enter Canada for six months. The Operational Manual provides:

> In most cases, a BSO should routinely authorize entry for a period of six months to a foreign national requesting entry as a temporary resident, even when the person requests entry for a very brief period. … Based on the information presented during an examination, a BSO at Immigration Secondary may decide to limit a temporary resident's stay to less than six months despite

92. Regulations, s. 50(1) and (2).
93. Regulations, s. 52.
94. Regulations, s. 52(2)(a) and (b).
95. Regulations, s. 52(f) and (g).
96. Regulations, s. 180.
97. Regulations, s. 183.
98. Regulations, s. 183(1)(b.1) and (b.2).

the length of time requested by the foreign national. If requested by the applicant and the BSO is satisfied that the foreign national is a temporary resident, is able to support themselves and accompanying family members financially, and is not inadmissible for reasons of health or security, the granting of entry for more than six months may be considered.[99]

X. Deposits and Guarantees

136. Where an officer is concerned that a temporary resident may not fulfil the conditions imposed on their entry, he or she may require the payment of a deposit or the posting of a guarantee.[100] The Operational Manual provides that:

> A deposit or guarantee may be warranted under [section 45 of the Regulations]:
>
> – if a foreign national indicates an intention to visit Canada for a short period, yet the BSO is concerned that they actually intend to remain permanently
> – if a foreign national presents themselves as a tourist and the BSO believes that their true intention is to work or study in Canada. The BSO could impose appropriate conditions set out in [section 183(1) of the Regulations] and require a deposit or a guarantee; or
> – if the BSO informs a foreign national who was originally seeking entry to work or study that such activities are not allowed and the foreign national agrees to come in as a tourist.[101]

The Manual makes it clear that a deposit and guarantee are not appropriate where the applicant is obviously inadmissible. In such cases, the Manual states, an officer should write an inadmissibility report, pursuant to section 44(1) of the Act.[102]

XI. Examination of Foreign Nationals Seeking Refugee Protection

137. Foreign nationals who arrive at a port of entry seeking Canada's protection[103] may be permitted entry to make a claim before the RPD of the IRB. The Operational Manual states that, 'A refugee claim is made when a person expresses

99. Citizenship and Immigration Canada, Operational Manual ENF4, *Port of Entry Examinations* (17 Jun. 2013) at ss 13.19 and 13.20.
100. Regulations, s. 45.
101. Citizenship and Immigration Canada, Operational Manual ENF4, *Port of Entry Examinations* (17 Jun. 2013) at s. 13.25.
102. *Ibid.*
103. Those who may be granted Canada's protection are identified in ss 96 and 97 of IRPA.

to a CIC or CBSA officer the need for Canada's protection.'[104] Further, the Manual also describes procedures for determining if there is a possible claim for refugee protection, even if none has been made, prior to issuing a removal order that would render an individual ineligible to claim refugee protection.[105] Officers at a port of entry have the authority to determine whether the person is eligible to have their claim referred to the RPD for determination.[106] Where the person is found ineligible, he or she will be refused entry. Where no decision is made within three days, or where the decision-making process has not been suspended for a justifiable reason the claimant is deemed to be eligible to make a claim.[107]

XII. Front End Screening at Port of Entry

138. The three-day period within which an officer must decide whether a claim is eligible to be referred to the RPD begins the moment the individual makes a claim to the officer.[108] The determination is preceded by 'front-end screening', which is an in-person examination and computerized database check that addresses questions of identity, admissibility, criminality, and security. The officer conducting the examination must address the language abilities and comprehension skills of the claimant and, where needed, an interpreter may be provided.[109] During the interview, the officers will ask the refugee claimants for information about why they are seeking Canada's protection. This information may be used later at a hearing before the RPD or on appeal to the RAD.

XIII. Criteria of Ineligibility

139. Section 101 of the Act identifies the grounds that render an individual ineligible to make a refugee claim before the RPD of the IRB.[110] Those who have already been given refugee protection in Canada are ineligible to make a second claim. A person might wish to do this in the unusual circumstance where they have been granted protection but subsequently issued a removal order. Were it permissible to make a second claim, this would delay the execution of the removal order. Similarly a person who has been recognized by another country to be a Convention refugee and can be returned there is ineligible to make a claim. A person who has

---

104. Citizenship and Immigration Canada, Operational Manual PP1, *Processing Claims for Refugee Protection in Canada, In-Canada Claims for Refugee Protection: Procedures at Inland Offices* (17 Feb. 2012) at s. 5.4.
105. Citizenship and Immigration Canada, Operational Manual ENF6, *Review of Reports under A44(1)* (12 Apr. 2007) at s. 8. Under s. 99(3) of IRPA, refugee claims may not be made by persons subject to removal orders.
106. IRPA, s. 100(1).
107. IRPA, s. 100(3).
108. Citizenship and Immigration Canada, Operational Manual PP1, *Processing Claims for Refugee Protection in Canada, In-Canada Claims for Refugee Protection: Procedures at Inland Offices* (17 Feb. 2012) at s. 5.7.
109. *Ibid.* at s. 9.1.
110. IRPA, s. 101.

made a claim to the IRB that has been rejected is also ineligible to make a second claim. Likewise, a person previously found to be ineligible to make a claim or to have withdrawn or abandoned a claim is also ineligible.

140. Two other grounds of ineligibility are worth noting. First, a person who has been determined to be inadmissible on grounds of security, violating human or international rights, serious criminality, or organized criminality is ineligible.[111] Second, claimants who have come to Canada through a country designated as a Safe Third Country may be declared ineligible and refused entry. To date only one country – the United States of America – has been designated. As described below, the agreement that establishes this rule of ineligibility and the regulations that give it legal effect in Canada allow a number of important exceptions.

XIV. Direct Back

141. 'Direct back' orders are authorized under section 41 of the Regulations.[112] They allow for an individual who has arrived at a port of entry at the land border with the United States to be returned temporarily to the United States. The individual is issued with a document indicating the proposed date, time, and place for a future examination. The policy has been highly controversial[113] and has resulted in refugee claimants being detained on their return to the United States, and thus being unable to return to Canada for their examination. In 2006, the Government committed to phasing out the policy as applied to refugee claimants.[114] The Operational Manual now advises officers at a port of entry that 'all efforts should be made to process refugee claimants at the time of arrival'.[115] The Manual further states that claimants should be 'directed back' to the United States only in exceptional circumstances. Exceptional circumstances might include when no officer is available from

111. Section 101 (2) of IRPA specifies that:

> 'A claim is not ineligible by reason of serious criminality … unless
>
> (a) in the case of inadmissibility by reason of a conviction in Canada, the conviction is for an offence under an Act of Parliament punishable by a maximum term of imprisonment of at least 10 years; or
>
> (b) in the case of inadmissibility by reason of a conviction outside Canada the conviction is for an offence that, if committed in Canada, would constitute an offence under an Act of Parliament punishable by a maximum term of imprisonment of at least 10 years.'

112. Regulations, s. 41.

113. The United Nations High Commissioner for Refugees expressed concern regarding Canada's policy of 'direct backs'. See, *Canada Newswire*, 10 Oct. 2007, available at: http://www.newswire.ca/en/story/120093/unhcr-expresses-deep-concern-over-canada-s-continued-policy-of-direct-backs (accessed 18 Jul. 2014).

114. Citizenship and Immigration Canada, A Partnership for Protection Year One Review (November 2006), Executive Summary, available at: http://www.cic.gc.ca/english/department/laws-policy/partnership/summary.asp (accessed 18 Jul. 2014).

115. Citizenship and Immigration Canada, Operational Manual ENF4, *Port of Entry Examinations* (17 Jun. 2013) at s. 18.4.

another port of entry to process the refugee claimant or when detention is not an option.[116] Officers are advised not to direct back unaccompanied minors.[117]

XV. Detention

142. The Act authorizes detention of foreign nationals or permanent residents, including those claiming refugee status, if necessary to complete an examination.[118] The Operational Manual advises officers that they should consider detaining individuals if it is not possible to complete the processing of their refugee claim at the port of entry.[119] The Manual further states that alternatives to detention should always be considered in the case of vulnerable persons and that, consistent with the Act, detention of children is always a last resort.[120]

---

116. *Ibid.* In 2012, provisions of the *Protecting Canada's Immigration System Act*, S.C. 2012, c. 17, came into force mandating the detention of 'designated foreign nationals' (DFNs) who are over 16 years of age: IRPA, s. 55(3.1). DFNs are foreign nationals whose arrival to Canada has been designated by the Public Safety Minister as 'irregular': IRPA, s. 20.1.
117. Citizenship and Immigration Canada, Operational Manual ENF4, *Port of Entry Examinations* (17 Jun. 2013) at s. 18.4.
118. IRPA, s. 55(3).
119. Citizenship and Immigration Canada, Operational Manual PP1, *Processing Claims for Refugee Protection in Canada, In-Canada Claims for Refugee Protection: Procedures at Inland Offices* (17 Feb. 2012) at s. 8.2.
120. *Ibid.* at ss 19.4 and 20.13. See IRPA, s. 60.

Chapter 3. Refusal of Entry

§1. Criteria for Refusal of Entry

I. Identity and Claimed Status

143. An officer at a port of entry may refuse entry to a person on a number of grounds. The most basic is that the principal applicant or family member is not the person they claim to be or does not have the required status that they claim to have. This might happen where the individual in question has insufficient documentation to prove their status or where the officer has reason to suspect the authenticity of the documentation.

II. Insufficient Reason to Grant Status: Prerequisites Not Met

144. An officer may also refuse entry on the ground that an applicant has failed to meet the formal prerequisites for entry. Thus, a foreign national who has failed to obtain a visa where required may be refused. A person holding a single entry visa may be refused entry where they have previously entered the country on that visa. A person intending to take up employment or intending to study who has failed to obtain the required permit may also be refused. A person who has been deported from Canada may not return without written authorization.

145. Similarly, an officer at a port of entry may refuse entry on the ground that the individual has not met the necessary substantive requirements. For example, a visa-exempt individual who is inadmissible may be refused a TRP on the ground that they have shown insufficient reason why their inadmissibility should not operate to exclude them. Likewise a person seeking to enter to make a claim for Canada's protection before the RPD of the IRB may be determined to be ineligible to make such a claim. Or further, where a person's situation has changed since they obtained a visa (where, for example, they have married someone), the ground for refusal may be the absence of opportunity to investigate the new circumstance (e.g., the opportunity to interview the new spouse).

III. Likelihood of Meeting Conditions

146. Similarly, entry may be refused where the officer is not satisfied that the individual will meet conditions for entry. Thus, where the officer has reason to believe that the individual seeking entry as a visitor may seek employment or may remain in Canada after their authorization has expired, the individual may be refused entry.

IV. Inadmissibility

147. The Act contains a set of ten grounds that render a person inadmissible to enter or remain in Canada: security, human or international rights violations, serious criminality, criminality, organized criminality, health, financial reasons, misrepresentation, non-compliance with the Act, and having an inadmissible family member. As noted, these factors apply differently to permanent residents and foreign nationals and are discussed in detail below.

§2. Procedures

I. Decision

148. Where, after examination at a port of entry, an officer is of the opinion that a person should not be permitted to enter Canada, a number of procedural options become available. Section 44 of the Act provides that the officer may prepare a report setting out the relevant facts for the consideration of another officer who exercises delegated authority from the Minister. The role of this second officer is to determine whether the report is well-founded and then to decide the appropriate action. Such actions might include referral of the matter to the ID of the IRB for an admissibility hearing or, in limited cases, making a removal order.

149. Section 44(1) of the Act deals with the decision of the first officer. It reads:

> An officer who is of the opinion that a permanent resident or a foreign national who is in Canada is inadmissible may prepare a report setting out the relevant facts, which report shall be transmitted to the Minister.[121]

150. Section 44(2) deals with the decision of the second officer. It reads:

> If the Minister is of the opinion that the report is well-founded, the Minister may refer the report to the Immigration Division for an admissibility hearing, except in the case of a permanent resident who is inadmissible solely on the grounds that they have failed to comply with the residency obligation under section 28 and except, in the circumstances prescribed by the regulations, in the case of a foreign national. In those cases, the Minister may make a removal order.[122]

151. Note that persons who arrive at a port of entry are assumed to be 'in Canada'. Unlike some other jurisdictions, Canadian law does not distinguish between those who are physically at the border and those who have gained entry.

121. IRPA, s. 44(1). The reference to the 'Minister' should be read as the 'Minister's delegate'.
122. IRPA, s. 44(2). Again, the reference to the 'Minister' should be read as the 'Minister's delegate'.

152. In addition, section 44 of the Act seems to give some discretion to each of the officers (by use of the word 'may') regarding whether or not to write or refer a report. In many circumstances, there may not be a requirement that a report be prepared, or when it is prepared, that it be referred to the ID or lead to a removal order. Section 42 of the Regulations expressly addresses one situation where a report will not be prepared with respect to a foreign national. It provides that where a foreign national who is seeking to enter Canada indicates that they want to withdraw their application they shall be allowed to do so. This provision, however, does not apply if a report is being prepared or has been prepared; in such cases the foreign national will not be allowed to withdraw their application and leave Canada unless the second officer does not refer the matter to the ID or make a removal order.[123]

153. The Federal Court of Appeal has considered the extent of the discretion accorded by section 44(2) and has determined that it is variable. In *Cha,* Décary JA states:

> Subsection 44(2) of the Act applies to all grounds of inadmissibility. These grounds encompass such diverse areas as security, human or international rights violations, serious criminality, criminality, organized criminality, health, financial reasons, misrepresentation and non-compliance with the Act. The complexity of the facts at issue varies from ground to ground. Some grounds have legal components, others not. The subsection applies to permanent residents and to foreign nationals, who are not usually subject to the same treatment under the terms of the Act. The subsection applies both to the power of the Minister's delegate to refer the report to the Immigration Division and to his power to issue the removal order himself.
>
> The scope of the discretion, therefore, may end up varying depending on the grounds alleged, on whether the person concerned is a permanent resident or a foreign national and on whether the report is referred or not to the Immigration Division. There may be a room for discretion in some cases, and none in others. This is why it was wise to use the term 'may'.[124]

He then concludes that where the ground of inadmissibility is criminality or serious criminality, it is not permissible for an officer to take into account individual circumstances when deciding whether or not to issue a removal order:

> In the circumstances, the use of the word 'may' does not attract discretion. 'May' is no more than an enabling provision, nothing more … 'than a signal from the legislator that an official … is being empowered to do something'.[125]

As a result of this decision, it is probably accurate to say that the level of discretion accorded by section 44 of the Act depends on the circumstances of the case but that

123. Regulations, s. 42(1) and (2).
124. *Cha v. Canada (Minister of Citizenship and Immigration)*, 2006 FCA 126 at paras 21–22.
125. *Ibid.* at para. 38.

there is little if any discretion to refrain from writing about individuals who are criminally inadmissible.

154. The Operational Manual identifies a lengthy list of extenuating factors that should be taken into account when determining whether a report should be written. The list focuses on such matters as the person's level of involvement in Canadian social life, whether there is a pattern of flouting immigration regulations, and whether the person has been counselled on the topic of their inadmissibility. Notwithstanding *Cha*, the Manual also leaves open the possibility of discretion being exercised in criminal cases. It suggests that the following questions be considered:

> In minor criminality cases, is a decision on rehabilitation imminent and likely to be favourable?
>
> Has the permanent resident been convicted of any prior criminal offence?
> Based on reliable information, is the permanent resident involved in criminal or organized criminal activities?
>
> What is the maximum sentence that could have been imposed?
>
> What was the sentence imposed?
>
> What are the circumstances of the particular incident under consideration?
>
> Did the conviction involve violence or drugs?[126]

155. An applicant must be accorded procedural fairness at the port of entry. In *Hernandez*, the Federal Court found that the duty of fairness owed by officers carrying out their mandate under section 44 was 'relaxed', but included the right to be informed of the purpose of the interview, the right to counsel, the right to have the officer inform the applicant of any information the applicant would not reasonably be expected to have, the right to make submissions either orally in writing, and the right to obtain a copy of the report.[127] The Court found in that case that the applicant, a permanent resident, was not accorded procedural fairness by a port of entry officer who interviewed him prior to preparing a report. Three reasons underlie the decision: The applicant was not advised of the purpose of the interview; he was not allowed to make submissions; and he was not given a copy of the officer's report.[128]

156. Section 44(2) of the Act provides two circumstances where a removal order may be issued at the port of entry without referring the matter to the ID of the IRB. First, where a permanent resident has been found to be inadmissible for failing to comply with the obligation, set out in section 28 of the Act, to reside in Canada for 730 days of every five-year period and second, where a foreign national has been found to be inadmissible solely on a ground or grounds set out in section 228 of the Regulations.[129] The grounds in section 228 of the Regulations are discussed below.

---

126. Citizenship and Immigration Canada, Operational Manual ENF5, *Writing 44(1) Reports* (20 Aug. 2013), s. 8.3.
127. *Hernandez v. Canada (Minister of Citizenship and Immigration)*, 2005 FC 429 at paras 70–71.
128. *Ibid.* at paras 76–77.
129. Regulations, s. 228.

157. Where the officer at the port of entry determines that a permanent resident fails to meet the residency requirement, the Minister's delegate at the port of entry may issue a removal order.[130] However, the permanent resident has a right to appeal the decision to the IAD of the IRB.[131] Section 49 of the Act provides that a removal order comes into force the day the appeal period expires if there is a right to appeal and no appeal is made or the day of the final determination of the appeal if an appeal is made.[132] The appeal period is thirty days.[133] Thus, although the removal order is issued, the permanent resident will be permitted to enter the country.

158. Section 228 of the Regulations identifies the circumstances in which the Minister's delegate at the port of entry may issue a removal order to a foreign national. He or she may do so where the individual is inadmissible solely on grounds of: (1) criminality or serious criminality, having been convicted of a criminal offence in Canada; (2) misrepresentation, where the RPD of the IRB has vacated a decision granting refugee protection for misrepresentation; (3) failure to comply with a requirement of the Act or regulations by, for example, failing to establish that he or she holds a visa when required; (4) having an inadmissible accompanying family member.[134] If the foreign national is inadmissible on grounds besides those listed in section 228, the officer may not issue the removal order.

159. Where the foreign national is either under the age of 18 years and unaccompanied by a parent or is unable to appreciate the nature of the proceedings, the officer does not have the authority to issue a removal order.[135]

160. In cases where the Minister's delegate does not have the authority to issue a removal order against the person seeking to enter Canada, the report may be referred to the ID of the IRB for a determination whether the person is inadmissible.

II. Detention and Detention Review

161. The officer conducting the port of entry examination may order that a person seeking entry be detained. Sections 55(2) and (3) of the Act provide:

> 55. (2) An officer may, without a warrant, arrest and detain a foreign national, other than a protected person:
> (a) who the officer has reasonable grounds to believe is inadmissible and is a danger to the public or is unlikely to appear for examination, an

130. IRPA, s. 44(2).
131. IRPA, s. 63(3). In addition, s. 63(4) allows an appeal to the IAD against a decision made outside Canada on the residency obligation under s. 28 of IRPA.
132. IRPA, s. 49(1)(b) and (c). In addition, a removal order may be ordered stayed by the Federal Court or may be stayed in other circumstances set out in s. 50 of the IRPA.
133. *Immigration Appeal Division Rules*, SOR/2002-230, rule 7(2).
134. Regulations, s. 228.
135. Regulations, s. 228(4).

admissibility hearing, removal from Canada, or at a proceeding that could lead to the making of a removal order by the Minister under subsection 44(2); or

(b) if the officer is not satisfied of the identity of the foreign national in the course of any procedure under this Act.

(3) A permanent resident or a foreign national may, on entry into Canada, be detained if an officer:

(a) considers it necessary to do so in order for the examination to be completed; or

(b) has reasonable grounds to suspect that the permanent resident or the foreign national is inadmissible on grounds of security, violating human or international rights, serious criminality, criminality or organized criminality.

162. Where a foreign national or permanent resident has been detained, notice must be provided to the ID of the IRB without delay.[136] The ID must review the detention order within forty-eight hours. A second review is required within seven days, and thereafter at least once every thirty days.[137] The purpose of the detention review is to determine whether the individual should continue to be detained.

163. The *Protecting Canada's Immigration System Act*[138] added provisions to the Act making it mandatory to detain foreign nationals whose arrival is designated as 'irregular' – such arrivals are deemed 'designated foreign nationals' (DFNs)[139] – by the Minister of Public Safety and Emergency Preparedness and who are 16 years of age or older.[140] While the ID must be notified without delay of a DFN's detention, the first detention review takes place within fourteen days rather than forty-eight hours. Subsequent detention reviews must take place six months after the previous review and no earlier, instead of within seven or thirty days.[141] Detention reviews for DFNs take place on a more limited basis.[142] If it orders release, the Act requires the ID to impose any conditions set out in the Regulations; at the time of writing, however, no such conditions had been prescribed.[143] Finally, the Minister may order the release of a DFN if exceptional circumstances warrant it or if, in the Minister's opinion, the reasons for detention no longer exist. The Minister may, but is not required, to impose conditions on release.[144]

136. IRPA, s. 55(4).
137. IRPA, s. 57.
138. S.C. 2012, c. 17.
139. IRPA, s. 20.1.
140. IRPA, s. 55(3.1).
141. IRPA, s. 57.1.
142. IRPA, s. 58(1.1).
143. IRPA, s. 58(4).
144. IRPA, s. 58.1.

164. Section 60 of the Act states that the detention of children is a measure that should be used only in the last resort.[145] However, a report published by the Canadian Council of Refugees in November 2009 indicates that children are detained in many circumstances that are not exceptional.[146]

165. In recent years, detention of individuals at ports of entry has increased dramatically. In 2009, 14,362 people were detained at the border compared to under 10,774 five years previously.[147]

III. The Inadmissibility Hearing

166. Where a report has been referred to the ID for determination of admissibility, the ID is required to hold a hearing where practicable. Notice of the hearing must be given to both the Minister and the permanent resident or foreign national (the 'party'). The admissibility hearing is adversarial in nature, but, the member of the ID is not bound by legal rules of evidence. The party is entitled to representation by counsel.[148]

167. Prior to the hearing, the Minister's counsel is required to provide to the ID and to the individual involved all relevant information and documents in his or her possession, including the evidence that is to be introduced. The Minister's counsel may, however, make an application for the non-disclosure of certain information.[149] Where this is done, the member of the ID is required to ensure the confidentiality of the information if he or she is of the opinion that its disclosure would be injurious to national security or endanger the safety of any person.[150] The member is also required to provide the individual with a summary of information and other evidence that enables them to be reasonably informed of the case made by the Minister in the proceeding but that does not include anything that, in the member's opinion, would be injurious to national security or endanger the safety of any person if disclosed.[151] The party is provided with a special advocate who is authorized to view the undisclosed evidence and argue on his or her behalf with respect to the adequacy of disclosure to the party and on the merits of inadmissibility issue.[152]

---

145. IRPA, s. 60. Section 249 of the Regulations sets out several factors to be considered by the ID of the IRB when conducting a detention review involving a minor.
146. See Canadian Council for Refugees, *Detention and the Best Interests of the Child,* available at http://www.ccrweb.ca/documents/detentionchildren.pdf (accessed 18 Jul. 2014); see also Delphine Nakache, 'The Human and Financial Cost of Detention of Asylum-Seekers in Canada' (2011), available at www.refworld.org/docid/4fafc44c2.html (accessed 18 Jul. 2014).
147. Kathleen Harris, 'Report: 14,000 suspected illegal immigrants detained last year', *Toronto Sun* (11 Jan. 2010), at: http://www.torontosun.com/news/canada/2010/01/11/12425881-qmi.html (accessed 18 Jul. 2014).
148. IRPA, ss 167(1) and 173.
149. IRPA, s. 86.
150. IRPA, s. 83(1)(d).
151. IRPA, s. 83(1)(e).
152. IRPA, s. 83(1)(b).

168. Where the party is an unaccompanied minor or is unable to appreciate the nature of proceedings a designated representative may be appointed by the presiding member to look after the party's interests.[153]

169. As a general rule, a hearing will be open to the public. However, the ID member is authorized to exclude the public where there is a serious possibility that the life, liberty or security of a person will be endangered if the proceeding is held in public, a real and substantial risk to the fairness of the proceeding such that the need to prevent disclosure outweighs the societal interest that the proceeding be conducted in public, or a real and substantial risk that matters involving public security will be disclosed. Before making any such order, the ID is required to consider whether alternative measures would be sufficient to protect the interests identified.[154]

170. Where the party before the ID is a refugee claimant, the hearing will generally be heard in the absence of the public although the ID is authorized to open it to the public 'where it is appropriate to do so' after taking into account the factors listed in the paragraph immediately above.[155]

171. A foreign national who is seeking to enter Canada has the burden of satisfying the member of the ID that they are not inadmissible. The burden is different where the person has been authorized to enter the country and is being removed. In these circumstances, the Minister has the burden of showing that the party is inadmissible.[156] The ID may also recognize the right to enter Canada of a citizen, registered Indian, or permanent resident; grant permanent resident status or temporary resident status to a foreign national if it is satisfied the foreign national meets the requirements under the Act; or authorize a permanent resident or foreign national to enter Canada for further examination.[157]

172. Where the party fails to meet the burden, the Board member must issue the applicable removal order – that is, a departure, deportation, or exclusion order.[158] The applicable removal orders are set out in the Regulations.[159]

153. IRPA, s. 167(2).
154. IRPA, s. 166.
155. IRPA, s. 166(c.1.).
156. IRPA, s. 45(d).
157. IRPA, s. 45(a)–(c).
158. IRPA, s. 45(d).
159. IRPA, ss 228 and 229.

Part II. Rights of Residence: General Provisions

Chapter 1. Short Stay Residence

173. As described in Part One, foreign nationals who are authorized to enter and remain in Canada as temporary residents are classified under four general headings: visitors, temporary workers, students and TRP holders. The last of these is exceptional: it applies to those who are permitted to reside in Canada despite falling within the criteria of inadmissibility. The laws regulating the residency of visitors and TRP holders are considered in this chapter. Part III addresses the laws regulating the residency of temporary workers and students.

§1. Conditions on the Residence of Visitors

174. The visitor class is defined by exclusion to encompass those who have been authorized to enter and remain temporarily in Canada but who have not been authorized to work or study.[160] It includes tourists, business visitors, and those who may work in Canada without a work permit.

175. 'Business Visitors' are described in the Regulations as foreign nationals who seek to engage in international business activities in Canada without directly entering the Canadian labour market.[161] A person will be held not to be directly entering the Canadian labour market only if two conditions are met: the primary source of their remuneration for their business activities must be outside Canada and their primary place of business and actual place of accrual of profits must be predominately outside Canada.[162] Specific categories of business visitor are also recognized, including those purchasing Canadian goods or services for a foreign business or government, those receiving or giving training within a Canadian parent or subsidiary of a corporation that employs them outside Canada and those selling

160. While s. 192 of the Regulations defines a visitor as a foreign national 'who has been authorized to enter and remain in Canada as a visitor', s. 195 refers to those who have been authorized to enter and remain as workers and s. 211 refers to those authorized to enter and remain as students.
161. Regulations, s. 187(1).
162. Regulations, s. 187(3).

goods on behalf of a foreign business or government (as long as the sales are not to the general public in Canada).[163]

176. The category of business visitor is also recognized in the North American Free Trade Agreement (NAFTA) and other international free trade agreements to which Canada is a signatory, including those with Peru, Columbia, Costa Rica, Chile, Israel, and the European Free Trade Association.[164]

177. In addition to business visitors, the Regulations identify a diverse group of foreign nationals who may work without authorization, and who consequently are considered visitors. Examples include performing artists undertaking a time-limited engagement, participants in sports activities and conference organizers.[165]

178. Visitors are authorized to enter Canada for a specified period of time – the default is six months[166] – and are required to leave the country when that period has expired unless they have been granted an extension. A period of time either greater or less than the default of six months may be imposed. The decision to impose a longer or shorter period of authorization will be based on three considerations: the individual's means of support in Canada, the period for which he or she applies to stay and the expiry date of the person's passport or other travel document.[167] Persons seeking visitor status will not be authorized to stay beyond their passport's date of expiry.[168]

179. Other conditions may also be imposed on visitors but they too are subject to qualification. Section 185 of the Regulations grants the power to officers to impose, vary or cancel specific conditions on temporary residents. It provides:

> An officer may impose, vary or cancel the following specific conditions on a temporary resident:
>
> (a) the period authorized for their stay;
> (b) the area within which they are permitted to travel or are prohibited from travelling in Canada; and
> (c) the times and places at which they must report for:
> (i) medical examination, surveillance or treatment, or
> (ii) the presentation of evidence of compliance with applicable conditions.

---

163. Regulations, s. 187(2).
164. The texts of Canada's Free Trade Agreements are available online at: http://www.international.gc.ca/commerce/index.aspx.
165. Regulations, s. 186. There are more than twenty categories of worker listed.
166. Regulations, s. 183(2).
167. Regulations, s. 183(2).
168. Citizenship and Immigration Canada, Operational Manual ENF4, *Port of Entry Examinations*, s. 13.20.

180. Border Services Officers are not empowered to use conditions as a deterrent to entry. The Operational Manual offers some limitations on the imposition of conditions. It provides:

> The [Border Services Officer] should not use conditions as a means of discouraging a foreign national from coming into Canada. The reasons for imposing conditions on a temporary resident are to ensure that the person complies with the period and purpose for which they sought entry into Canada and to make the temporary resident aware of the need for formal authorization before extending that period or varying the purposes of the visit.[169]

181. The Operational Manual gives two examples where conditions may be imposed on movement within Canadian territory:[170] first, where a person is being admitted to stand trial or be a witness in legal proceedings and second, where they are in transit to another country and therefore have no reason to leave the airport.

182. The Manual also specifies that it would be appropriate to impose the condition of a medical examination where the foreign national has a dormant medical condition that could pose a danger to public health if it became active. Where such a condition is imposed, it also states that it would appropriate to impose the further condition of providing evidence of compliance.[171]

183. At the end of the period of authorization, the visitor loses status automatically unless they have received an extension of their authorization.[172] The matter does *not* require an official determination.[173] However, in limited circumstances, those who have lost their status as temporary residents by remaining beyond their authorized date of departure may have their status restored.

184. Section 182 of the Regulations provides that a visitor may apply for restoration of status within ninety days after losing temporary resident status as a result of failing to abide by the time limits on their authorization. Section 182 also provides that the Minister *shall* restore the status if it is established that 'the visitor … meets the initial requirements for their stay and has not failed to comply with any other conditions imposed'. The language implies that there is no discretion to refuse if the conditions are met.

185. The application form for restoration of status is the same as that used for extension of status, as described immediately below.

169. *Ibid.* at s. 13.22.
170. *Ibid.*
171. *Ibid.* at s. 13.23.
172. IRPA s. 47(a).
173. IRPA s. 47(a).

§2. Maintaining Residence: Administrative Procedures and Documents

186. A foreign national may apply for an extension of their authorization to remain in Canada as a visitor. While the Regulations specify only that the application must be made before the period of authorization expires,[174] CIC informs temporary residents on its website that they must apply for an extension thirty days before their authorization expires.[175]

187. The application for an extension of authorization is usually made by mail.[176] The Regulations require an applicant to satisfy the officer that any conditions imposed on entry have been fulfilled and that he or she 'continues to meet the requirements' that apply to the grant of a visa.[177] The language of this legal provision is odd since the applicant may have been visa-exempt and thus it may never have been determined that he or she meets the criteria for a visa. The best interpretation of the regulation would require the officer to grant an extension to a visa-exempt foreign nationals where they continue to meet the original criteria for entry that are found in sections 20 and 22 of the IRPA, namely that they have proper documentation (a passport or travel document), that they intend to leave Canada by the end of the period of extended authorization and are not inadmissible.

188. The application for an extension requires that applicants provide: full details of why they want to stay longer, proof of identity, proof of current status in Canada, and evidence of how they will support themselves or be supported in Canada and how they will pay for transportation to leave Canada. It is suggested that the latter evidence may be provided by a guarantor's letter or a bank statement.

189. The Operational Manual offers a series of questions and guidelines that are considered relevant to the officer charged with deciding whether the extension should be granted. They include the following:

- Consider the intentions of the client: What is the client doing in Canada? How long has the applicant been here? How long is the request for?
- Officers must consider the reason given by the client for applying for the extension. Are the plans well thought out or merely frivolous? Taking the applicant's situation in their home country into consideration, is a prolonged stay in Canada reasonable?
- Determine whether the client has the means to support themselves or whether someone else is willing to provide adequate support.
- Assess the client's ability to leave Canada. Officers should consider whether the applicant has the means to either return to their home country or to proceed onward to a third country.

---

174. Regulations, s. 181.
175. See: http://www.cic.gc.ca/english/visit/extend-stay.asp.
176. The Guide for making an application for an extension is available online at: http://www.cic.gc.ca/english/information/applications/guides/5551ETOC.asp.
177. Regulations, s. 181(2).

- What was the original purpose of the visit to Canada? Has it been fulfilled? If no, was sufficient time originally granted to fulfil the purpose?
- What family, employment or other responsibilities and obligations has the person left behind and how have they been discharged? Is the proposed extension logical, reasonable and feasible in light of these circumstances?[178]

190. Where the application for an extension has been submitted, the applicant will retain status until a decision is made even where the decision is made after the date on which the original authorization expires. A person in this position is described as having 'implied status'.

191. Foreign national with implied status who leave the country may be granted re-entry if they are visa-exempt or have a multiple entry visa. However, those who have been issued a single entry visa will not be permitted to re-enter, (although visits to the United States are permissible).[179]

§3. Legal Position of Visitors

192. Unlike temporary workers and students, who may be accorded some limited benefits depending on their province of residence, visitors are excluded from both federal and provincial plans that provide social or economic benefits. In the case of contributory benefit regimes, such as Employment Insurance and the Canada Pension Plan, they are excluded because the plan requires that the beneficiary has worked for a specified number of hours made earlier contributions to the fund. Similarly visitors are ineligible for benefits under the Federal Old Age Security Pension and the various provincial social assistance plans.[180]

193. However, visitors are protected by some of the provisions of the Canadian Charter of Rights and Freedoms. Various provisions of the Charter, including those that fall under the heading 'Fundamental Freedoms' and those falling under the heading 'Legal Rights' guarantee rights to 'everyone', a catch-all category that is sufficiently broad to include visitors.[181]

§4. Position of Family Members

194. As outlined in Part I, an application to enter and remain in Canada as a visitor may include accompanying family members, all of whom will be granted the

178. Citizenship and Immigration Canada, Operational Manual IP6, *Processing Temporary Resident Extensions*, s. 5.1.
179. Regulations, s. 190 (3)(f).
180. In addition visitors who become reliant on social assistance become inadmissible under the terms of s. 39 of IRPA.
181. In *Singh v. Canada (Minister of Employment and Immigration)* [1985] 1 SCR 177, Wilson J. states, 'I am prepared to accept that the term ["everyone"] includes every human being who is physically present in Canada and by virtue of such presence amenable to Canadian law.'

same status. The category of 'family member' includes one's spouse or common-law partner, a dependent child, the spouse or common law partner's dependent child and the dependent child of a dependent child.[182] The inadmissibility of an accompanying family member is a ground of inadmissibility that applies to all foreign nationals who wish to enter or remain in Canada. Should a visitor become inadmissible, their accompanying family will also become inadmissible.[183]

195. The grant of temporary resident status to a visitor does not provide any benefits to family members of the grantee who are outside Canada.

196. Applications for extensions of authorization may include family members. The Application Form (IMM 1249) covers applications by all members of the family and must be accompanied by a photocopy of a marriage certificate or statutory declaration of common law union (if appropriate), photocopies of passport pages and a receipt that applicable fees have been paid. Where the applicant has paid a representative to assist in the application, a further form (IMM 5401) must be included.

§5. Loss of Status

197. A visitor may lose status in two circumstances: automatically, at the end of the period for which they are authorized to remain in Canada[184] and second, on a determination by an officer or the ID of the IRB that they have failed to comply with any other requirement of the Act, and thereby become inadmissible.[185]

198. The alleged ground of inadmissibility determines the identity of the administrative actor charged with deciding the question. The issue will be decided by a delegate of the Minister in four circumstances: criminality or serious criminality in relation to offences committed in Canada; misrepresentation; failure to comply with the Act (e.g., working or studying without a permit); and inadmissible family member.[186] Where the allegation relates to other grounds of inadmissibility, the matter will be determined by the ID of the IRB.

199. In proceedings before the ID relating to the inadmissibility of an individual who has been authorized to enter Canada as a temporary resident, the onus is on the government to show on the balance of probabilities that the person is inadmissible.[187] This differs from an admissibility hearing relating to a person who seeks to enter Canada, where the person seeking admission bears the onus of proving that they are not inadmissible.

---

182. Regulations, s. 1.
183. IRPA s. 42.
184. *Ibid.* s. 47(a).
185. *Ibid.* s. 47 (b).
186. Regulations, s. 228.
187. IRPA s. 45(d).

200. A visitor who is found to be inadmissible by either a Minister's delegate or the ID may apply for leave to seek judicial review from the Federal Court.

201. At any time the visitor may also apply to the Minister for permission to remain in Canada on humanitarian or compassionate (H&C) grounds.[188] The application for H&C consideration must be in writing and must accompany an application to remain in Canada as a permanent resident. An H&C decision must take into account the best interests of any child directly affected by the decision.

§6. Conditions on Residence of Temporary Resident Permit Holders

202. An individual who is inadmissible to enter Canada will normally be denied entry either by a visa officer or at port of entry. An inadmissible individual who is already in Canada is subject to removal. However, in exceptional circumstances such individuals may apply for a TRP. While a visa officer outside Canada may approve a TRP, such a permit may be issued only at a port of entry or within Canada. The IRPA authorizes an officer to issue a TRP to persons who are otherwise inadmissible where he or she is 'of the opinion that it is justified in the circumstances'.[189] The reasons for issuing a permit may be reasons of public policy, national interest or humanitarian and compassionate considerations.

203. A TRP may be issued both to individuals who seek to remain in Canada temporarily but have been found to be inadmissible and to those who seek to remain permanently.

204. A holder of a TRP is authorized to remain in Canada for the period of validity which may extend from one day to three years.[190]

205. A TRP will be issued only where the circumstances are compelling. The Operational Manual specifies:

> An inadmissible person's need to enter or remain in Canada must be compelling and sufficient enough (sic) to overcome the health or safety risks to Canadian society. The degree of need is relative to the type of case. Even if the inadmissibility or violation is relatively minor, a permit may be unwarranted in the absence of compelling need. For example, the temporary resident visa program would lack integrity if temporary residents without visas obtained temporary resident permits at ports of entry.
>
> The following includes points and examples, which are **not** exhaustive, but illustrate the scope and spirit in which discretion to issue a permit is to be applied.
>
> Officers may issue a permit if:

188. IRPA s. 25.
189. IRPA s. 24.
190. Citizenship and Immigration Canada, Operational Manual IP1, *Temporary Resident Permits*, s. 5.3.

– the need to enter or remain in Canada is compelling and sufficient to overcome the risk;
– the risk to Canadians or Canadian society is minimal and the need for the presence in Canada outweighs the risk. ... Restoration of status is not an option.[191]

206. A TRP may be cancelled at any time. Before the cancellation becomes effective, the holder is contacted in writing and is informed of the reasons for the cancellation and is offered the opportunity to make representations in writing or in person to the officer who intends to cancel the permit.[192]

§7. Applications for TRPs and extensions

207. There is no formal procedure for applying for a TRP. The initial grant of a TRP will follow a negative determination made in relation either to another application, for example for a visa or for authorization to enter Canada or to the issuance of a removal order.

§8. TRPs and Human Trafficking

208. Persons who self-identify as victims of human trafficking may be granted a TRP to allow them to regularize their status in Canada and escape the influence of the trafficker. In such cases, a two-part process is frequently adopted, with the grant of a short-term permit (under 180 days) being issued while the officer investigates the circumstances and the allegations of trafficking followed by a more complete examination where a longer term permit is requested.[193]

209. Victims of trafficking are eligible for health benefits and counselling under the Interim Federal Health Programme (IFHP).[194]

210. An application form (IMM1249) is available for an extension of a TRP. It must be accompanied by the following documents: (a) a passport or acceptable travel document is normally required for proof of identity. US citizens may supply a birth certificate instead; (b) a photocopy of current TRP and any other document issued by CIC; (c) supporting documentation of action taken to resolve the inadmissibility; (d) evidence of means of future financial support; (e) A letter specifying the compelling reasons for extending the permit and any changes in personal circumstances, any further grounds of inadmissibility that apply.

191. *Ibid.* s. 5.8.
192. *Ibid.* s. 23.1.
193. *Ibid.* s. 16.
194. See: http://www.cic.gc.ca/EnGLIsh/inFORMation/applications/trp.asp.

211. While the Regulations merely state that the application for an extension be made before authorization expires,[195] the Operational Manual stipulates that the application for an extension of a permit must be made at least thirty days before the expiry of the permit. This could only be applicable to permits that are valid for a longer period.

§9. Legal Position of TRP Holders

212. The benefits of holding a TRP are substantial. While a TRP holder may not work or study without a further permit, such a permit may be obtained from within Canada. Moreover, a work permit may be issued to a TRP holder without the need of a LMO[196] where the period of validity of the TRP is at least six months and where the holder is unable to support themselves without working.[197]

213. TRP holders are in some circumstances eligible for benefits which are denied to visitors. For example, specific reference is made to TRP holders in the Ontario Health Insurance Plan which provides coverage after a three-month waiting period.

214. The most important benefit attached to the TRP is that, in some circumstances, it allows the holder to apply for permanent resident status from within Canada. Permit holders are subject to a unique set of selection criteria. Assuming no further grounds of inadmissibility beyond those that prevented their original entry, a permit holder who is medically inadmissible will obtain status after three years of continuous residence. Five years of continuous residence is required for those inadmissible on other grounds, except where the ground of inadmissibility is security (section 34), violation of human or international rights (section 35), serious criminality (section 36(1)) or organized criminality (section 37). In these latter cases, the TRP holder is ineligible for permanent resident status.

215. The requirement of continuous residence entails that if a TRP expires and the holder applies for a new permit, the residence period is calculated from the date that the second permit is issued. A break in continuity will also occur where the holder leaves Canada without seeking prior authorization to re-enter.

216. The TRP may also be used to regularize the status of a person who has been determined to be a Convention refugee or a protected person but who is not granted permanent resident status because of inadmissibility for reasons of security, human rights violations, serious criminality organized criminality or danger to public health and safety.

---

195. Regulations, s. 181.
196. See Part III.
197. Regulations, s. 208(b).

217. A TRP holder who leaves Canada may not re-enter unless pre-authorization has been given. Departure from Canada without obtaining pre-authorization renders the permit invalid.[198]

§10. Position of Family Members

218. Each person is required to make an individual application for a TRP.

219. Similarly, each TRP holder may apply for permanent resident status only on behalf of himself or herself. Each accompanying family member must submit a separate application.[199]

198. Regulations, s. 63(b).
199. *Ibid.* p. 36.

Chapter 2. Long-Term Residence

§1. Conditions of Residence for Permanent Residents

220. All permanent residents must meet a residence requirement in order to maintain their status and their entitlement to stay in the country. The basic requirement is outlined in section 28 of the IRPA, which provides:

> a permanent resident complies with the residency obligation with respect to a five-year period if, on each of a total of at least 730 days in that five-year period, they are:
>
> (i) physically present in Canada,

221. Three exceptions to this requirement are recognized. A permanent resident may reside outside Canada for a longer period where: (a) they are accompanying a Canadian citizen who is their spouse or common-law (or a parent if they are a child); (b) they are outside Canada employed on a full-time basis by a Canadian business or in the public service of Canada or of a province; or (c) they are an accompanying spouse, common-law partner or child of a permanent resident who is outside Canada and is employed on a full-time basis by a Canadian business or in the public of Canada or of a province. The Operational Manual gives detailed guidance on each of these exceptions.[200]

222. The use of the phrase 'physical presence' in section 28 is now mirrored in the Strengthening Canadian Citizenship Act's requirement that residence for purposes of citizenship eligibility requires physical presence in Canada.[201] The amendment resolved years of inconsistency in the Federal Court's interpretation of residence for citizenship purposes.[202]

223. Failure to meet the residency requirement outlined in section 28 does not automatically lead to loss of status. A determination by the appropriate authority must first be made. Moreover, the officer may determine that humanitarian and compassionate considerations justify the retention of status in the particular circumstances of a case.[203]

224. The Operational Manual lists a lengthy set of factors that may be taken into account when determining whether humanitarian and considerations outweigh the

200. Citizenship and Immigration Canada, Operational Manual ENF23, *Loss of Permanent Resident Status*, s. 7.9.
201. Strengthening Canadian Citizenship Act s. 3(1), amending s. 5(1)(c) of the Citizenship Act.
202. See, for example, *Canada (Minister of Citizenship and Immigration) v. Zhou* [2008] FCJ No. 1170 and *Islam v. Canada (Minister of Citizenship and Immigration),* [2009] FCJ No. 14.
203. IRPA s. 28(2)(c).

breach of the residency requirement.[204] They are categorized under four general headings: the extent of the non-compliance; circumstances beyond the person's control, including consideration of whether the person was under the authority of a parent when they left Canada; establishment outside Canada, including consideration of whether the person has acquired permanent resident status elsewhere; and presence and degree of consequential hardship, including consideration of the impact of loss of status on other Canadian permanent residents and citizens.

225. In addition, where a person has been a permanent resident for more than five years, it is sufficient to show that residency requirement was met for the five-year period immediately before the date of determination. Thus, a permanent resident who has resided outside Canada for more than three years but who subsequently returned to reside in Canada for 730 days during the next five years would meet the residency requirement.

226. Where a person has been a permanent resident for less than five years, it is sufficient to show that they will be able to meet the residency requirement for the five-year period following the grant of status.[205]

227. A further condition is placed on individuals who were granted permanent resident status after applying under the former entrepreneur programme.[206] Entrepreneurs are granted status with the caveat that they must meet conditions relating to the establishment of a business within a specified period of time. Section 98 of the Regulations provides three conditions that must be met: the entrepreneur must control 33.33% or more of the equity of a qualifying Canadian business; they must provide ongoing management of the business; and they must create at least one full-time job for a citizen or permanent resident. In order to get status the entrepreneur is required to state in writing that they intend and will be able to meet these conditions. The conditions must be met for one year within three years of getting status and the entrepreneur must report and provide evidence on their attempts to comply within the relevant period.

228. Each entrepreneur is provided with a kit called the 'Entrepreneur Counselling and Monitoring Guide', which contains guides and forms relating to the fulfilment of conditions. Within six months the entrepreneurs is required to provide an address to CIC. On receipt, the entrepreneur is interviewed and counselled on the conditions that must be met. A second monitoring period occurs between eighteen and twenty-four months after status is granted. A second interview allows the officer

204. Citizenship and Immigration Canada, Operational Manual, OP10, *Permanent Residency Status Determination*, s. 14.

205. IRPA s. 28(2)(b)(i).

206. In 2014, CIC cancelled the federal entrepreneur program. It has been replaced by a new 'start-up visa' as a five-year pilot project. Unlike the former entrepreneur programme, there are no additional conditions imposed on permanent residents accepted under the start-up visa programme. Subsequent references to 'entrepreneurs' refer to individuals accepted under the programme before it was suspended in 2011 and ultimately terminated. See, http://www.cic.gc.ca/english/immigrate/business/entrepreneurs/index.asp (accessed 11 Jun. 2014).

to provide feedback on the level of compliance that has been achieved. After entrepreneurs comply with the conditions, they are required to submit an application to cancel conditions. Where the conditions have not been met, the officer may prepare a report (under section 44 of the IRPA) indicating that the entrepreneur is inadmissible. The officer may recommend against an admissibility hearing in the section 44 report, 'in cases where the conditions were only partially met, but where entrepreneurs have acted in good faith and have made reasonable efforts to meet the conditions but did not succeed for reasons beyond their control'.[207]

229. Family members of an entrepreneur are subject to the condition that the entrepreneur meet these conditions. Thus, a determination that an entrepreneur has failed to meet these conditions leads to loss of status for both the entrepreneur and their family members.[208]

§2. Administrative Procedures and Documents

230. Each permanent resident is issued a permanent resident card that indicates status and facilitates re-entry into Canada should they leave. The card is valid for a five-year period. A permanent resident card is issued only in Canada. A person who is in possession of the card is presumed to have permanent resident status. However, a person who is outside Canada without a status card is presumed not to have permanent resident status.

231. A permanent resident who is outside Canada without a status card and who wishes to return to Canada must apply to a visa office for a travel document.

232. The Officer will issue the travel document only if satisfied that the individual has met the residency requirement or has been allowed to retain status for humanitarian and compassionate reasons, or seeks to return to Canada to appeal an earlier decision that they have lost status for having failed to meet the residency requirement. Where an officer overseas decides that a person has not met the residency requirement, the individual may appeal the decision to the IAD of the IRB. For this last provision to apply, the individual must have been physically present in Canada at least once within the previous 365 days.

233. In order to obtain the relevant travel document the individual must submit an application form (IMM524E), a valid passport from another country which guarantees re-entry to that country, and evidence to show that they meet the residency requirement. This may include employment documents and financial documents such as Revenue Canada assessment forms. A variety of other documents may provide proof that the person has been physically present in Canada in the previous 365 days.

207. Citizenship and Immigration Canada, Operational Manual IP7, *Entrepreneur Program*, s. 12.8.
208. Regulations, s. 98(6).

234. The decision that a person has failed to meet the residency requirement may also be made at the port of entry. The decision will be made by the Minister's delegate when considering a report issued by a CBSA officer that a person is inadmissible. Where the Minister's delegate decides that the permanent resident has failed to meet the residency requirement, he or she may issue a removal order. This is the only circumstance where the Minister's delegate may issue a removal order against a permanent resident. In all other circumstances, it is only the ID of the IRB that may issue such an order after an admissibility hearing. The removal order only comes into force after an appeal to the IAD of the IRB has failed or the time allowed to make an appeal has expired where no appeal has been made.

§3. Legal Position of Permanent Residents

235. The status of a permanent resident roughly approximates that of a Canadian citizen, with some notable exceptions. The Supreme Court of Canada has held that discrimination against permanent residents is analogous to discrimination on the basis of grounds specifically prohibited in section 15 of the Charter. Thus, a provincial law that permitted only Canadian citizens to practice law in the province was held to be unconstitutional for discriminating against permanent residents who were similarly qualified.[209]

236. Permanent residents have the same capacity as citizens to sponsor members of their family who are themselves applying for permanent resident status.

237. However, there are important differences between the status of permanent resident and citizen. The guarantee of equality rights is subject to the qualification found in section 1 of the Charter which stipulates that all rights and freedoms are subject to such reasonable limits prescribed by law as can be demonstrably justified in a free and democratic society. The Supreme Court of Canada has held that it is justifiable to retain some privileges for citizens to promote social cohesion and to create an incentive for people to naturalize.[210]

238. Various statutes reserve specific benefits and obligations for citizens and exclude permanent residents. For example, under the federal Public Service Employment Act, citizens are shown preference in some instances of hiring and promotion. In several provinces, the Jury Act excludes permanent residents and foreign nationals from serving on a jury.

239. Moreover, because the Charter itself distinguishes between citizens and permanent residents in relation to the right to enter, remain in and leave Canada, differentiation between citizens and permanent residents in the field of immigration has been determined to be constitutional. It is not an infringement to differentiate between citizens and permanent residents in relation to entry and removal. The

209. *Andrews, supra* n. 6.
210. *Lavoie, supra* n. 7.

Charter also appears to reserve democratic rights (the right to vote or to be a member of the House of Commons or a provincial legislature) to citizens.

240. The Supreme Court of Canada has determined that the mere deportation of a permanent resident does not engage his or her constitutional rights to life, liberty and security of the person nor the constitutional rights of family members. In *Medovarski*, the Court stated:

> The most fundamental principle of immigration law is that non-citizens do not have an unqualified right to enter or remain in Canada: *Chiarelli v. Canada (Minister of Employment and Immigration)*, [1992] 1 S.C.R. 711, at p. 733. Thus the deportation of a non-citizen in itself cannot implicate the liberty and security interests protected by s. 7 of the *Canadian Charter of Rights and Freedoms.*

The Court went on to state that even if these rights were engaged by the process of deportation, the process of deportation was in accordance with principles of fundamental justice.

241. The United Nations Human Rights Committee has also considered complaints by Canadian permanent residents who were ordered deported. In the 1993 decision *Stewart v. Canada*,[211] the applicant had arrived in Canada as a child but had never taken out citizenship. He argued that the decision to remove him from Canada after determining that he was inadmissible on grounds of criminality, infringed his right to enter 'his own country' guaranteed by Article 12(4) of the International Covenant on Civil and Political Rights (ICCPR). The Committee rejected the argument that Canada was Stewart's 'own country' because Canada 'facilitated acquiring its nationality', and Stewart's choice not to naturalize, and/or to commit acts disqualifying him from naturalizing, prevented Canada from becoming '"his own country" within the meaning of Article 12'.[212] The Committee also determined that the interference with family relations consequent to deportation was not unlawful or arbitrary.[213] In 2011, a majority of the Human Rights Committee came to the opposite conclusion on both issues with respect to Jama Warsame, a Saudi-born Somali citizen who arrived in Canada at the age of 4 years from Saudi Arabia and acquired permanent resident status:[214] Canada was Jama Warsame's 'own country', and deportation would deprive him of the right to enter and remain in it. Deportation would also violate his right to family relations under Articles 17 and 23.[215]

211. Communication No. 538/1993, available online at: http://www.worldlii.org/int/cases/IIHRL/1996/84.html.
212. *Ibid.* at para. 12.5.
213. *Ibid.* at para. 12.10.
214. *Jama Warsame v. Canada*, Communication No. 1959/2010, UN Doc. CCPR/C/102/D/1959/2010 (2011).
215. *Ibid.* at para. 8.

242. Between the *Stewart* and *Warsame* cases, Canadian law had been amended to remove an appeal to the IAD when the case involves serious criminality. However, the Minister may still consider the impact of deportation on family life where an H&C application is made by the individual to the Minister, although an H&C application does not stay a deportation order pending the decision.

§4. Position of Family Members

243. Children born in Canada are Canadian citizens whatever the status of their parents. However, the citizen-child of a permanent resident does not have a constitutional right that his or her parent not be deported. In *Langner v. Canada (Minister of Employment and Immigration)*,[215a] the Federal Court of Appeal held that the decision to deport a foreign national did not infringe the constitutional rights of their citizen-child. The child had no Charter right to 'demand that the Canadian Government not apply, to their parents the penalties provided for violation of Canadian immigration laws. The decision of the parent to take their child or leave him in Canada is regarded a private decision'.

244. However, the best interests of a Canadian child are a relevant factor that must be taken into account where the person under removal order has made an application to the Minister to be permitted to remain in Canada on humanitarian and compassionate grounds, or where an appeal has been made to the IAD.

245. In most circumstances where a permanent resident has been found to be inadmissible, this will have no bearing on the permanent resident status of family members. There is one exception, noted above. Where an entrepreneur has failed to meet the conditions that qualify their status, family members will also be found to have failed to meet a condition.

§5. Loss of Permanent Resident Status

246. Permanent residents who become Canadian citizens will lose their permanent resident status. However, this has a positive impact on their right of residence since citizens enjoy a more secure status, which can be revoked in more limited circumstances that the citizen misrepresented or withheld relevant information in their citizenship application (or in their previous application for permanent resident status), or have been convicted for crimes designated as 'national security offences', or have served in an enemy armed force.[216]

215a. (1995), 184 NR 230 FCA.

216. Citizenship Act, s. 10, as amended by Strengthening Canadian Citizenship Act, s. 10.1–10.7 (not in force as of Feburary 2015). See also, Citizenship and Immigration Canada, Operational Manual CP9, *Acquisition and Loss of Canadian Citizenship*, s. 12.2.

247. As noted above, permanent residents will also lose status when a final determination is made that they have failed to comply with the residence requirement.

248. Permanent residents will also lose status when a removal order issued by the ID of the IRB comes into force. Such an order will be issued where the permanent resident has been found to be inadmissible.

249. The grounds of inadmissibility that apply to permanent residents overlap with those that apply to foreign nationals but are less strict. The inadmissibility of a family member (section 42) does not render a permanent resident inadmissible; Likewise, only foreign nationals are inadmissible on the ground that they are or will be unable to support themselves financially (section 39) or do not meet the health requirements (section 38), or on grounds of mere (as opposed to serious) criminality (section 36).

250. When deciding the issue of inadmissibility, the ID does not have discretion to take into account the length of time that the permanent resident has spent in Canada.

251. The decision of the ID may be appealed to the IAD of the IRB unless the individual has been found to be inadmissible on grounds of security, violating human rights, serious criminality[217] or organized criminality.

252. The IAD may allow an appeal where it finds that the original decision is wrong in law, in fact or mixed law and fact; where it finds that a principle of natural justice was not observed; or where sufficient humanitarian and compassionate considerations warrant special relief in light of all the circumstances of the case, taking into account the best interests of any child directly affected.

253. Specific rules also apply to individuals who have been granted permanent resident status after having made a successful claim for refugee protection. Where the earlier decision is vacated on the ground that it was obtained through misrepresentation or where there is a determination that protected status has ceased, the permanent resident status may be lost.[218]

---

217. A foreign national or permanent resident is inadmissible for 'serious criminality' for: (a) having been convicted in Canada of an offence under an Act of Parliament punishable by a maximum term of imprisonment of at least ten years, or of an offence under an Act of Parliament for which a term of imprisonment of more than six months has been imposed; (b) having been convicted of an offence outside Canada that, if committed in Canada, would constitute an offence under an Act of Parliament punishable by a maximum term of imprisonment of at least ten years; or (c) committing an act outside Canada that is an offence in the place where it was committed and that, if committed in Canada, would constitute an offence under an Act of Parliament punishable by a maximum term of imprisonment of at least ten years. (IRPA s. 36(1)).

218. IRPA, s. 46 (1)(c.1)(d).

Part III. Rights of Residence for Specific Categories of Migrants

254. This part addresses the specific legal rules applicable to sub-categories of permanent and temporary residents. Chapter 1 deals with temporary residents who also work or study, and Chapter 5 deals with the preferential entry granted business persons and professionals who enter and work temporarily under the NAFTA and the General Agreement on Trade in Services (GATS). Chapter 2 covers certain foreign nationals who can transition from temporary to permanent residence within Canada. Chapter 3 deals with the family and economic classes, who enter Canada as permanent residents. Chapter 4 deals with refugees and other protected persons. Refugee or protected person status affords permanent residence or a pathway to it in all but exceptional cases. It is possible to be protected from removal but also to be inadmissible at the same time.

255. The rules with respect to admissibility cannot be understood separately from the rules of inadmissibility. The basic rule is that no foreign national or permanent resident will be admitted to or allowed to remain in Canada if inadmissible on any of the grounds contained in sections 34–42 of the Act, subject to exceptions. Grounds of inadmissibility include security concerns, human or international rights violations, serious and non-serious criminality, organized criminality, public health concerns, financial reasons, misrepresentation and non-compliance with the Act. They and the procedures for enforcing them are detailed in Part IV.

Chapter 1. Temporary Residents

256. Part II, Chapter 1, addresses the general rules governing admission and residence of temporary residents. This chapter addresses the specific rules applicable to temporary residents who wish to study or work in Canada.

§1. Students

257. Study has historically been recognized as a valid reason for entry into Canada. The government's rationale for admitting foreign students has shifted in emphasis over time. For instance, during a period of race-based restrictions on the immigration of Chinese to Canada in the early twentieth century, the Canadian government explained the exception for Chinese students on the basis that these students would serve as 'missionaries of trade' upon return home.[219] Later, foreign student admission was promoted as a form of quasi-development assistance, whereby nationals from less developed countries obtain the benefits of a Canadian education (in the formal and informal sense), and then return and contribute to the advancement of their home countries. Today, admission of foreign students is rationalized in terms of their economic and academic contribution to Canada and Canadian post-secondary institutions. Importantly, foreign students are now viewed as a pool of potential economic class immigrants to Canada.[220] Entry of students into Canada is listed in the Act as one of the objectives of Canada's immigration policy and it is considered a priority by the Ministry.[221] In 2012, more than 100,000 foreign students entered and a total of 265,404 foreign students resided in Canada.[222] The top five source countries in 2012 were China, India, the Republic of Korea, Saudi Arabia, and the United States.[223]

258. Study permits are required for full- or part-time studies undertaken at a university or college, or for any academic, professional, or vocational training.[224] They are not required for courses of general interest or self-improvement, distance learning (unless part of the programme must be undertaken in Canada) or audited courses. Some foreign nationals, such as private diplomatic staff or individuals pursuing courses of study shorter than a visitor's authorized period of stay – for example, an English as a second language programme less than six months long

---

219. N. Kelley & M. Trebilcock, *The Making of the Mosaic: A History of Canadian Immigration Policy* 152–153, 203 (*2d ed.,* U. Toronto Press, 2010).
220. Citizenship and Immigration Canada, 'OP12 – Students' (15 Dec. 2008) at 7 (hereinafter 'OP12').
221. IRPA, s. 3(1)(g).
222. Citizenship and Immigration Canada, Facts and Figures, 2012, Immigration Overview: Permanent and Temporary Residents – Total entries of foreign students by source country, and foreign students present on 1 December, by source country, http://www.cic.gc.ca/EnGLish/resources/statistics/facts 2012/index.asp (accessed 11 Jun. 2014).
223. *Ibid.* Total entries of foreign students by source country, http://www.cic.gc.ca/EnGLish/resources/statistics/facts2012/temporary/13.asp (accessed 11 Jun. 2014).
224. Regulations, ss 1(1) ('studies'), 212.

– do not require a permit.[225] Educational institutions in Canada are generally sensitive to immigration requirements and will not allow a foreign national to commence a course of study without a permit.[226]

259. The basic rule for foreign nationals who wish to study in Canada is that they must apply for a study permit from outside the country concurrent with their application for a temporary resident visa or TRV, if required.[227] Foreign nationals from the United States, Greenland, and the French-held islands of St Pierre and Miquelon south of Newfoundland may apply for study permits at a port of entry into Canada.[228] Others, such as holders of study permits that are about to expire or that have recently expired, holders of valid work permits, and refugee claimants, may apply for study permits in Canada.[229] Family members of study-permit holders and family of some other foreign nationals – for example, family of foreign journalists – may also apply for study permits in Canada.[230] Permits are not required for minor children of legally admitted foreign nationals for pre-school, primary, or secondary school other than the children of temporary residents not authorized to work or study.[231]

260. An immigration officer is required to issue a study permit if the foreign national has applied in accordance with the Regulations, will leave Canada at the end of the period authorizing their stay and, in most cases, has been screened medically.[232] The foreign national must not be inadmissible on health or other grounds. The study permit will usually be issued for the length of the course of study.[233]

261. All applicants must submit an acceptance letter from the institution where they will study.[234] Students must also demonstrate that they possess sufficient funds (without having to work in Canada) to pay tuition, maintain themselves and accompanying family members, and pay the cost of transportation to and from Canada for themselves and accompanying family. Financial sufficiency need only be shown for the first year of studies, although '[o]fficers should be satisfied … that the probability for future funding does exist … '.[235] Officers exercise discretion as to the nature of documentation they can request to verify financial sufficiency. They may be less strict in requiring proof of funds for applicants from developed countries, whereas for students from 'very high-risk environments', the Regulations and Operational Manual instruct officers that 'requiring and systematically verifying substantial history of funds and supplementary individual or family financial and employment

225. Regulations, ss 9(2)m 188–189.
226. Lorne Waldman, *Immigration Law and Practice*, Loose-leaf (2d ed., LexisNexis-Butterworths, 2003) at s. 14.218.
227. Regulations, ss 9(1) and 213.
228. Regulations, s. 214.
229. Regulations, s. 215(1).
230. Regulations, s. 215(2).
231. IRPA, s. 30(2).
232. Regulations, s. 216(1).
233. OP12, s. 7.14.
234. Regulations, s. 219(1).
235. OP12, s. 7.17.

documentation may be necessary to ensure that only genuine students well able to support their programme of studies are accorded study permits'.[236]

262. Permits can be denied if an immigration officer doubts the applicant's intention to study, but any such denial must be based on information related to the specific case. Cultural context and historical migration patterns of co-nationals, for example, are not by themselves considered valid reasons for denying a study permit. Applicants must be made aware of an officer's concerns, if based on information not on the record, and given an opportunity to address them.[237] In the assessment of an applicant's *bona fides*, the Operational Manual recommends considering the proposed length of stay, the applicant's means of support, the applicant's obligations and ties to his or her home country, the applicant's likelihood of leaving Canada should an application for permanent residence be refused, and the applicant's record of compliance with the Act and the Regulations.[238] The Federal Court of Appeal has said officers may consider:

> ties to the country of origin, whether there are credible reasons for wishing to study in Canada, the age of the applicant, whether prior acceptance has been obtained from an educational institution in Canada and the likelihood of return to the country of origin.[239]

The long-term goals of the applicant may also be considered.[240] Linguistic facility will also be a factor.[241]

263. In *Kim v. Canada (Minister of Citizenship and Immigration)*, a case that involved an application for a study-permit renewal, Mosley J. listed some relevant considerations to take into account when considering whether a student has been a *bona fide* student while in Canada:

> The percentage of course load undertaken, an applicant's grades and the length of time taken to pursue a study programme, including intervals where an applicant was not studying, are all relevant considerations in assessing whether an applicant continues to be a *bona fide* student.[242]

---

236. Regulations, s. 220 and OP12, s. 7.7.
237. See *Mohamed v. Canada (Minister of Citizenship and Immigration)*, [2001] F.C.J. No. 1536 (T.D.); *Mittal v. Canada (Minister of Citizenship and Immigration)*, [1998] F.C.J. No. 727 (T.D.).
238. OP12, s. 5.15.
239. *Wong (Guardian) v. Canada (Minister of Citizenship and Immigration)*, 1999 CanLII 8201 (F.C.A.), at para. 13, n. 3.
240. *Ibid.* at para. 13.
241. Waldman, s. 14.229–14.230. For two decisions quashing officers' refusals due to a purported lack of bona fides, see *Wang v. Canada (Minister of Citizenship and Immigration)*, [2001] F.C.J. No. 95 (T.D.); *Lin v. Canada (Minister of Citizenship and Immigration)*, [2004] F.C.J. No. 106 (F.C.).
242. *Kim v. Canada (Minister of Citizenship and Immigration)*, 2004 FC 55 at para. 26.

264. Full-time students registered at an educational institution and who hold valid study permits are entitled to work on campus without a work permit. 'On campus' means within campus boundaries or at different locations on a campus within the same municipality.[243] Under an Off-Campus Work Permit Programme, students in degree-granting programmes may apply to work off-campus part-time during the academic year and full-time on scheduled breaks without first obtaining a labour market opinion (LMO), an opinion from Employment and Social Development Canada (ESDC) certifying that their job will have a neutral or positive effect on the labour market in Canada. (Such opinions are discussed below, III.3.2.) Certain other students are allowed to work off campus with a permit but without a LMO, such as students who have become destitute due to circumstances outside their control.[244]

265. Under a Post-Graduate Work Permit Programme, full-time foreign students can obtain a work permit for between eight months and three years, depending on their period of study. There are no restrictions on the type of job a graduating student can obtain. Students who have completed a programme that lasted less than eight months and students who have in the past received a work permit following a programme of study are ineligible. Also ineligible are participants in certain exchange programmes, such as a Canada-Chile Equal Opportunity Scholarship or the Canada-China Scholars' Exchanges Programme.[245] Certain students who have worked in higher-skilled occupations will be able to apply for permanent residence inside Canada under the Canadian Experience Class. (For the Canadian Experience Class, see III.2.2.)

§2. Temporary Workers

266. Until recently, temporary work permits were an instrument to enable foreign nationals to fill temporary gaps in the labour market caused by insufficient numbers of qualified Canadian citizens and permanent residents. Subject to two exceptions, the system was not designed to fill chronic gaps in the labour market caused by the unwillingness of employers to offer wages and working conditions sufficient to attract and retain Canadian citizens and permanent residents. The two major exceptions were temporary worker programmes to admit live-in caregivers ('nannies') and seasonal agricultural workers, discussed below. In the last decade, however, the Canadian government has dramatically expanded the temporary worker regime in three respects. First, the government has created new temporary work permits for skilled workers that enable transition to permanent resident status. Second, the government has eased the restrictions on some private employers' requirement to demonstrate adequate efforts to recruit, train and employ Canadians and permanent residents as a precondition to hiring foreign workers. Third, the federal government has entered into agreements that devolve authority to provinces to select temporary and permanent residents. Some provinces have, in turn, created

---

243. Regulations, s. 186(f) and OP12, s. 5.20.
244. Regulations, s. 208(a) and OP12, s. 5.22.
245. See OP12, s. 5.34.

their own temporary worker regimes. In 2012, Canada issued 213,573 Temporary Foreign Worker (TFW) work permits, compared to 138,450 in 2006.[246]

267. In general, foreign nationals who work in Canada in jobs that are normally remunerated must be authorized by issuance of a permit or must fall under one of twenty-three different categories of exemptions listed in the Regulations.[247] Among those exempted are business visitors;[248] accredited diplomats and their families; full-time students working on campus; performing artists; visiting athletes and coaches; foreign journalists reporting on events in Canada (a category that includes the landing crew for the Goodyear Blimp); foreign crew members of trains, planes, or ships; and foreign nationals who have remained in Canada after expiry of their initial work permit and have applied for an extension.[249]

268. If a permit and visa are required, these must in most cases be obtained prior to entry into Canada after receiving a job offer from a Canadian employer.[250] The permit and visa will generally be issued at the same time. Nationals or permanent residents of the United States and residents of Greenland or St Pierre and Miquelon, the French-controlled islands south of Newfoundland, may apply for a work permit at the port of entry. Some categories of persons may apply for a work permit from within Canada, such as foreign nationals applying for an extension; study-permit holders; and professionals, intra-company transferees, traders, or investors covered by the NAFTA.[251]

269. An officer 'shall' issue a work permit if it has been properly applied for; if satisfied the foreign national will leave Canada at the end of his or her authorized stay; if the foreign national needs to be and has been screened medically; and if the foreign national has been offered employment and the officer has determined that the 'offer is genuine', and that the employment is likely to result in a neutral or positive effect on the labour market in Canada.[252] This last condition applies in most cases, but not all. Various humanitarian exceptions exist. Permits will be issued without a Labour Market Opinion (LMO)/Labour Market Impact Assessment (LMIA) certifying the impact on the labour market if, for example, the applicant is a refugee claimant or foreign national subject to an unenforceable removal order; a student who has become destitute through no fault of their own; or a holder of a

246. Citizenship and Immigration Canada, Facts and Figures 2012 – Immigration Overview: Permanent and Temporary Residents – Total entries of foreign workers by yearly sub-status, http://www.cic.gc.ca/EnGLish/resources/statistics/facts2012/temporary/05.asp (accessed 11 Jun. 2014).
247. Regulations, ss 8(1), 186, 196; see also generally Part 11 of the Regulations.
248. Business visitors are defined in s. 187 of the Regulations. A business visitor is anyone 'who seeks to engage in international business activities in Canada without directly entering the Canadian labour market' (s. 187(1)).
249. Regulations, s. 186.
250. Regulations, s. 8(1) and Citizenship and Immigration Canada, 'FW1 – Foreign Worker Manual' (29 Jan. 2013), s. 5.10 (hereinafter 'FW1'). Section 198 of the Regulations states foreign nationals may apply for a work permit at a point of entry if they come from a visa-exempt country. This exemption, however, only applies if no LMO is needed, and so will in general not apply.
251. Regulations, s. 199.
252. Regulations, s. 200(1) and s. 203(1).

TRP issued under section 24(1) of the Act.[253] Permits will also be issued without LMO/LMIAs to members of certain specialized immigration classes able to apply for permanent residence from within Canada – such as live-in caregivers, protected persons, members of the spouse-in-Canada class, and individuals who have applied for permanent residence on humanitarian and compassionate grounds – so they can work while their applications are in process.[254] Certain kinds of work are also exempted from the LMO/LMIA requirement, such as work covered by an international agreement or work that advances certain Canadian interests.[255] Under new regulations, in such cases if a foreign national has already secured an offer of employment it must be determined whether the offer is 'genuine'.[256]

270. A work permit will not be issued if there are reasonable grounds to believe the foreign national is unable to perform the work; if, in the case of employment in Québec, no *Certificat d'acceptation du Québec* has been issued; if employment of the foreign national is likely to disrupt an ongoing labour dispute or the employment of a permanent resident or Canadian national involved in that dispute; if the foreign national has failed to comply with the conditions of a previous work or study permit and less than six months have passed since the unauthorized work or study has stopped;[257] or if the foreign national wants to enter Canada under the live-in-caregiver programme but has not met that programme's requirements.[258] Foreign nationals seeking to enter Canada to work must not be inadmissible.

271. As of April 2011, a work permit will not be issued to a foreign national who has worked temporarily in Canada for a cumulative period of four years, unless four additional years has passed since his or her last work authorization.[259] There are exemptions from this requirement for foreign workers whose employment is covered by an international agreement or who intend to perform work that would create or maintain significant social, cultural, or economic benefits or opportunities for Canadian citizens or permanent residents. The government states that this regulation is meant to ensure that employers do not use the TFW programme as a means

253. Regulations, ss 200(1)(c)(i) and 206, 208. For the exemption from LMO/LMIAs, see Regulations, s. 203(1). See also, Citizenship and Immigration Canada, 'See if you need a labour market opinion' (4 Jun. 2014), http://www.cic.gc.ca/english/work/apply-who-permit.asp (accessed 11 Jun. 2014).
254. Regulations, ss 200(1)(c)(i) and 207. For the exemption from LMO/LMIAs, see Regulations, s. 203(1).
255. Regulations, ss 200(1)(c)(ii) and 204, 205. For the exemption from LMOs, see Regulations, s. 203(1).
256. Regulations, s. 200(1)(c)(ii.1).
257. There are exemptions to this restriction. For example, work permits will be issued to foreign nationals provided they only breach conditions specifically imposed by an officer when admitting them for temporary residence; in the case of refugee claimants or foreign nationals subject to an unenforceable removal order; or in the case of foreign nationals subsequently issued a temporary resident permit under s. 24(1) of IRPA: Regulations, s. 200(3)(e)(ii), (iii), and (iv).
258. Regulations, s. 200(3).
259. Regulations, s. 200(3)(g).

of indefinitely employing foreign workers who would not be admissible on a permanent basis. The so-called four in, four out rule.is meant to emphasize the 'temporary' nature of temporary work permits, but it does not prevent or discourage employers from replacing one temporary worker with another temporary worker indefinitely.[260] It will particularly affect temporary workers who are not eligible for transitional programmes that enable temporary workers to qualify for permanent resident status. This regulation marks an explicit shift away from the policy that the temporary worker regime is primarily designed to fill temporary labour market needs, toward a 'guest worker' policy whose objective is to prevent workers who fill certain chronic labour market shortages from ever being able to claim or acquire permanent residence.

272. An officer shall refuse to issue a work permit to an otherwise qualified foreign national in order to further the public policy of protecting 'foreign nationals who are at risk of being subjected to humiliating or degrading treatment, including sexual exploitation'.[261] The objective of this provision is to protect foreign nationals (especially women) from trafficking by prohibiting their entry into Canada.

273. Work is defined in the Regulations as 'an activity for which wages are paid or commission is earned, or that is in direct competition with the activities of Canadian citizens or permanent residents in the Canadian labour market'.[262] Wages or commission are described in broad terms as 'salary or wages paid by an employer to an employee, remuneration or commission received for fulfilling a service contract, or any other situation where a foreign national receives payment for performing a service'.[263]

274. The question of whether an activity is 'in direct competition' with Canadian citizens or permanent residents introduces a threshold issue that may not be capable of clear resolution. The Operational Manual instructs officers considering this issue to consider a range of factors directed at answering the question of whether the foreign national will be 'doing an activity that a Canadian or permanent resident should really have an opportunity to do'.[264]

275. The general practice is that before issuing a permit, an officer must determine whether the job offer is genuine and whether the employment of the foreign

260. Canada Gazette, 'Regulations Amending the Immigration and Refugee Protection Regulations (Temporary Foreign Workers)' Vol. 143, no. 41 (10 Oct. 2009) available online at: http://gazette.gc.ca/rp-pr/p1/2009/2009-10-10/html/reg1-eng.html (accessed 6 Jun. 2013). See proposed s. 200 (3)(g) (hereinafter 'TFW Regulations').
261. IRPA, s. 30(1.6).
262. Regulations, s. 2. See *Juneja v. Canada (Minister of Citizenship and Immigration)*, 2007 FC 301 (F.C.); *Georgas v. Canada (Minister of Employment and Immigration)*, [1979] 1 F.C. 349 (C.A.); *Bernardez v. Canada (Minister of Citizenship and Immigration)*, [1995] F.C.J. No. 1297 (T.D.).
263. FW1, s. 5.1.
264. *Ibid.*

national is likely to have a neutral or positive economic effect on the labour market in Canada on the basis of a LMO/LMIA provided by ESDC.[265]

276. In determining whether a job offer should be considered genuine, the officer will consider the following factors: (1) whether the employer is actively engaged in the business in respect of which the offer is made; (2) whether the offer is consistent with the reasonable employment needs of the employer; (3) whether the offer's terms can be reasonably fulfilled by the employer; and (4) past compliance of the employer or of the employer's recruiter with legislation regulating employment and the recruitment of employees.[266] An offer will not be deemed genuine if an employer in the two years previous has provided a foreign national with wages or working conditions significantly different from those offered or has employed a foreign national in an occupation significantly different than that which was offered. The Ministry is to maintain a list on its website of employers whose offers have been deemed not genuine, for purposes of determining employer ineligibility to hire temporary foreign workers for two years following a violation of the terms of employment offered to a temporary foreign worker.[267]

277. The LMIA (formerly known as LMO) is the most cumbersome step in the work permit application process.[268] LMIAs provided by ESDC regarding the effect of a job on the Canadian labour market must consider six factors: (1) whether employment of the foreign national is likely to result in job creation or job retention for Canadian citizens or permanent residents; (2) whether employment of the foreign national is likely to lead to the creation or transfer of skills or knowledge for the benefit of Canadian citizens or permanent residents; (3) whether employment of the foreign national is likely to fill a labour shortage; (4) whether wages offered to the foreign national match prevailing wage rates and whether conditions at the proposed workplace meet generally accepted Canadian standards; (5) whether the employer has made or agreed to make reasonable efforts to hire or train Canadian citizens or permanent residents; and (6) whether employment of the foreign national is likely to adversely affect the settlement of any labour dispute in progress or the employment of any person involved in such a dispute.[269]

278. As part of its efforts to prevent exploitation of foreign workers, the government in April 2009 stopped granting LMO extensions. Employers must apply for

265. Regulations, ss 200, 203.
266. Regulations, s. 200(5).
267. Regulations, s. 203(5), 203(6).
268. An 'expedited labour market opinion' pilot project was launched in Alberta and British Columbia in 2007. Under the project, employers hiring foreign workers for work in one of thirty-three different occupations may receive an LMO in three to five days. Among the occupations are carpenters, civil engineers, delivery drivers, ironworkers, pharmacists, and retail salespersons and clerks. The government ended the pilot project on 15 Apr. 2010 once an LMO-processing backlog had ended. See Citizenship and Immigration Canada, 'Temporary Foreign Workers – Federal Roles' (18 Aug. 2010), at http://www.cic.gc.ca/english/department/media/backgrounders/2010/2010-8-18.asp (accessed 6 Jun. 2013).
269. Regulations, s. 203(3).

a new LMIA upon expiry of the previous one. Effective 31 December 2013, amendments to the Regulations and new Ministerial Instructions came into force to further address long-standing concerns in relation to abuse of temporary foreign workers. Employers applying for LMO/LMIAs were subject to new conditions, including the requirement to demonstrate that they 'have made reasonable efforts to provide a workplace that is free of abuse which includes physical, sexual, psychological or financial abuse'.[270] ESDC has expanded authority to conduct inspections and compliance reviews and non-compliant employers will be subject to a range of sanctions including: a ban of two years and their name, address and period of ineligibility published on the CIC website; a negative LMIA being issued for any pending applications; and/or revocation of previously-issued LMO/LMIAs.[271]

279. There are several exceptions to the LMIA requirement. No LMIA is required if: (1) the job being filled by the foreign national would create or maintain significant social, cultural, or economic benefits or opportunities for Canadian citizens or permanent residents; (2) the job would create or maintain reciprocal employment for Canadian citizens or permanent residents abroad; (3) the permit is sought by a refugee claimant or protected person or if certain other humanitarian concerns are present; (4) the Minister has designated the job as related to a research, educational, or training programme for which 'limited access to Canadian labour market is necessary for reasons of public policy relating to the competitiveness of Canada's academic institutions or economy'; or (5) the job is of a religious or charitable nature.[272] International reciprocal employment arrangements falling under ministerial designation range from high-level trade agreements such as the NAFTA or the GATS to such narrowly tailored endeavours as the International Pacific Halibut Commission, a Malaysian accounting trainee programme, and the North American Cooperative Waterfowl Survey and Banding Programme.[273] If no LMIA is required, in some cases an individual may be issued an open work permit. Open permits may be unrestricted or restricted to a particular occupation or occupations.[274]

280. In practice, an employer will generally receive a favourable LMIA and work permit for the foreign national if it has advertised in a manner consistent with industry practices for jobs of similar skill levels and posted its opening for at least fourteen days in an online national job bank maintained by the government.[275]

---

270. Employment and Social Development Canada, 'New Requirements for Employer Compliance' (30 Dec. 2013) http://www.esdc.gc.ca/eng/jobs/foreign_workers/employer_compliance.shtml (accessed 11 Jun. 2014).
271. *Ibid.* and Employment and Social Development Canada, 'Regulatory Amendments and Ministerial Instructions Coming Into Force' (6 Jan. 2014). http://www.edsc.gc.ca/eng/jobs/foreign_workers/notices/reg_change.shtml (accessed 11 Jun. 2014). As of February 2015, the government has conducted zero on-site inspections of employers: 'Power to inspect TFW employers without a warrant hasn't been used', Globe and Mail, 5 Feb. 2015, available for download at http://www.theglobeandmail.com/news/politics/power-to-inspect-tfw-employers-without-a-warrant-hasnt-been-used/article22798600/ (last accessed 17 Feb. 2015).
272. Regulations, ss 205–207.
273. For a listing of international agreements under which LMOs are not required, see FW1, s. 5.27.
274. FW1, s. 10.
275. Job Bank http://www.jobbank.gc.ca/ (accessed 6 Jun. 2013).

LMIAs may be unfavourable if it is determined that temporary employment of a foreign national will disrupt an ongoing strike or lockout. The Regulations also state that work permits can be refused if:

> the specific work that the foreign national intends to perform is likely to adversely affect the settlement of any labour dispute in progress or the employment of any person involved in the dispute, unless all or almost all of the workers involved in the labour dispute are not Canadian citizens or permanent residents and the hiring of workers to replace the workers involved in the labour dispute is not prohibited by the Canadian law applicable in the province where the workers involved in the labour dispute are employed ... [276]

Temporary foreign workers in Canada may find themselves caught up in a strike at their place of employment. In such cases, the Ministry allows temporary foreign workers to remain in Canada on strike pay for the length of their permit, return home, or seek other employment and apply for a new work permit. A temporary foreign worker who cannot or does not want to change jobs but is worried about falling out of status must apply for an extension. Filing of the application provides the temporary foreign worker with implied status for four months. Once four months are up, the foreign worker has an additional thirty days to get an LMO/LMIA, after which his or her application will be refused.

281. In July 2002, the government launched a pilot project for temporary foreign workers in low-skilled occupations. The jobs required at most a high school diploma or two years' training. Work permits can be issued in such cases for a maximum of two years. Initially, foreign nationals then had to return home for a minimum of four months 'to ensure that [temporary foreign workers] maintained a connection with their home country'.[277] Under changes that came into effect in May 2009, however, foreign workers were allowed to apply for new permits from within Canada so long as their employer procured a new LMO/LMIA, a new employment contract was signed, the original work permit had not expired, and in accordance with 2011 regulatory change, the foreign worker's total presence in Canada did not exceed four years.[278] Employers seeking to take advantage of the low-skilled foreign worker programme must consult with their workplace union and offer wages comparable to any provided for in their collective bargaining agreement. They must also extend the same benefits to foreign workers as are given to Canadian or permanent resident employees. Employers must help foreign workers find suitable accommodation and provide medical coverage until they become eligible for

---

276. Regulations, s. 200(3).
277. Citizenship and Immigration Canada, Operation Bulletin 113 (12 May 2009), available online at: http://www.cic.gc.ca/english/resources/manuals/bulletins/2009/ob113.asp (accessed 20 Oct. 2009).
278. *Ibid*. Citizenship and Immigration Canada, 'Pilot project for workers with lower levels of formal training' (11 Oct. 2012), http://www.cic.gc.ca/english/work/low-skill.asp (accessed 6 Jun. 2013).

coverage under provincial health plans. Finally, they must cover transportation costs.[279]

281.1. The Seasonal Agricultural Worker Programme (SAWP) is distinctive in Canada because it operates through interstate agreements between Canada and sending states in the Caribbean and Mexico. The Canadian government has facilitated recruitment of agricultural workers for seasonal work since 1966, when 263 farm workers first came over from Jamaica. Under long-standing bilateral memoranda of understanding, agricultural workers from Mexico and eleven Caribbean countries may be hired to work in any province except Newfoundland (which, like the territories of Nunavut, Yukon, and the Northwest Territories, has limited agriculture). The job offer must be for at least 240 hours of work over six weeks or less, for a maximum duration of eight months between 1 January and 15 December, by which date every worker must be repatriated. The workers must receive free housing with a usable kitchen[280] and must be paid prevailing wages or the rate being paid by the employer to Canadians doing the same work. An LMIA is required under the programme.

282. Beginning in the late 1990s, the government has continued to create ad hoc programmes for temporary foreign workers that modify, streamline, or reduce the prerequisites for employers seeking to recruit specified classes of foreign worker. These have included information technology (IT) professionals and foreign workers sought by Petro-Canada to work in the oil sands in northern Alberta. In 2012, the Canadian government authorized employers of temporary foreign workers to pay up to 15% less than the prevailing average wage in high-skilled occupations and up to 5% less in low-skilled occupations. Since then, the temporary foreign worker programme has been subject to an increasing degree of scrutiny amidst allegations that the programme has been failing to protect vulnerable foreign workers. At the same time, a number of cases emerged in which employers had intentionally bypassed Canadian workers in favour of non-nationals willing to work for lower wages.[281] In April 2013, the government ended so-called wage flexibility for employers of temporary foreign workers. In April 2014, an immediate moratorium on the food service sector's access to the temporary foreign worker programme was announced,

279. Human Resources and Skills Development Canada, 'Temporary Foreign Worker Program: Pilot Project for Occupations Requiring Lower Levels of Formal Training (NOC C and D)' (16 Sep. 2009), http://www.hrsdc.gc.ca/eng/workplaceskills/foreign_workers/lowskill.shtml (accessed 20 Oct. 2009).

280. Except in British Columbia: see Human Resources and Skills Development Canada, 'Seasonal Agricultural Worker Program' (10 Jun. 2009), http://www.hrsdc.gc.ca/eng/workplaceskills/ foreign _workers/ei_tfw/sawp_tfw.shtml (accessed 20 Oct. 2009).

281. As an example, in April 2013, it was revealed that the Royal Bank of Canada was planning to use a United States-based outsourcing firm to assist in the transfer of information technology work performed by Canadians to foreign workers. See, 'Conservatives crack down on abuses of foreign worker program' *Toronto Star*, 29 Apr. 2013. See also, Human Resources and Skills Development Canada, 'Evaluation of the Labour Market Opinion Streams of the Temporary Foreign Worker Program' (September 2012) http://www.esdc.gc.ca/eng/publications/evaluations/skills_and_employment/2013/temporary_foreign.pdf (accessed 11 Jun. 2014).

and the government confirmed its intent to pursue 'significant reforms' to the programme as a whole.[282]

283. On 20 June 2014, the government lifted the food service sector moratorium and announced a major overhaul of the TFW programme.[283] The government suggested that reforms were necessary to 'ensure the TFW programme is only used as intended, as a last and limited resort to fill acute labour shortages on a temporary basis when qualified Canadians are not available'.[284] The TFW programme has been reorganized into two distinct programmes: the TFW programme, referring to those streams under which employers request the admission of foreign workers to fill specific jobs; and the newly created International Mobility Programmes (IMPs), intended for workers who will 'advance Canada's broad economic and cultural national interest'.[285] IMPs are not based on employer demand but rather, reciprocal international agreements,[286] arrangements that facilitate permanent immigration, or initiatives to recruit highly-skilled workers and international students. Employment and Social Development Canada is identified as the lead agency for the TFW programme while CIC is the lead for IMPs. Many of the reforms were effective immediately, while others are being phased in over the course of the following eighteen months.[287]

284. The overhaul consists of three basic pillars:

(i) limiting access to ensure that Canadians are first in line for available jobs;
(ii) more and better labour market information for stronger screening; and
(iii) more effective enforcement and tougher penalties.

285. In terms of the first pillar, new measures include: a cap on the number of low-wage temporary foreign workers an employer can hire per work site; replacing the Labour Market Opinion through a more rigorous LMIA which requires employers to confirm the number of Canadians that applied for a particular job, the number of Canadians interviewed and an explanation if Canadian applicants were not hired; barring applications for the lowest-wage, lowest-skill, entry-level occupations in the food services, accommodation and retail trade sectors in regions with unemployment rates of 6% or higher; reducing LMIAs for low-wage temporary foreign workers from the current two-year standard duration to one-year periods; and reducing

282. Statement by the Honourable Minister Jason Kenney, Minister of Employment and Social Development (24 Apr. 2014) http://news.gc.ca/web/article-en.do?mthd=index&crtr.page=1&nid=842269 (accessed 11 Jun. 2014).

283. See, Employment and Social Development Canada, 'Government of Canada Overhauls Temporary Foreign Worker Programme Ensuring Canadians are first in line for available jobs' (20 Jun. 2014) http://news.gc.ca/web/article-en.do?mthd=advSrch&crtr.mnthndVl=7&crtr.mnthStrtVl=1&crtr.page=1&nid=859859&crtr.yrndVl=2014&crtr.kw=overhaul+temporary+foreign+worker&crtr.yrStrtVl=2002&crtr.dyStrtVl=1&crtr.dyndVl=29 (accessed 29 Jul. 2014).

284. *Ibid.*

285. *Ibid.*

286. See, para. 279 *supra.* The NAFTA and the GATS are considered in greater detail in Ch. 5.

287. See, Employment and Social Development Canada, 'Timeline of Measures Coming into Force' http://www.esdc.gc.ca/eng/jobs/foreign_workers/reform/timeline.shtml (accessed 29 Jul. 2014).

the cumulative period during which general low-wage temporary foreign workers will be allowed to remain in Canada.[288] In addition, the use of the National Occupation Classification (NOC) system has been replaced by wage levels as the basis for administering the TFW programme. Positions where the prevailing wage is below the provincial/territorial median wage are considered low-wage, while positions where the prevailing wage is at or above the provincial/territorial median wage are considered high-wage.[289]

286. Elements of the second pillar in relation to stronger screening include the creation of a new job matching service that is intended to identify jobs for Canadians that match their experience and skills (and reduce reliance by employers on temporary foreign workers); as well as new job vacancy and wage surveys to be conducted by Statistics Canada.[290]

287. Measures adopted under the third pillar in relation to enforcement and penalties include an increase in the number of inspections, the introduction of fines imposed for non-compliance by employers (up to CAD 100,000); expanding the ability to publicly list employers who have been suspended and are under investigation or have been banned from using the programme; as well as additional funding for the CBSA so it can pursue more criminal investigations.[291]

288. The government has indicated that the costs for administering the reformulated TFW programme will be 'borne entirely by employers who use the programme, not by taxpayers'.[292] The application fee employers must pay per worker requested will increase from CAD 275 to CAD 1,000. In addition ESDC intends to impose an estimated CAD 100 'privilege fee' to offset the costs of federal investments in skills and job training.[293]

---

288. Employment and Social Development Canada, 'Government of Canada Overhauls Temporary Foreign Worker Program Ensuring Canadians are first in line for available jobs' (20 Jun. 2014).
289. Government of Canada, 'Overhauling the Temporary Foreign Worker Program: Putting Canadians First' (2014): http://www.esdc.gc.ca/eng/jobs/foreign_workers/reform/overhauling_TFW.pdf (accessed 30 Jul. 2014) at 8. Pending amendments to the *Regulations* and policy manuals, this publication is the primary source for details about the new TFWP. It sets out the key features of the five discrete categories within the programme; high-wage; low-wage; highest – demand/highest-paid/or shortest duration; primary agricultural stream and live-in caregiver programme.
290. For further details, see, Employment and Social Development Canada, 'Government of Canada Overhauls Temporary Foreign Worker Program Ensuring Canadians are first in line for available jobs' (20 Jun. 2014).
291. *Ibid.*
292. *Ibid.*
293. *Ibid.*

Chapter 2. Transitional Programmes

289. Certain immigration programmes enable temporary foreign workers to 'audition' for permanent residence by entering as temporary foreign workers and then transition to permanent residence if they meet stipulated criteria. This chapter deals with the three principal categories of temporary foreign workers who may transition from temporary to permanent residence. Two of these – the Live-In Caregiver Programme and the Canadian Experience Class – are aimed directly at Canada's economic and labour market needs. The third, long-term temporary residence permits, is a discretionary category for foreign nationals who would otherwise be inadmissible.

§1. LIVE-IN CAREGIVERS

290. Canadians have long relied on female foreign nationals to perform live-in domestic labour.[294] Since the early 1970s, live-in domestic workers were confined to temporary work permits, with no prospect of permanent residence. Job loss led to deportation. Following public controversy sparked by the attempted deportation of seven Jamaican workers initially recruited under an earlier Caribbean Domestic Scheme, the government reformed its policy in 1981. Under the new Foreign Domestic Movement Programme foreign domestic workers could apply for permanent residence from within Canada after two years of live-in domestic work. Although the worker could change employers, she could not change employment. That remains the basic requirement under the Live-in Caregiver Programme in the current Act.

291. The Ministry today says that the Live-In Caregiver Programme was established to 'meet a labour market shortage of live-in caregivers in Canada, while providing an avenue for these individuals to work and eventually apply for permanent residence from within Canada'.[295] Live-in care under the Regulations involves three components: (1) the foreign national must provide child care, senior home-support care, or care of a disabled person; (2) without supervision; (3) in a private household in which he or she also lives.[296] The government consistently defends the 'live-in' requirement of the programme by claiming that there is no shortage of 'live-out' care in Canada.[297] In 2010, 7,664 live-in caregivers (94% female), and 6,245

294. For a summary of the history of Canadian immigration law and policy regarding domestic workers, see Audrey Macklin, 'On the Inside Looking In: Foreign Domestic Workers in Canada' in *Maid in the Market* 13–18, 27–37 (W. Giles & S. Arat-Koc, eds., Fernwood Press, 1992).
295. Citizenship and Immigration Canada, OP14, *Processing Applicants for the Live-in Caregiver Program*, (2009) at 4 (hereinafter 'OP14').
296. Regulations, s. 2.
297. See, e.g., Government response to the report of the Standing Committee on Citizenship and Immigration: 'Temporary Foreign Workers and Non-Status Workers' (19 Aug. 2009), http://www2.parl.gc.ca/HousePublications/Publication.aspx?Language=E&Mode=1&Parl=40&Ses=2&DocId=4017803&File=0 (accessed 6 Jun. 2013).

dependents were granted permanent residence through the programme.[298] According to the government, 90% of the participants in the programme apply for permanent resident status; of these, 98% are successful.[299]

292. Most participants in the live-in caregiver programme are Filipino women. Live-in caregivers enter as temporary workers, and so must apply for a live-in caregiver work permit and also a temporary resident visa, or TRV, if required.[300] To receive a temporary work permit, the applicant must have: (1) completed the equivalent of Canadian secondary school; (2) one-year's paid work experience or six months' training under a formal educational programme related to the employment sought, such as training in early childhood education or geriatric care; (3) sufficient knowledge of English or French to be able to communicate effectively in an unsupervised setting; and (4) an employment contract that complies with the programme's requirements, as well as an LMO/LMIA from HRSDC/ESDC. Applicants to Québec must also obtain a *Certification d'acceptance du Québec,* or CAQ.[301] Applicants must also be screened for medical and other grounds of inadmissibility.

293. If an officer concludes all the requirements have been met, he or she will issue a work permit for up to three years and three months, provided the length corresponds to that set out in the LMO. According to the Operational Manual, live-in caregivers are not normally allowed to bring family, unless they can show they can support them and have the permission of their future employer to have family members live in their home.[302]

294. Concerns about abuse dog the Live-In Caregiver Programme: 'Foreign live-in caregivers' precarious status, the obligation to live in the home of the employer, and their general situation of dependence on their employer make for an often highly stressful and potentially abusive workplace environment.'[303] It was largely to address abuse concerns that the requirement of an employment contract with certain specified content (e.g., employment contracts must provide expressly that the caregiver will be given a private room with a lock)[304] has been added to the Regulations. The Regulations under the new Act also allow caregivers to change employers more easily, although they still have to obtain a new work permit for each

298. Citizenship and Immigration Canada, Facts & Figures 2010, 'Permanent Residents by Category', http://www.cic.gc.ca/english/resources/statistics/facts2010/permanent/03.asp (accessed 6 Jun. 2013).
299. Canada Gazette, 'Regulations Amending the Immigration and Refugee Protection Regulations,' Vol. 143, no. 51 (19 Dec. 2009), http://gazette.gc.ca/rp-pr/p1/2009/2009-12-19/html/reg3-eng.html (accessed 6 Jun. 2013).
300. Regulations, s. 111.
301. Regulations, ss 112, 200(3)(d). See discussion of the requirements in Citizenship and Immigration Canada, OP14, *Processing Applicants for the Live-In Caregiver Program*, (27 Oct. 2010), s. 5.2 to 5.5 (hereinafter OP14).
302. OP14, s. 5.10.
303. Carasco, Emily et al., *Immigration and Refugee Law: Cases, Materials, and Commentary* (Emond Montgomery, 2007) at 261.
304. OP14, s. 5.7.

new job.[305] In November 2014, the government announced reform of the Live-Caregiver Programme: The live-in requirement was made optional, but access to permanent residence was made more restrictive and capped at an annual quota of 5,500, evenly divided by those who care for children and those who care for people with high medical needs.[306] Since certain aspects of the new policy are inconsistent with the Regulations, it is not apparent that the policy change is sourced in law.[307]

295. Technically, live-in caregivers are temporary foreign workers until they apply for permanent residence under the programme, at which point they become part of the 'live-in caregiver class' of permanent resident applicants.[308] Caregivers may apply for permanent residence after having completed two years of full-time employment, provided they meet the requirements of section 113(1) of the Regulations. The most important criterion is that the caregiver must have provided child, elder, or disabled care for at least two years within the three years following entry. In *Turingan*, the Federal Court found that officers have limited discretion to refuse permanent resident status once it has been determined that a participant has worked the required twenty-four months.[309]

§2. Canadian Experience Class

296. In 2008, the government established the Canadian Experience Class (CEC), which allows certain foreign students and temporary foreign workers to apply for permanent residence (in any province except Québec) on the basis of a pass/fail evaluation rather than a points system.[310] The government stated that the new programme seeks to address the Skilled Worker Programme's unresponsiveness to labour shortages, which has apparently caused some employers to shift to long-term reliance on the temporary foreign worker programme. By facilitating swifter admission to Canada than under the Skilled Worker Programme, the new class is supposed to make Canada a more attractive destination to immigrants with desired skills at a time when global competition for skilled workers is intensifying.[311] Currently, admissions under the CEC are subject to an annual cap of 12,000 new applications.[312]

305. Canada Gazette, 'Immigration and Refugee Protection Regulations', Vol. 135, no. 50 (15 Dec. 2001) at 4530-31 (hereinafter 'RIAS').
306. Citizenship and Immigration Canada, 'Improving Canada's Caregiver Program', http://news.gc.ca/web/article-en.do?nid=898719&_ga=1.80238935.1713352821.1374540577 (accessed 17 Feb. 2015).
307. See, e.g., Regulations, s. 113.
308. Regulations, s. 113(1).
309. *Turingan v. Minister of Employment and Immigration* (1993), 72 FTR 316.
310. The new class was created pursuant to ss 12(2) and 14 of IRPA.
311. Canada Gazette, 'Regulations Amending the Immigration and Refugee Protection Act (Canadian Experience Class)' Vol. 142, no. 32 (9 Aug. 2008), http://gazette.gc.ca/rp-pr/p1/2008/2008-08-09/html/reg1-eng.html (accessed 14 Nov. 2009).
312. See, Canada Gazette, Government Notices, Vol. 148, 26 Apr. 2014, Department of Citizenship and Immigration, Updated Ministerial Instructions 12 (MI 12).

297. The Regulations create two streams of the experience class, the temporary foreign worker and post-graduation streams. Under the temporary foreign worker stream, an applicant must have the equivalent of two years full-time experience in a management position, a professional occupation, technical occupation, or skilled trade. Ministerial Instructions stipulate that there are six ineligible occupations: Administrative officers; Administrative assistants; Accounting technicians and bookkeepers; Retail sales supervisors; Food service supervisors; and Cooks.[313] In addition, self-employment does not count. The experience must have been acquired legally in Canada within the three years prior to the application.[314] Under the post-graduation stream, an applicant must have completed a Canadian programme of study, in which they were enrolled full-time for two years, not including any full-time course in English or French as a second language.[315] The applicant must demonstrate they have had the equivalent of one year's full-time legally authorized work experience in a management position, a professional occupation, technical occupation, or skilled trade since graduation. The experience must be acquired in the two years prior to applying for permanent residence.[316] Again, the work cannot include periods of self-employment.

298. Both streams require proficiency in French or English and the submission of results of an independent language test administered by a CIC-designated agency.[317] Applicants must have come lawfully to Canada to work or study and have temporary resident status at the time of their application and they must apply while working in Canada or within one year of leaving a job in Canada.[318] In addition to undocumented work, this excludes work garnered as a refugee claimant.[319]

299. CEC applicants are not required to submit proof of funds. However, in common with all categories of applicants for permanent resident status, they are assessed to determine whether they fall under the general criteria of inadmissibility.

§3. Temporary Resident Permit Holders

300. Section 24(1) of the Act, grants immigration officers the discretion to issue a temporary resident permit, or TRP that enables the entry of a person who is otherwise inadmissible to Canada:

> A foreign national who, in the opinion of an officer, is inadmissible or does not meet the requirements of this Act becomes a temporary resident if an officer is

313. MI 12, 'Canadian Experience Class'. See also, Citizenship and Immigration Canada, Operational Manual OP25-A, *Canadian Experience Class* (30 Jan. 2014), ss 5.1, 10 and 11.1 (hereinafter 'OP25-A').
314. Regulations, s. 87.1(2)(a)(ii).
315. Regulations, s. 87.1(3)(e).
316. Regulations, s. 87.1(2)(a)(i).
317. Regulations, s. 87.1(2)(b).
318. Regulations, s. 87.1(3)(c).
319. Citizenship and Immigration Canada, OP10, *Permanent Residency Status*, s. 5.1.

of the opinion that it is justified in the circumstances and issues a temporary resident permit, which may be cancelled at any time.

Officers must follow any instructions issued by the Minister in issuing permits.[320] Foreign nationals admitted as temporary permanent residents will be granted permanent residence if they remain in Canada continuously, without adding new grounds of inadmissibility, for three or five years.[321]

301. In 2012, 13,564 permits were issued. The largest group of permits were issued to foreign nationals inadmissible on grounds of non-serious criminality (7,014). Next came permits for individuals inadmissible because of non-compliance with the Act (5,206) and serious criminality (888).[322] Based on the most recent data available, in 2012 only sixty-seven TRP holders became permanent residents, less than one-tenth of 1% of the new permanent resident cohort.[323] This suggests that few TRP holders actually transition to permanent resident status.

302. To be eligible for a TRP, a foreign national must be: (1) inadmissible and seeking to come to Canada; (2) in Canada and inadmissible, subject to a section 44(1) inadmissibility report, reportable for a violation of the Act, or otherwise in breach of the Act; or (3) not eligible for restoration of a legal status that has been lost.[324] Interviews may or may not be conducted. In general they will not be held if the grounds of inadmissibility are relatively minor and if credibility or merit is not an issue.[325]

303. It is instructive to contrast the discretionary power under section 24(1) with the broader discretion provided in section 25(1) of the Act, under which foreign nationals may be admitted as temporary or permanent residents or receive other relief for humanitarian and compassionate reasons. Section 24(1) permits are distinguishable from humanitarian and compassionate relief by virtue of the fact that: (1) they are only temporary and merely provide a basis for a later application for permanent residence; (2) the statute expressly stipulates that they may be cancelled at any time; and (3) the possible reasons for granting such permits are not limited at all by the wording of the provision and, indeed, the Operational Manual makes reference to economic and labour market needs as well as the need to avoid public controversy. For all these reasons, TRPs have been described by the courts as a 'highly discretionary' tool – i.e., more discretionary than humanitarian and compassionate leave[326] – to be used only in compelling cases. In *Nasso*, the Federal Court said:

320. IRPA, s. 24(3).
321. Regulations, s. 65 and 65.1.
322. Citizenship and Immigration Canada, Annual Report to Parliament on Immigration, 2013 at 23.
323. Citizenship and Immigration Canada, Facts and Figures 2012, 'Permanent Residents by Category' at 6-7.
324. Citizenship and Immigration Canada, Operational Manual IP1, *Temporary Resident Permits* (19 Jun. 2007), s. 5.5 (hereinafter 'IP1').
325. IP1, s. 10.
326. *Farhat v. Canada (Minister of Citizenship and Immigration)*, 2006 FC 1275.

> It seems to me that an applicant who cannot satisfy an officer that he has a requirement or, to use the words of the decision under review, a compelling need to enter Canada, cannot establish that a permit is justified in the circumstances. In other words, to be granted a TRP in these exceptional circumstances requires more than showing that one has a wish or desire to enter Canada – it requires much more – otherwise, it is not an exceptional circumstance.[327]

304. Like the courts, the Operational Manual stresses the exceptional nature of TRPs. Section 24(1) is intended for cases where there are 'compelling reasons for an officer to issue a TRP to allow a person who does not meet the requirements of the Act to enter or remain in Canada'.[328] Elsewhere, it states: 'Officers should issue permits with caution and only in special circumstances.'[329] The Manual instructs officers not to issue TRPs in cases where someone has lost or faces the loss of their status as a visitor, foreign student, or foreign worker. In such cases, the foreign national must apply for an extension within ninety days of expiration; TRPs are not to be used as an end-run around this requirement. TRPs are not to be issued if a sponsor, host, or employer is not 'reputable or accountable' or if an officer has 'reasonable grounds to believe that the person's presence in Canada may be expected to result in public disorder'. Finally, officers are instructed not to issue TRPs to deal with criminal inadmissibility cases where rehabilitation may be demonstrably available; such rehabilitated individuals would no longer be inadmissible.[330]

305. In all other cases, officers are told to weigh various factors, including the needs of the foreign national, the benefit admission would bring to Canadian society, the seriousness of the inadmissibility ground, and risks to health and safety posed by entry. At other points in the Manual, officers are told to consider factors such as family ties; attendance at conferences or other events; economic imperatives, like labour market needs; if medical treatment is involved, its availability outside Canada; the 'tangible' and 'intangible' benefits that may accrue to others upon admission; and the identity of any sponsor, host, or employer. If the beneficial effects are purportedly in the public interest, these should normally relate to the 'economic or employment security of Canadian citizens or permanent residents'.[331] Examples of cases that may not warrant permits following such discretionary balancing include inadmissible sponsored parents if there are other children or family members in the home country to provide elder care, or criminally inadmissible spouses who are a risk to reoffend.[332]

306. Special procedures apply in medical cases. Officers are instructed to consider issues such as the contagiousness of the foreign national's condition; the

---

327. *Nasso, supra* n. 65, at para. 15.
328. IP1, s. 5.1.
329. IP1, s. 5.7. This is a position that has been endorsed by the Federal Court: *Farhat, supra* n. 64, paras 22–24.
330. IP1, s. 18.7.
331. IP1, s. 12.3.
332. IP1, s. 12.2.

feasibility of protective public health measures; the degree of need for health and social services; and whether there are arrangements to cover the costs of treatment.[333] The officer's initial report must be considered by a senior Ministry official, who makes a final decision on admission in consultation with the provincial health authority. Health care falls within provincial jurisdiction in Canada; an objection by a provincial health authority, while not determinative, weighs against a permit application.[334]

307. In criminal cases, officers are instructed to consider the seriousness of the offence that lies behind inadmissibility, the chances of successful settlement without further offences, evidence of reform or patterns of criminal behaviour, and the controversy or risk caused by the person's presence in Canada, among other factors.[335] A criminal offence may be deemed minor if, for instance, it did not involve drugs, violence, or property damage.[336] In other cases, officers are instructed to consider questions such as whether there is a pattern of violations of the Act, credibility, and the potential for public controversy.[337]

308. Permits may be issued for a maximum of three years, after which they may be renewed from within Canada.[338] Permit holders have the obligation to comply with any conditions imposed on their authorization, as well as with the requirements of the Act. They are also required to leave Canada at the end of their authorized stay, unless they become permanent residents.[339] If they fail to meet their obligations, they may be subject to a section 44(1) inadmissibility report and may not be eligible for permanent residence.

309. Permit holders must apply for renewal at least thirty days before expiration. The Manual says: 'Permit extensions cannot be refused if the only reason for the refusal is to preclude the person from becoming eligible to apply for permanent residence in the permit holder class.'[340] Permits lose validity once a permit holder leaves Canada, regardless of the listed expiration date. However, a permit may provide for advance authorization to re-enter Canada. Permits are not considered travel documents, and a permit holder seeking to return to Canada must be issued a special travel document, known as a 'counterfoil', for their passport.[341]

310. Under the Act, permits may be cancelled at any time; the Manual adds the proviso 'if circumstances change'.[342] Officers must provide a permit holder with

333. IP1, s. 13.1.
334. IP1, s. 13.6.
335. IP1, s. 14.1.
336. IP1, s. 15.3.
337. IP1, s. 15.1.
338. Regulations, s. 63(d).
339. IRPA, s. 29(2).
340. IP1, s. 5.16.
341. IP1, s. 17.5.
342. IP1, s. 25.

notice of the intention to cancel, set out the reasons for cancellation, and allow the permit holder to respond. Officers are also instructed to obtain concurrence from the Ministry office that issued the original permit. Once a permit has been cancelled, a foreign national may be subject to a removal order.[343]

311. There is no discretion in granting permanent residence to permit holders if the requirements of the Regulations have been met: 'Persons who remain continuously in Canada on a permit for the specified time and do not become inadmissible on other grounds will be granted permanent residence.'[344] Family members cannot be granted permanent residence as part of the application, although family members may be sponsored by a permit holder who has become a permanent resident.[345]

312. Permit holders inadmissible for medical reasons relating to themselves or family members are eligible for permanent residence after three years of continuous residence.[346] In all other cases, permit holders are eligible after five years.[347] Continuous residence can be interrupted in one of two ways. A permit holder might leave Canada without authorization to re-enter, in which case the permit is automatically cancelled. Alternatively, a permit holder might allow his or her permit to lapse without applying for an extension. Officers are instructed that a short break in continuity, outside a foreign national's control – for example, because of illness or processing delays –, not necessarily be an impediment in extending TRP status.[348] Permit holders inadmissible on grounds of security, international criminality, organized criminality, or serious criminality will not be eligible to apply for permanent residence.[349]

313. Permit holders can apply inland for work and study permits.[350] Work permits may be 'open' – that is, not tied to any particular employer and exempted from the requirement for a LMO.[351] Permit holders may have access to health and social services.[352]

314. Finally, the Regulations also create a 'protected temporary residents class' for foreign nationals who hold a TRP and who became a temporary resident for

343. IP1, s. 23.3.
344. IP1, s. 5.7. If a new ground of inadmissibility has arisen, the foreign national may be granted a new permit: IP1, at 36.
345. IP1, s. 22.2.
346. Regulations, s. 65(b)(i). See RIAS at 4532: 'This change reflects the fact that, unlike other inadmissibility grounds, persons with a medical inadmissibility do not have recourse or measures to eliminate their inadmissibility such as rehabilitation or a pardon.'
347. Regulations, s. 65(b)(ii).
348. IP1, s. 5.15.
349. Regulations, s. 65(b)(ii).
350. Regulations, ss 199(d), 215(1)(e).
351. Regulations, s. 208(b).
352. IP1, s. 5.4.

protection reasons after applying for refugee status outside Canada.[353] This class was created to allow refugees in urgent need of protection to apply for permanent residence from within Canada, but without the delay associated with the broader TRP holder class.[354]

353. Regulations, s. 151.1(2).
354. IP1, s. 6.4.

Chapter 3. Long Stay Residents

§1. The Family Class and Economic Class

315. The next two chapters focus on immigrants who are authorized to reside in Canada as permanent residents. The three main classes of permanent resident, set out in section 12(1) of the IRPA, are the economic, family, and refugee classes. The economic class consists of foreign nationals admitted on the basis of their prospective economic contribution. Members of the family class are admitted because of their relationship to a Canadian or permanent resident. Canada admits refugees in fulfilment of international legal obligations and for humanitarian reasons. This chapter deals with the family and economic classes. Refugees are dealt with separately in Chapter 4.

§2. The Family Class

316. It is important to emphasize at the outset the distinction between members of the family class and 'family members'. Principal applicants in the economic, family, and refugee class are permitted to bring with them accompanying 'family members'. The category of 'family members' includes spouses, common-law partners (same or opposite sex), dependent children, and dependent children of dependent children.[355] The 'family class' is a broader category to which separate rules of admission apply.

317. Members of the family class today are permitted to come to Canada as permanent residents because they have a close relative who is a Canadian citizen or permanent resident, and who is willing to sponsor them. The same rules apply to citizen and permanent residents. Historically Canada did not set formal quotas or caps on the number of family class immigrants admitted each year, but the resources allocated to processing applications, and the bureaucratic prioritizing of applications, made it possible for the Minister to predict and modulate numbers.[356]

318. In 2011, in the wake of a long-standing backlog in the processing of sponsorship applications for parents and grandparents, the government announced a temporary suspension for this category. No new applications to sponsor parents or grandparents were accepted for processing between 5 November 2011 and 1 January 2014.[357] The sponsorship programme for parents and grandparents resumed on

355. Regulations, s. 1(3).
356. For projected admissions targets for 2012 with regard to the family class, see, Citizenship and Immigration Canada, 'Supplementary Information for the 2012 Immigration Levels Plan' (14 Nov. 2011) at: http://www.cic.gc.ca/english/department/media/notices/notice-levels2012.asp. (accessed 6 Jun. 2013).
357. See: CIC, 'Sponsoring your family', at: http://www.cic.gc.ca/english/immigrate/sponsor/index.asp (accessed July 2012). A new 'super visa' specifically for parents and grandparents was introduced when the temporary suspension was announced to facilitate visits (rather than long stays) to Canada

2 January 2014 with an annual cap of 5,000 applications[358] and a number of new requirements, outlined in section *A* below.

319. The basic framework for the family class programme is established by sections 12(1) and 13(1) of the Act together with sections 116–137 of the Regulations. The regulation of family class migration is animated by two concerns: first, defining which relationships qualify as sufficiently proximate to warrant inclusion; second, defining the financial obligations of Canadian citizens and permanent residents who sponsor family class members, with a view to ensuring that newly admitted family members do not impose a fiscal burden by accessing Canada's income assistance programmes. Thus, both the nature of the familial relationship and the acceptability of sponsorship arrangements in effect provide the selection criteria for this class.

320. To be admitted through the family class, a foreign national who is the principal applicant must: (1) have a relative who is a Canadian citizen, permanent resident, or registered Indian willing and eligible to sponsor them; (2) prove their identity, age, and relationship to the sponsor through documentation, by answering truthfully in the course of an examination, or, in the last resort, through a DNA test;[359] (3) not be inadmissible, nor have family members (accompanying or non-accompanying) who are inadmissible;[360] and (4) have valid passports or travel documents.[361] If a non-accompanying family member is not examined as part of the application, or is explicitly exempted from examination, he or she may not be sponsored later on.

321. This section will first outline in section 1 the family members included in the family class. The rules for dependent children and adoption are set out in section 1.2. Finally, section 3 deals with the special spouse-in-Canada class created to allow for the sponsorship of foreign national spouses living in Canada other than by seeking humanitarian and compassionate discretion under section 25 of the Act.

I. Family Class Members

322. Section 12(1) of the IRPA states that a foreign national may be selected as a member of the family class on the basis of their relationship as the spouse,

---

for up to two years. Eligible applicants must meet a number of conditions, including the requirement to purchase Canadian medical insurance for at least one year. See, CIC, 'Visiting Canada: Parent and Grandparent Super visa – who can apply' at: http://www.cic.gc.ca/english/visit/supervisa-who.asp.(accessed July 2012).

358. Canada Gazette, Government Notices, Vol. 147, 13 Jun. 2013, Department of Citizenship and Immigration, Ministerial Instructions 9 (MI 9), 'Parents and Grandparents'.

359. See IRPA, ss 16, 127; and Citizenship and Immigration Canada, OP1, *Procedures*, ss 5.9–5.12, 13, and 14.

360. Two categories of person are not covered by this requirement: first, separated spouses and second, children no longer in the legal custody of the applicant, dependent child of the applicant, or any other accompanying family member. See Regulations, s. 23.

361. Citizenship and Immigration Canada, OP2, *Processing Members of the Family Class*, s. 5.1.

common-law partner, child, parent, or prescribed family member of a Canadian citizen or permanent resident. Relatives that may be members of the family class are set out in section 117(1) of the Regulations:

- spouses, common-law partners, and conjugal partners – including same-sex partners;
- dependent children under 19 years or, in stipulated circumstances of dependency, over 18 years;[362]
- mothers and fathers;
- grandparents;
- orphaned minors who are the sponsor's sibling, niece or nephew, or grandchild;
- a minor child who the sponsor intends to adopt;
- any relative if there is no aunt, uncle, or family member from the list above who is already a Canadian citizen, Indian, or permanent resident or any relative from the list above who could be sponsored (the 'wild card' relative).[363]

Notably omitted are fiancées and siblings. The former were included under previous legislation, the 1978 Immigration Act. However, now they must apply either under section 25 of the Act for humanitarian and compassionate grounds review or, if they qualify, as common law or conjugal partners. At present, siblings of a Canadian citizen or permanent resident may qualify and enter only as accompanying family members of a parent who is the principal applicant.

323. A 'dependent child' is defined in the Regulations as a biological or adopted child who is under 19 years of age and unmarried, or is 19 years of age or older, and has depended on the parent since before they were 19 years, and is unable to

362. See Regulations, s. 2. In 2002, the Regulations raised the age for dependent children from 18 years to 21 years. The government gave two reasons for changing the definition of dependency at that time: first, in some cultures unmarried children will continue to live with their parents; second, increasingly children continue to live with and depend on their nuclear family while pursuing higher education prior to entering the labour force. See *Immigration and Refugee Protection* Regulations, and Regulatory Impact Analysis Statement, PC 2002-997, 11 Jun. 2002, online: http://publications.gc.ca/gazette/archives/p2/2002/2002-06-14-x/pdf/g2-136x9.pdf at 257 (accessed 31 Jul. 2014). Effective 1 Aug. 2014, however, the definition of a dependent child returned to 18 years and under; and the exception for full-time students was also removed. The government stated changes were necessary because older dependent children had lower economic outcomes and Canada needed to focus more on meeting the country's economic needs. The exception for older dependent children pursuing full-time studies created 'significant challenges' and processing inefficiencies. See, *Regulations Amending the Immigration and Refugee Protection Regulations*, and Regulatory Impact Analysis Statement, P.C. 2014-619 29 May 2014: http://canadagazette.gc.ca/rp-pr/p2/2014/2014-06-18/html/sor-dors133-eng.php (accessed 30 Jul. 2014); and Government of Canada, 'Notice – Changes to the definition of a dependent child' (23 Jun. 2014): http://www.cic.gc.ca/english/department/media/notices/2014-06-23.asp (accessed 30 Jul. 2014).

363. Regulations, s. 117(1). Note that the class of relatives admissible under the family class is broader than those included in the definition of family member at s. 1(3) of the Regulations. Section 1(3) expressly states that it is not applicable to s. 12 of IRPA, that is, that it does not define the family class.

support themselves because of a physical or mental condition.[364] In this latter case, there is a risk that in establishing the physical or mental condition necessitating dependency, the child will be found inadmissible on medical grounds.[365] 'Biological child' includes children who are born with the help of assisted human reproductive technologies, so long as the applicant or the applicant's spouse, common-law partner, or conjugal partner gave birth to the child. Where a child is born through surrogacy, a parental relationship must be established through adoption.[366]

324. 'Spouse' is not defined in the Regulations but a definition of 'marriage' is found in section 2:

> 'marriage', in respect of a marriage that took place outside Canada, means a marriage that is valid both under the laws of the jurisdiction where it took place and under Canadian law.

This has been interpreted to mean that the relationship must meet the formal criteria of validity of the country where it took place and the essential criteria of validity of both countries. However, there is authority to the effect that only essential criteria of validity recognized in Canada must be met.

The Operational Manual adds to the definition by stipulating that: 'Marriage is a status-based relationship existing from the day the marriage is legally valid until it is severed by death or divorce.'[367] This would include same-sex marriage where the conditions of mutual legality are met. All Canadian provinces and territories now recognize same-sex marriage, so same-sex marriages that occurred in Canada after legalization count as spousal relationships. Marriage in a foreign jurisdiction that also recognizes same-sex marriage will create a spousal relationship under the Act. In 2012, there were ten countries, six American states, and one US district where same-sex marriages were performed and recognized or had been recognized for a limited period.[368]

325. The Regulations define 'common-law partner' to mean 'in relation to a person, an individual who is cohabiting with the person in a conjugal relationship, having so cohabited for a period of at least one year'.[369] Common-law partners also include 'an individual who has been in a conjugal relationship with a person for at

364. Regulations, s. 2. Note that in *Gilani v. Canada (Minister of Citizenship and Immigration)*, [2005] F.C.J. No. 1880 (F.C.) the Federal Court held that the physical or mental condition need not have been diagnosed before the child reached 22 years (the age limit for dependency in place at that time) nor need it have persisted continuously since then.

365. This point is made in Waldman, *supra* at s. 13.58. See Act, s. 38(1), although the child himself or herself cannot be excluded on the ground that they will make excessive demands on health and social services: IRPA, s. 38(2)(a).

366. OP2, s. 5.14.

367. OP2, s. 5.25.

368. These are Netherlands, Belgium, Spain, Canada, South Africa, Norway, Sweden, Portugal, Iceland and Argentina; the State of Massachusetts, the State of Connecticut, the State of Iowa, the State of Vermont, New Hampshire, New York and the District of Columbia (as of 2012).

369. Regulations, s. 1(1).

least one year but is unable to cohabit with the person, due to persecution or any form of penal control'.[370]

326. 'Conjugal partner' is defined to mean 'in relation to a sponsor, a foreign national residing outside Canada who is in a conjugal relationship with the sponsor and has been in that relationship for a period of at least one year'.[371] This definition is meant to capture marriage-like relationships where cohabitation is impossible, typically because of immigration law. Only conjugal-partner relationships between sponsors and foreign nationals count for the purposes of the family class. Conjugal partners of sponsored individuals, therefore, cannot be brought into Canada as accompanying family members unless they did not cohabit due to 'persecution or any form of penal control'.

327. The categories of spouse, common law partner, and conjugal partner are intended to capture relationships 'of some permanence, where individuals are interdependent – financially, socially, emotionally, and physically – where they share household responsibilities, and where they have made a serious commitment to one another'.[372] Therefore, in assessing whether a spousal, common-law, or conjugal partner relationship actually exists, officers are instructed to consider whether a relationship is characterized by a mutual commitment to a shared life to the exclusion of all other conjugal relationships. This requirement denotes, among other things, a requirement of monogamy.[373] The Manual also tells officers to consider the circumstances under which the couple met, the evidence of a relationship and of cohabitation, and whether the couple has combined their affairs and achieved an expected degree of interdependence.[374]

328. Section 117(9) of the Regulations expressly excludes certain spousal, common law, or conjugal partners from the ambit of the family class:

- spouses, common-law partners, or conjugal partners who are under 16 years of age;
- spouses, common-law partners, or conjugal partners, if the sponsor is still under sponsorship obligations towards a former spouse, common-law partner, or conjugal partner;

370. Regulations, s. 1(2). Conjugal partners unable to cohabit for reasons of penal control or fear of persecution are included in the definition of 'common-law' partner in order to enable such conjugal partners to be accompanying family members of principal applicants in the economic, family, or refugee class.
371. Regulations, s. 2.
372. OP2, s. 5.25.
373. Bigamous and polygamous arrangements are not recognized according to s. 117(9)(c) of the Regulations.
374. OP2, s. 5.25. In *M. v. H.*, [1999] 2 S.C.R. at para. 59, the Supreme Court of Canada adopted the following as generally accepted characteristics of a conjugal relationship: shared shelter, sexual and personal behaviour, services, social activities, economic support and children, as well as the societal perception of the couple.

- spouses if either the foreign national or the sponsor has another spouse, common-law partner, or conjugal partner;[375]
- a foreign national who was a former spouse or common law partner of the sponsor at the time the sponsor applied to for permanent residence, if the visa officer neither examined nor waived examination of the former spouse or common law partner.[376]

329. This last exclusion is meant to enforce the requirement that all family members be declared and, with few exceptions, examined when applying for permanent residence. This requirement is meant to 'to encourage honesty and prevent applicants from circumventing immigration rules'. In specific cases, officers may consider applying humanitarian and compassionate discretion to admit foreign nationals excluded from the family class by this provision.[377] Finally, it may be possible to achieve admission for unexamined family members if they are not directly sponsored, but merely enter as family members of a sponsored person.[378]

330. The Regulations contain blanket exclusions to weed out bad faith relationships. Section 4 of the Regulations says any spousal, common-law, conjugal or adoptive relationship will not be recognized if it 'is not genuine and was entered into primarily for the purpose of acquiring any status or privilege under the Act'.[379] This provision is to be read conjunctively: '[T]he questioned relationship must be both not genuine and entered into primarily for the purpose of acquiring any status or privilege under the Act.'[380] So a relationship will be excluded on the basis of bad faith only if both requirements are met. Of further note are the verb tenses used. The first prong of the test asks whether a relationship is now genuine. The second asks about the purpose envisioned at the time the relationship began. In theory, a non-genuine relationship entered into for immigration purposes can metamorphose into a genuine one that ought not to be captured by section 4.[381]

331. In deciding whether a relationship is genuine, the courts and the IAD of the IRB have emphasized that a number of factors must be considered. For example, the IAD has said:

375. There are some complexities here. To be disqualified, either the foreign national or the sponsor must have had, at the time of their marriage, another spouse. The foreign national is disqualified if the sponsor has another conjugal partner who is a foreign national or if the foreign national is the conjugal partner of another sponsor: Regulations, s. 117(9).
376. The exceptions are for non-accompanying family members who an officer had determined did not need to be examined: Regulations, s. 117(10).
377. OP2, s. 5.12. The examples of given cases where humanitarian and compassionate discretion might be appropriate are: (1) cases where the best interests of a child are at issue, (2) cases where it was clearly not possible to produce a relative for examination, (3) cases involving a refugee who believed his or her relatives were dead or who did not know their whereabouts, and (4) cases where the existence of a child born out of wedlock was not disclosed because of cultural stigma.
378. Regulations, s. 70(4). OP2, s. 5.12.
379. Note that s. 4 and 4.1 of the Regulations apply to all parts of IRPA, not just the family class.
380. *Donkar v. Canada (Minister of Citizenship and Immigration)*, 2006 FC 1089 at para. 12.
381. *Ibid.* at para. 18.

> The genuineness of the marriage is based on a number of factors. They are not identical in every appeal as the genuineness can be affected by any number of different factors in each appeal. They can include, but are not limited to, such factors as the intent of the parties to the marriage, the length of the relationship, the amount of time spent together, conduct at the time of meeting, at the time of an engagement and/or the wedding, behaviour subsequent to a wedding, the level of knowledge of each other's relationship histories, level of continuing contact and communication, the provision of financial support, the knowledge of and sharing of responsibility for the care of children brought into the marriage, the knowledge of and contact with extended families of the parties, as well as the level of knowledge of each other's daily lives.[382]

The second prong of the test under section 4 requires that admission or some other privilege under the Act be more than simply a factor in deciding to enter a relationship. It must be 'the dominant driving force' behind the relationship.[383] The Federal Court has clarified that the privilege or status need not have been achieved; nor need it have accrued to the person applying for permanent residence.[384]

332. Section 4.1 of the Regulations further excludes spousal, common-law, and conjugal relationships if they had previously been dissolved for the purposes of obtaining status for a sponsor, the foreign national seeking permanent residence or another foreign national.[385] An example is *Mariano*, in which the sponsor divorced her spouse, who was medically inadmissible, and thus removed him from her application for permanent residence when she herself immigrated to Canada. She subsequently remarried and applied to sponsor him. The IAD held that section 4.1 of the Regulations applied to exclude the relationship.[386]

333. All sponsored foreign nationals and their dependents must undergo a medical examination. Section 38(2) of the Act exempts spouses, common-law partners, and dependent children from inadmissibility on the grounds that they have a medical condition that will place excessive demands on health or social services. Note,

---

382. *Chavez, Rodrigo v. Minister of Citizenship and Immigration* (IAD TA3-24409), Hoare, 17 Jan. 2005 at para. 3; cited in Legal Services, Immigration and Refugee Board of Canada, Sponsorship Appeals (1 Jan. 2008) Ch. 6, at 6.
383. *Singh, Ravinder Kaur v. M.E.I.*(I.A.B. 86-10228), Chu, Suppa, Eglington (dissenting), 8 Aug. 1988, at 5; cited in Sponsorship Appeals, Ch. 6, at 7. This was an interpretation of similar provisions under the former Immigration Act and Regulations.
384. *Gavino, Edwin Dorol v. M.C.I.*(F.C., No. IMM-3249-05), Russell, 9 Mar. 2006; 2006 FC 308; cited in Sponsorship Appeals, Ch. 6, at 7.
385. Non-genuine adoptive relationships where the adoption has not yet taken place are excluded by virtue of s. 117(1)(g)(i) of the Regulations. Bad faith adoptions of children over 18 years old are covered by s. 117(4)(c) of the Regulations.
386. *Mariano, Edita Palacio v. M.C.I.*(IAD WA5-00122), Lamont, 20 Sep. 2006; cited in Sponsorship Appeals, Ch. 6, at 29. When applying to immigrate to Canada, Mariano would have been inadmissible because she had a medically inadmissible family member (her spouse). Once she became a permanent resident however, she could legally sponsor her spouse because medical inadmissibility is not a bar to sponsoring a spouse.

however, that any demand placed on social services will lead to default of a sponsorship agreement. Section 24 of the Regulations provides this same exemption to conjugal partners and children who will be adopted.[387]

334. In 2012, the government introduced a regulation that alters the status of sponsored spouses. Historically, foreign nationals who successfully applied to be sponsored as members of the family class were admitted to Canada as permanent residents. The new regulation confers conditional status on spouses, common law partners and conjugal partners in a relationship of two years or less with their sponsor and who have no children in common with their sponsor at the time they submit their sponsorship application. They will be able to retain permanent resident status at the end of a two-year period in Canada unless there is evidence that their relationship is not genuine. The government's stated objective is to deter 'marriages of convenience'.[388]

II. Dependent Children and Adoptions

335. The most important provision affecting the sponsorship of dependent children is section 117(9)(d) of the Regulations. Where a person seeking to come to Canada as a permanent resident does not make available a child for examination, they will later be disallowed from sponsoring that child. This harsh provision was determined to be constitutionally valid by the Federal Court of Appeal in *de Guzman*.[389] Moreover in the same case the provision was not held to be contrary to Canada's international human rights obligations because it is qualified by section 25(1) of the IRPA, which permits exemptions to be made on humanitarian and compassionate grounds.

336. The regulations dealing with the admission of adopted children were developed partly to comply with the Convention on Protection of Children and Cooperation in Respect of Intercountry Adoption ('Adoption Convention') and the United Nations Convention on the Rights of the Child ('CRC'). These conventions impose an obligation to safeguard the best interests of children brought into Canada through international adoption.

337. The adoption provisions apply to all international adoptions, including the adoption of orphaned relatives. Adopted children will not be admitted unless the

387. Regulations, s. 24. All such family members could still be inadmissible on the other health-related grounds, that is, if they have a health condition that is likely to be a danger to public health or safety. IRPA, s. 38(1)(a) and (b).

388. See Canada Gazette, 'Regulations Amending the Immigration and Refugee Protection Regulations: Regulatory Impact Analysis Statement and Proposed Regulatory Text', Vol. 146, No. 10–10 Mar. 2012, http://gazette.gc.ca/rp-pr/p1/2012/2012-03-10/html/reg1-eng.html (accessed 6 Jun. 2013); and Regulations, s. 72.1.

389. *de Guzman v. Canada (Minister of Citizenship and Immigration)*, 2005 FCA 436. Note that s. 117(9)(d) does not just apply to dependent children, but to all unaccompanying family members who are not examined.

intended parents have confirmed they have obtained information with respect to the children's medical condition.[390] An exclusionary provision also applies to all so-called bad faith adoptions – those undertaken 'primarily for the purpose of acquiring any privilege or status under the Act'[391] – and adoptions where there is evidence of child trafficking or undue gain.[392]

338. There are no stipulated criteria in the Act or Regulations for identifying adoptions of convenience, but the Operational Manual instructs officers to consider, among other things, the circumstances of the adoption; the whereabouts and circumstances of the biological parents; whether the child continued to live with his or her biological parents after adoption; and the reasons given for the adoption.[393] In *de Guzman*, the IAD also listed a number of factors that can be considered when judging the authenticity of an adoption. These include the motivation of the adopting parents; to a lesser extent, the motivation of the natural parents; the authority and suasion of the adopting parents over the child; the relationship between the child and the natural parents after adoption; treatment by the adopting parents of the adopted child versus any natural children; changes to official records, etc.; and arrangements and actions relating to child care and otherwise providing for the adopted child.[394]

339. The rules for admitting adopted children to permanent residence depend on the place and manner where the adoption has taken or will take place, as well as on the province or territory[395] where the child will live with his or her new family.[396] In this, the Regulations reflect the fact that in Canada the provinces, and not the federal government, have legislative authority over children's rights and welfare. To bring an adopted child to Canada as a member of the family class, the province where the family will live must issue one of three kinds of letter approving the adoption. No-objection letters state that the provincial authority does not object to the adoption. No-involvement letters state, in the case of adoptions finalized abroad, that the province had no involvement with the adoption but will recognize it. Letters or notices of agreement state that the province and the adoptive parents agree to the adoption.

340. If the adoption is to take place in Canada, and both the province and the country of origin are signatories to the Adoption Convention, then a competent authority in both jurisdictions must issue a letter approving the adoption.[397] If the adoption is to take place in Canada and either the province or the country of origin is not party to the Adoption Convention, the child will be admitted if the adoption

390. Regulations, s. 118.
391. Regulations, ss 4, 117(1)(g)(i), 117(4)(c), and 117(7).
392. Citizenship and Immigration Canada, OP3, Adoptions (3 Apr. 2009), at 8 (hereinafter 'OP3').
393. OP3, at 7.
394. *de Guzman v. Canada (Minister of Citizenship and Immigration)*, [1995] I.A.D.D. No. 1248, 33 Imm. L.R. (2d) 28.
395. In what follows, the references to a province or provinces include territories.
396. A matrix of the requirements is found in OP3, at 5.
397. Regulations, s. 117(1)(g)(ii).

is shown to be legal, there is no evidence of child trafficking or undue gain, and the province issues a letter saying it does not object to the adoption.[398]

341. If the adoption has already taken place, inside or outside Canada, it must be established that the adoption was in the best interests of the child, according to certain factors set out in the Regulations.[399] These include: (1) that a competent authority has conducted or approved a study by an accredited social worker of the adoptive parents' household (a home study); (2) that the child's biological parents gave free and informed consent to the adoption; (3) that the adoption created a genuine parent-child relationship; (4) that the adoption conformed to local law; (5) that the adoption conformed to the laws of the sponsor's place of residence and, if the sponsor lived in Canada at the time of adoption, that his or her province of residence has issued a letter stating that it has no objection to the adoption; (6) that, if both the province of residence and the country of origin are parties to the Adoption Convention, competent authorities in both jurisdiction have issued letters approving the adoption; and (7) if either the province or the country of origin are not parties to the Adoption Convention, that there is no evidence of child trafficking or undue gain.[400] Officers are instructed in general to accept a valid adoption order from the country of origin as proof that the foreign adoption-law requirements have been met. All Canadian provinces except Québec recognize adoptions that are valid according to the laws of the country of origin; it is not open to an officer to second-guess the validity of legally recognized adoptions.[401] In Québec, specialized tribunals must grant recognition once the child arrives in Canada.[402]

342. The above requirements deal with the adoption of minors. Sponsorship of foreign nationals adopted when 18 years of age (but under 19 years, pursuant to changes in the definition of dependency in 2014) is also possible. In such cases, the adoption must comply with local law, a genuine parent-child relationship must have been established prior to the child's eighteenth birthday, and the adoption must not have been undertaken primarily to gain entry to Canada.[403]

343. Children adopted internationally are barred from later sponsoring their biological parents, since the relationship is deemed severed.[404] Also, if an adoption is later revoked, the former adoptee can only sponsor another foreign national 'if the revocation of the adoption was not obtained for the purpose of sponsoring that application'.[405]

---

398. Regulations, s. 117(1)(g)(iii).
399. Regulations, s. 117(2).
400. Regulations, s 117(2) and (3).
401. See *Wee v. Canada (Minister of Employment and Immigration),* [1992] I.A.D.D. No. 205, 18 Imm. L.R. (2d) 103.
402. OP3, at 6.
403. Regulations, s. 117(4).
404. Regulations, s. 3(2); OP3, at 8.
405. Regulations, s. 133(5).

Subject to some restrictions, adoptive parents have the option of obtaining citizenship for the adopted child without first sponsoring the child as a permanent resident. The process does not differ substantially from the sponsorship process, except that the status conferred on the child is citizenship rather than permanent resident status.[406]

A. *Sponsorships*

344. Sponsorship entails an obligation to ensure that the financial needs of the sponsored person are met without resort to publicly administered social assistance which is defined in section 2 of the Regulations as:

> any benefit in the form of money, goods or services provided to or on behalf of a person by a province under a program of social assistance, including a program of social assistance designated by a province to provide for basic requirements including food, shelter, clothing, fuel, utilities, household supplies, personal requirements and health care not provided by public health care, including dental care and eye care.

345. Failure to meet the obligation can lead to two major adverse consequences. First, sponsors in default may not sponsor another individual as long as they remain in default.[407] Second, sponsors may be required to pay in full any social assistance received by their sponsored relatives during the stipulated period, regardless of whether the relationship persists or whether the economic situation of the sponsor has deteriorated.[408]

346. The right to sponsor is granted by section 13(1) of the Act and section 130(1) of the Regulations to Canadian citizens and permanent residents who are at least 18 years of age and who live in Canada. The Operational Manual adds: 'Registered Indians were unintentionally omitted from [section 13(1)], but are nonetheless administratively included.[409] Section 130(2) further extends the right of sponsorship to Canadian citizens living abroad who wish to sponsor a spouse, common-law partner, conjugal partner, or dependent child, so long as the sponsor will reside in Canada after the sponsored foreign national becomes a permanent resident. The onus is on the sponsoring citizen to satisfy immigration officials of their intention to return to live in Canada.[410] Misrepresentation in a sponsorship

406. This option was introduced in 2008 for adoptive parents in circumstances where, *inter alia* at least one adoptive parent was born or naturalized in Canada and was a Canadian citizen when the adoption took place. See, CIC, 'Intercountry Adoption: Which Process to Use' at: http://www.cic.gc.ca/english/immigrate/adoption/choose.asp. (July 2012).
407. Regulations, s. 133(1)(g)(i).
408. *Canada (Attorney General) v. Mavi*, [2011] 2 S.C.R. 504.
409. Citizenship and Immigration Canada, Operational Manual IP2, *Processing Applications to Sponsor Members of the Family Class* (15 Oct. 2013) at 15 (hereinafter 'IP2').
410. IP2, at 15, 42–43.

application can lead to removal of a permanent resident sponsor and the inadmissibility of sponsored relatives.[411] Canadian citizens who make misrepresentations are subject to possible criminal penalties.[412]

347. Sponsors must meet several requirements to be approved.[413] They must intend to meet their obligations in the undertaking. They must not be subject to a removal order, including stayed orders.[414] They must not be detained in any penitentiary, jail, reformatory, or prison. They must not have been convicted of any sexual offence. They must not have been convicted of any offence causing bodily harm against a spouse, son or daughter, or any other relative or relative of his or her spouse.[415] They must not be in default of any undertaking or any court-ordered child or spousal support payments. They must not be in default of any other debts under the Act. They must not be undischarged bankrupts. They must meet minimum income requirements, except if sponsoring spouses, common-law or conjugal partners, or dependant or adopted children.[416] They must not be on social assistance, except for reasons of disability. Note, however, that if a sponsor is receiving social assistance due to a disability, the sponsored family member may be found inadmissible on financial grounds.[417]

348. Sponsorship involves two contracts, each with legislated content: an 'undertaking' made to the Minister of Citizenship and Immigration or a provincial authority and a 'sponsorship agreement' between the sponsored individual or individuals, the sponsor, and any co-signor.

349. In an undertaking, a sponsor promises to provide 'food, clothing, shelter, fuel, utilities, household supplies, personal requirements and other goods and services, including dental care, eye care and other health needs not provided by public health care' and that 'the sponsored person and his or her family members will not need to apply for social assistance'. Each undertaking further states: 'I understand that the sponsored person and his or her family members will be admitted solely on the basis of their relationship to me (as sponsor) and that they do not need to have the financial means to become established in Canada.' It also sets out the length of the undertaking and that:

---

411. IRPA, s. 40(1)(a) and (b) and 40(2)(b).
412. IRPA, ss 127 and 128.
413. Regulations, s. 133(1).
414. For the clarification regarding stayed orders, see IP2, at 21.
415. There are exceptions to the criminality exclusions. For convictions in Canada, a sponsor will not be disqualified if: (1) he or she has been pardoned; (2) there has been a final determination of an acquittal in the case; or (3) five years or more have passed since completion of the sentence. See Regulations, s. 133(2). For convictions outside Canada, disqualification will not follow if: (1) there has been a final determination of acquittal; or, (2) five or more years have passed since completion of the sentence and the applicant is demonstrably rehabilitated. See Regulations, s. 133(3).
416. Regulations, s. 133(4). Sponsors of parents and grandparents must meet the minimum income requirements, plus 30%, for each of the three consecutive taxation years immediately preceding the application. See, Regulations, s. 133 (1) (j) B.
417. IRPA, s. 39.

> I understand that the undertaking remains in effect no matter what may change in my life. For example, if I am divorced, change jobs, become unemployed, and/or go back to school, I will still be responsible to the sponsored person and his or her family members I am sponsoring or for whom I am co-signing.

Each undertaking further explains the acts that lead to default and the consequences of default. In language that has proven significant in the only major case dealing with undertakings, the standard undertaking also states:

> The Minister and the province concerned may choose not to take enforcement action to recover money from me if the default is the result of abuse or in other circumstances. The decision not to act at a particular time does not cancel the debt. The Minister and the province concerned may recover the debt when circumstances have changed.[418]

350. The binding nature of undertakings is established by section 13(3) of the Act. Further, section 132 of the Regulations provides that 'the sponsor's undertaking obliges the sponsor to reimburse Her Majesty in right of Canada or a province for every benefit provided as social assistance to or on behalf of the sponsored foreign national and their family members' for the statutorily specified period.[419]

351. The legislated duration of the undertaking varies according to the relationship with the sponsored individual. It is three years for spouses, common-law partners, or conjugal partners, which coincides with the residency requirement for citizenship eligibility. For dependent children and children whose adoption takes place in Canada, it is either ten years or the day the child turns 25 years, whichever comes first.[420] It is three years for dependent children who are 19 years or older when they become permanent residents. For parents, grandparents and their accompanying family members, the undertaking lasts twenty years.[421] For all other family class members, the undertaking lasts for ten years.[422] In most cases, the duration of the undertaking begins on the date the sponsored family member becomes a permanent resident. Provinces can legislate earlier expiration dates, though only Québec has done so.[423]

---

418. See form IMM1344AE, p. 5, at http://www.cic.gc.ca/english/pdf/kits/forms/IMM1344E.PDF. (accessed 6 Jun. 2013).
419. Regulations, s. 132(1).
420. This means that the maximum duration of the undertaking decreases depending on the age of the child. Undertakings range from ten years for a 15-year old to four years for a 21-year old.
421. Regulations, s. 132 (1)(b) iv.
422. Regulations, s. 132 (1) (b) v.
423. Regulations, s. 133(3). See also s. 133(2), which establishes default rules for undertakings given to provinces concerning children. For dependent children under 22 years old, the undertaking lasts until the later of either the twenty-second birthday of the child or 10 years following their accession to permanent residence. For children under 22 years who are not dependents, the undertaking lasts ten years. (In Québec, the duration of undertakings are: three years for spouses, common-law partners, and conjugal partners; ten years or until age 18 years, whichever comes first, for dependent children; and ten years for all other family members. Sponsors who move from Québec must

352. Section 145(2) of the Act makes debts owing under an undertaking payable 'on demand' and recoverable by either the federal or provincial governments.[424] Section 146 of the Act allows the government to file a certificate with the Federal Court stating an amount owed, after which that amount becomes recoverable in the same manner as any court judgment. The government may garnish wages or other payments owing to sponsors who have defaulted on an undertaking.[425]

353. Provincial social assistance authorities provide information to the Ministry about sponsored permanent residents.[426] A sponsor will be in default of the undertaking if any sponsored family member receives *any* form of social assistance, including assistance related to disability, during the period of validity or if there is breach of any other obligation contained in the undertaking, such as the obligation to provide for the essential needs of sponsored relatives. Default ends when the sponsor repays the benefits received from the provincial government 'in full or in accordance with an agreement with that government' or otherwise ceases to be in breach.[427] The end of the undertaking's prescribed duration or the death of a sponsored individual does not nullify an undertaking. If a defaulting sponsor dies, the government will not seek compensation unless there is a co-signor.[428]

354. Sponsors, co-signors,[429] and the sponsored family members must also enter into a sponsorship agreement acknowledging and clarifying the sponsorship relationship. The agreement must include: (1) a statement that the sponsor will provide for the sponsored family members' 'basic requirements' for the duration of the undertaking; (2) a declaration by sponsors and co-signors that their financial obligations do not prevent them from honouring their obligations to the Minister; and (3) a statement by the sponsored family member that he or she 'will make every reasonable effort to provide for their own basic requirements and those of their accompanying family members'. No agreement is required if a sponsored foreign national is under 19 years and is not the spouse, common-law partner, or conjugal partner of the sponsor.[430] Sponsorship agreements are meant to ensure 'sponsors focus on their obligations' and 'confirms their understandings of their mutual

---

sign a new undertaking and agreement. See IP2, at s. 6.5. Citizenship and Immigration Canada, Operational Manual OP6, *Federal Skilled Workers* (8 May 2009) at s. 11).

424. Section 145(3) of IRPA further provides: 'A debt may be recovered at any time.'

425. IRPA, s. 147.

426. IP2, at 23.

427. Regulations, s. 135.

428. IP2, at 19.

429. Requirements for co-signors are set out in s. 132(5) of the Regulations. A co-signor must be a spouse or common-law partner of the sponsor and must otherwise meet all the sponsorship eligibility requirements, other than having filed a sponsorship application. Co-signors take on all the obligations of the sponsor, but they do not have all the rights. For example, they may not continue with an application if the sponsor withdraws and they have no right of appeal against a refused permanent resident visa: See IP2, at section 5.28.

430. Regulations, s. 132(4). However, co-signors may continue with an appeal following the death of a sponsor if there is evidence of joint sponsorship: *Annor, Gladys v. M.C.I.*(IAD TA4-04677), Whist, 28 Sep. 2005; cited in Sponsorship Appeals at p. 4.

obligations and responsibilities'.[431] Nonetheless, the legal effect of sponsorship agreements is unclear. If sponsored family members receive social assistance after not making reasonable efforts to provide for themselves, the sponsor will still be found in default. Even if legally enforceable, it is doubtful that, as a practical matter, sponsors would be able to collect from sponsored family members in breach of their obligations.

355. Undertakings and sponsorship agreements tether sponsors to sponsored family members, regardless of subsequent changes to their relationship. This complicates fulfilment of sponsorship obligations by sponsors; the life choices of sponsored relatives; and the enforcement by the government of undertakings. Under the old Act, undertakings were enforced by suit in court and sponsors occasionally succeeded in having their debts lowered or eliminated.[432]

356. In 2011, the Supreme Court of Canada confirmed that in dealing with defaulting sponsors, 'the government must act fairly having regard to their financial means to pay and the existence of circumstances that would militate against enforcement of immediate payment (such as abuse)'.[433] The Court held that in exercising its discretion, the government's duty of procedural fairness includes the following obligations:

> (a) to notify a sponsor at his or her last known address of the claim; (b) to afford the sponsor an opportunity within limited time to explain in writing his or her relevant personal and financial circumstances that are said to militate against immediate collection; (c) to consider any relevant circumstances brought to its attention keeping in mind that the undertakings were the essential conditions precedent to allowing the sponsored immigrant to enter Canada in the first place; (d) to notify the sponsor of the government's decision; (e) without the need to provide reasons.[434]

The Court further noted that governments had discretion to defer collection but not forgive debt.[435]

III. Spouses, and Common-Law Partners, in Canada

357. The Regulations create a separate class for spouses and common-law partners who may apply for permanent residence from within Canada.[436] This class

431. IP2, at 19–20.
432. See, for example, *Manitoba v. Khaleghi-Hashemian*, 2002 MBQB 1 (CanLII); *Her Majesty the Queen in Right of the Province of Manitoba v. Barkman et al.*, 2007 MBQB 54 (CanLII). See also *Her Majesty the Queen in Right of the Province of Manitoba v. Kabamba et al.*, 2006 MBQB 201 (CanLII), in which the sponsor did not succeed.
433. *Canada (Attorney General)*, *supra* n. 408, at para. 63.
434. *Ibid.* para. 79 (iv).
435. *Ibid.* para. 79 (i).
436. Regulations, s. 123.

includes all foreign nationals who are spouses and common-law partners cohabiting with a Canadian citizen or permanent resident and who are the subject of a sponsorship application.[437] The sponsorship must be approved pursuant to the rules set out above. In addition, the sponsorship must cover any accompanying family members of the foreign national spouse or a common-law partner. The application must include a request to have these family members remain in Canada as permanent residents.[438] They must not be inadmissible.[439]

358. Section 124(b) of the Regulations requires that sponsored spouses have valid temporary resident status. However, a policy statement issued in 2005, purportedly under authority of section 25(1) of the Act, effectively eliminated the requirement of valid temporary resident status, thereby permitting the inclusion of spouses without lawful status.[440]

§3. Economic Class

359. Section 12(2) of the Act provides for selection of immigrants as members of the economic class based on their ability to become economically established in Canada. This is consistent with the general statements of purpose found in section 3 of the Act that the legislation aims 'to pursue the maximum social, cultural and economic benefits of immigration' and 'to support the development of a strong and prosperous Canadian economy'. Economic class migrants represent the largest group of permanent residents admitted annually to Canada, with 160,819 economic class permanent residents accepted into Canada in 2012. However, more than half of this number – 92,553 permanent residents – are the spouses or dependents of the principal applicant.[441] The economic class comprises a number of different subclasses: federal skilled workers, federal skilled tradespersons, business immigrants, provincial nominees, Québec-selected immigrants, and live-in caregivers. In this section, we discuss the first five of these; while live-in caregivers are discussed briefly above. The federal skilled worker and federal skilled tradespersons are discussed first in sections 3.1 and 3.2, with the requirements for business immigrants, provincial nominees and Québec-bound immigrants dealt with in sections 3.3 and 3.4. A new initiative, the Express Entry programme, will be briefly elaborated in section 3.5.

437. Regulations, s. 124. The same general exclusions from the family class in s. 117(9) of the Regulations apply to the In-Canada class under s. 125 of the Regulations.
438. Regulations, s. 128.
439. Regulations, s. 129.
440. Under this policy, applicants are exempt from s. 124(b) of the Regulations and from the requirements under s. 21(1) of IRPA and s. 72(1)(e)(i) of the Regulations that they not be inadmissible due to lack of status. All other requirements of the class continue to apply. The policy is set out in Citizenship and Immigration Canada, Operational Manual IP8, '*Spouse or Common-law partner in Canada Class*' (16 Oct. 2006) at Appendix D–H.
441. Citizenship and Immigration Canada, Annual Report to Parliament on Immigration, 2013 at 14.

I. Federal Skilled Workers

360. Section 75(1) of the Regulations defines the federal skilled worker class 'as a class of persons who are skilled workers and who may become permanent residents on the basis of their ability to become economically established in Canada and who intend to reside in a province other than the Province of Québec'.

361. The processing of skilled worker applications first focuses on eligibility. At the initial stage, their eligibility for the programme is assessed. The basic requirements found in the Regulations is that the applicant must have one year of continuous full-time or part-time equivalent experience within the last ten years in an occupation that falls under classifications O, A, or B in the National Occupational Classification (NOC) matrix;[442] they must meet a minimum language threshold; and they must have either a Canadian educational credential or provide an assessment by a CIC-designated organization confirming their credential is equivalent to a completed Canadian one.

Ministerial Instructions promulgated in 2010 restricted the number of eligible occupations and constituted the first step in the government's plan to ensure that workers were better equipped to secure employment upon arrival in Canada. Only those with experience in one of twenty-nine specified job classifications, those who worked or studied legally for a year in Canada, or those with arranged employment were eligible. A further set of Ministerial Instructions announced in June 2011 and effective 1 July 2011 imposed a numerical annual cap of 10,000 federal skilled worker applications in total and within the 10,000 cap, a maximum of 500 federal skilled worker applications per eligible occupation.[443] In July 2012, the federal skilled worker programme was subject to a 'temporary pause', pending implementation of new selection criteria. The pause did not apply to individuals with a qualifying job offer or those applying under a special stream for PhD students. Effective 1 May 2014, the programme re-opened with an annual cap of 25,000 new applications in total, a new list of fifty eligible occupations and a maximum of 1,000 applications accepted per eligible occupation. In the new programme, a maximum of 500

442. The NOC matrix describes the duties, skills, aptitudes and work settings for more than 500 different occupations in the Canadian labour market, each of which is described in detail. The matrix is divided into NOC O (management occupations), A (professional occupations, which usually require university education), B (technical, skilled trades, and paraprofessional occupations, which usually require college education), C (occupations that usually require secondary school or occupation-specific training), and D (occupations that require on-the-job training). The matrix's chief function is now to screen applications for immigrants who have arranged employment or who have spent a year in Canada as a student or temporary foreign worker. The matrix is redundant for applicants who have the minimum one year's experience in one of the occupations listed under the ministerial instructions, all of which fall under the NOC O, A, or B classifications.

443. Listed occupations included management consultants, restaurant and food service managers, insurance adjusters and claims examiners, biologists, various health care practitioners (specialist physicians, general practitioners and family physicians, physiotherapists, registered nurses, etc.), chefs and cooks, contractors and supervisors in the carpentry and mechanic trades and heavy equipment construction, electricians (except industrial and power system electricians), plumbers, and a number of others. See also, http://www.cic.gc.ca/english/immigrate/skilled/apply-who-instructions.asp#list (Citizenship and Immigration Canada, OP6, *Federal Skilled Workers* (8 May 2009) at p. 11).

PhD students are accepted per year while applicants with arranged employment are not subject to any intake caps.[444]

362. Eligible applicants are assessed according to six selection factors under a point system to see if they have the requisite number of points indicating a general ability to establish themselves in Canada.

363. The criteria under the revised point system are:

- *Education*: An applicant receives up to twenty-five points for his or her educational achievements, according to the level of the degree and the number of degrees or diplomas obtained.[445]
- *Language*: An applicant receives up to twenty-eight points for his or her ability in Canada's official languages, French and English.[446] The applicant must specify which official language is to be considered his or her first official language. Language proficiency must then be assessed by a designated institution, or other written evidence of linguistic proficiency must be given.
- *Employment experience*: An applicant gets up to fifteen points based on the amount of experience he or she has in an NOC O, A, or B category occupation (a managerial or professional position, or skilled or technical trade), specified by him or her, over the previous ten years.[447] To qualify, the applicant must have experience performing certain key functions and duties associated with the occupation.[448] The officer need not assess the applicant's experience in any occupation other than those specified in the application.[449] The experience also cannot be in an occupation designated by the Minister as 'restricted', although currently there are no such occupations.[450]

---

444. See, Canada Gazette, Government Notices, Vol. 148, 26 Apr. 2014, Department of Citizenship and Immigration, Updated Ministerial Instructions 12 (MI 12); and Citizenship and Immigration Canada, Fact Sheet – Federal Skilled Worker Programme, http://www.cic.gc.ca/english/resources/publications/employers/federal-skilled-worker-program.asp (accessed 21 May 2014).
445. Regulations, s. 78.
446. Regulations, s. 79. Note that officer discretion is quite carefully controlled with respect to assessment of language proficiency. Interviews with an officer are not supposed to be used for linguistic assessment; an officer must either rely on official test results or evaluate written evidence of proficiency against published government standards. Officers may not consider any claim that test results are not an accurate reflection of an applicant's true abilities. They may not override the test results and substitute their own evaluation of language abilities. They may not accept results of any test administered by a non-approved organization. See OP6, at 34–40.
447. Regulations, s. 80.
448. In *Nakamine v. Canada (Minister of Citizenship and Employment)* (1998), 41 Imm. L.R. 2d 255, [1998] FCJ No. 3 (TD), the Immigration officer discounted all of the applicant's work experience, including Canadian experience, because he had no formal academic training or apprenticeship. Evidence showed occupational skills for this job (chef-cook) were typically acquired on the job. The court set the refusal aside. See *Dogra v. Canada (Minister of Citizenship and Employment)* (1999), 166 FTR 264, [1999] FCJ No. 560 (TD).
449. Regulations, s. 80(6).
450. OP6, at 13.

– *Age*: Applicants can receive up to twelve points for their age.[451] Individuals between eighteen and thirty five years of age receive the maximum number of points. People in that age bracket are thought most likely to successfully establish themselves. The number of points awarded declines with each year above and below these outer limits, down to zero for individuals younger than 18 years or older than 46 years of age.
– *Arranged Employment*: Applicants receive up to ten points for having arranged employment in Canada if there has been an official determination that the employment will have a neutral or positive effect on the labour market in Canada.[452] Arranged employment is 'an offer of indeterminate employment in Canada'. An offer of employment will be approved if it is genuine, if it is not part-time or seasonal, and if the wages and working conditions are sufficient to attract and retain Canadian citizens. While arranged employment counts toward a positive point-system evaluation, having no arranged employment does not automatically disqualify an applicant.[453]
– *Adaptability*: Applicants receive up to ten points for general adaptability.[454] Such points can be awarded to a skilled worker based on the educational credentials of his or her spouses or common-law partner, their spouse or partner's Canadian work experience, or for having a relative who is a citizen or permanent resident living in Canada.

364. Only those applicants who achieve the pass mark of sixty-seven may be admitted.[455] Under section 76(2) of the Regulations, the pass mark is based on a number of factors: (1) the number of applications by skilled workers as members of the skilled worker class currently being processed; (2) the number of skilled workers projected to become permanent residents according to a report published by the Government of Canada;[456] and (3) the potential, taking into account economic and other relevant factors, for the establishment of skilled workers in Canada. The pass mark may be revised any time and can be applied retroactively against existing applications.[457]

365. The Regulations grant discretion to immigration officers to substitute their own evaluation for the results of the point system if in their view 'the number of points awarded is not a sufficient indicator of whether the skilled worker may become economically established in Canada'.[458] Any such exercise of discretion

451. Regulations, s. 81.
452. Regulations, s. 82.
453. Regulations, s. 76(1)(b)(ii).
454. Regulations, s. 83.
455. Regulations, s. 76(2) empowers the Minister to set the pass mark. The pass mark is available online at the Ministry website.
456. This report is mandated by IRPA, s. 94.
457. On retroactivity in this context, See *Kazi v. Canada (Minister of Citizenship and Immigration)*, [2004] 1 FCR 161.
458. Regulations, s. 76(3).

requires a second officer's concurrence.[459] When the Regulations were first promulgated, the Ministry explained: 'A selection system can be designed to reflect the factors that would lead to economic success for the majority of applicants; it cannot, however, reflect the specific personalized elements that might lead to success or failure for every applicant. Therefore, the continuation of discretion has been considered desirable.'[460] Officers must consider exercising discretion in an applicant's favour when asked to do so.[461] This discretion is not the same as humanitarian and compassionate consideration, and it cannot be used to override refusal due to insufficient funds, failure to meet the definition of a skilled worker, or failure to meet the eligibility requirements under the 2010 Ministerial Instructions.

366. In addition an applicant who does not have arranged employment is expected to support themselves and their family members while trying to establish themselves in Canada and so must show they have enough funds – unencumbered, available, and transferable – to do so.

367. The amount of funds needed is 'equal to half the minimum necessary income applicable in respect of the group of persons consisting of the skilled worker and their family members'.[462] The income requirement is half of what Canada's statistics ministry (Statistics Canada) says is necessary for a family the same size as the applicant's (including accompanying and non-accompanying dependents) to survive in an urban area of 500,000 or more.[463] For example, an applicant with a family of four must show he or she has CAD 21,971 available.[464]

368. Lastly applicants are assessed to determine whether they fall under the general criteria of inadmissibility.

II. Federal Skilled Tradespersons

369. Section 87.2 of the Regulations defines the federal skilled trades class 'a class of persons who are skilled trades workers and who may become permanent residents on the basis of their ability to become economically established in Canada in a skilled trade occupation and their intention to reside in a province other than

459. Regulations, s. 76(4).
460. RIAS at 4516.
461. See, OP6, at 35: 'Federal Court case law indicates that if an applicant or their representative requests orally or in writing that the officer consider exercising these powers in the applicant's favour, officers must examine the circumstances. There is no requirement that an interview be conducted in all cases when the applicant did not make a compelling case for substituted evaluation. If officers do not consider substituted evaluation appropriate in the circumstances, they should indicate this in file notes and in the refusal letter. Officers do not need the concurrence of the designated officer to deny requests for the use of positive substituted evaluation.' See also *Yan v. Canada (Minister of Citizenship and Immigration)*, [2003] FCT 510.
462. Regulations, s. 76(1)(b)(i).
463. OP6 at 18.
464. See, CIC, 'Proof of funds – Federal Skilled Workers' (3 Apr. 2014), http://www.cic.gc.ca/english/immigrate/skilled/funds.asp (accessed 8 Jun. 2014).

the Province of Quebec'. Launched in 2013, this programme uses a modified selection system that places greater emphasis on practical training and work experience rather than formal education.[465]

370. Membership in the federal skilled trades class is based on a pass/fail system in which applicants must meet all the requirements set out in Regulation 87.2 (3). All applicants must:

- Have either a one-year qualifying job offer or a Provincial/Territorial certificate of qualification in a qualifying skilled trade;
- Meet minimum language proficiency thresholds in either English or French;
- Have at least two years of full time or equivalent part-time work experience within the last five years in an eligible skilled trade (not combined partial year experience in multiple occupations); and
- Satisfy the employment requirements set out in the NOC with the exception of licensing requirements, which are addressed separately.[466]

Altogether, there are ninety occupations currently eligible for processing under the FSTP. There is an annual cap of 5,000 applications, with sub-caps of 100 for each occupation.[467]

371. In addition to meeting the experience/skills and language criteria listed above, Regulation 87.2 (5) stipulates that the applicant must also have sufficient funds available for settlement in Canada. This requirement is waived, if the applicant has an offer of employment as defined in Regulation 87.2(3)(d)(ii), (iii) and (v). The settlement funds must be: available and transferable; and unencumbered by debts or other obligations. Visa officers 'must be satisfied that the applicant has at their disposal, with sufficient liquidity, and with the ability to transfer those assets, the necessary threshold of funds to support their establishment in Canada on arrival'.[468] The amount of funds required is based to the applicant's family size. Temporary foreign workers already settled and working in Canada do not have to provide proof of funds.[469]

372. Lastly applicants are assessed to determine whether they fall under the general criteria of inadmissibility.

465. See, Citizenship and Immigration Canada, Fact Sheet – Federal Skilled Trades Program (5 May 2014), http://www.cic.gc.ca/english/resources/publications/employers/federal-skilled-trades-program.asp (accessed 8 Jun. 2014).
466. Regulations, s. 87.2(3). See also, Citizenship and Immigration Canada, Operational Manual OP26, *Federal Skilled Trades Class* (2 Jan. 2013), ss 5.1, 6.1 and 10.1 (hereinafter 'OP26').
467. For a list of the ninety eligible skilled trades and further details regarding the Federal Skilled Trades program, see, Citizenship and Immigration Canada, 'Applications being accepted – Skilled Trades' (1 May 2014), http://www.cic.gc.ca/english/immigrate/trades/applications.asp (accessed 10 Jun. 2014); See also, OP26, s. 10.1; and Canada Gazette, Government Notices, Vol. 148, 26 Apr. 2014, Department of Citizenship and Immigration, Updated Ministerial Instructions 12 (MI 12), 'Federal Skilled Trades Class'.
468. OP26, s. 9.9.
469. *Ibid.*

III. Federal Business Class Immigrants (Self-Employed and Start-up Business Class)

373. Over the years Canada's business immigration programme was subject to a range of criticisms for being administratively burdensome, lacking sufficient measures of accountability and failing to deliver meaningful economic benefits.[470] By 2011, the federal government appeared to agree with this assessment, suspending the entrepreneur programme and a year later, the immigrant investor programme as well. Both programmes were terminated in 2014 and at the same time, Canada's business class immigration programme was significantly revamped. The programme currently consists of two sub-classes: self-employed persons and the start-up business class.

374. Self-employed. The self-employed programme currently recognizes only self-employed artists or cultural workers, athletes, and farmers.[471] To be admitted as a self-employed immigrant, an applicant must have two years' related experience, the intention and ability to continue in that line of work, and the potential to contribute significantly to their field once in Canada.[472]

375. If applicants under the self-employed programme meet the criteria for this class, they are then assessed according to a point system tailored for business immigrants. They receive up to thirty-five points for previous experience (depending on the number of years, with thirty-five for five years and zero for less than two); ten points if they are between 21 years and 49 years old; up to twenty-five for their education; up to twenty-four points for language proficiency in French or English; and up to six points for adaptability (with points given for previous work or study in Canada, relatives in Canada, as well as the level of education attained by a spouse or common law partner).[473] They require only thirty-five points to pass but they must possess adequate settlement funds to support their family upon arrival in Canada. As with skilled workers, immigration officers have discretion to substitute their own evaluation, with the concurrence of a second officer, of the applicant's ability to become economically established in Canada.[474]

---

470. See, for example, *Report of the Auditor General of Canada to the House of Commons*. 'Chapter 3: Citizenship and Immigration Canada – The Economic Component of the Canadian Immigration Program', April 20000 at 3-18; and David Ley, 'Seeking Homo Economicus: The Canadian State and the Strange Story of the Business Immigration Program' (2003) Annals of Association of American Geographers, Vol. 93, Issue 2, online: http://www.tandfonline.com/doi/abs/10.1111/.U5fKsBZ_XVs (accessed 10 Jun. 2014).
471. RIAS at 4523–4525. See also, Citizenship and Immigration Canada, Operational Manual OP 8, *Entrepreneur and Self-Employed* (7 Aug. 2008), s. 11 (hereinafter 'OP 8').
472. Regulations, s. 88(1). A permanent resident admitted under another category (skilled worker, family class, refugee) remains free to set up his or her own business.
473. Regulations, s. 108; and Citizenship and Immigration Canada, 'Selection Factors – Self-Employed' (23 Oct. 2012), http://www.cic.gc.ca/english/immigrate/self_employed/selection_factors.asp (accessed 10 Jun. 2014).
474. Regulations, s. 109.

376. Start-up Business Class. Launched in 2013, the start-up business class is a five year pilot programme which is limited to entrepreneurs who intend to reside outside of Quebec and already have the support of a designated Canadian venture capital firm and a minimum investment of CAD 200,000 or an angel investor group and a minimum investment of CAD 75,000. A limited number of business incubator programmes are also designated – in which case no investment is required but the applicant must be accepted into the programme.[475]

377. According to the government, the Start-up Business Class pilot programme will:

- test the potential for increased economic benefit to Canada by linking foreign entrepreneurs with Canadian private sector partners ... that have experience and expertise dealing with start-up businesses;
- enable entrepreneurs to create jobs in Canada and build innovative companies that can compete on a global scale; and
- provide private sector firms access to a broader range of entrepreneurs, including the best and brightest minds from around the world.[476]

378. In addition to having a commitment certificate or letter of support from a designated partner, applicants must meet settlement fund requirements, provide proof that they have at least one year of post-secondary education and meet or exceed the minimum language proficiency thresholds in either English or French. Membership in the class in determined on a pass/fail basis – applicants must meet the minimum qualifying criteria for all requirements for their application to be approved. [477] As with skilled workers, immigration officers have discretion to substitute their own evaluation, with the concurrence of a second officer, of the applicant's ability to become economically established in Canada.[478]

379. The government expects to issue a maximum of 2,750 visas for each year of the five year pilot programme.[479] The first two applicants were accepted in July 2014.[480]

475. Canada Gazette, Government Notices, Vol. 147, 30 Mar. 2013, Department of Citizenship and Immigration, Ministerial Instructions Respecting the Start-up Business Class 7 (MI 7), s. 2; and Government of Canada, 'Start-up Visa': http://www.cic.gc.ca/english/immigrate/business/start-up/index.asp?utm_source=slash-startup&utm_medium=short-url&utm_campaign=generic (accessed 11 Jun. 2014).
476. Citizenship and Immigration Canada, IP13/OP 27, *Start-up Business Class* (1 Apr. 2014) at s. 2. (hereinafter 'IP13/OP27').
477. *Ibid.*, at s. 10.1.
478. *Ibid.*, at s. 10.2.
479. Ibid., at s. 5.1.
480. 'Canada's Start-up visa program accepts first two applicants' *The Canadian Press*, 16 Jul. 2014: http://www.huffingtonpost.ca/2014/07/16/canada-start-up-visa-program_n_5593126.html (accessed 30 Jul. 2014).

IV. Québec Immigrants and Provincial Nominees

380. The Provincial Nominee Programme gives provinces and territories that enter into an agreement with the federal government a direct role in nominating economic-class immigrants.[481] Currently ten jurisdictions have signed agreements under the programme – one with each province except Québec, which is subject to its own accord, plus the Yukon Territory.[482] It remains the preserve of the federal government to determine general classes of admissibility and inadmissibility and to make final determinations in individual cases. The Québec accord supplants the federal economic class immigration programme. All other provincial and territorial programmes supplement it. In addition to the Provincial Nominee Programme, some provinces operate temporary worker programmes and also use the Provincial Nominee Programme as a transitional programme to grant permanent resident status.[483] A common feature of all provincial programmes is that once a foreign national obtains permanent resident status, he or she has a constitutionally protected right under section 6(1) of the Canadian Charter of Rights and Freedoms to move anywhere in Canada. Provinces can only encourage, but not compel, permanent residents admitted under a provincial programme to remain in that province.

381. The federal-provincial agreements allow the provinces to nominate prospective permanent residents to meet specific labour market or economic development needs. Canada retains responsibility for defining immigrant categories, setting immigration levels, and establishing admissibility and inadmissibility criteria under the Act. Use of the programme has climbed steadily over the past decade. In 2001, 1,274 permanent residents were admitted under it; by 2004, the number had risen to 6,248;[484] by 2012, to 40,899.[485]

382. After an individual has been nominated by a province, he or she must submit a separate application to CIC for permanent residence. An officer may issue a permanent resident visa, or PRV, so long as: (1) the foreign national is named in a provincial nomination certificate; (2) the foreign national intends to reside in the nominating province;[486] (3) the foreign national has not been nominated solely because he or she has provided capital or has participated in an 'immigration-linked investment scheme'; (4) the foreign national is not inadmissible; and (5) none of the foreign national's family members, accompanying or not, are inadmissible. Federal officers have discretion, with the concurrence of a second officer, to substitute their own judgment of a foreign national's ability to become economically established in

481. IRPA, s. 8.
482. Below, the use of 'province' denotes provinces and territories.
483. See description of Alberta programme, below at para. 375.
484. Citizenship and Immigrartion Canada, Annual Report to Parliament on Immigration 2005 at 22.
485. Citizenship and Immigration Canada, Facts and Figures 2012, 'Permanents Residents by Category', http://www.cic.gc.ca/english/resources/statistics/facts2012/permanent/02.asp (accessed 29 Jul. 2014).
486. Regulations, s. 87(2).

Canada. Prior to exercising this discretion or refusing admission on any other ground, officers are required to consult with the nominating government.[487]

383. The bar on provincial nominees who are investors is meant to ensure the integrity of the federal business immigrant class, discussed above. An immigration-linked investment scheme is one in which an investment is made in order to facilitate immigration or the acquisition of a status or privilege under the Act. Investment will not be a bar to immigration if: (1) the investment is in a business that is not operated primarily for the purpose of deriving investment income; (2) the foreign national controls or will control more than CAD 1 million or one-third of the business's equity; (3) the foreign national will provide acting and ongoing management of the business from inside the nominating province; and (4) the terms of the investment in the business do not include a redemption option allowing the foreign national to withdraw his or her money soon after being admitted to Canada.[488]

384. As an example, in Alberta employers may apply to provincial authorities for approval to recruit a specified number of foreign candidates. Employers must establish, among other things, that the employee position cannot be filled by a Canadian citizen or permanent resident, that it is full-time, meets provincial employment and wage standards, and is being offered to a qualified individual.[489] The programme allows employers to nominate foreign nationals already in Alberta under a work permit. Also, employees may be approved if recruited by a pre-approved Alberta employer and given a valid job offer. A successful applicant under the programme obtains permanent resident status.

385. The most enduring and comprehensive cooperative governance arrangement over immigration is with Québec. Québec established its own department of immigration in 1968, with a view to promoting an immigration framework consistent with its aspirations to sustain and enhance its autonomy and francophone status. Thereafter, a series of agreements gave the province an increasing voice in immigrant selection. In 1971, the Canadian and Québec governments signed their first agreement on immigration, allowing the province to have representatives in Canadian embassies to counsel prospective immigrants. A 1975 agreement allowed Québec to interview foreign nationals and make recommendations to visa officers. A 1978 agreement for the first time allowed Québec to define its own selection criteria. The Canada-Québec Accord Relating to Immigration and Temporary Admission of Aliens, still in force, was signed in February 1991. The Accord gives Québec exclusive (and not just parallel) authority over admission of all economic class immigrants who indicate they intend to settle in the province.

386. Unlike other federal-provincial agreements, the Accord has a national/cultural component, in that it expressly aims to respect the 'distinct identity' and

487. Regulations, s 87(3) and (4).
488. Regulations, s. 87(6).
489. Alberta Economic Development, Alberta's Provincial Nominee Program (June 2005): http://www.alberta-canada.com/pnp/ (accessed December 2009).

preserve the 'demographic importance' of Canada's only francophone-majority province.[490] It also gives Québec a far greater say over the selection of permanent and temporary residents and does not allow for Canadian visa officers to substitute their own judgment of a foreign national's ability to establish successfully in the province or in Canada. There is also an across-the-board requirement that permanent residents intending to live in Québec meet the provincial selection criteria.[491]

387. In common with the federal programme, Québec's selection process is points based, but the actual selection factors and the weight assigned to each factor are specifically tailored to Québec's interests.[492] In 2011, the provincial government initiated a public consultation on immigration planning with a view to consolidating a number of new policy directions for the period 2012–2015. The directions identified include gradually raising the proportion of principal applicants in the skilled worker category with training in areas that correspond to labour market needs to 50%; maintaining a majority of individuals in overall admissions who know French; raising the level of knowledge of French; and maintaining the proportion of individuals under 35 years of age to between 65% and 75% of overall admissions.[493]

388. Priority processing is currently accorded to applicants with a validated employment offer or preferred areas of training.[494] The Québec Ministère de l'Immigration et des Communautés Culturelles (MICC):

---

490. Section 2 of the *Canada-Québec Accord Relating to Immigration and Temporary Admission of Aliens, 1991* states: 'An objective of this Accord, is among other things, the preservation of Québec's demographic importance within Canada and the integration of immigrants to that province in a manner that respects the distinct identity of Québec.' Online: http://www.cic.gc.ca/english/department/laws-policy/agreements/quebec/can-que.asp#Accord. (accessed 7 Jun. 2013).

491. Regulations, s 70(3) and 70(4)(b) (accompanying family members). See Art. 12(b) of the Canada-Québec Accord. 'Canada shall admit any immigrant destined to Québec who meets Québec's selection criteria, if the immigrant is not in an inadmissible class under the law of Canada' and Art. 12(c): 'Canada shall not admit any immigrant into Québec who does not meet Québec's selection criteria'.

492. The framework for the Québec skilled worker class is set out in s. 86 of the Regulations. For more detailed information about Québec-selected immigration and the skilled-worker programme in particular, see Québec Immigration, 'Requirements of the Immigration Program for skilled workers' at: http://www.immigration-quebec.gouv.qc.ca/en/immigrate-settle/permanent-workers/official-immigration-application/requirements-programs/index.html. A summary table (in French) of the factors and criteria used to select skilled workers as well as how they are weighted and the passing scores that apply to skilled workers is available online: http://www.immigration-quebec.gouv.qc.ca/publications/fr/divers/Grille-synthese.pdf.

493. See, Immigration et Communautés culturelles Québec, 'Québec Immigration Planning for the Period 2012–2015, Summary' (2011): http://www.micc.gouv.qc.ca/publications/en/planification/planning-levels-summary-20122015.pdf.

494. 'The *2009 List of areas of training* is intended to identify candidates who have earned diplomas or degrees in areas with good medium-term job prospects. It is compiled with particular regard to Québec job market requirements. The diploma or degree must have been obtained in the five years previous to applying for a Québec Selection Certificate (QSC). If this is not the case, the applicant must have worked for at least one year out of the five years in question in a field directly related

legislates by Ministerial Order, the number of points that can be allocated to each of the selection factors; the authority to create, eliminate and/or modify a mandatory minimum number of points which applicants can be required to obtain for each of the selection factors within each class of immigrants; and the authority to retrospectively enact regulatory amendments which could apply to applicants submitted prior to an amendment and which have not proceeded to a specified point in the assessment process.[495]

389. If the candidate is selected, he or she will receive a *certificat de sélection du Québec* (CSQ – Québec selection certificate), the official immigration document issued by the Government of Québec. At that stage the individual then applies to the federal government for admission as a permanent resident and will be required to undergo medical and security checks.

390. With respect to family class members, Québec does not regulate the definition of the family class, but it does provide its own criteria for sponsorship undertakings. Sponsorships must be three years for spouses and common-law or conjugal partners and ten years in all other cases. The federal government retains authority over enforcement.[496]

391. Québec employs its own selection and sponsorship criteria for refugees selected from abroad, in addition to the federal statutory and international law tests for protected persons. However, the federal government retains exclusive jurisdiction over asylum seekers (inland refugee claimants).[497] Québec has its own form of equitable relief applied, pursuant to section 71 of the Regulations and Article 3.1 of the Act Respecting Immigration to Québec, to foreign nationals 'in a particularly distressful situation'.[498]

---

to the diploma or degree obtained and for which assessment is being made.' Immigration et Communautés Culturelles Québec, '2009 List of Areas of Training': http://www.immigration-quebec.gouv.qc.ca/en/immigrate-settle/permanent-workers/official-immigration-application/requirements-programs/list-areas-training.html.

495. See, Colin R. Singer, 'Québec Immigration Rules' (2009): http://www.immigration.ca/permres-qc-rules.asp.

496. See, Immigration et Communautés Culturelles Québec, 'Sponsors and sponsored persons': http://www.immigration-quebec.gouv.qc.ca/en/immigrate-settle/sponsors-sponsored/index.html. See also, IP2, at 52–54; Regulations, s. 137; and Canada-Québec Accord, Arts 13–16, 21.

497. Canada-Québec Accord, Arts 17–20. The provisions in the Regulations dealing with protected persons destined for Québec are: ss 139(1)(h); 141(1)(e); 151.1(2.1); 158; 175(3).

498. Regulations, s. 71. See *An Act Respecting Immigration to Québec*, R.S.Q., c. I-0.2, s. 3.1. The provision reads:

> Notwithstanding the third or fourth paragraph, the Minister may, in accordance with the regulations, issue a selection certificate to a foreign national in a particularly distressful situation, in particular, in the case of Convention refugees as defined in the Immigration Act (Revised Statutes of Canada, 1985, chapter I-2), or in any other case where the Minister considers that the results obtained following the application of the selection criteria do not reflect whether or not the foreign national will be able to become successfully established in Québec. Conversely, the Minister may refuse to issue such a certificate to a foreign national who meets the conditions and criteria of selection if he has reasonable grounds to believe that the foreign national does

392. Foreign nationals need a *certificate d' acceptation du Québec* – (CAQ – Québec certificate of acceptance) if coming to the province temporarily as workers, students, or to receive medical treatment.[499] Foreign nationals must meet provincial selection criteria to transition from being a temporary resident permit, or TRP, holder to a permanent resident who intends to live in Québec.[500] They must also meet provincial selection criteria if applying to become a permanent resident in Québec on humanitarian and compassionate grounds.[501]

V. Express Entry

393. Set to launch in January 2015, the 'Express Entry' system represents an attempt to respond to concerns that there is a misalignment between Canada's labour market needs and the ability of economic class immigrants to find suitable employment upon arrival in Canada.[502] Express Entry is an expedited electronic management system for permanent resident applications under the Federal Skilled Worker Programme, the Federal Skilled Trades Programme and the Canadian Experience Class. It will also be available for a portion of Provincial Nominee Programmes. There will be no application caps or occupation lists and the government has committed to processing completed applications within six months. CIC asserts that Express Entry will result in faster and more efficient service to potential skilled immigrants. It will also allow the Government of Canada to be more flexible and responsive to Canada's changing economic conditions and priorities.[503]

394. Express Entry will involve two steps. First, potential candidates complete an online profile documenting their skills, work experience, language ability and other details. Those who meet the criteria of one of the designated economic immigration programmes will be ranked against others in a pool of candidates. Those

---

not intend to settle in Québec or is unlikely to settle successfully in Québec or that the settlement of the foreign national would be contrary to public interest.

499. Canada-Québec Accord, Art. 22. Regulations, ss 7(3) (medical treatment); 200(3)(b), 203(4) (temporary work permits); 216(3) (study permits).
500. Regulations, s. 65(d) and 65.1(2).
501. Regulations, ss 67(a), 68(a), and, for accompanying family members, 69(1)(b) and (2)(b).
502. For an appraisal of the new system, initially referred to as the 'Expression of Interest' immigration model, see, Alberta Association of Immigrant Serving Agencies, 'Expression of Interest: An In-Depth Review of a New Immigration Model', Research Brief, Issue 2, 2013/2014 (December 2013): http://aaisa.ca/wp-content/uploads/2013/02/EOI-BRIEF-DRAFT.pdf (accessed 29 Jul. 2014). For a critique of the government's current direction in relation to economic immigration reform, see, Naomi Alboim, 'Adjusting the Balance: Fixing Canada's Economic Immigration Policies' (Toronto: Maytree, July 2009): http://www.maytree.com/wp-content/uploads/2009/07/adjustingthebalance-final.pdf (accessed 29 Jul. 2014).
503. Citizenship and Immigration Canada, 'Express Entry': http://www.cic.gc.ca/english/immigrate/express/express-entry.asp (accessed 30 Jul. 2014).

who do not already have a job offer (which will be subject to a LMIA) or a provincial/territorial nomination will be required to register with the federal Job Bank which will attempt to match their skills with the labour needs of employers, provinces and territories. At step two, the highest ranking candidates in the pool based on their skills and experience[504] and those with offers of arranged employment or provincial/territorial nominations, will be invited to apply for permanent residence. 'They will have 60 days to submit an electronic application for permanent residence. Candidates who do not receive an Invitation to Apply for permanent residence after 12 months may resubmit their profile and re-enter the pool if they still meet the criteria.'[505] The government notes that this provision should avoid backlogs and facilitate quick processing times, thereby fulfilling the function of inventory control that the prior system did not achieve.[506]

504. As of 30 Jul. 2014, CIC had not published information regarding the actual ranking criteria.
505. Citizenship and Immigration Canada, 'Express Entry': http://www.cic.gc.ca/english/immigrate/express/express-entry.asp (accessed 30 Jul. 2014).
506. *Ibid.*

Chapter 4. Refugees and Other Humanitarian Immigrants

395. Canada's refugee protection regime has two components, the refugee and humanitarian resettlement programme for those seeking protection from outside Canada and the inland asylum process for persons making refugee protection claims within Canada. The key distinguishing factor in this scheme – the location of the applicant – affects the substantive and procedural rights of the person, who may be either a foreign national or a permanent resident, seeking protection.

396. The legislative framework for the protection regime begins with section 95(1) of the Act, under which refugee protection may be conferred on three classes of persons: (1) persons determined, outside Canada, to be refugees under the 1951 *Convention relating to the Status of Refugees* or 'person[s] in similar circumstances' under a visa application; such individuals are granted permanent residence or protected temporary residence; (2) persons in Canada determined to be Convention refugees or 'person[s] in need of protection' by the RPD or the RAD of the IRB; and (3) persons granted protection by the Minister after a pre-removal risk assessment (PRRA).[507] Section 95(2) defines a 'protected person' as someone on whom refugee protection has been conferred in one of these three ways, so long as this status has not been found to have ceased or been vacated.

397. Protected persons admitted to Canada as permanent residents enjoy the rights associated with that status. Those who are not admitted as permanent residents are granted several important rights under the Act that other foreign nationals do not enjoy. First, most protected persons may apply for permanent resident status from within Canada unless inadmissible on one of several grounds.[508] As part of this application, neither they nor their family members may be found inadmissible on the ground that they are likely to impose excessive demands on Canadian health and social services,[509] although they are subject to other inadmissibility criteria. Second, a protected person cannot be arrested and detained without warrant by an immigration officer.[510] Third, protected persons are granted a statutory right against refoulement to a country where they would be at risk,[511] unless they are the subject of a danger opinion.[512]

398. Protected persons and refugee claimants are also granted certain social and economic rights. Refugee claimants, protected persons, and their family members

507. Note that under reforms to the PRRA process included in the *Balanced Refugee Reform Act*, S.C. 2010, c. 8 and the *Protecting Canada's Immigration System Act*, S.C. 2012, c. 17, most PRRA applications will be considered by the RPD. At the time of writing, these reforms had not yet come into force. The Government of Canada announced that it expected them to be brought into force in December 2014.
508. IRPA, s. 21(2).
509. IRPA, s. 38(2)(c).
510. IRPA, s. 55(2).
511. IRPA, s. 115(1).
512. IRPA, s. 115(2).

are eligible to apply for study permits from inside Canada and do not need to provide biometric information to do so.[513] Refugee claimants, protected persons, and the family members of protected persons may also apply for work permits without first obtaining a labour market opinion, or LMO.[514] Minor children of individuals with work or study authorization do not need permits for pre-school, primary, or secondary education.[515] Resettled refugees are also eligible for certain forms of financial assistance.[516]

399. Some refugee claimants, resettled refugees, and others who are unable to pay for health care may be eligible for limited benefits under the IFHP.[517] In 2012, the government promulgated two orders significantly amending the programme by restricting access to health care for some previously eligible groups and by making different levels of health care available to different groups.[518] For example, under the new orders, hospital, physician, and laboratory services, and other supplemental benefits, were available to resettled refugees who receive income support from the federal government. However, refugee *claimants* in Canada received hospital, physician, or laboratory services only if urgent or essential. Claimants also received coverage for medications and vaccines only if needed to treat a disease that poses a risk to public health or to treat a condition that is a safety concern. Others, such as refugee claimants from designated countries of origin (DCOs)[519] and rejected refugee claimants, only received services of any kind if needed to deal with a public health or public safety concern. Some groups, such as refugee claimants who had abandoned or withdrawn their applications for refugee protection, received no coverage at all.[520] The government said that the aim of the amendments to the IFHP was to contain the costs of the programme and to support other aspects of refugee reform also brought into force in 2012.[521]

400. The changes to the IFHP led to significant criticism. Several Canadian provinces, including Alberta, Manitoba, Nova Scotia, Ontario, Quebec, and

513. Regulations, ss 206, 207, 215 and 216.
514. Regulations, ss 200(1), 203(1), 206 and 207. However, note that refugee claimants who are nationals of a designated country of origin (DCO) may not apply for work permits until 180 days have passed since their claim was referred to the RPD: see Regulations, s. 206(2).
515. IRPA s. 30(2).
516. See Government of Canada, 'Financial Assistance – Refugees' (11 Oct. 2012), available at: http://www.cic.gc.ca/english/refugees/outside/resettle-assist.asp (accessed 19 Jul. 2014).
517. See Government of Canada, 'Health Care – Refugees' (27 Nov. 2013), available at: http://www.cic.gc.ca/english/refugees/outside/arriving-healthcare.asp (accessed 21 Jul. 2014).
518. Order in Council, P.C. 2012-443 ('Order Respecting the Interim Federal Health Care Program, 2012') (25 Apr. 2012); Order in Council, P.C. 2012-945 ('Order Amending the Order Respecting the Interim Federal Health Program, 2012') (28 Jun. 2012).
519. Designated Countries of Origin (DCOs) are countries designated by the Minister under criteria set out in s. 109.1 of IRPA and in certain ministerial orders. These criteria appear to be intended to identify countries that are generally safe. The consequences of designation, such as shorter timelines for the hearing of refugee claims, are discussed below.
520. Government of Canada, 'Interim Federal Health Program: Summary of Benefits' (14 Dec. 2012), available at: http://www.cic.gc.ca/english/refugees/outside/summary-ifhp.asp (accessed 23 Jul. 2014).
521. These explanations, among others, are set out in *Canadian Doctors for Refugee Care v. Canada (Attorney General)*, 2014 FC 651 at paras 49–56.

Saskatchewan, announced plans to provide some forms of health care funding not available under the amendments to the IFHP.[522] In addition, in July 2014, the Federal Court decided that the two orders amending the IFHP contravene the *Canadian Charter of Rights and Freedoms* and therefore were of no force and effect. In particular, the Federal Court found the restrictions to health care under the amended programme 'constituted cruel and unusual treatment', contrary to section 12 of the Charter, and were discriminatory, contrary to section 15.[523] At the time of writing, the government's appeal of the Federal Court's decision was before the Federal Court of Appeal but had not yet been heard.[524]

401. The remainder of this chapter describes Canada's overseas refugee programme in section 1 and its inland asylum regime in section 2. In section 3, Canada's system of imposing a moratorium on removing foreign nationals to certain dangerous countries is discussed.

§1. Convention Refugees Abroad and Humanitarian Persons Abroad

402. Canadian resettlement policy generally targets refugees in specific situations. In recent years, Canada has focused on resettlement of refugees from Colombia, Afghanistan, Iraqis from Syria and Jordan, Karens from Thailand, Rohingyas from Bangladesh, and Bhutanese from Nepal.[525] In all, Canada resettled 5,430 government-assisted and 4,220 privately sponsored refugees in 2012.[526] These were below the government's announced targets of 7,500 government-assisted and 5,500 privately-sponsored refugees.[527] The government announced a commitment to increase the annual number of refugees resettled from abroad to 14,500 in 2013 and

522. See, e.g., Government of Ontario, 'Backgrounder: Ontario Temporary Health Program' (9 Dec. 2013), available at: http://news.ontario.ca/mohltc/en/2013/12/ontario-temporary-health-program.html (accessed 23 Jul. 2014).

523. *Canadian Doctors for Refugee Care, supra* n. 521, at paras 49–56.

524. Laura Payton, 'Federal government to appeal ruling reversing "cruel" cuts to refugee health', *CBC News* (4 Jul. 2014), at: http://www.cbc.ca/news/politics/federal-government-to-appeal-ruling-reversing-cruel-cuts-to-refugee-health-1.2696311 (accessed 23 Jul. 2014).

525. For example, in 2006, Canada first agreed to resettle Burmese Karen refugees living in Thailand: Government of Canada, 'Backgrounder – Group resettlement of Karen refugees in Mae La Oon Camp, Thailand' (20 Jun. 2006), available at: http://www.cic.gc.ca/english/department/media/backgrounders/2006/2006-06-20.asp (accessed 25 Jul. 2014). Of the 26,000 Rohingya living in two Bangladeshi camps, 100 were selected for resettlement in 2006 and 2007. 200 more were expected to be selected in 2008. In 2007, Canada announced plans to resettle, over several years, 5,000 of the 107,000 Bhutanese refugees living in Nepalese camps. As of June 2009, 340 Bhutanese had been resettled in Canada. Citizenship and Immigration Canada, 'Resettling Bhutanese Refugees – Update on Canada's Commitment' (18 Jun. 2009), available online: http://www.cic.gc.ca/english/refugees/outside/bhutanese.asp (accessed 30 Oct. 2009).

526. Citizenship and Immigration Canada, Annual Report to Parliament on Immigration, 2013 at 17, available at: www.cic.gc.ca/english/pdf/pub/annual-report-2013.pdf (accessed 21 Jul. 2014).

527. Citizenship and Immigration Canada, 'Notice – Supplementary Information for the 2012 Immigration Levels Plan' (4 Nov. 2011): http://www.cic.gc.ca/english/department/media/notices/notice-levels2012.asp (accessed 25 Jul. 2014).

ultimately admitted 5,756 government-assisted and 6,277 privately-sponsored refugees, which was 2,497 short of the stated goal.[528] Most of these refugees are brought to Canada as permanent residents. A small number come as protected temporary residents and transition to permanent residence once in Canada.

403. There are two main classes of person who are eligible for resettlement in Canada: the 'Convention refugees abroad class' and the 'country of asylum class'. Except where specification is necessary, this section uses the term 'refugee' in a non-technical manner to cover both classes.

404. To be eligible under the 'Convention refugee abroad class', a person must have been determined by an officer to be a Convention refugee outside of Canada.[529] The requirements of the Convention refugee definition are discussed below.

405. To be eligible under the 'country of asylum class', a person must be determined by an officer to be in need of resettlement because they have been, and continue to be, seriously and personally affected by civil war, armed conflict, or massive violations of human rights in their countries of nationality or habitual residence.[530] Individuals in this class must also be outside their countries of nationality and habitual residence.[531] The Operational Manual stipulates that a 'massive violation of human rights' does not include violations directed either at a specific individual or even a collection of individuals, but only those violations that target an entire group or population. Nor can a massive violation of human rights be a one-time event, even if horrific, without either a history or a reasonable expectation of a recurrence.[532] The Manual further defines 'seriously and personally affected' to mean that an applicant must suffer from a sustained, effective denial of basic human rights.[533] The Federal Court appears to have accepted these definitions.[534]

406. In addition to these two classes, there is also the 'protected temporary residents class'. The Operational Manual states that this class was designed to allow refugees in urgent need of protection to apply for permanent residence from within

528. Citizenship and Immigration Canada, Annual Report to Parliament on Immigration, 2013 at 17, available at: www.cic.gc.ca/english/pdf/pub/annual-report-2013.pdf (accessed 21 Jul. 2014) and Citizenship and Immigration Canada, Annual Report to Parliament on Immigration, 2014, available at www.cic.gc.ca/english/resources/publications/annual-report-2014/index.asp (accessed 17 Feb. 2015).
529. Regulations, s. 145.
530. Regulations, s. 147.
531. *Ibid.*
532. Citizenship and Immigration Canada, Operational Manual OP5, *Overseas Selection and Processing of Convention Refugees Abroad Class and Members of the Humanitarian – Protected Persons Abroad Classes* (13 Aug. 2009) at s. 6.28.
533. Citizenship and Immigration Canada, Operational Manual OP5, *Overseas Selection and Processing of Convention Refugees Abroad Class and Members of the Humanitarian – Protected Persons Abroad Classes* (13 Aug. 2009) at s. 6.9.
534. *Sivakumaran v. Canada (Minister of Citizenship and Immigration)*, 2011 FC 590; *Bakhtiari v. Canada (Citizenship and Immigration)*, 2013 FC 1229; *Adel v. Canada (Citizenship and Immigration)*, 2014 FC 203.

Canada.[535] This includes persons authorized to enter Canada under a TRP issued pursuant to section 24(1) of the Act for protection reasons after applying for a visa under the Convention refugee abroad class. It also includes foreign nationals who entered Canada on a Minister's permit under the former Act for protection reasons.[536]

407. Overseas refugees do not qualify for permanent residence simply by meeting the refugee definition or falling within one of the two other 'refugee-like' classes established in the Regulations. Among other things, the Regulations require that: (1) there be no 'reasonable prospect' within a 'reasonable period' of either voluntary repatriation or resettlement in the country that the foreign national has fled, local integration in their country of refuge, or resettlement in another country;[537] (2) the foreign national must have sufficient funds – either their own money or through a private sponsorship or government assistance – to help them settle in Canada;[538] and (3) the foreign national must be capable of successfully establishing in Canada.[539]

408. Canada also applies inadmissibility criteria to applicants for resettlement. There are some exceptions. If an applicant otherwise meets the requirements of the programme, they will not be barred on financial grounds[540] or on the ground that they might reasonably be expected to cause excessive demand on health or social services.[541] Refugees may not be excluded for some forms of material misrepresentation,[542] though applicants are still obligated to be truthful upon examination[543] and the Minister can apply to have refugee protection vacated if it was obtained through misrepresentation.[544] Other grounds of inadmissibility continue to apply so, for example, a resettlement candidate may be inadmissible for contravention of the Act or if they are likely to be a danger to public health or safety.[545] Accordingly, they must undergo medical screening and security and criminality checks. Further, applicants will be refused if they fall under the exclusion provisions of the Convention.[546]

409. The legislative scheme attempts to remove administrative and other barriers to protection for some special cases of refugees – those with 'urgent need of protection' or those deemed 'vulnerable'. These refugees are exempt from requirement

535. Citizenship and Immigration Canada, Operational Manual IP1, *Temporary Resident Permits* (19 Jun. 2007) at s. 6.4.
536. Regulations, s. 151.1(1) and (2).
537. Regulations, s. 139(1)(d).
538. Regulations, s. 139(1)(f).
539. Regulations, s. 139(1)(g).
540. IRPA, s. 39 and Regulations, s. 21.
541. IRPA, s. 38(1)(c).
542. Regulations, s. 22.
543. IRPA, s. 16.
544. IRPA, s. 109.
545. IRPA, ss 40, 41, and 38(1)(a) and (b).
546. IRPA, s. 98.

found in section 139(1)(g) of the Regulations of demonstrating an ability to become successfully established in Canada.[547]

410. 'Vulnerable' cases are supposed to be processed in one to four months.[548] They are defined to mean:

> in respect of a Convention refugee or a person in similar circumstances, that the person has a greater need of protection than other applicants for protection abroad because of the person's particular circumstances that give rise to a heightened risk to their physical safety.[549]

411. A person in 'urgent need of protection' is defined to include members of both classes (the Convention refugee abroad and country of asylum classes) whose life or physical safety is under immediate threat and who is likely to be killed; subjected to violence, torture, sexual assault, or arbitrary imprisonment; or returned to their country of nationality or former habitual residence if not protected.[550] Cases of persons in urgent need of protection are supposed to receive immediate attention, to be decided within twenty-four hours, and those refugees accepted under the category are supposed to be en route to Canada within three to five days, usually under a TRP.[551]

412. Notwithstanding these special categories, and despite the exemption from inadmissibility for financial reasons, the assessment of applicants' financial sufficiency and support remains an important element of the resettlement programme. Refugees other than those deemed vulnerable or in urgent need of protection must have independent means or support from the government and/or private sponsors. An officer must also determine that they have the ability to establish themselves successfully in Canada. The ability to establish means that the person, with the help of family members, will be able to provide for themselves and their family members and will not have to rely on social assistance for food and shelter after either three or five years. The determination is to be based on factors set out in the Regulations, including personal resourcefulness and initiative, the presence of relatives in Canada, potential for employment, and ability to learn either French or English.[552] When a determination is negative, officers are instructed to further consider whether

547. Regulations, s. 139(1)(g) and 139(2).
548. Citizenship and Immigration Canada, Operational Manual OP5, *Overseas Selection and Processing of Convention Refugees Abroad Class and Members of the Humanitarian – Protected Persons Abroad Classes* (13 Aug. 2009) at s. 24.1.
549. Regulations, s. 138(1).
550. Regulations, s. 138(1).
551. Citizenship and Immigration Canada, Operational Manual OP5, *Overseas Selection and Processing of Convention Refugees Abroad Class and Members of the Humanitarian – Protected Persons Abroad Classes* (13 Aug. 2009) at s. 23.2.
552. Regulations, s. 139(1)(g) and Citizenship and Immigration Canada, Operational Manual OP5, *Overseas Selection and Processing of Convention Refugees Abroad Class and Members of the Humanitarian – Protected Persons Abroad Classes* (13 Aug. 2009) at s. 13.13.

establishment would be possible with limited assistance under specific forms of government or private sponsorship.[553]

413. All refugees accepted for resettlement need to secure some source of funding. Apart from those refugees who have independent means, there are three forms of support – private, government, and joint government/private sponsorships. Government and joint sponsorships tend to be reserved for more vulnerable or urgent cases.[554] Private sponsors apply in Canada to be matched with government-identified refugees or to bring in refugees that they themselves have identified through contacts abroad. They must go through a separate application process in Canada parallel to the foreign national's application for resettlement at an overseas Ministry office.

414. Government-assisted refugees are those supported by the federal government's Resettlement Assistance Programme.[555] They are given income support from CIC at approximately the equivalent of provincial social assistance rates and provided with a range of other essential services. Income support can be provided for up to twelve months for ordinary government-assisted refugees; twenty-four months for special-needs cases under the joint-assistance programme; and thirty-six months for minors. Monthly income support covers only the most basic needs. Start-up items like furnishings may be provided.[556] Other forms of integration help may be provided by Ministry-funded non-governmental agencies.

415. Joint assistance sponsorships facilitate resettlement in Canada of refugees and other protected persons who have special needs. 'Special needs' refugees include those with large families, with medical disabilities, or who suffer from the effects of systemic discrimination or from trauma resulting from violence or torture.[557] Under this programme, the government works with private sponsors toward the resettlement of special-needs persons who would not otherwise be accepted on account of financial insufficiency or an inability to establish successfully in Canada. The government provides income support through the Resettlement Assistance Programme and private sponsors provide moral, emotional, and practical support and guidance. Special needs groups are expected to be able to adapt to life in Canada

553. Citizenship and Immigration Canada, Operational Manual OP5, *Overseas Selection and Processing of Convention Refugees Abroad Class and Members of the Humanitarian – Protected Persons Abroad Classes* (13 Aug. 2009) at s. 13.14.

554. Sasha Jones & Martin Baglay, *Refugee Law* (Irwin Law, 2007) at 189.

555. Citizenship and Immigration Canada, Operational Manual OP5, *Overseas Selection and Processing of Convention Refugees Abroad Class and Members of the Humanitarian – Protected Persons Abroad Classes* (13 Aug. 2009) at s. 6.25.

556. Citizenship and Immigration Canada, Operational Manual OP5, *Overseas Selection and Processing of Convention Refugees Abroad Class and Members of the Humanitarian – Protected Persons Abroad Classes* (13 Aug. 2009) at s. 6.44.

557. Regulations, s. 157(2). See also Citizenship and Immigration Canada, Operational Manual OP5, *Overseas Selection and Processing of Convention Refugees Abroad Class and Members of the Humanitarian – Protected Persons Abroad Classes* (13 Aug. 2009) at s. 6.42.

with additional attention and care. Assistance is available for up to twenty-four months or, in rare cases, up to thirty-six.[558]

416. Private sponsors may be religious, ethnic, community, or service organizations that have entered into an agreement with the Ministry to sponsor refugees on a one-time or regular basis. In addition, any group of five or more Canadian citizens or permanent residents may apply to privately sponsor a refugee.[559] All private sponsors must be located or have a representative in the community where the refugee will settle; must provide a proposed settlement plan and an undertaking; and must not have defaulted on a previous undertaking.[560] Sponsorship applications will be approved if an officer determines that the sponsoring group has the financial means to meet its obligations under the settlement plan for the duration of the undertaking and has made adequate arrangements for the arrival of the refugee and his or her family members.[561] Private sponsors commit to receiving the refugees and providing them with lodging, care, settlement assistance, and financial support. Such support can include financing for basic expenses, selecting a physician or dentist, enrolling children in school, and helping adult refugees find jobs.[562] The period of care must last at least one year, up to a maximum of three in exceptional cases. If during the sponsorship period a resettled refugee chooses to move to a community where the sponsoring group does not have a representative, a new sponsoring group may need to be found.[563]

417. One of the goals of the resettlement programme is rapid family reunification. Family members are defined under the Regulations to include spouses or common-law partners, dependent children, and dependent grandchildren.[564] The Manual emphasizes the importance of family reunification and unity: 'If one family member is accepted as meeting resettlement criteria, then every effort should be made to deal with other family members in the same way.'[565] There is a flipside to the importance placed on family unity. Under section 42 of the Act, if a family member is inadmissible then the rest of the family is rendered inadmissible, a policy justified in the resettlement context by the need to keep families together.[566]

---

558. Citizenship and Immigration Canada, Operational Manual OP5, *Overseas Selection and Processing of Convention Refugees Abroad Class and Members of the Humanitarian – Protected Persons Abroad Classes* (13 Aug. 2009) at s. 6.31.
559. Citizenship and Immigration Canada, Operational Manual OP5, *Overseas Selection and Processing of Convention Refugees Abroad Class and Members of the Humanitarian – Protected Persons Abroad Classes* (13 Aug. 2009) at s. 6.39.
560. Regulations, s. 153(1).
561. Regulations, s. 154(1).
562. Sasha Jones & Martin Baglay, *Refugee Law* (Irwin Law, 2007) at 189–190.
563. *Ibid.* at 190.
564. Regulations, s. 1(3).
565. Citizenship and Immigration Canada, Operational Manual OP5, *Overseas Selection and Processing of Convention Refugees Abroad Class and Members of the Humanitarian – Protected Persons Abroad Classes* (13 Aug. 2009) at s. 13.6.
566. Citizenship and Immigration Canada, Operational Manual OP5, *Overseas Selection and Processing of Convention Refugees Abroad Class and Members of the Humanitarian – Protected Persons Abroad Classes* (13 Aug. 2009) at s. 13.6. Note that this ground of inadmissibility no longer applies once an individual becomes a protected person: IRPA, s. 42.

418. The Operational Manual instructs officers to 'be flexible in determining who is a member of a refugee family, as it is not unusual in many refugee situations to find that families have been split or reconfigured for reasons relating to the departure from the country of nationality or last permanent residence'.[567] In furtherance of this objective, the Manual makes provision for 'de facto' family members – individuals who do not meet the statutory definition of family but who have a relationship of long-standing financial and emotional dependency with the principal applicant. Examples of de facto family members given in the Manual include: unmarried adult daughters in cultures where it is normal for unmarried daughters to remain dependent; widowed sisters or sisters-in-law in cultures where it is expected that the applicant would take on responsibility for their care and support; young children for whom the family has been caring and whose biological parents are missing or have been killed; elderly aunts, uncles, or cousins who have resided with the principal applicant for a substantial period of time and/or who are dependent on the principal family unit for care, shelter, and emotional support. Unlike family members falling under the regulatory definition, each de facto family member must meet the definition of refugee independently, they must be living with the principal applicant at the time of the principal applicant's application, and they must be processed concurrently with the principal applicant.[568]

419. The Regulations also seek to facilitate rapid reunion in Canada with the 'one-year window of opportunity' programme.[569] This programme allows for reunification with family members as defined in the Regulations – spouses, common-law partners, dependent children, and dependent grandchildren. De facto family members are not eligible. Family members must have been identified on the principal applicant's PRV application before he or she departed for Canada.[570] If family members do not accompany the principal applicant or fall within the one-year window, they must be sponsored as family class immigrants.

420. There are three ways applicants can apply for resettlement from abroad: through referral organizations, private sponsorships, and direct access. Referrals may come from the United Nations High Commissioner for Refugees (UNHCR) or any organization with which the Minister has entered a memorandum of understanding related to resettlement.[571] They may also come from private sponsors.[572]

567. Citizenship and Immigration Canada, Operational Manual OP5, *Overseas Selection and Processing of Convention Refugees Abroad Class and Members of the Humanitarian – Protected Persons Abroad Classes* (13 Aug. 2009) at s. 13.6.
568. Citizenship and Immigration Canada, Operational Manual OP5, *Overseas Selection and Processing of Convention Refugees Abroad Class and Members of the Humanitarian – Protected Persons Abroad Classes* (13 Aug. 2009) at s. 13.7.
569. Regulations, s. 141.
570. *Ibid.* See also Citizenship and Immigration Canada, Operational Manual OP5, *Overseas Selection and Processing of Convention Refugees Abroad Class and Members of the Humanitarian – Protected Persons Abroad Classes* (13 Aug. 2009) at ss 6.36 and 25.
571. Regulations, s. 138. Section 143 of the Regulations empowers the Minister to enter into such memoranda of understanding. There does not appear to be a list of referral organizations on the CIC website.
572. IRPA, s. 13(1).

Direct access is an exceptional means of securing protection. It is available only in geographic areas designated by the Minister because, among other factors, of the relative importance of resettlement needs in the area within the context of resettlement needs globally.[573]

421. Applicants undergoing consideration have limited rights. They are entitled to procedural fairness, including the right to counsel depending on the circumstances.[574] The duty of fairness for overseas applications, however, is considerably attenuated compared to the procedural fairness afforded to inland claimants.

422. The Manual sets out special procedures for processing applications made in countries that are signatories to the 1951 *Refugee Convention* and that provide 'fair and effective protection for refugees and asylum seekers'.[575] If there is such protection, an officer may refuse the application on the grounds that the foreign national might have access to a durable solution in that country.[576] Whether a country provides fair and effective protection is to be assessed keeping in mind the fundamental rights of refugees and the conditions in the country at issue. Officers are directed to consider whether access to refugee protection is given in a non-arbitrary and procedurally fair way; whether the country interprets its refugee obligations as broadly as Canada (e.g., do they conform to Canadian guidelines regarding gender-based persecution); whether additional non-refugee classes, like the country of asylum classes, are protected; the risks faced by the individual while waiting for protection; and so on. If the individual has filed for protection in the country and been refused, his or her application must be considered.[577] In the case of countries that have not signed the Convention, there is a presumption that a durable solution is not available. This presumption may be defeated, but 'such cases are rare'.[578]

§2. Inland Refugee Claimants (Asylum Seekers)

I. The Protection Provisions of the Act

423. The substantive criteria for conferring refugee protection and protected person status in Canada are found in two provisions of the Act. Section 96 incorporates the Convention refugee definition. Section 97 creates the complementary category 'persons in need of protection' to cover individuals who would face a risk of torture, loss of life, or cruel and unusual treatment or punishment if returned to their

573. Regulations, s. 140.2(2) and (3).
574. *Ha v. Canada (Minister of Citizenship and Immigration)*, 2004 FCA 49 at paras 66–69.
575. Citizenship and Immigration Canada, Operational Manual OP5, *Overseas Selection and Processing of Convention Refugees Abroad Class and Members of the Humanitarian – Protected Persons Abroad Classes* (13 Aug. 2009) at s. 7.2.
576. Regulations, s. 139(1)(d).
577. Citizenship and Immigration Canada, Operational Manual OP5, *Overseas Selection and Processing of Convention Refugees Abroad Class and Members of the Humanitarian – Protected Persons Abroad Classes* (13 Aug. 2009) at s. 7.2.
578. *Ibid.*

country of origin. Also, as in other states, the judiciary and administrative decision-makers often cite decisions from other jurisdictions as well as the UNHCR Handbook and other international law sources. The text that follows in section §2.I.A offers a cursory summary of Canadian cases interpreting the Convention refugee definition. In section §2.I.B, we address interpretive issues concerning complementary protection under section 97 of the Act. Exclusion from refugee protection is dealt with in section §2.I.C and non-refoulement in section §2.I.D. Finally, the procedural aspects of seeking refugee protection in Canada before the RPD and RAD of the IRB are discussed in section §2.II.

A. *Convention Refugees*

424. Section 96 of the Act incorporates into Canadian law the refugee definition from the 1951 Convention relating to the Status of Refugees:

> A Convention refugee is a person who, by reason of a well-founded fear of persecution for reasons of race, religion, nationality, membership in a particular social group or political opinion,
>
> (a) is outside each of their countries of nationality and is unable or, by reason of that fear, unwilling to avail themself of the protection of each of those countries; or
>
> (b) not having a country of nationality, is outside the country of their former habitual residence and is unable or, by reason of that fear, unwilling to return to that country.

425. A significant body of jurisprudence interpreting the refugee definition exists in Canada. Many administrative decisions rendered by the first-level RPD and the appellate-level RAD are published and accessible, as are most judicial review decisions by the Federal Court, the Federal Court of Appeal, and the Supreme Court of Canada. The IRB produces and from time to time revises a distillation of the Canadian jurisprudence.[579]

426. The Chair of the IRB is authorized by the Act to enact guidelines to assist decision-makers in interpreting and applying the refugee definition. Guideline 4, *Women Refugee Claimants Fearing Gender-Related Persecution* ('Gender Guidelines'), first issued in 1993, set a global precedent that has led to similar initiatives in other states as well as by the UNHCR. The Gender Guidelines, which were revised in 1996 but not since, offer decision-makers guidance on how to interpret

579. See, IRB Legal Services, *Interpretation of the Convention Refugee Definition in the Case Law* (2005; updated 2010).

and apply the refugee definition in a gender-sensitive manner. The Gender Guidelines attend to gender-specific forms of persecution, gender-related reasons for persecution, and gender as the basis for particular social group designation. The Gender Guidelines also address procedural concerns, such as the possible reluctance of women to disclose sexual abuse in front of a male decision-maker. The IRB has issued seven other guidelines (many, but not all, concerning refugee status determination) to assist decision-makers on both substantive and procedural issues. They include guidelines on *Civilian Non-Combatants Fearing Persecution in Civil War Situations,* on *Child Refugee Claimants*, as well as on *Procedures with Respect to Vulnerable Persons.*[580]

427. Standard of proof. The burden of proof in making a refugee claim lies with the claimant. Under section 96, the claimant must prove that he or she faces a 'reasonable chance', a 'serious possibility', or 'more than a mere possibility' of persecution on one of the listed grounds.[581] These different formulations are generally treated as equivalent by the courts and the IRB. Note that they provide only the legal test to be met; the facts establishing this level of risk must be proven on a balance of probabilities.[582]

428. Well-founded fear. The claimant's fear of persecution must be well-founded. Well-foundedness of a fear has a subjective and an objective component.[583] Given that virtually any claimant (other than a very young or a mentally challenged claimant) will testify that he or she fears persecution, the subjective dimension is frequently understood as related to the claimant's credibility. The claimant who is believed generally satisfies the decision-maker that he or she subjectively fears persecution;[584] the claimant who is not credible often fails to do so. The objective component requires evidence that the subjective fear is realistic and supportable. Consideration of objective well-foundedness often involves tendering evidence of past persecution of the claimant or those similarly situated to the claimant. However, the refugee definition is forward-looking and such evidence serves only to establish the likelihood of future persecution.[585] In 2005, the Federal Court of Appeal in *Fernandopulle* held there is no rebuttable presumption that a person who has faced persecution in the past faces a well-founded fear of persecution in

580. For the full text of all eight of the current IRB Chairperson's Guidelines, see: http://www.irb-cisr.gc.ca/Eng/BoaCom/references/pol/guidir/Pages/index.aspx (accessed 24 Jul. 2014).

581. *Adjei v. Canada (Minister of Employment and Immigration)*, [1989] F.C.J. No. 67 (F.C.A.). See also *Ponniah v. Canada (Minister of Employment and Immigration)*, [1991] F.C.J. No. 359 (C.A.). For a recent discussion of these various formulations, see *Sivaraththinam v. Canada (Citizenship and Immigration)*, 2014 FC 162 at paras 41–56.

582. *Li v. Canada*, [2005] F.C.J. No. 1 (F.C.A.) at paras 10–12.

583. *Rajudeen v. Canada (Minister of Employment and Immigration)*, [1984] F.C.J. No. 601 (C.A.). See also, *Canada (Attorney General) v. Ward* [1993] 2 SCR 689; *Chan v. Canada (Minister of Employment and Immigration)* [1995] 3 SCR 593.

584. *Shanmugarajah v. Canada (Minister of Employment and Immigration)*, [1992] F.C.J. No. 1049 (C.A.).

585. *Oyarzo v. Canada (Minister of Employment and Immigration)*, [1982] 2 F.C. 779 at 781 and 782–783 (C.A.).

the future, a presumption that it was argued is suggested by the UNHCR Handbook.[586]

429. Persecution. Persecution is not defined in the Act, just as it is not defined in the Convention. Courts in Canada, as well as the IRB, have generally followed James C. Hathaway in defining persecution as a 'sustained or systemic violation of basic human rights demonstrative of a failure of state protection'.[587] The agent of persecution need not be the state. It may also be a private actor.[588]

430. Serious threats to life and threats and infringements of liberty will always amount to persecution,[589] however, they are not essential elements.[590] Persecution can result from a single event, if serious enough, and need not necessarily be sustained.[591] At the same time, cumulative harassment and discrimination may amount to persecution even if no single incident would qualify. In some cases, denial of the right to work[592] or denial of education[593] can amount to or be part of a pattern of persecution. Prosecution for a criminal offence does not per se constitute persecution. However, prosecution can be persecutory where it is undertaken for a Convention reason, where the law criminalizes the exercise of a fundamental human right, or where the punishment for the crime is so grossly disproportionate to the offence as to amount to persecution.[594]

431. The Supreme Court of Canada has specifically referred to the availability of state protection with respect to the assessment of the objective component of the well-founded fear of persecution: '[I]f a state is able to protect the claimant, then his or her fear is not, objectively speaking, well-founded.'[595] The requirement to show inadequate state protection can be a significant hurdle for refugee claimants. Claims are often rejected on this basis alone.

432. States are presumed to be able to protect their nationals or residents from the kinds of harm that may qualify as persecution, and the claimant must provide

586. *Fernandopulle v. Canada (Minister of Citizenship and Immigration)*, 2005 FCA 91 at para. 19. See UNHCR, Handbook on Procedures and Criteria for Determining Refugee Status Under the 1951 Convention and the 1967 Protocol relating to the Status of Refugees, HCR/IP/4/Eng/REV.1 (Geneva, January 1992) at para. 45.

587. James C. Hathaway, *The Law of Refugee Status* 104–105 (Butterworths, 1991).

588. *Canada (Attorney General), supra* n. 583.

589. *Ibid.* at paras 64–69.

590. *Amayo v. Canada (Minister of Employment and Immigration)*, [1982] 1 F.C. 520 at 520–521 (C.A.).

591. *Saad v. Canada (Minister of Citizenship and Immigration)*, [2000] F.C.J. No. 1140 (T.D.).

592. *He v. Canada (Minister of Employment and Immigration)*, [1994] F.C.J. No. 1243 (T.D.); *Xie v. Canada (Minister of Employment and Immigration)*, [1994] F.C.J. No. 286 (T.D.).

593. *Ali v. Canada (Minister of Citizenship and Immigration)*, [1996] F.C.J. No. 1392 (T.D.); *Oyarzo, supra* n. 585.

594. See, *Cheung v. Canada (Minister of Employment and Immigration)*, [1993] 2 F.C. 314 (C.A.); *Chan, supra* n. 583, per La Forest J. (dissenting) at 632. Although Justice LaForest's decision is a dissent, it is considered persuasive authority by the IRB.

595. *Canada (Attorney General), supra* n. 583, at 712.

'clear and convincing evidence' of the state's unwillingness or inability to protect.[596] The Supreme Court of Canada has said, however, that to prove an absence of adequate state protection a refugee claimant will have to have approached the authorities to seek protection, unless such protection might not reasonably have been forthcoming.[597] Further, the Federal Court of Appeal has said that 'the more democratic the state's institutions, the more the claimant must have done to exhaust all the courses of action open to him or her' to rebut the presumption of adequate state protection.[598] In *Flores Carillo,* the Federal Court of Appeal adopted the view that state protection fails where it does not lower the likelihood of future persecution below the threshold of 'serious risk' or 'more than a mere possibility'.[599] More recent case law from the Federal Court has emphasized the need to undertake a 'contextual' analysis of whether state protection is or is not available by examining: (1) the nature of the human rights violation; (2) the profile of the alleged human rights abuser; (3) the efforts that the victim took to seek protection from authorities; (4) the response of the authorities to requests for their assistance; and (5) the available documentary evidence.[600] The Federal Court has recently struck down many decisions of the RPD for failing to assess the 'operational adequacy' of state protection; good intentions, unimplemented initiatives, and serious efforts without actual results will not be enough.[601]

433. Nexus. The feared persecution must be 'for reasons of' one of the five grounds listed in the Convention refugee definition: race, religion, nationality, membership in a particular social group or political opinion. In establishing the nexus between the feared persecution and one of these grounds, the Supreme Court has said that the relevant consideration is the perspective of the agent of persecution, since that is the perspective that is determinative in inciting the persecution.[602] The perception of the persecutor need not reflect a correct interpretation of the claimant's true beliefs, intentions, or actions.[603]

434. The courts have recognized that agents of persecution sometimes act out of mixed motives, and it is sufficient if one of these implicates a listed ground of

596. *Ibid.* at 724; *Hinzman v. Canada (Minister of Citizenship and Immigration)*, 2007 FCA 171 at para. 44.
597. *Canada (Attorney General), supra* n. 583, at 723–24.
598. *Canada (Minister of Citizenship and Immigration) v. Kadenko*, (1996), 143 DLR (4th) 532. See also *Hinzman, supra* n. 596.
599. *Flores Carrillo v. Canada (Minister of Citizenship and Immigration)*, 2008 FCA 94, [2008] 4 F.C.R. 636.
600. *Gonzalez Torres v. Canada (Minister of Citizenship and Immigration)*, 2010 FC 234 at paras 37–42.
601. *Y.M.V. v. Canada (Minister of Citizenship and Immigration)*, 2011 FC 1364; *Hercegi v. Canada (Minister of Citizenship and Immigration)*, 2012 FC 250. See *Kina v. Canada (Minister of Citizenship and Immigration)*, 2014 FC 284 at para. 48 for a list of such cases.
602. *Canada (Attorney General), supra* n. 583, at 747.
603. *Ibid.*

persecution.[604] A decision-maker has an obligation to consider each possible nexus based on the facts of the claim.[605]

435. Race, Religion & Nationality. The meanings of race, religion, and nationality are not the subject of extensive jurisprudence in Canada. Race has featured in only a handful of Canadian court cases. The IRB has referred its members to the UNHCR Handbook, which states 'race … has to be understood in its widest sense to include all kinds of ethnic groups that are referred to as "races" in the common usage'.[606] Nationality has not been restricted to legal status and has been taken to include ethnic and linguistic groups.[607] Religion has also been treated broadly by Canadian courts:

> [T]he concept of religion should be broadly interpreted to allow for claims based on a person's religious beliefs, even if those are not part of an organized religion. This can even be extended to cover cases where a person's religious beliefs are such that he or she rejects religion altogether. If a person is persecuted by reason of such a belief, then there will be a sufficient nexus to the claim.[608]

The courts and tribunals have therefore included in the scope of religion theistic, non-theistic, and atheistic beliefs,[609] although there has been some inconsistency with respect to devil worship cults.[610] Freedom of religion includes the right to manifest the religion in public or private in teaching, practice, worship, and observance.[611] The religion at issue need not be the victim's; it may be sufficient if the persecution is motivated by the persecutor's beliefs.[612] In all these cases, the perception of the persecutors remains determinative. Once again, a person may be persecuted because of race, religion, or nationality even if the persecutor has misidentified these personal characteristics.

---

604. *Zhu v. Canada (Minister of Employment & Immigration)*, [1994] F.C.J. 80 (C.A.); *Gonsalves v. Canada (Minister of Citizenship and Immigration)*, 2011 FC 648.
605. *Canada (Attorney General), supra* n. 583, at 745.
606. UNHCR, Handbook on Procedures and Criteria for Determining Refugee Status Under the 1951 Convention and the 1967 Protocol relating to the Status of Refugees, HCR/IP/4/Eng/REV.1 (Geneva, January 1992) at para. 68; IRB Legal Services, Interpretation of the Convention Refugee Definition in the Case Law (2005; updated 2010), s. 4.2.
607. *Hanukashvili, Valeri v. M.C.I.* (F.C.T.D., no. IMM-1732-96), Pinard, 27 Mar. 1997. See IRB Legal Services, Interpretation of the Convention Refugee Definition in the Case Law (2005; updated 2010), s. 4.3; Sasha Jones & Martin Baglay, *Refugee Law* (Irwin Law, 2007) at 127–128.
608. *Hui Qing Yang v. Canada (Minister of Citizenship and Immigration)*, [2001] F.C.J. No. 1463 (F.C.). The Federal Court is here citing with approval a passage from Lorne Waldman, *Immigration Law and Practice* at s. 8.268.
609. IRB Legal Services, Interpretation of the Convention Refugee Definition in the Case Law (2005; updated 2010), s. 4.4 and the cases cited therein.
610. Sasha Jones & Martin Baglay, *Refugee Law* (Irwin Law, 2007) at 129 and cases cited therein.
611. See IRB Legal Services, Interpretation of the Convention Refugee Definition in the Case Law (2005; updated 2010), s. 4.4 and the cases cited therein. See also, Sasha Jones & Martin Baglay, *Refugee Law* (Irwin Law, 2007) at 128–129.
612. *Chabira v. Canada (Minister of Employment and Immigration)* (1994), 27 Imm. L.R. (2d) 75 (F.C.T.D.).

436. Membership in a particular social group. In two decisions, the majority opinion in *Ward* and the dissenting opinion in *Chan*, the Supreme Court of Canada has provided extensive discussion of this ground. In *Ward*, the Court listed three potential categories of social groups: (1) groups defined by an innate or unchangeable characteristic; (2) groups whose members associate for reasons so fundamental to their human dignity that they should not be forced to forsake the association; and (3) groups associated by a former voluntary status, unalterable due to its historical permanence.[613] The Court elaborated:

> The first category would embrace individuals fearing persecution on such bases as gender, linguistic background and sexual orientation, while the second would encompass, for example, human rights activists. The third branch is included more because of historical intentions, although it is also relevant to the anti-discrimination influences, in that one's past is an immutable part of the person.[614]

In *Chan*, Justice La Forest wrote that the *Ward* categories ought not to be applied in an 'unyielding deterministic' way. He further clarified that the second category from *Ward* need not refer to formal and active associations.[615] Nonetheless, it is clear that not just any group can be a particular social group for purposes of the Convention refugee definition. In *Ward*, the claimant's membership in the Irish National Liberation Army, an organization committed to achieving its political goals through any means, including violence, was not considered integral to his human dignity.[616] The Court also held in *Ward* that a particular social group cannot be defined tautologically as a group that happens to be persecuted.[617] Some of the 'particular social groups' recognized by Canadian courts and the RPD include: families, homosexuals (sexual orientation), trade unions, the poor, women, and persons suffering from mental illness.[618] Some more recent groups that have been proposed and rejected have included 'young, impoverished and uneducated teenagers living in small, gang-riddled rural communities who refuse to be recruited because of a strongly held political opinion that disagrees with Mara [gang] activities'[619] and 'Tamil males who were passengers on the *MV Sun Sea*'.[620] The *MV Sun Sea* is a ship that arrived in Canada in August 2010 carrying 492 Sri Lankan Tamil passengers, most of whom applied for refugee protection.

---

613. *Canada (Attorney General), supra* n. 583, at 739.
614. *Ibid.*
615. *Chan, supra* n. 583, at 642. As noted above, Justice LaForest's decision is a dissent, but it is considered persuasive authority by the IRB. See, IRB Legal Services, s. 4.5.
616. *Canada (Attorney General), supra* n. 583, at 745.
617. *Canada (Attorney General), supra* n. 583, at 729–733.
618. See, IRB Legal Services, Interpretation of the Convention Refugee Definition in the Case Law (2005; updated 2010), s. 4.5 and the cases cited therein.
619. *Ayala Sosa v. Canada (Citizenship and Immigration)*, 2014 FC 428 at paras 28–29. But see more recently, *Banegas v. Canada (Citizenship and Immigration)*, 2015 FC 45.
620. Canada (Citizenship and Immigration) v. B380, 2012 FC 1334 at paras 24–27.

437. Political opinion. In *Ward*, the Supreme Court of Canada said the political opinion ground embraces 'any opinion on any matter in which the machinery of state, government, and policy may be engaged'.[621] The Supreme Court further clarified two aspects of the approach to political opinion. First, the political opinion need not have been expressed outright.[622] The relevant issue is whether the agent of persecution considered the claimant's conduct to be political or attributed political activities to him or her. Second, the beliefs imputed to the claimant need not conform to his or her true beliefs. Nor need the claimant have actually set out to engage in political action. The test:

> is not whether the decision maker considers that the applicant engaged in political activities, but whether the persecutor in the country from which he claims to be a refugee considers his conduct political activity.[623]

The breadth of the approach under the *Ward* definition is to an extent illustrated by *Klinko*, in which the Federal Court of Appeal ruled that the claimant's complaints about corruption among regional government officials expressed a political opinion even though the central government of Ukraine did not officially condone corruption.[624]

438. State protection. As noted above, *Ward* made the question of state protection integral to the analysis of whether there is a well-founded fear of persecution. However, the question of state protection also arises separately in a later clause of the definition, which requires that a claimant be 'unable or, by reason of that fear, unwilling to avail themself of the protection' of their country of nationality or of former habitual residence. Nevertheless, the Federal Court has said, 'given that a lack of state protection is inherent in the finding of a well-founded fear of persecution, it is unlikely that the question of unwillingness or inability to avail oneself of state protection will require serious inquiry'.[625]

439. Internal Flight Alternative. Canadian courts, like those of other countries, have inferred a requirement that refugee claimants demonstrate that they are not safe anywhere in their country from the idea that refugee protection is surrogate protection, i.e., available only when one's home state cannot itself offer protection. The Federal Court of Appeal in *Rasaratnam* adopted a two-prong test for determining whether an internal flight alternative is a bar to refugee protection. The first question is whether there is a serious possibility of persecution in the purportedly safe internal destination. The second question is whether or not it would be reasonable

---

621. *Canada (Attorney General), supra* n. 583, at 746. Here the Supreme Court was endorsing a definition taken from Guy S. Goodwin-Gill, *The Refugee in International Law* (Oxford: Clarendon Press, 1983) at 31.
622. *Ibid.*
623. *Chen v. Canada (Minister of Employment and Immigration)* (1994), 22 Imm. L.R. (2d) 160) (F.C.T.D.); *Inzunza v. Canada (Minister of Employment and Immigration)* (1979) 103 D.L.R. (3d) 105 (F.C.A.).
624. *Klinko v. Canada (Minister of Citizenship and Immigration)*, [2000] F.C.J. No. 228 (C.A.).
625. *Zhuravlvev v. Canada (Minister of Citizenship and Immigration)*, [2000] 4 F.C. 3 at para. 18.

in all the circumstances for the claimant to go there.[626] The threshold of 'reasonableness' is extremely low, as was made clear by the Federal Court of Appeal in *Thirunavukkarasu*:

> An IFA cannot be speculative or theoretical only; it must be a realistic, attainable option. Essentially, this means that the alternative place of safety must be realistically accessible to the claimant. Any barriers to getting there should be reasonably surmountable. The claimant cannot be required to encounter great physical danger or to undergo undue hardship in travelling there or in staying there. For example, claimants should not be required to cross battle lines where fighting is going on at great risk to their lives in order to reach a place of safety. Similarly, claimants should not be compelled to hide out in an isolated region of their country, like a cave in the mountains, or in a desert or a jungle, if those are the only areas of internal safety available. But neither is it enough for refugee claimants to say that they do not like the weather in a safe area, or that they have no friends or relatives there, or that they may not be able to find suitable work there. If it is objectively reasonable in these latter cases to live in these places, without fear of persecution, then IFA exists and the claimant is not a refugee.[627]

In the same case, the Federal Court of Appeal clarified that the burden of proof on questions of internal flight alternative lies with the claimant; however, the Minister or RPD must give notice that the issue will be raised.[628]

440. Outside the country of nationality or habitual residence. Canadian decision-makers have followed UNHCR's Handbook on Procedures and Criteria for Determining Refugee Status in interpreting 'country of nationality' to mean 'country of citizenship'.[629] If a claimant has a country of nationality, the claim should be assessed against that country and not against a country where he or she has residence.[630] In the case of multiple nationalities, the claim must be assessed against each country.[631] Claims of stateless persons must be assessed against his or her country of 'former habitual residence'. The Federal Court of Appeal has found that 'if it is within the control of the applicant to acquire the citizenship of a country with respect to which he has no well-founded fear of persecution, the claim for refugee status will be denied'.[632] And further: '[W]here citizenship in another country is *available*, an applicant is expected to make attempts to acquire it and will be denied

626. *Rasaratnam v. Canada (Minister of Employment and Immigration)*, [1992] 1 FC 706 (FCA).
627. *Thirunavukkarasu v. Canada (Minister of Employment and Immigration)*, 22 Imm. L.R. (3d) 241 (FCA).
628. *Ibid.*
629. UNHCR, Handbook on Procedures and Criteria for Determining Refugee Status Under the 1951 Convention and the 1967 Protocol relating to the Status of Refugees, HCR/IP/4/Eng/REV.1 (Geneva, January 1992) at para. 87.
630. See IRB Legal Services, *Interpretation of the Convention Refugee Definition in the Case Law* (2005; updated 2010) at 2.1.
631. *Ibid.*
632. *Canada (Minister of Citizenship and Immigration) v. Williams*, 2005 FCA 126 at para. 23.

refugee status if it is shown that it is within his power to acquire that other citizenship.'[633]

B. Complementary Protection

441. Section 97 establishes a residual category of 'persons in need of protection', intended to meet Canada's obligations under the Convention against Torture (CAT) and the International Covenant on Civil and Political Rights (ICCPR). Claims under section 97 would be deemed 'complementary' or 'subsidiary' in international refugee law. In Canada, they are sometimes referred to under the heading of 'consolidated grounds' claims, because such claims 'consolidate' various protection grounds formerly scattered throughout the old Immigration Act. Section 97 reads as follows:

> 97. (1) A person in need of protection is a person in Canada whose removal to their country or countries of nationality or, if they do not have a country of nationality, their country of former habitual residence, would subject them personally:
>
> (a) to a danger, believed on substantial grounds to exist, of torture within the meaning of Article 1 of the Convention Against Torture; or
>
> (b) to a risk to their life or to a risk of cruel and unusual treatment or punishment if
>
> (i) the person is unable or, because of that risk, unwilling to avail themself of the protection of that country,
>
> (ii) the risk would be faced by the person in every part of that country and is not faced generally by other individuals in or from that country,
>
> (iii) the risk is not inherent or incidental to lawful sanctions, unless imposed in disregard of accepted international standards, and
>
> (iv) the risk is not caused by the inability of that country to provide adequate health or medical care.

Section 97(2) allows for other categories of persons in need of protection to be prescribed by the Regulations, though to date this regulatory power has not been used.

442. 'Torture', the 'risk to life', and the risk of 'cruel and unusual treatment or punishment' all specify forms of abuse that might amount to persecution under section 96. Thus there is some overlap with respect to the forms of mistreatment and suffering that the two provisions seek to prevent. The major difference between them is that section 97 does not require claimants to demonstrate a nexus between the anticipated treatment and their race, religion, nationality, membership in a particular social group, or political opinion. Torture, as defined, must be intentionally

633. *Ibid.* at para. 27. Emphasis in original.

aimed at such purposes as eliciting information, punishment, intimidation or coercion, or for any discriminatory purposes; meanwhile, the risk to life or of cruel and unusual treatment or punishment can, in theory, be wholly unintentional.

443. Another significant difference lies in the burden a claimant must meet to win protection. The standard of proof in section 97 is the same as for section 96. Proof of every necessary factual element must be established on a balance of probabilities. However, these factual elements must demonstrate a higher degree of likelihood of mistreatment than under section 96. In *Li v. Canada*, the Federal Court and the Federal Court of Appeal held that the risk of torture under section 97(1)(a) must be more likely than not, i.e., the likelihood of being tortured must surpass the balance of probabilities:

> Proof on a balance of probabilities is the standard of proof the panel will apply in assessing the evidence adduced before it for purposes of making its factual findings. The test for determining the danger of torture is whether, on the facts found by the panel, the panel is satisfied that it is more likely than not that the individual would personally be subjected to a danger of torture.[634]

The Court later extended the same reasoning to section 97(1)(b), so that the same risk threshold must be proven for alleged risks to life or of cruel and unusual treatment or punishment.[635] *Li*, therefore, imposes a different and higher risk threshold for persons in need of protection than for refugee claimants under section 96, who must establish a reasonable chance or a serious possibility of persecution.

444. The Federal Court has said that analyses under sections 96 and 97 ordinarily should be carried out separately. In particular, credibility determinations may be dispositive of a section 96 but not a section 97 claim.[636] That is, even if a tribunal disbelieves a claimant's purported level of fear and his or her account of past abuses, objective evidence of country conditions might establish a section 97 risk:

> There may well be instances where a refugee claimant, whose identity is not disputed, is found to be not credible with respect to his subjective fear of persecution, but the country conditions are such that the claimant's particular circumstances make him/her a person in need of protection. It follows that a negative credibility determination, which may be determinative of a refugee claim under s. 96 of the Act, is not necessarily determinative of a claim under subsection 97(1) of the Act. The elements required to establish a claim under section 97 differ from those required under section 96 of the Act where a well-founder [*sic*] fear of persecution to a convention ground must be established. Although the evidentiary basis may well be the same for both claims, it is essential that both claims be considered as separate. A claim under section 97

634. *Li v. Canada (Minister of Citizenship and Immigration)*, 2005 FCA 1 at para. 28; aff'g 2003 FC 1514.
635. *Ibid.* at paras 38–39.
636. *Bouaouni v. Canada (Minister of Citizenship and Immigration)*, [2003] F.C.J. No. 1540 (F.C.).

> of the Act requires that the Board apply a different test, namely whether a claimant's removal would subject him personally to the dangers and risks stipulated in paragraphs 97 (1) (a) and (b) of the Act.[637]

The only exceptions to the requirement of a separate analysis are cases where there is 'absolutely no evidence that could support a claim that a person is in need of protection'.[638]

445. Danger of Torture. Section 97(1)(a) expressly incorporates the definition of torture from the CAT, which is set out in the Schedule to the Act:

> For the purposes of this Convention, 'torture' means any act by which severe pain or suffering, whether physical or mental, is intentionally inflicted on a person for such purposes as obtaining from him or a third person information or a confession, punishing him for an act he or a third person has committed or is suspected of having committed, or intimidating or coercing him or a third person, or for any reason based on discrimination of any kind, when such pain or suffering is inflicted by or at the instigation of or with the consent or acquiescence of a public official or other person acting in an official capacity. It does not include pain or suffering arising only from, inherent in or incidental to lawful sanctions.[639]

Torture must be intentional, committed with the involvement of official state agents, and it must result in severe physical or mental suffering.

446. Risk not Faced Generally by Others. Section 97(1)(b)(ii) of the Act creates a confusing exception the application of which has been important in recent years. Under this provision, a claimant will not be a 'person in need of protection' if they face a risk to life or of cruel and unusual treatment of punishment that is not faced 'in every part' of their country of origin or that is 'faced generally by other individuals in or from that country'. The second part of this provision is now commonly referred to as the 'generalized risk' exception. It has often been applied by the RPD to deny claims that the tribunal sees as stemming from criminal activity in countries where criminality is rife. In some cases, the Federal Court has seemed to endorse the idea the exception may apply where 'the risk of all forms of criminality is general and felt by all'.[640] However, more recently several Federal Court decisions have criticized the RPD for equating criminality and generalized risk without undertaking an individualized inquiry into the situation of the claimant before

637. *Ibid.* at para. 41; see also, *Dunkova v. Canada (Minister of Citizenship and Immigration)* 2010 FC 1322 at para. 28; and *Kaleja v. Canada (Minister of Citizenship and Immigration),* 2010 FC 252 at paras 23–25.

638. *Anthonimuthu v. Canada (Minister of Citizenship and Immigration)*, 2005 FC 141 at para. 52.

639. *Convention against Torture and other Cruel, Inhuman or Degrading Treatment or Punishment*, Can. T.S. 1987 No. 36; G.A. res. 39/46 [annex, 39 UN GAOR Supp. (No. 51) at 197, UN Doc. A/39/51 (1984)], Art. 1(1)].

640. *Prophète v. Canada (Minister of Citizenship and Immigration)*, 2008 FC 331 at para. 23; *aff'd* 2009 FCA 31.

them.[641] Instead, this recent case law has stressed the need to first appropriately characterize the nature of the risk faced by asking such questions as whether the claimant faces an ongoing or future risk, what the risk is, and whether it is a risk to life or of cruel and unusual treatment or punishment. Next, it must be asked whether a significant group in the same country faces risk of the same nature and degree. If the risk faced by the claimant is not the same as that faced by a larger group, then the exception will not apply.[642] A recent Federal Court case states that a 'consensus has emerged' in favour of this approach.[643]

447. Lawful Sanctions. Section 97(1)(b)(iii) creates an exception for risks to life or of cruel and unusual treatment or punishment that are 'inherent or incidental to lawful sanctions, unless imposed in disregard of accepted international standards'. This exception does not cover pain or suffering inherent or incidental to all lawful sanctions, only those that stem from sanctions that are legitimate from an international perspective. Indeed, the Federal Court has held it is an error of law for the RPD to fail to consider whether an otherwise lawful sanction has been imposed in disregard of accepted international standards.[644] An intriguing question under section 97(1)(b)(iii) is whether an individual facing lawful execution would qualify for protection. In *Burns*, not a refugee case, the Supreme Court of Canada held that it would be unconstitutional to extradite an individual to face trial in a foreign jurisdiction for a capital crime without assurances that the death penalty would not be imposed or carried out. The Court found that, while there was no international law norm against it, there was 'significant movement' internationally toward abolition of the death penalty.[645] Further, it found that in 'the Canadian view of fundamental justice, capital punishment is unjust and it should be stopped'.[646] That suggests that an individual potentially facing the death penalty might be granted protection under section 97.[647]

448. Risk of Cruel and Unusual Treatment or Punishment. Cruel and unusual punishment has been considered in detail by the Supreme Court of Canada in *Smith*, a criminal case brought under the Canadian Charter of Rights and Freedoms. The Court held that such punishment would have to be 'so excessive as to outrage

---

641. See, e.g., *Vivero v. Canada (Citizenship and Immigration)*, 2012 FC 138 at paras 28–29; *Vaquerano Lovato v. Canada (Citizenship and Immigration)*, 2012 FC 143 at para. 14; *Loyo de Xicara v Canada (Minister of Citizenship and Immigration)*, 2013 FC 593 at paras. 17–18.
642. *Portillo v. Canada (Citizenship and Immigration)*, 2012 FC 678 at paras 40–41; see also *Corado Guerrero v. Canada (Citizenship and Immigration)*, 2011 FC 1210 at paras 27–30.
643. *Chinchilla v. Canada (Citizenship and Immigration)*, 2014 FC 546 at para. 27.
644. See *Klochek v. Canada (Minister of Citizenship and Immigration)*, 2010 FC 474 at paras 10–11; *Canada (Minister of Citizenship and Immigration) v. Harvey*, 2013 FC 717 at para. 45.
645. *United States v. Burns* [2001] 1 SCR 283, 2001 SCC 7 at para. 89.
646. *Ibid.* at para. 84. See also the earlier case of *Kindler v. Canada (Minister of Justice)*, [1991] 2 S.C.R. 779.
647. Waldman asserts that 'it would always be a violation of [Canada's] concept of acceptable international standards to return a person to a country where they would be at risk of losing their life through "lawful sanctions"': Lorne Waldman, *Immigration Law and Practice*, Loose-leaf (2d ed., LexisNexis-Butterworths, 2003) at s. 8.40.

standards of decency'[648] and that 'the effect [of the punishment] must not be grossly disproportionate to what would have been appropriate'.[649] Assessment requires first consideration of what an appropriate punishment would be, in light of factors such as the gravity of the offence, the person's personal characteristics, and the particular circumstances of the case. Next, the effect of the punishment must be considered by looking at, among other things, the length of a proposed sentence and the conditions under which it will be served.[650] The Court added:

> some punishments or treatments will always be grossly disproportionate and will always outrage our standards of decency: for example, the infliction of corporal punishment, such as the lash, irrespective of the number of lashes imposed, or, to give examples of treatment, the lobotomisation of certain dangerous offenders or the castration of sexual offenders.[651]

449. The category of 'treatment' seems to be a broad one that encompasses a wide range of acts inflicted otherwise than for purposes of criminal punishment. There is some discussion of the definition of 'cruel and unusual treatment' in Canadian constitutional law, but this case law has concerned situations where the government is alleged to have inflicted such treatment outside of penal or non-penal contexts.[652] Since claims under section 97 often involve risks originating with private actors, many of the considerations suggested by this case law – which largely involve an evaluation of the treatment relative to the government's legitimate aims – will not always be applicable.[653] However, the Federal Court has suggested that considerations might also 'include whether the treatment in question is unacceptable to a large segment of the population, whether it accords with public standards of decency or propriety, whether it shocks the general conscience, and whether it is unusually severe and hence degrading to human dignity and worth'.[654] Jones and Baglay further suggest that the following questions be considered when a claim invokes the possibility of cruel and unusual treatment: (1) Is the treatment not in accord with public standards of decency and propriety? (2) Is it unnecessary because of the existence of adequate alternatives? (3) Can it not be applied upon a rational basis in accordance with ascertained and ascertainable standards?[655] They cite in support a case, *I.D.Q.*, a case decided by the RPD under the old Immigration Act:

---

648. *R. v. Smith*, [1987] 1 SCR 1045 at para. 54, citing *R. v. Miller and Cockriell* [1977] 2 SCR 680 at 688. See more recently *R. v. Wiles*, 2005 SCC 84.
649. *R. v. Smith, ibid.*
650. *Ibid.*
651. *Ibid.* at para. 57.
652. For discussion, see *Canadian Doctors For Refugee Care, supra* n. 521, at paras 577–692. See also *Peter v. Canada (Public Safety and Emergency Preparedness)*, 2014 FC 1073 at paras 227–28.
653. *Ibid.* at para. 614.
654. *Ibid.*
655. Sasha Jones & Martin Baglay, *Refugee Law* (Irwin Law, 2007) at 179. The authors cite *Soenen v. Thomas*, (1983) 8 C.C.C. (3d) 224 (Alta. Q.B.).

> Treatment that is inhuman or degrading has been equated with cruel and unusual treatment. Inhuman treatment has been described as premeditated, applied for hours at a stretch and causing, if not bodily injury, intense physical and mental suffering. Degrading treatment has been described as arousing in its victims' feelings of fear, anguish and inferiority capable of humiliating and debasing them and possibly breaking their physical and moral resistance.[656]

Cruel and unusual treatment has been found to include kidnapping,[657] kidnapping of an individual's children,[658] and the receipt of plausible threats.[659] Ostracism amounting to discrimination has been found not to be cruel and unusual treatment.[660]

450. Risk Not Caused by Inability to Provide Adequate Health or Medical Care. Section 97(1)(b)(iv) specifically denies protection in cases where a risk arises due to the inadequacy of health or medical care in a country. The courts and the RPD have so far rejected all claims where a person faced a medical risk to their life because of poverty, while carving out a possible exception where the denial of proper care amounts to persecution based on a Convention ground:

> [T]he provision in issue is meant to be broadly interpreted, so that only in rare cases would the onus on the applicant be met. The applicant must establish, on the balance of probabilities, not only that there is a personalized risk to his or her life, but that this was not caused by the inability of his or her country to provide adequate health care. Proof of a negative is required, that is, that the country is not unable to furnish medical care that is adequate for this applicant. This is no easy task and the language and the history of the provision show that it was not meant to be.
>
> The ability of the different countries of the world to provide adequate health care varies dramatically. Some might contend that even countries such as Canada, the United Kingdom and the United States, though financially able, are not providing 'adequate' health care to some of their people. These countries might respond that they are 'unable' to provide more care, given their other financial obligations. Some might disagree and argue that these countries would, if they altered their priorities, be able to provide more. Whether this reluctance to provide more means that a country is unable to provide more is not a task that Courts can easily assess, except in cases such as the denial of health care on persecutorial grounds or other similar bases. This will be a difficult evidentiary hurdle to overcome.[661]

656. [2002] R.P.D.D. No. 189 (QL) at para. 34. Internal citations omitted.
657. [2002] R.P.D.D. No. 189 (QL).
658. *Ibid.*
659. TA1-15686 (unreported). Cited in Sasha Jones & Martin Baglay, *Refugee Law* (Irwin Law, 2007) at 180.
660. TA1-02673 [2003] R.P.D.D. No. 487. Cited in Sasha Jones & Martin Baglay, *Refugee Law* (Irwin Law, 2007) at 180.
661. *Covarrubias v. Canada (Minister of Citizenship and Immigration),* 2006 FCA 365 (Linden J.A.) at paras 31–32.

The Court later elaborated on the exception to the general rule as follows:

> The wording of the provision clearly leaves open the possibility for protection where an applicant can show that he faces a personalized risk to life on account of his country's unjustified unwillingness to provide him with adequate medical care, where the financial ability is present. For example, where a country makes a deliberate attempt to persecute or discriminate against a person by deliberately allocating insufficient resources for the treatment and care of that person's illness or disability, as has happened in some countries with patients suffering from HIV/AIDS, that person may qualify under the section, for this would be refusal to provide the care and not inability to do so. However, the applicant would bear the onus of proving this fact.[662]

C. *Exclusion*

451. Section 98 of the Act incorporates the Refugee Convention's exclusion clauses, Articles 1E and 1F:

> E. This Convention shall not apply to a person who is recognized by the competent authorities of the country in which he has taken residence as having the rights and obligations which are attached to the possession of the nationality of that country.
>
> F. The provisions of this Convention shall not apply to any person with respect to whom there are serious reasons for considering that:
>
> (a) he has committed a crime against peace, a war crime, or a crime against humanity, as defined in the international instruments drawn up to make provision in respect of such crimes;
> (b) he has committed a serious non-political crime outside the country of refuge prior to his admission to that country as a refugee;
> (c) he has been guilty of acts contrary to the purposes and principles of the United Nations.

The Act applies these clauses to both sections 96 and 97, even though section 97(1)(a) incorporates the CAT into Canadian law, and the CAT does not include exclusion clauses.

452. Article 1E states that refugee protection is not available to persons 'recognized by the competent authorities of the country in which he has taken residence as having the rights and obligations which are attached to the possession of the nationality of that country'. In *Zeng*, the current leading case, the Federal Court of Appeal laid out the following framework of analysis for Article 1E:

662. *Ibid.* at para. 39. See also, *Laidlow v. Canada (Minister of Citizenship and Immigration)*, 2012 FCA 256.

> Considering all relevant factors to the date of the hearing, does the claimant have status, substantially similar to that of its nationals, in the third country? If the answer is yes, the claimant is excluded. If the answer is no, the next question is whether the claimant previously had such status and lost it, or had access to such status and failed to acquire it. If the answer is no, the claimant is not excluded under Article 1E. If the answer is yes, the RPD must consider and balance various factors. These include, but are not limited to, the reason for the loss of status (voluntary or involuntary), whether the claimant could return to the third country, the risk the claimant would face in the home country, Canada's international obligations, and any other relevant facts.[663]

In a much earlier case, the Federal Court of Appeal held that the question to be asked is whether the claimant was, when applying for admission to Canada, still recognized by the competent authorities of the putative Article 1E country as a permanent resident.[664] Especially crucial is whether the putative Article 1E country recognizes the claimant's right to return there, even if his or her travel documents have expired, and not whether in international law, or from Canada's perspective, that country has formal or legal responsibility for the claimant.[665] The rights conferred need not be identical, but merely comparable, to those of nationals,[666] although some basic rights must be included such as the right to return to the country of residence; the right to work freely without restrictions; the right to study; and full access to social services.[667] As questions regarding the application of foreign law, these are treated as questions of fact to be decided on a balance of probabilities.[668] The initial onus is on the Minister, the RPD, or the RAD, as the case may be. Once the prima facie grounds for exclusion have been established, however, the claimant must show why his or her right of residence cannot be acted upon by renewing their residency status or otherwise.[669]

453. Article 1F(a) excludes individuals when there are 'serious reasons for considering that' they have 'committed a crime against peace, a war crime, or a crime against humanity, as defined in the international instruments drawn up to make provision in respect of such crimes'. The 'serious reasons for considering' evidentiary threshold is 'something more than suspicion or conjecture, but something less than the balance of probabilities'.[670] There is no need to balance the nature of the

---

663. *Canada (Citizenship and Immigration) v. Zeng*, 2010 FCA 118 at para. 28.
664. *Canada (Minister of Citizenship and Immigration) v. Mahdi* (1995), 32 Imm. L.R. (2d) 1 (F.C.A.).
665. *Wassiq v. Canada (Minister of Citizenship and Immigration)* (1996), 33 Imm. L.R. (2d) 238 (F.C.T.D) at 242.
666. *Kroon v. Canada (Minister of Employment and Immigration)* (1995), 28 Imm. L.R. (2d) 164 (F.C.T.D) at 167.
667. *Shamlou v. Canada (Minister of Citizenship and Immigration)* (1995), 32 Imm. L.R. (2d) 135 (F.C.T.D).
668. *Ibid.*
669. *Shahpari v. Canada (Minister of Citizenship and Immigration)* (1998), 44 Imm. L.R. (2d) 139 (F.C.T.D.).
670. *Sivakumar v. Canada (Minister of Employment and Immigration)*, [1994] 1 F.C. R. 433 (C.A.) at 445.

international crime against the feared persecution.[671] Some defences are available, such as duress, superior orders, and military necessity.[672] The IRB relies on international instruments such as the Charter of the International Military Tribunal, the Rome Statute of the International Criminal Court, and the Geneva Conventions in defining international crimes.[673] Further the Supreme Court of Canada has made clear that recourse to international jurisprudence is necessary when assessing allegedly excludable international crimes.[674] There have been no Federal Court or tribunal decisions dealing with crimes against peace. There have been only a relatively small number dealing with war crimes. In *Ramirez*, the Federal Court of Appeal held that a refugee claimant who had aided and abetted the torture and killing of civilians during the Salvadoran civil war was excludable for either a war crime or a crime against humanity; the Court chose not to specify, employing instead the term 'international crime'.[675] In a later case, *Bermudez*, the Federal Court held that war crimes were confined to crimes committed against the civilians of another country during an international war.[676]

454. Crimes against humanity have received the most detailed treatment and have been the subject of two major Supreme Court of Canada decisions, first in *Finta*,[677] a criminal prosecution, and more recently in *Mugesera*,[678] an inadmissibility case involving a permanent resident. In *Mugesera*, the Court held that the following four factors must be made out to support a finding that an act was a crime against humanity:

(i) An enumerated proscribed act was committed (this involves showing that the accused committed the criminal act and had the requisite guilty state of mind for the underlying act);
(ii) The act was committed as part of a widespread or systematic attack;
(iii) The attack was directed against any civilian population or any identifiable group of persons; and
(iv) The person committing the proscribed act knew of the attack and knew or took the risk that his or her act comprised a part of that attack.

The first three elements describe the physical criminal act, or *actus reus*. The fourth describes the mental element, or *mens rea*. The 'proscribed acts' suggested by the

---

671. *Gonzalez v. Canada (Minister of Employment and Immigration)*, [1994] 3 F.C. 646 (C.A.) at 657; *Canada (Minister of Citizenship and Immigration) v. Malouf* (1995), 190 N.R. 230 (F.C.A.).
672. IRB Legal Services, *Interpretation of the Convention Refugee Definition in the Case Law* (2005; updated 2010) at 10.2.5.1-3.
673. *Ibid.* at 10.2. Note that the Federal Court has held that the definitions in the Rome Statute cannot be applied retroactively: *Ventocilla v. Canada (Minister of Citizenship and Immigration)*, 2007 FC 575 (F.C.).
674. *Ezokola v. Canada (Citizenship and Immigration)*, 2013 SCC 40 at paras 42–46; *Mugesera v. Canada (Minister of Citizenship and Immigration)*, 2005 SCC 40 at para. 126.
675. *Ramirez v. Canada (Minister of Employment and Immigration)*, [1992] 2 F.C. 306 (C.A.).
676. *Bermudez v. Canada (Minister of Citizenship and Immigration)*, [2000] F.C.J. No. 860 (T.D.) at para. 12.
677. *R. v. Finta*, [1994] 1 S.C.R. 701.
678. *Mugesera*, *supra* n. 674.

Court are murder, extermination, enslavement, deportation, persecution, or 'any other inhumane act or omission'.[679] Both the physical and mental element of the underlying proscribed act must be made out. The second and third elements of the Court's test in *Mugesera* require an interpretation of the context to see whether the underlying crime was committed as part of a widespread or systematic attack directed against a civilian population or identifiable group.[680] The civilian population or identifiable group must be the primary object of the attack; its members must not be mere collateral victims.[681] Finally, the mental element of a crime against humanity requires that an individual know of the widespread or systematic attack and that his or her actions are part of it or take the risk that they will be part of it. Knowledge, and not intention, is all that is required.[682]

455. One of the issues that commonly arises under Article 1F(a) is when an individual may be found complicit in a war crime or crime against humanity that he or she did not personally commit. In *Ezokola*, the Supreme Court of Canada criticized the Federal Court (and, by implication, the RPD) for overextending the test for complicity in such crimes.[683] To avoid findings of mere '[g]uilt by association',[684] the Supreme Court held that to exclude a claimant under Article 1F(a), 'there must be serious reasons for considering that the claimant has voluntarily made a significant and knowing contribution to the organization's crime or criminal purpose'.[685] Whether this test is met on the facts of a particular case requires the assessment of a non-exhaustive set of factors: the size and nature of the organization; the part of the organization with which the refugee claimant was most directly concerned; the refugee claimant's duties and activities within the organization; the refugee claimant's position or rank in the organization; the length of time the refugee claimant was in the organization, particularly after acquiring knowledge of the group's crime or criminal purpose; and the method by which the refugee claimant was recruited and the refugee claimant's opportunity to leave the organization.[686] Finally, a full contextual analysis of these factors would include any viable defences, including the defence of duress.[687]

456. Article 1F(b) excludes an individual from refugee protection when there are 'serious reasons for considering that … he has committed a serious non-political crime outside the country of refuge prior to his admission to that country as a refugee'. As with Article 1F(a), the 'serious reasons for considering' standard calls for 'something more than suspicion or conjecture, but something less than the

679. *Ibid.* at para. 129.
680. *Ibid.* at para. 151. Each aspect of this test receives detailed treatment in *Mugesera*.
681. *Ibid.* at paras 161–162.
682. *Ibid.* at paras 174–174. See also the definition of 'crimes against humanity' and 'war crimes' in s. 4(3) of the *Crimes Against Humanity and War Crimes Act*, S.C. 2000, c. 24.
683. *Ezokola, supra* n. 674, at paras 78–83.
684. *Ibid.* at para. 3.
685. *Ibid.* at para. 84; see also para. 8.
686. *Ibid.* at para. 91.
687. *Ibid.* at para. 100.

balance of probabilities'.[688] A valid warrant or conviction issued by a foreign country, absent claims that the charges were fabricated or that there were serious due process concerns, by itself may satisfy the evidentiary requirement.[689] Previously, the courts have also taken the same approach to complicity in ordinary criminal activity as under Article 1F(a).[690] Whether the test for complicity set out by the Supreme Court in *Ezokola* will also find its way into the case law regarding Article 1F(b) – in light of statements by the Court in *Ezokola* distinguishing complicity in criminal law and complicity under Article 1F(a)[691] – remains to be seen.

457. If it is established that there are serious reasons for considering that a crime was committed by the refugee claimant, then the central questions in any Article 1F(b) case will be whether a crime is 'non-political' and whether it is 'serious'. With respect to the question of whether or not a crime is political, the Federal Court of Appeal has established a two-part test. There must first be a political disturbance related to a struggle to abolish either a government or government policy. Second, there must be a rational connection between the crime and accomplishment of the political objective.[692] The question of rational connection has come to involve an assessment of whether the crime was proportional to the objective; such proportionality, moreover, will be assessed within the context of the political system in which the struggle is waged. A grave crime such as murder may not result in exclusion when targeting a brutally repressive regime, though it would as an act of protest within a democracy: 'To put the matter in concrete terms, the plotters against Hitler might have been able to claim refugee status; the assassin of John F. Kennedy could never do so.'[693] The crime must have occurred outside Canada and before the claimant sought refuge here.

458. The serious nature of the crime may be established under section 105(3) of the Act, which deems an individual excludable if he or she has been ordered surrendered under the Extradition Act[694] for a crime that in Canada would carry a ten-year minimum sentence.[695] Beyond that set of circumstances, which is in practice unusual, the evaluation of whether a crime will be considered 'serious' until recently has followed a framework established by the Federal Court of Appeal in *Jayasekara.*[696] Under this approach, a decision-maker must first ask whether the crime that the claimant is alleged to have committed is one that, in Canada, would be punishable by a maximum term of imprisonment of at least ten years. If so, it is

688. *Sivakumar, supra* n. 670
689. *Qazi v. Canada (Citizenship and Immigration)*, 2005 FC 1204; *Biro v. Canada (Citizenship and Immigration)*, 2005 FC 1428; *Betancour v. Canada (Citizenship and Immigration)*, 2009 FC 767.
690. *Zrig v. Canada (Minister of Citizenship and Immigration)* 2003 FCA 178.
691. *Ezokola, supra* n. 674, at para. 46.
692. *Gil v. Canada (Minister of Employment and Immigration)*, [1995] 1 F.C. 508 (C.A.) at 528–529 and 533.
693. *Ibid.* at 535.
694. *Extradition Act*, S.C. 1999, c-18.
695. IRPA, s. 105(3).
696. *Jayasakera v. Canada (Minister of Citizenship and Immigration)*, 2008 FCA 404.

presumed to be serious.[697] The presumption of seriousness (or non-seriousness, as the case may be) may be rebutted by considering 'the elements of the crime, the mode of prosecution, the penalty prescribed, the facts and the mitigating and aggravating circumstances underlying the conviction'.[698] Importantly, the Federal Court of Appeal in *Jayasekara* added that there is to be 'no balancing, however, with factors extraneous to the facts and circumstances underlying the conviction such as, for example, the risk of persecution in the state of origin'.[699] The same court subsequently concluded that, although the presumption is to be established by examining Canadian criminal law at the time the refugee claim is being determined,[700] post-commission conduct or other considerations, such as subsequent rehabilitation or whether the claimant is a danger to the public in Canada, cannot be taken into account.[701] It should be noted that under this framework, an individual may be excluded for a purely economic offence.[702] In *Febles*, a decision released in late 2014, the Supreme Court of Canada appears to have left intact the framework of analysis established in *Jayasekara*, agreeing that if a crime would be punishable by ten years' imprisonment it will generally be considered serious but warning that 'the ten-year rule should not be applied in a mechanistic, decontextualized, or unjust manner'.[703]

459. Article 1F(c) excludes a person when there are 'serious reasons for considering that … he has been guilty of acts contrary to the purposes and principles of the United Nations'. Some of the same rules apply here as in the case of Article 1F(a) and (b). The 'serious reasons for considering' threshold implies 'something more than suspicion or conjecture, but something less than the balance of probabilities'.[704] Once again, with respect to Article 1F(c) the Canadian courts have held that the persecution feared should not be balanced against the excludable act in deciding whether to grant refugee status.[705]

460. In *Pushpanathan*, the Supreme Court of Canada said that the purpose of Article 1F(c) was:

> to exclude those individuals responsible for serious, sustained or systemic violations of fundamental human rights which amount to persecution in a non-war setting. Article 1F(c) may be applicable to non-state actors. Although it may be more difficult for a non-state actor to perpetrate human rights violations on a scale amounting to persecution without the state thereby implicitly adopting those acts, the possibility should not be excluded *a priori*.[706]

---

697. *Ibid.* at para. 40.
698. *Ibid.* at para. 44.
699. *Ibid.*
700. *Sanchez v. Canada (Citizenship and Immigration)*, 2014 FCA 157 at para. 9; aff'g 2013 FC 913.
701. *Hernandez Febles v. (Citizenship and Immigration)*, 2012 FCA 324 at para. 35; see also *Feimi v. Canada (Citizenship and Immigration)*, 2012 FCA 325.
702. *Xie v. Canada (Citizenship and Immigration)*, 2004 FCA 250 (C.A.).
703. *Febles v. Canada (Citizenship and Immigration)*, 2014 SCC 68 at para. 62.
704. *Sivakumar, supra* n. 670.
705. *Pushpanathan v. Canada (Minister of Citizenship and Immigration)*, [1996] 2 F.C. 49 (C.A.); *Canada (Minister of Citizenship and Immigration), supra* n. 671.
706. *Pushpanathan v. Canada (Minister of Citizenship and Immigration)*, [1998] SCR 982 at 1029.

It continued:

> Article 1F(c) will thus be applicable where there is consensus in international law that particular acts constitute sufficiently serious and sustained violations of fundamental human rights as to amount to persecution, or are explicitly recognized as contrary to the UN purposes and principles. First, where a widely accepted international agreement or UN resolution explicitly declares that the commission of certain acts is contrary to the UN purposes and principles, then there is a strong indication that those acts will fall within Art. 1F(c). Where such declarations or resolutions represent a reasonable consensus of the international community, then that designation should be considered determinative. A second category of acts which fall within the scope of Art. 1F(c) are those which a court is able, for itself, to characterize as serious, sustained and systemic violations of fundamental human rights constituting persecution. Where the rule which has been violated is very near the core of the most valued principles of human rights and is recognized as immediately subject to international condemnation and punishment, then even an isolated violation could lead to an exclusion under Art. 1F(c). The status of a violated rule as a universal jurisdiction offence would be a compelling indication that even an isolated violation constitutes persecution. A serious and sustained violation of human rights amounting to persecution may also arise from a particularly egregious factual situation, including the extent of the complicity of the claimant.[707]

Examples of the first kind of act included enforced disappearances, torture, and international terrorism.[708] A majority of the Supreme Court of Canada determined that conspiring to traffic in a drug is not contrary to the purposes and principles of the United Nations.[709]

461. Questions of complicity can arise under Article 1F(c), just as they often do under Article 1F(a). It appears that the courts and the IRB will apply the approach to complicity set out by the Supreme Court of Canada in *Ezokola* to Article 1F(c).[710]

462. In addition to the exclusion clauses, rejection of a claim is possible for reasons grouped under the heading of 'cessation' in section 108(1) of the Act. Under this provision, a refugee claim may be rejected if: (1) a claimant has voluntarily re-availed themselves of the protection of their country of nationality; (2) a claimant has voluntarily reacquired their nationality; (3) a claimant has acquired a new nationality and enjoys protection in the country of that nationality; (4) a claimant

707. *Ibid.* at 1032.
708. *Ibid.* at 1030.
709. *Ibid.* at 1035.
710. *Alam v. Canada (Citizenship and Immigration)*, 2014 FC 556. See also *X (Re)*, 2013 CanLII 88064 (RAD file no. VB3-01770).

has voluntarily become re-established in the country in which they claim to be facing a threat; or (5) the reasons that provided the foundation for the claim have ceased to exist.[711] This last ground for rejection may not apply if because of past persecution, torture, treatment, or punishment there are compelling reasons not to send an individual back to his or her home country.[712] The IRB must turn its attention to whether such compelling reasons exist in all cases where it has found past persecution and also that there has been a change in circumstances.[713] Note that applications for cessation may be brought even after a positive determination by the RPD; if successful, the claim is deemed to have been rejected.[714] Such cessation would mean, among other things, that a refugee claimant would no longer be able to obtain permanent resident status.[715]

D. Non-refoulement

463. For most persons granted protected person status under the Act, section 115(1) of the Act provides assurance against non-refoulement:

> A protected person or a person who is recognized as a Convention refugee by another country to which the person may be returned shall not be removed from Canada to a country where they would be at risk of persecution for reasons of race, religion, nationality, membership in a particular social group or political opinion or at risk of torture or cruel and unusual treatment or punishment.

Statutory protection against refoulement does not apply to a person 'who is inadmissible on grounds of serious criminality and who constitutes, in the opinion of the Minister, a danger to the public in Canada'.[716] It also does not apply to persons who are 'inadmissible on grounds of security, violating human or international rights or organized criminality if, in the opinion of the Minister, the person should not be allowed to remain in Canada on the basis of the nature and severity of acts committed or of danger to the security of Canada'.[717] Foreign nationals who are excluded from refugee protection under Articles 1E and 1F of the Refugee Convention are also not protected from refoulement under section 115.[718] Such excludable persons may nonetheless be protected against removal through the PRRA process described below. If the Minister concludes through a PRRA that a likely destination

711. The Minister may also apply on any of these grounds for the cessation of refugee protection that has previously been conferred: IRPA, s. 108(2).
712. IRPA, s. 108(4).
713. *Yamba v. Canada (Minister of Citizenship and Immigration)* (2000), 254 N.R. 388 at para. 6 (F.C.A.).
714. IRPA, s. 108(3).
715. Regulations, s. 177(a).
716. IRPA, s. 115(2)(a).
717. IRPA, s. 115(2)(b).
718. That is because a foreign national who is excluded from refugee protection cannot become a 'protected person' in Canada and is unlikely to be 'a person who is recognized as a Convention refugee by another country', as is required to enjoy the guarantee against refoulment in s. 115(1) of IRPA.

country is unsafe, removal will be stayed temporarily with respect to that country.[719] However, even under a PRRA, the Minister may balance the need for protection against the severity of the acts committed or against the danger posed by an individual to the Canadian public or security.[720] In the 2002 *Suresh* case, the Supreme Court of Canada ruled that it would generally violate the Charter to return a person to a country where he or she faces a substantial risk of torture, save in unspecified 'exceptional circumstances'.[721] This qualification on the scope of non-refoulement under the Act may breach Canada's international obligations under the CAT, not to remove persons to another state where there are substantial grounds for believing that they would be in danger of being subjected to torture.[722]

464. Non-refoulement is also ensured by automatic stays of removal orders that take effect when an individual has a pending claim for protection,[723] a pending judicial review of a negative RAD decision on a refugee protection claim,[724] or has filed a PRRA application.[725] However, automatic stays pending judicial review are not granted to refugee claimants who do not have a right of appeal from the RPD to the RAD.[726]

II. The Inland Refugee Claim Process

465. Inland refugee claimants are usually foreign nationals but may be permanent residents within Canada. The RPD and the new RAD of the IRB are tasked with deciding whether such claimants should be granted refugee protection, which confers protected person status unless such status is subsequently vacated under section 109 or determined to have ceased under section 108 of the Act.[727]

466. Foreign nationals or permanent residents can make a refugee claim to a Canadian immigration officer at any port of entry, CIC office, or CBSA office. An officer first interviews the refugee claimant to determine his or her eligibility to make a claim; the burden is on the claimant to establish eligibility.[728] Refugee

719. IRPA, s. 114(1)(b).
720. IRPA, s. 113(d).
721. *Suresh v. Canada (Minister of Citizenship and Immigration),* [2002] 1 S.C.R. 3, 2002 SCC 1 at para. 78.
722. The United Nations Committee Against Torture has recommended that these restrictions on protection for persons covered by the Convention Against Torture be lifted: see *Conclusions and recommendations of the Committee against Torture: Canada. 07 Jul. 2005. CAT/C/CR/34/CAN. (Concluding Observations/Comments)*, esp. comments 4(c), 4(d), and 5(b). See also Canadian Council for Refugees, 'Comments on Canada's Compliance with Article 3 of the Convention Against Torture' (28 Apr. 2005), available at: http://www.web.ca/ccr/catcompliance.html (accessed 3 Nov. 2009).
723. IRPA, s. 49(2).
724. Regulations, s. 231.
725. Regulations, s. 232.
726. This exception arises through the joint operation of s. 110(2) of IRPA and s. 231(1) of the Regulations. There are other exceptions as well under s. 231(2)–(4).
727. IRPA, s. 95.
728. IRPA, s. 100(4).

claimants who make a claim at the port of entry are required to submit a 'Basis of Claim' (BOC) document to the RPD within fifteen days of the date on which their claim is referred to the RPD for determination.[729] Those who make a claim at an office inside Canada must submit their completed BOC to the officer on the day the officer determines the eligibility of the claim.[730] Decisions on eligibility are to be made within three days, failing which claims are referred automatically to the RPD.[731] When the refugee claim is made by a foreign national, an officer will issue a conditional removal order on collateral grounds such as financial insufficiency or non-compliance with the Act.[732] The conditional order will take effect if a claim is found ineligible or is otherwise rejected, withdrawn, abandoned, or terminated.[733]

467. Refugee claims may be ineligible for referral to the RPD if: (1) the claimant has already been granted refugee protection or had a claim rejected by the IRB; (2) the claimant has been recognized as a Convention refugee by another country to which he or she may safely return; (3) the claimant came directly or indirectly to Canada from a designated 'safe-third country' (only the United States is so designated); (4) the claimant has been determined to be inadmissible on grounds of security, violating human or international rights, serious criminality, or organized criminality.[734] Notwithstanding the Supreme Court decision *Singh*,[735] which found that refugee claimants have a right to due process under the Canadian Charter of Rights and Freedoms, it has been held that there is no constitutional right to due process during eligibility determinations.[736]

468. In 2004, Canada and the United States implemented a Safe Third Country Agreement. The Agreement states that a refugee claimant who seeks to enter Canada via the territorial border with the United States will be sent back to the United States for determination of refugee status and vice versa. Canada had long sought such an agreement with the United States, because many more asylum seekers entered Canada via the United States than the reverse. Under the terms of the Agreement, exceptions exist for unaccompanied minors, asylum seekers who have relatives in the destination state, or citizens of visa-exempt countries.[737] Immediately upon its declaration in force, a coalition of civil society organizations, as well as a Colombian asylum seeker ('John Doe'), challenged the designation of the

729. Regulations, s. 159.8(2). The RPD may extend the time limit for submitting the BOC for reasons of fairness and natural justice: Regulations, 159.8(3); *Refugee Protection Division Rules*, SOR/2012-256, rule 8.
730. Regulations, s. 159.8(1).
731. IRPA, s. 110(3).
732. Citizenship and Immigration Canada, Operational Manual PP1, *Processing Claims for Refugee Protection in Canada* (February 17, 2012), s. 3.16.
733. IRPA, s. 49(2). A claim may be 'terminated' on several grounds after it has been referred to the RPD. For example, termination is possible if it is discovered that the claim was ineligible or if the finding of eligibility resulted directly or indirectly from a misrepresentation.
734. IRPA, s. 101.
735. *Singh v. Minister of Employment and Immigration*, [1985] 1 S.C.R. 177.
736. *Berrahma v. Canada*, [1991] F.C.J. No. 180 (T.D.); *Raza v. Canada (Minister of Citizenship and Immigration)*, [1999] 2 F.C. 185 (T.D.).
737. IRPA, s. 101(1)(e); Regulations, s 159.1–159.9.

United States as a safe country for asylum seekers. They contended that by deflecting Canada-bound asylum seekers to the asylum regime in the United States, Canada breached asylum seekers' rights under the Canadian Charter of Rights and Freedoms. The challenge succeeded before the Federal Court, but was overturned by the Federal Court of Appeal.[738]

469. Eligible claims are referred to the RPD of the IRB for a hearing, which in most cases is to take place within sixty days of referral.[739] Hearings before the RPD are meant to be non-adversarial.[740] Members of the Canadian refugee bar questioned whether this is in fact the case in the context of a court challenge to an IRB Guideline establishing procedural standards for RPD hearings.[741] To make out a claim, claimants must satisfy the RPD that they meet the criteria for refugee status under section 96 of the Act or for persons in need of protection under section 97. They may also have to show they should not be excluded under section 98 of the Act, if a prima facie case for exclusion is established. There is a right to counsel at a hearing.[742] The provinces of Ontario, British Columbia, and Québec provide limited public funding for counsel.

470. Pursuant to reforms that came into force on 15 December 2012, the government now has the authority to designate certain countries – which are then referred to as 'designated countries of origin' (DCOs) – based on certain qualitative or quantitative criteria that appear to be designed to identify relatively safe countries.[743] When the number of claims from a country surpasses a threshold, established by order of the Minister, the power to make a designation is triggered when a certain percentage of claims from that country have been rejected, withdrawn, or abandoned. Alternatively, in cases where the number of claims from a country is below the minimum threshold established, the Minister may designate that country as a DCO if he or she is of the opinion that: (i) the country in question has an independent judiciary, (ii) recognizes basic democratic rights and freedoms and makes available a mechanism for redress if those rights or freedoms are infringed, and (iii) civil society organizations exist.[744]

471. DCO claimants face accelerated timelines for hearings at the RPD; their hearings take place within either thirty or forty-five days, rather than sixty days,

738. *Canadian Council for Refugees, Canadian Council of Churches, Amnesty International and John Doe v. Her Majesty the Queen*, 2007 FC 1262; rev'd 2008 FCA 229; Supreme Court of Canada Bulletin, 6 Feb. 2009 (application for leave dismissed): http://scc.lexum.umontreal.ca/en/bulletin/2009/09-02-06.bul/09-02-06.bul.html.

739. Regulations, s. 159.9(1)(b).

740. IRPA, s. 165.

741. *Canada (Minister of Citizenship and Immigration) v. Thamotharem*, 2007 FCA 198, leave to appeal refused [2007] S.C.C.A. No. 394 (QL). See also *Benitez v. Canada (Minister of Citizenship and Immigration)*, 2007 FCA 199. These cases challenged the IRB's *Chairperson's Guideline 7: Concerning Preparation and Conduct of a Hearing in the Refugee Protection Division* (15 Dec. 2006; updated 15 Dec. 2012), available at: http://www.irb-cisr.gc.ca/Eng/BoaCom/references/pol/GuiDir/Pages/GuideDir07.aspx (accessed 25 Jul. 2014).

742. IRPA, s. 167.

743. IRPA, s. 109.1.

744. *Ibid.*

depending on whether they make their claim at a port of entry or inside Canada.[745] They are denied an appeal to the Refugee Appeal Division (RAD).[746] The denial of a right of appeal to the RAD means, further, that such claimants do not benefit from a statutory stay of removal when applying for judicial review of a negative RPD decision,[747] although they may seek a stay from the court.[748] Finally, failed refugee claimants from DCOs are not eligible to apply for a PRRA for thirty-six months following a negative RPD decision.[749] At the time of writing, the Minister had designated thirty-seven countries.[750]

472. A single RPD member typically presides over a hearing into a refugee claim.[751] Such claims are generally held in the absence of the public, but a member of the public may apply to attend a hearing.[752] Representatives of UNHCR have a right to attend any hearing unless national security evidence is before the panel.[753] The Minister may intervene in any refugee hearing upon providing a notice to the claimant stating the purpose of intervention and, if exclusion is believed to be an issue, the facts upon which the Minister will rely.[754] Claimants and the Minister have the right to be represented by legal or other counsel.[755] To represent a claimant for a fee or other form of consideration, however, counsel must be either a lawyer or an immigration consultant in good standing, or a student-at-law acting under supervision of a lawyer in good standing; otherwise, counsel can be anyone but must be unremunerated.[756] Parties may call witnesses, including experts. All testimony is given under oath or by solemn affirmation. In assessing a claimant's case, RPD members may receive and base their decision on 'evidence that is adduced in the proceedings and considered credible and trustworthy in the circumstances';[757] in practice, this usually involves assessing the claimant's credibility, other witnesses' testimony, and personal documentary evidence provided by a claimant as

745. Regulations, s. 159.9(1)(a).
746. IRPA, s. 110(2)(d.1).
747. The lack of a statutory stay is the result of s. 231(1) of the Regulations, which only grants such stays for the duration of applications for judicial review of decisions by the RAD. Therefore, if there is no right of appeal to the RAD there is no statutory stay.
748. IRPA, s. 50(a).
749. IRPA, s. 112(2)(b.1) and (c). The Minister may create exemptions to this thirty-six-month bar.
750. See Citizenship and Immigration Canada, 'Designated Countries of Origin' (17 Jun. 2013), available at: http://www.cic.gc.ca/english/refugees/reform-safe.asp (accessed 25 Jul. 2014). The countries designated at time of writing were Australia; Austria; Belgium; Chile; Croatia; Cyprus; Czech Republic; Denmark; Estonia; Finland; France; Germany; Greece; Hungary; Iceland; Ireland; Israel (excludes Gaza and the West Bank); Italy; Japan; Latvia; Lithuania; Luxembourg; Malta; Mexico; Netherlands; New Zealand; Norway; Poland; Portugal; Slovak Republic; Slovenia; South Korea; Spain; Sweden; Switzerland; United Kingdom; and United States of America.
751. IRPA, s. 163.
752. IRPA, s. 166(c) and (d); see also the *Refugee Protection Division Rules*, SOR/2012-256, rule 57.
753. IRPA, s. 166(e) and (f).
754. *Refugee Protection Division Rules*, SOR/2012-256, rule 29; IRPA, s. 170(c)–(e).
755. IRPA, s. 167.
756. IRPA, s. 91. A challenge on federalism grounds to the former legislation authorizing immigration consultants to appear before the IRB was unsuccessful: *Law Society of British Columbia v. Mangat*, [2001] 3 SCR 113.
757. IRPA, s. 170(h).

well as general documentary evidence attesting to conditions in the country of reference. In almost all claims, such documentary evidence will include a 'national documentation package' maintained by the IRB with respect to most countries worldwide.[758]

473. RPD members must provide either oral or written reasons for all decisions.[759] If the claim was rejected and the RPD member is of the opinion that there was no credible or trustworthy evidence on which it could have made a favourable decision, the reasons must say as much.[760] Similarly, if the RPD member was of the opinion that the claim was clearly fraudulent, it must state in its reasons for decision that the claim is manifestly unfounded.[761] A statement of either kind – that a claim has no credible basis or is manifestly unfounded – has the effect of eliminating a right of appeal to the RAD and, consequently, the benefit of a statutory stay of removal.[762]

474. Claimants whose claims have been rejected by the RPD, or the Minister seeking to challenge a positive determination, may challenge a decision through one of three mechanisms: a motion before the RPD to reopen their claim, an appeal to the RAD of the IRB, or an application for leave and judicial review in the Federal Court. There is no right of appeal to the RAD for certain failed refugee claimants or from certain kinds of decisions. Specifically, there is no right of appeal to the RAD in respect of: (1) a decision by the RPD allowing or rejecting the claim of a 'designated foreign national';[763] (2) a determination by the RPD that a claim has been withdrawn or abandoned; (3) a decision by the RPD rejecting a claim where the RPD states in its reasons that the claim is manifestly unfounded or has no credible basis; (4) a decision by the RPD with respect to a claimant who was eligible to make a refugee claim notwithstanding having come to Canada from a designated safe third country (i.e., the United States); (5) a decision by the RPD allowing or rejecting a claim by a national of a DCO; (6) a decision by the RPD allowing or rejecting an application by the Minister for a determination that refugee protection has ceased; and (7) a decision by the RPD allowing or rejecting an application by the Minister to vacate a decision allowing refugee protection.[764] In such cases, a claimant or the Minister has recourse only to an application to reopen or to the Federal Court. The RPD must not allow an application to reopen unless it is established that there was a failure to observe a principle of natural justice.[765] Applications to

758. See IRB, 'National Documentation Packages' (7 Mar. 2014), available at: http://www.irb-cisr.gc.ca/Eng/ResRec/NdpCnd/Pages/ndpcnd.aspx (accessed 25 Jul. 2014).

759. IRPA, s. 169(b).

760. IRPA, s. 107(2).

761. IRPA, s. 107.1. The provision came into force in 2012. The *Balanced Refugee Reform Act*, S.C. 2010, c.8, originally provided RPD members with a discretionary power ('may') to declare claims manifestly unfounded if clearly fraudulent. The *Protecting Canada's Immigration System Act*, S.C. 2012, c. 17, removed this discretion and made the statement by the RPD mandatory.

762. IRPA, s. 110(2)(c) and Regulations, s. 231.

763. A 'designated foreign national' (DFN) is a foreign national whose arrival has been designated as 'irregular' by the Public Safety Minister under s. 20.1 of IRPA.

764. IRPA, s. 110(2).

765. Refugee Protection Division Rules, SOR/2012-256, rule 62(6).

reopen at the RPD may not be brought once the Federal Court has made a final determination with respect to the application for leave or for judicial review of a claim.[766]

475. Appeals to the RAD, for those claims where there is a right of appeal, are generally conducted only in writing. Appellants, whether the Minister or refugee claimants, have fifteen calendar days from the date they receive the written reasons of the RPD to file a notice of appeal and thirty calendar days to file an appeal record. The Act restricts the ability of refugee claimants to present evidence to the RAD that was not before the RPD. They may present only evidence 'that arose after the rejection of their claim or that was not reasonably available, or that the person could not reasonably have been expected in the circumstances to have presented' at the time of the RPD's rejection of their claim.[767] The Minister faces no such evidentiary limits, although if the Minister presents evidence to the RAD, the refugee claimant will similarly be unrestricted with respect to evidence presented in response to the Minister's evidence.[768] The RAD may hold an oral hearing to decide credibility issues with respect to a refugee claimant that are raised by new evidence and central to a claim.[769]

476. In disposing of an appeal, the RAD may choose to confirm the RPD's determination, substitute its own determination, or send a matter back to the RPD for redetermination.[770] The RAD must render its decisions in writing.[771] If an appeal to the RAD is dismissed, either the Minister or a failed refugee claimant may apply for leave and judicial review of the RAD decision at the Federal Court or may apply to reopen the RAD's decision. As with the RPD, the RAD must only reopen an appeal if it is established that there was a failure to observe a principle of natural justice.[772] Also, similarly to the RPD, the RAD may not reopen an appeal if the Federal Court has made a final determination on an application for leave or judicial review with respect to the same refugee claim.[773]

477. The provisions of the Act implementing the RAD only came into force on 15 December 2012. As a result, most of the statutory provisions governing the RAD have yet to be interpreted by the courts. One of the first issues that confronted the RAD was what standard of review, if any, it should apply in considering appeals from the RPD. In the first year and a half of its existence, the RAD mainly reviewed

766. IRPA, s. 170.2.
767. IRPA, s. 110(4). This legislative provision appears to be modelled on a nearly-identical provision governing the evidence that may be presented with a PRRA application: IRPA, s. 113(a). The RAD has in general interpreted s. 110(4) using a test developed by the Federal Court of Appeal for the application of s. 113(a): *Raza v. Canada (Citizenship and Immigration)*, 2007 FCA 385.
768. IRPA, s. 110(5).
769. IRPA, s. 110(6).
770. IRPA, s. 111.
771. IRPA, s. 169(c). This provision was amended by the *Balanced Refugee Reform Act*, S.C. 2010, c. 8., to allow the RAD to render decisions orally. However, the amended version had not yet come into force at the time of writing.
772. *Refugee Appeal Division Rules*, SOR/2012-257, rule 49(6).
773. IRPA, s. 171.1.

the RPD's decisions on issues of fact and mixed fact and law on a deferential standard of 'reasonableness'. It mainly reviewed the RPD's decisions on issues of law on a more exacting 'correctness' standard.[774] In a series of decisions, the Federal Court has upheld this approach only once[775] and otherwise rejected it more than thirty times.[776] In *Huruglica*, the Federal Court decided that the RAD should show deference to the RPD only with respect to credibility findings and in other areas where the RPD has an advantage:

> Having concluded that the RAD erred in reviewing the RPD's decision on the standard of reasonableness, I have further concluded that ... the RAD is required to conduct a hybrid appeal. It must review all aspects of the RPD's decision and come to an independent assessment of whether the claimant is a Convention refugee or a person in need of protection. Where its assessment departs from that of the RPD, the RAD must substitute its own decision.
>
> In conducting its assessment, it can recognize and respect the conclusion of the RPD on such issues as credibility and/or where the RPD enjoys a particular advantage in reaching such a conclusion but it is not restricted, as an appellate court is, to intervening on facts only where there is a 'palpable and overriding error'.[777]

In other cases, however, the Court has said the RAD should apply a seemingly deferential standard of 'palpable and overriding error' to issues of fact and mixed fact and law decided by the RPD, and a standard of correctness to issues of law.[778] At the time of writing, an appeal of the decision in *Huruglica* had been filed but not yet scheduled for a hearing.

478. Claimants or the Minister can also apply for leave for judicial review by the Federal Court of a decision of the RPD or the RAD. If it grants leave, the Federal Court generally reviews decisions on a deferential standard of reasonableness with respect to issues of fact and mixed fact and law and, in most cases, a non-deferential standard of correctness on issues of law. However, following the Supreme Court of Canada's decision in *Dunsmuir v. New Brunswick*,[779] in which the Court substantially revised administrative law doctrine regarding standards for judicial review, the Federal Court has occasionally applied a standard of reasonableness to issues of law.[780] This has created some uncertainty.

---

774. See, e.g., *X(Re)*, 2013 CanLII 84910 (IRB) at paras 6–24.
775. *Iyamuremye v. Canada (Citizenship and Immigration)*, 2014 FC 493 at para. 2.
776. See, e.g., *Huruglica v. Canada (Citizenship and Immigration)*, 2014 FC 799; *Spasoja v. Canada (Citizenship and Immigration)*, 2014 FC 913; *Alyafi v. Canada (Citizenship and Immigration)*, 2014 FC 952; *Djossou v. Canada (Citizenship and Immigration)*, 2014 FC 1080.
777. *Huruglica, ibid.* at paras 54–55.
778. *Spasoja, supra* n. 776; *Aloulou v. Canada (Citoyenneté et Immigration)*, 2014 CF 1236.
779. [2008] 1 S.C.R. 190.
780. See discussions in, e.g., the Federal Court of Appeal decision in *Hernandez Febles, supra* n. 701, as well as discussion in the Federal Court decisions in *Canada (Citizenship and Immigration), supra* n. 620; *Canada (Citizenship and Immigration) v. B472*, 2013 FC 151; *Portillo, supra* n. 642.

479. According to a recent study, 14.44% of judicial review applications are granted leave by the Federal Court. In cases where leave is granted, the success rate at the merits stage is 43.98%.[781] An appeal to the Federal Court of Appeal is only allowed when the Federal Court judge has certified that a question of general importance is raised by the claimant's case.[782] If the IRB's decision is set aside by the Federal Court or the Federal Court of Appeal, it is usually sent back to the RPD or the RAD, as the case may be, for a new determination by a different decision-maker.

480. The conditional removal order, usually a departure order,[783] issued to a foreign national during the determination of their eligibility to claim refugee protection comes into force fifteen days after the claim has been rejected by either the RPD or the RAD, as the case may be.[784] If a refugee claimant seeks judicial review of a RAD decision, the removal order will come into force upon the unsuccessful end of the judicial review process.[785] Stays are not available, except by court order,[786] to refugee claimants who do not have a right of appeal to the RAD, who are inadmissible on grounds of serious criminality, or who are a resident of the United States or St Pierre and Miquelon.[787] Once the stay is lifted, or if no stay was available, the claimant is required to leave Canada within thirty days under a departure order and to verify their departure; if he or she does not, the departure order becomes a deportation order and the claimant will be barred from returning to Canada in the future without permission from the Minister.[788]

481. Unsuccessful refugee claimants can pursue other processes under the Act, such as an application for permanent residence on humanitarian and compassionate (H&C) grounds or a PRRA, although these processes are not intended as appeals or reviews of decisions by the RPD or RAD. An H&C application is an application for discretionary relief under section 25 of the Act. H&C applications are discussed in detail in Part VI, Chapter 1.

482. Until recently, once a removal order was in force but prior to removal, individuals were notified by the officer in charge of removal that they were eligible to apply for a PRRA.[789] PRRA review was not available to persons facing extradition

781. See, Sean Rehaag, 'Luck of the Draw? Judicial Review of Refugee Determinations in the Federal Court of Canada (2005–2010)', (2012) 38 Queen's L. J. 1 at 23.
782. IRPA, s. 74(d).
783. Regulations, ss 228(3) and 229(2).
784. IRPA, s. 49(2).
785. Regulations, s. 231
786. IRPA, s. 50(a).
787. Regulations, s. 231. The Regulations state, at s. 231(2), that refugee claimants who are nationals of DCOs or who are Designated Foreign Nationals (DFNs) do not benefit from an automatic stay of removal when seeking judicial review. (A DFN is a foreign national whose arrival has been designated as 'irregular' by the Public Safety Minister under s. 20.1 of the Act.) Subsection 231(2), however, appears to be redundant. Under s. 110(2) of the Act, such refugee claimants do not have a right of appeal to the RAD, and so would not be granted a stay under s. 231(1).
788. Regulations, s. 224(1) and (2).
789. IRPA, s. 112(1). See also Regulations, s. 160.

or to those deemed ineligible to make a refugee claim because they came to Canada through a designated safe third country (i.e., through the United States).[790] Pursuant to amendments made under the *Balanced Refugee Reform Act* and the *Protecting Canada's Immigration System Act*, which came into force in 2012, unsuccessful refugee claimants facing removal are now denied access to a PRRA if it has been less than twelve months since they were the subject of a negative RPD or RAD decision, as are other persons who have received a negative PRRA decision within the previous twelve months.[791] The Minister may exempt from these twelve-month bars nationals or former habitual residents of a country; nationals or former habitual residents who lived in a given part of a country; or a class of nationals or former habitual residents of a country.[792] Unsuccessful claimants from DCOs are barred from applying for a PRRA for thirty-six months following a negative RPD or PRRA decision.[793] The *Balanced Refugee Reform Act* also includes provisions that will have the effect of transferring most PRRA applications to the RPD for determination, with the exception of applications by foreign nationals who have been determined to be inadmissible on grounds of security, violating human or international rights, organized criminality, or (with some limitations) serious criminality; determined to be excluded from refugee protection under Article 1F; or have been named in a security certificate.[794] The measures transferring responsibility for most PRRA applications to the RPD are not yet in force.[795]

483. For most claimants currently eligible for a PRRA, removals are stayed once a PRRA application has been filed, unless the removal order has been made at a port of entry.[796] The PRRA process is in almost all cases a written one, in which applicants may present 'only new evidence that arose after the rejection [of their refugee claim] or was not reasonably available, or that the applicant could not reasonably have been expected in the circumstances to have presented, at the time of the rejection'.[797] Oral hearings may be held if there is such new evidence that raises a serious issue of credibility with respect to the applicant that, if accepted, would justify allowing the application for protection.[798] Negative PRRA reviews can be the subject of judicial review. Successful application may be vacated in cases of misrepresentation.[799] The success rate for PRRA applications is generally below 3%.[800]

790. IRPA, s. 112(2)(a) and (b).
791. IRPA, s. 112(b.1) and (c). The twelve-month PRRA bar was found to be constitutional in *Peter, supra* n. 652.
792. IRPA, s. 112(2.1).
793. IRPA, s. 112(b.1) and (c).
794. See the *Balanced Refugee Reform Act*, S.C. 2010, c. 8, ss 15–16. See also IRPA, s. 112(3).
795. The government had announced that it expected the transfer to take place by December 2014: see, Immigration and Refugee Board of Canada, 'Changes to the Refugee Protection Division' (6 Nov. 2013), available at: http://www.irb-cisr.gc.ca/Eng/RefClaDem/Pages/RpdSprC31Impact.aspx (accessed 13 Jul. 2014). However, these plans had yet to be carried through at the time of writing.
796. Regulations, s. 166 and s. 232.
797. IRPA, s. 113(a).
798. Regulations, s. 167.
799. IRPA, s. 114(3).

484. In standard cases, a PRRA officer will consider the protection needs of the person using the criteria set out in section 96 (the Convention refugee definition), section 97 (consolidated-grounds protection), and section 98 (the exclusion clauses of the Refugee Convention).[801] Successful claimants are granted refugee protection and in most cases become eligible to apply for permanent residence.[802]

485. In the case of foreign nationals inadmissible or excluded on grounds of security, international criminality, or organized criminality, the PRRA officer will consider only whether the individual qualifies for protection under section 97 – that is, if he or she faces a risk of torture, a risk to their life, or a risk of cruel and unusual treatment or punishment if returned to their country of origin.[803] Also in those cases, the officer will balance the risk to the applicant against either: (1) the danger posed to the Canadian public by their continued presence, in cases of serious criminality; or (2) the nature and severity of the acts committed or the danger posed the Canadian security.[804] In cases of applicants inadmissible for serious criminality because of a conviction in Canada punishable by a maximum term of at least ten years but for which a penalty of less than two years was imposed, the assessment is also made under sections 96 to 98, but the same balancing is to be carried out as in the case of other applicants inadmissible or excluded on the grounds just listed.[805] In such cases, a successful PRRA results not in refugee protection but only in the stay of a removal to a country in which the applicant was determined to be at risk.[806] Such stays can be re-examined by the Minister, with notice to the foreign national, and can be cancelled if the grounds for protection are thought no longer to exist.[807]

486. Most persons who receive refugee protection are eligible anytime to apply for permanent residence within Canada. Family members may be included in the application for permanent residence. Family outside Canada will be issued a PRV if they are included in the original application and they apply to a Canadian officer outside Canada less than a year after the original applicant becomes a permanent resident.[808] All family members are subject to screening for inadmissibility, although not all grounds of inadmissibility will apply.[809]

487. There is one exception the general rule of immediate eligibility. The *Protecting Canada's Immigration System Act* created a new power for the Minister of

800. Government of Canada, 'Formative Evaluation of the Pre-Removal Risk Assessment Program' (February 2008), available at: http://www.cic.gc.ca/english/resources/evaluation/prra/section4.asp (accessed 13 Jul. 2014).
801. IRPA, s. 113(c).
802. IRPA, s. 114(1) and s. 21(2).
803. IRPA, s. 113(d).
804. IRPA, s. 113(d).
805. IRPA, s. 113(e). This exception also applies to applicants who have been convicted abroad of a crime which would be punishable in Canada by a maximum term of at least ten years, unless they are found to be excluded from refugee protection under Art. 1F.
806. IRPA, s. 114(1)(b).
807. IRPA, s. 114(2).
808. Regulations, s. 176.
809. Regulations, s. 176(3).

Public Safety and Emergency Preparedness to designate groups of foreign nationals as 'irregular arrivals' if certain conditions are met.[810] These conditions are: (1) where the Minister is of the opinion that examinations of the persons in the group, particularly for the purpose of establishing identity or determining inadmissibility, and any other investigations cannot be conducted in a 'timely manner'; or (2) the Minister has reasonable grounds to suspect that, in relation to the arrival of the group of foreign nationals proposed for designation, there has been, or will be, human smuggling for the benefit or profit of, at the direction of, or in association with, a criminal organization or terrorist group.[811] Members of a designated group are deemed to be 'designated foreign nationals' (DFNs).[812] DFNs who become protected persons may not apply for permanent residence for five years after a positive RPD decision on their claim.[813] DFNs may also not file an H&C application for five years.[814] Until they become permanent residents, they are also barred from applying for a travel document[815] or initiating the sponsorship process for family members outside Canada.[816] They are also subject to reporting obligations.[817] Contrary to expectations, at the time of writing, only a small number of designations have been made.[818]

488. Also ineligible for permanent residence are foreign nationals whose refugee protection status has been determined to have ceased under section 108 of the Act or has been vacated under section 109 of the Act and those who already have status as a citizen, permanent resident, or Convention refugee in a country where they do not face persecution or another risk covered by the Act.[819] Another potential obstacle to becoming a permanent resident is proof of identity. The Regulations in general require applicants for permanent residence to provide proof of identity.[820] However, a protected person 'who does not hold' an identity document that

810. IRPA, s. 20.1.
811. IRPA, s. 21.2(1).
812. IRPA, s. 21.2(2).
813. IRPA, s. 20.2(1).
814. IRPA, s. 25(1.01).
815. IRPA, s. 31.1. This section states: 'For the purposes of Article 28 of the Refugee Convention, a designated foreign national whose claim for refugee protection or application for protection is accepted is lawfully staying in Canada only if they become a permanent resident or are issued a temporary resident permit under section 24.' Article 28 of the Refugee Convention states: 'The Contracting States shall issue to refugees lawfully staying in their territory travel documents for the purpose of travel outside their territory unless compelling reasons of national security or public order otherwise require ...' Therefore, for the purposes of Art. 28 of the Refugee Convention, s. 31.1 deems DFNs not to be 'lawfully staying' in Canada, even if they have been granted refugee protection, until they become either a permanent resident or a holder of a Temporary Resident Permit (TRP). DFNs are also barred from applying for TRPs for five years: IRPA, s. 24(5).
816. IRPA s. 12(1).
817. IRPA s. 98.1. See also Regulations, 174.1. In addition, conditions may be imposed on DFNs if ordered released from detention by either the Immigration Division (ID) or an officer: IRPA, s. 58(4) and 58.1(3).
818. Only four orders have been made: Canada Gazette, 'Designation of Irregular Arrivals' Vol. 146, no. 150 (15 Dec. 2012), available online at: http://gazette.gc.ca/rp-pr/p1/2012/2012-12-15/html/notice-avis-eng.html (accessed 13 Jul. 2014).
819. Regulations, s. 177.
820. Regulations, s. 50(1).

would otherwise be required under the Regulations may instead submit: (1) any identity document issued outside Canada prior to entry or (2) statutory declarations by the foreign national and by someone who knew him or her prior to entry.[821] Notwithstanding this flexibility, some applicants still have difficulty establishing their identity and end up as protected persons with no straightforward prospect of permanent residence.[822]

489. Refugees who become permanent residents acquire all the rights attaching to that status. They may sponsor family members to come to Canada through the family class; they may travel to and from Canada; and they may apply for citizenship if they have resided in Canada for three of the four years immediately preceding their application.

§3. Moratorium Countries

490. Section 230 of the Regulations allows the Minister of Public Safety and Emergency Preparedness to impose a temporary stay of removals with respect to a country or a place if the circumstances in that country or place pose a generalized risk to the entire civilian population as a result of armed conflict, environmental disaster, or any other situation that is temporary and generalized. Countries so designated are often referred to in shorthand as 'moratorium countries'. Such stays do not apply to persons inadmissible on grounds of security, international criminality, serious and non-serious criminality, or organized criminality. They are also not applicable to persons excluded from refugee protection under Article 1F of the Convention or to persons who provide written consent to be removed to the designated country. The Public Safety Minister may cancel the stay once the generalized danger has dissipated.[823]

491. As of December 2014, the moratorium countries are Afghanistan, the Democratic Republic of Congo and Iraq. In July 2009, the Minister of Public Safety lifted the moratorium for removals to Burundi, Liberia, and Rwanda, and Haiti and Zimbabwe were lifted in December 2014.[824] The Minister introduced a special programme to defer removal of nationals of these three countries if they choose to submit an application for permanent residence on H&C grounds; the deferral will continue until the application is decided.[825]

492. Nationals of moratorium countries receive the same employment and social benefits as other temporary foreign workers. They are entitled to attend school,

821. *Ibid.*
822. Sasha Jones & Martin Baglay, *Refugee Law* (Irwin Law, 2007) at 90.
823. Regulations, s. 230.
824. Citizenship and Immigration Canada, 'Operational Bulletins 136 (Modified) – July 16, 2013': http://www.cic.gc.ca/english/resources/manuals/bulletins/2009/ob136.asp (accessed 13 Jul. 2014); Citizenship and Immigration Canada, 'Operational Bulletin 600 – January 23, 2015': http://www.cic.gc.ca/english/resources/manuals/bulletins/2015/ob600.asp (accessed 3 April 2015).
825. *Ibid.*

though they do not benefit from subsidized post-secondary education. They have access to health care under the IFHP only if their conditions pose a public health or safety risk.[826] Unless they pursue alternate means under the Act, such as the refugee process or humanitarian and compassionate (H&C) leave under section 25(1), nationals of moratorium countries will have limited rights and no path to permanent residence. Indeed, the government has been criticized for not creating a new admissions class for granting permanent residence for moratorium-country nationals not otherwise eligible for permanent residence under the Act.[827]

826. For general discussion of the changes to the IFHP program, see Citizenship and Immigration Canada, 'Health care – Refugees' (27 Nov. 2013), available at: http://www.cic.gc.ca/english/refugees/outside/arriving-healthcare.asp (accessed 25 Jul. 2014). However, information on the effect of the changes on nationals of moratorium countries is not available at this site and is difficult to find elsewhere on the CIC website. The effect of the amendments to the IFHP on a national of a moratorium country is discussed in *Canadian Doctors For Refugee Care, supra* n. 521, at paras 63, 174–81.

827. Canadian Council for Refugees, 'Lives on Hold: Nationals of Moratoria Countries Living in Limbo' (July 2005), available at: http://ccrweb.ca/livesonhold.pdf (accessed 13 Jul. 2014).

Chapter 5. Nationals with Preferential Treatment

493. As outlined above, Canada has formalized a number of trading partnerships with other countries and groups of countries. Each of these agreements extends privileges to citizens of the various countries to enter Canada and do business there. By way of example, this chapter considers two such agreements – the NAFTA and the GATS. Admissions pursuant to both of these agreements are administered by CIC within its IMP. Qualified individuals admitted under NAFTA or GATS can enter Canada more easily because they are not subject to a LMIA, a screening process conducted by Employment and Social Development Canada to determine whether an equivalent Canadian worker is available to perform the job.[828]

§1. North American Free Trade Agreement

494. In 1994, Canada, the United States, and Mexico entered into the NAFTA. Chapter 16 of NAFTA, titled 'Temporary Entry for Business Persons', allows select categories of temporary workers from each signatory access to the other countries' markets. The categories of temporary workers admitted under NAFTA are: (1) business visitors, (2) traders and investors, (3) intra-company transferees, and (4) professionals.[829]

495. To qualify, business visitors must engage in an enumerated business activity, such as technical or scientific research and design; marketing, sales, and distribution; or various tourism-related services.[830]

496. Traders must demonstrate that they are seeking to carry on substantial trade in goods or services between two of the state parties. Investors must provide evidence that they are seeking to establish, develop, administer or provide advice or key technical services to the operation of an investment to which his or her business has committed a substantial amount of capital.[831] Traders or investors must be performing duties that are supervisory, executive or involve essential skills.[832]

---

828. For further details of the LMIA process, see Part III, Chapter 1, s. 2 above. As part of a review of Canada's Temporary Foreign Worker Program in 2014, a number of new rules and application fees will apply to entrants under NAFTA and GATS. As a pre-condition to obtaining a work permit under NAFTA or GATS, the employer will be required to submit the job offer itself to CIC for an 'opinion request' to ensure the job offer merits LMIA exemption. Additional application fees will take effect in the summer of 2015: the Employer Compliance fee of CAD 230 for employer specific work permits and CAD 100 privilege fee for open work permits. See, Government of Canada, 'Overhauling the Temporary Foreign Worker Program: Putting Canadians First' (2014): http://www.esdc.gc.ca/eng/jobs/foreign_workers/reform/overhauling_TFW.pdf (accessed 30 Jul. 2014) at 27–28.
829. NAFTA, annex 1603.
830. NAFTA, appendix 1603.A.1.
831. NAFTA, annex 1603, s. B.
832. NAFTA, annex 1603, s. B.1.

497. The intra-company transferee category allows managers, executives, or employees with specialized knowledge to transfer to an affiliated company in another NAFTA country, provided they have been employed by an affiliate for at least one full year of the previous three.

498. Finally, NAFTA lists sixty-four professions, each with its own qualifications, entitled to work in one of the three countries, provided they have an employment offer and will be performing professional-level duties.

499. Only citizens of the three signatories are covered by NAFTA; permanent residents are not. Entry under NAFTA requires: (1) proof of citizenship; (2) documentation demonstrating the purpose of entry, including the duties of the business person; and (3) proof that the intended duration of entry is not permanent.[833] NAFTA removes the need for a LMIA for all business persons covered by it. It removes the need for a work permit for business visitors. For professionals and intra-company transferees, it allows for the issuance of a work permit at the port of entry.

500. NAFTA is complementary to the normal immigration regime. American and Mexican business persons are still eligible to apply for entry under the Act through other avenues. It has no effect on permanent residence applications. It also does not affect the general provisions in the Act dealing with temporary workers, inadmissibility criteria, travel and identity documents, or licensing and certification requirements for foreign professionals.

§2. General Agreement on Trade in Services (GATS)

501. Established in 1994 at the conclusion of the Uruguay Round of the General Agreement on Tariffs and Trade, the GATS is a multilateral agreement signed by 148 members of the World Trade Organization, including Canada. Its primary aims include the liberalization of trade in services and the gradual phasing out of government barriers to international competition in the services sector. To this end, GATS provides a framework of principles and rules designed to facilitate the temporary movement of business persons among Member States.

502. 'Trade in services' is defined as the supply of a service from the territory of one member into the territory of another. 'Supply of a service' is defined to include the production, distribution, marketing, sale, and delivery of a service.[834] To facilitate the free flow of such services, GATS permits the facilitated entry to Member States of business visitors, intra-company transferees, and professionals, all of whom are defined in the agreement. Qualified individuals in these three categories can enter Canada more easily because they do not need a LMIA or in the case of business visitors, a work permit.

833. NAFTA, annex 1603, s. A.1.
834. GATS, Art. 1.

503. To gain entry: (1) a foreign national must be a citizen of and resident in a signatory country (the country of citizenship and residence need not be the same); (2) the foreign national must work in either business, communications, construction, distribution, an environment-related industry, finance, tourism and travel, or transport;[835] (3) the foreign national must be seeking temporary entry only; and (4) the foreign national must otherwise comply with all requirements of Canada's immigration legislation.[836]

504. Business visitors and intra-company transferees qualify under the generally applicable immigration provisions contained in the Act and Regulations.[837] GATS creates unique rules for the entry of professionals. These must have their credentials recognized by the relevant Canadian professional association and, in some cases, must have been granted a licence. There are two groups of professionals. Group 1 comprises of engineers, agrologists, architects, forestry professionals, geomatics professionals, and land surveyors. Group 2 comprises foreign legal consultants, urban planners, and senior computer specialists. Professionals under Group 2 are subject to the additional requirement that their Canadian employer be engaged in 'substantive business' – that is, it must not be a shell company established to facilitate entry of foreign workers. Professionals are admitted for a maximum of three months. Specifically excluded are professionals who provide services in the education, health, or recreational, culture, and sport sectors.[838]

835. GATS, Annex on Movement of Natural Persons Supplying Services under the Agreement.
836. Citizenship and Immigration Canada, Operational Manual FW 1, *Temporary Foreign Worker Guidelines* (29 Sep. 2009) at 115–118 (hereinafter 'FW1').
837. Regulations, ss 186(a) and 187; 205(a).
838. FW1 at 115–118.

Part IV. Inadmissibility

505. Canada's first post-confederation Immigration Act, of 1869, contained exclusion provisions, only haphazardly enforced, under which the government could prohibit 'the landing of pauper or destitute Immigrants … until such sums of money as may be found necessary are provided and paid … by the master of the vessel carrying such Immigrants, for their temporary support'.[839] The next Immigration Act, passed three years later in 1872, excluded any 'criminal or other vicious class of immigrants'.[840] These early exclusions, aimed at all prospective newcomers, were soon accompanied by a series of legislative measures specifically targeting immigrants from China and other parts of Asia. Between 1878 and 1908, a series of exclusionary measures were passed in the province of British Columbia. Since the provincial legislature was largely acting outside its authority, many of these were either struck down or disallowed. The federal government, however, responded to anti-Chinese sentiment by enacting a head tax on Chinese immigrants, which rose from CAD 50 in 1885,[841] to CAD 100 in 1900,[842] to CAD 500 in 1903.[843] In 1923, the federal government passed The Chinese Immigration Act, *1923* prohibiting the entry of most Chinese into the country, which remained in force until it became a post-World War II embarrassment in 1947.

506. The head tax on, and later outright prohibition of, Chinese immigration was part of a wide array of direct and indirect regulatory strategies aimed at excluding unwanted races.[844] Other government initiatives included landing-money requirements; attempts to negotiate voluntary restrictions on emigration with governments of origin; and selective criminalization, such as the Opium Act, which targeted use of opium among the Chinese but left non-Chinese pharmacists and doctors free of sanction.[845] Beginning with the Immigration Act, 1906, exclusionary measures were often carried out through the grant of broad discretionary powers of exclusion to the executive.[846] The Minister of the Interior responsible for the 1906 Act explained that its sole purpose was 'to enable the Department of Immigration to deal with undesirable immigrants' by providing new means of control. Under its authorization, the

839. Quoted in Galloway 1997 at 10. See also Kelley and Trebilcock at 63–64.
840. *Ibid.*
841. Chinese Immigration Act, S.C. 1885, c. 71.
842. Chinese Immigration Act, *1900*, S.C. 1900, c. 32, s. 6.
843. Chinese Immigration Act, *1903*, S.C. 1903, c. 8, s. 6.
844. Kelley and Trebilcock at 111.
845. Kelley and Trebilcock at 156.
846. Galloway 1997 at 13.

list of prohibited immigrants was expanded to include the insane, epileptic, deaf and dumb, blind, infirm, those suffering from 'loathsome' contagious diseases, paupers, the destitute, and those convicted of crimes of 'moral turpitude' like prostitution and pimping.[847] The government also created a 'continuous passage rule' by executive order, prohibiting from landing immigrants who had not arrived on a continuous voyage from their countries of origin. This rule effectively barred all immigrants of Asian origin. Later enshrined legislatively, it led to a standoff between a group of 376 Indians who arrived in Vancouver from Hong Kong aboard the steamship *Komagata Maru* in 1914. The passengers were confined to the ship in unsanitary conditions while their legal challenges made their way through the courts. When these failed, two months later, the ship returned to India, where their arrival was met with a riot in which twenty-three of the passengers were killed by police.[848]

507. The country's immigration policies began to shift away from racial bias following World War II. In 1962, the government passed regulations removing racial background as a criterion of selection, except in cases of family reunification. In 1967, the racially neutral, economically focused point system was promulgated and the discrimination built into family-sponsorship rules was eliminated.[849] The 1976 Immigration Act replaced the former, archaic classes of inadmissible persons (such as 'idiots, imbeciles, and morons') with broader prohibitions on individuals liable to endanger public health or security or those likely to place an excessive burden on health and social services. The ban on persons convicted of crimes of moral turpitude was replaced by one on persons convicted of crimes prohibited by Canadian law.[850] In 1992, the government passed amendments that restructured the rules on security and medical inadmissibility. On the first score, it barred entry of persons suspected of having links to terrorist or criminal organizations. On the second, it greatly increased the discretion of medical officers in reviewing cases for medical inadmissibility. The amendments also sought to greatly enhance the government's enforcement powers, expanding search-and-seizure provisions and increasing penalties for smuggling immigrants.[851]

508. The current IRPA and Regulations carry forward these changes. The Act's approach to inadmissibility is guided by the objectives set out in section 3 – 'to protect the health and safety of Canadians and to maintain the security of Canadian society'[852] and 'to promote international justice and security by denying access to Canadian territory to persons, including refugee claimants, who are security risks or serious criminals'.[853] The vertebrae of the inadmissibility regime are sections 33–42 of the Act, which set out the substantive grounds of inadmissibility, including

847. Kelley and Trebilcock at 138.
848. Galloway 1997 at 14. Kelley and Trebilcock at 152–154.
849. Galloway 1997 at 18.
850. Kelley and Trebilcock at 408.
851. Kelley and Trebilcock at 410.
852. IRPA, s. 3(1)(h) and 3(2)(g).
853. IRPA, s. 3(2)(h). See also s. 3(1)(i), which reads: 'to promote international justice and security by fostering respect for human rights and by denying access to Canadian territory to persons who are criminals or security risks'.

grounds related to health, criminality, and security, among others. If found inadmissible on one of these grounds entry to Canada as a foreign national or permanent resident may be refused; temporary or permanent legal status may be lost; or removal from Canada may result. Because of Canada's constitutional and international law commitments, however, enforcement of an inadmissibility decision can be lengthy and complex. Among the commitments that most evidently shape the statutory enforcement mechanisms are the prohibition against deportation to persecution or torture (i.e., non-refoulement); the commitment to ensure that the best interests of children affected by immigration law are attended to; and the duty under the Canadian Charter of Rights and Freedoms to ensure no person in Canada is deprived of their life, freedom, or security of the person except in accordance with the principles of fundamental justice.

509. This part deals with substantive grounds of inadmissibility in Chapter 1 and with the enforcement of these grounds in Chapter 2. As will be clear throughout, many of the enforcement functions under the Act are the jurisdiction of the CBSA, under direction of the Minister of Public Safety.[854] However, references to the 'Minister' and the 'Ministry' continue to be to the Minister of Citizenship and Immigration and CIC. References to the 'ministers' will be used when responsibility for an area is held by both ministers. No attempt is made to distinguish actions taken by CBSA or CIC officers, as their functions often overlap; therefore references in this part to 'officers', unless specified, can be either officers of the Ministry or CBSA.

510. The inadmissibility regime raises several familiar issues. It is riddled with discretion at both the front and back ends of the enforcement process. Immigration or border security officers have the discretion whether or not to write a report recommending someone for inadmissibility and discretion over whether or not to arrest and detain an individual. The two ministers also have discretion to grant certain equitable and non-equitable relief from inadmissibility, such as TRPs; humanitarian and compassionate leave; protection under PRRA applications; and discretionary admission in the 'national interest' of persons otherwise inadmissible for reasons of security, organized criminality, and some types of international crime.

511. Another issue is the danger of prolonged and arbitrary detention. Although the Act provides for a rigorous system of detention review, there is no independent oversight of the detention programme, such as an ombudsman might provide. Detainees are often held for long periods in provincial or municipal jails, which are not designed to for such long-term needs. They are usually held alongside criminal detainees or, for their safety, in segregation units.

512. Most controversial, and dovetailing with general concerns over discretion and detention, is the treatment of security and criminal cases. Two special enforcement tools have proved particularly contentious: the issuance of so-called danger opinions and security certificates. Under security certificates, individuals may be

854. IRPA, s. 4(2).

detained for years and deemed inadmissible without ordinary rights to see and challenge all the evidence against them. Under danger opinions, a person inadmissible on one of several grounds may no longer be protected against refoulement.[855] Such persons may be returned to countries where they face a risk of persecution, torture and other threats to their personal security.

855. IRPA, s. 115(2).

Chapter 1. Inadmissibility and Loss of Residence

513. This chapter outlines the different substantive grounds of inadmissibility in the Act. There are many ways of dividing these up. They may be thought of in terms of those that aim at protecting key Canadian interests, such as the interest in public safety or the interest in preventing drains on the public fisc; those aimed at promoting international justice, for example, by not providing a safe harbour for war criminals or persons who have committed crimes against humanity; and those aimed at preserving the integrity of Canadian immigration policy, by rendering inadmissible those who have failed to comply with the Act or made material misrepresentations. Some of the inadmissibility grounds apply exclusively to foreign nationals. Those that relate to security, criminality, misrepresentation and non-compliance with the Act also apply to permanent residents. Determinations of inadmissibility at the first instance may be made either by an immigration officer or a panel of the ID of the IRB.

§1. Health

514. Section 38(1) of the Act renders inadmissible any foreign national on various health-related grounds:

> 38. (1) A foreign national is inadmissible on health grounds if their health condition:
>
> (a) is likely to be a danger to public health;
> (b) is likely to be a danger to public safety; or
> (c) might reasonably be expected to cause excessive demand on health or social services.

As can be seen from the text of the provision, this ground of inadmissibility is inapplicable to permanent residents. Further, inadmissibility on this ground requires the existence of a current health condition; past health conditions are not relevant.[856] 'Health services' means 'any health services for which the majority of the funds are contributed by governments, including the services of family physicians, medical specialists, nurses, chiropractors and physiotherapists, laboratory services and the supply of pharmaceutical or hospital care'. 'Social services' means 'any social services, such as home care, specialized residence and residential services, special education services, social and vocational rehabilitation services, personal support services and the provision of devices related to those services' that are funded primarily by the government.[857]

515. A medical examination is required for almost all foreign nationals seeking permanent residency and for their family members whether accompanying or

856. Waldman, s. 5.49.
857. Both definitions are found in s. 1 of the Regulations.

not.[858] It is also required for those seeking refugee protection in Canada. Those seeking temporary residence are generally exempted.[859] Those not exempted include foreign nationals coming to Canada to work in an occupation for which protection of public health is essential; foreign nationals seeking or renewing a work or study permit for longer than six months; foreign nationals who have lived or sojourned in an area determined by the Minister, in consultation with the Minister of Health, to have a higher incidence of serious communicable disease than Canada; and all foreign nationals entering Canada who may apply for protection through a PRRA.[860] Further, officers may require any foreign national to undergo a medical examination if there are reasonable grounds for believing they are inadmissible on health-related grounds.[861] Family members of protected persons not included in the person's application to remain in Canada as a permanent resident[862] and non-accompanying family members of foreign nationals applying for refugee protection from outside Canada are exempt.[863]

516. In cases of applicants from abroad or who arrive by land or ferry from the United States, medical examinations are conducted outside Canada. For applicants arriving at airports, temporary entry can be granted conditional on completion of a medical examination to be arranged by an officer. If an applicant appears to be an immediate public health or safety risk, he or she may be detained.[864] Medical examinations must be conducted by Ministry-approved physicians.[865] The results of examinations are reviewed by a medical officer, who provides an opinion on admissibility to the reviewing immigration officer or possibly the ID of the IRB. The immigration officer or ID may be under an obligation to determine the medical officer's decision is reasonable, coherent and understandable.[866]

517. Any concerns raised by the medical officer must be relayed to the foreign national so that he or she has an opportunity to respond.[867] Before concluding that an applicant's health condition might pose a danger to public health in Canada an officer or the ID must consider the communicability of any disease carried by the applicant and the impact the disease would have on others in Canada.[868] Applicants

---

858. The exception is those who are members of the Live-in Caregiver Class who are required to take an examination to become a member of that class. See Regulations s. 30(1) (g).
859. See Regulations, s. 30(1)(a).
860. Regulations, s. 30(1)(a)(i)–(vi).
861. IRPA, s. 16(2)(b) and Regulations, s. 30(a)(iv).
862. Regulations s. 30(1)(e).
863. Regulations, s 30(I)(f).
864. Citizenship and Immigration Canada, ENF 2, *Evaluating Inadmissibility*, s. 8.
865. Citizenship and Immigration Canada, *Medical Requirements* online at: http://www.cic.gc.ca/english/resources/tools/medic/assess/index.asp.
866. Waldman, s. 5.51, citing *Fei v. Canada (Minister of Citizenship and Immigration)*, [1997] F.C.J. No. 950 (T.D.). See also Waldman, s. 5.74–5.80.
867. *Canada (Minister of Citizenship and Immigration) v. Bhagwandass*, (2001) F.C.J. No. 341 (C.A.).
868. Regulations, s. 31.

may be admitted to Canada under 'medical surveillance'; currently, the most common reason for such admissions is tuberculosis.[869] Medical officers might also decide that a person currently inadmissible may become admissible after treatment; in such cases a final decision can be deferred until treatment is administered and a second examination is conducted.[870] In considering the danger to public safety posed by an applicant's medical condition, officers or the ID are to consider the risk of sudden incapacity or of unpredictable or violent behaviour related to the condition.[871]

518. 'Excessive demand' is defined in the Regulations as demand for either health or social services the cost of which exceeds average per capita costs over a five- or ten-year period.[872] Alternately, it may be a demand that would add to existing waiting lists and result in a rise in the rate of mortality and morbidity among permanent residents and citizens.[873] Excessive demand on health services can consist in demand for costly medical care or treatment or care or treatments beset by long waiting lists.[874] Ability to pay for care and treatment available through government-funded health services is not a relevant factor.[875] However, the ability to pay for social services is.[876] In the past, the courts have found that assessment on this ground must vary depending on whether the foreign national is seeking to come to Canada as a temporary or permanent resident[877] and on whether the foreign national is a principal or dependent.[878] In light of the clarity of the current Regulations in defining 'excessive demand', it is not obvious that these principles continue to apply.

519. Section 38(2) of the Act exempts two groups from inadmissibility due to potential excessive demand on health or social services: (1) protected persons or refugee claimants; and (2) spouses, common-law partners and children who are members of the family class. Accompanying family members (i.e., those who are not family-class members) are not exempted, unless they are the spouse, common law partner, dependent child or other prescribed family member of a foreign national falling within one of the two exempted categories.

520. Courts have reviewed negatively decisions by officers in which individuals have been deemed inadmissible due to the mere 'possibility' of excessive demand. As stated by the Supreme Court of Canada in the cases of *Hilewitz* and *De Jong*: 'The threshold is reasonable probability, not remote possibility. It should be more

869. Citizenship and Immigration Canada, *Medical surveillance and notifications* online at http://www.cic.gc.ca/english/resources/tools/medic/surveillance/index.asp.
870. Waldman, s. 5.63.
871. Regulations, s. 33.
872. Regulations, s. 1(1).
873. *Ibid.*
874. *Deol v. Canada (Minister of Citizenship and Immigration)*, (2003) 1 FC 301 (CA).
875. *Ibid.*
876. *Hilewitz v. Minister of Citizenship and Immigration, de Jong v. Minister of Citizenship and Immigration*, 2005 SCC 57, (2005) 2 S.C.R. 706.
877. See *Ahir v. Canada (Minister of Employment and Immigration)*, (1984) 1 F.C. 1098 (C.A.).
878. See *Chu v. Canada (Minister of Citizenship and Immigration)*, (1996) F.C.J. No. 74 (T.D.).

likely than not, based on a family's circumstances, that the contingencies will materialize.'[879] The Supreme Court has emphasized that assessment on this ground must be individualized, since generic assessments based on the classification of different impairments would result in the exclusion of some persons who 'would not cause, or would not reasonably be expected to cause, excessive demands on public funds'.[880] Following *Hilewitz* and *De Jong*, as well as the Federal Court of Appeal decision in *Colaco*,[881] the CIC has instructed officers to consider 'all evidence presented by an applicant, before making a decision of inadmissibility due to excessive demand on social services. Evidence regarding both ability and intent to mitigate the cost of social services in Canada must be considered, if presented'.[882] A medical officer must consider the availability and feasibility of any alternatives to publicly funded social services that individuals plan to pay for themselves. If the planned care would reduce the amount of demand to the point where it is no longer excessive, an immigration officer must then assess whether the applicant has the intent and funds to follow through with the plan.[883]

521. It has been Canadian policy since 1991 that people living with HIV/AIDS do not represent a danger to public health or safety by virtue of their HIV-positive status. Therefore, such persons are generally only excluded on the ground that they might impose excessive demands on health or social services under section 38(1)(c) of the Act.[884] That means inadmissibility decisions based on HIV status will be considered individually, based on the applicant's current health and whether or not they are taking anti-retroviral medication. It also means HIV-positive status will generally not prevent admission of those seeking protected status or those applying as a spouse, common-law partner or dependent child of a Canadian citizen or permanent resident.[885] It does not mean that having HIV/AIDS will necessarily count as a ground of persecution under the Convention refugee definition.

522. The standard medical examination performed on foreign nationals includes HIV screening for all persons over the age of 15 years, as well as children who have received blood or blood products and children with HIV-positive parents. HIV screening is supposed to be accompanied by counselling. Until 2006, all applicants for TRVs had to disclose their HIV status, but such disclosure is no longer required and therefore in general foreign nationals wishing to come as short-term visitors do not need to disclose their HIV status.

---

879. *Ibid.* at para. 58.
880. *Ibid.* at para. 56.
881. *Canada (Minister of Citizenship and Immigration) v. Colaco*, 2007 FCA 282.
882. OB63, available at http://www.cic.gc.ca/english/resources/manuals/bulletins/2008/ob063.asp. Also see *Medical refusals and inadmissibility* online at http://www.cic.gc.ca/english/resources/tools/medic/admiss/index.asp.
883. *Ibid.*
884. See *Singh v. Canada (Minister of Citizenship and Immigration)*, (2000) F.C.J. No. 1297 (T.D.).
885. A very informative description of Canadian admissions policies and HIV/AIDS is found in Canadian HIV/AIDS Legal Network, 'Canada's immigration policy as it affects people living with HIV/AIDS' (May 2009), available online at http://www.aidslaw.ca/publications/publicationsdocEN.php?ref=97.

§2. CRIMINALITY, ORGANIZED CRIMINALITY AND INTERNATIONAL CRIMINALITY

523. Sections 36 and 37 of the Act specify criminality, serious criminality and organized criminality as grounds of inadmissibility. Section 35 deals with individuals guilty of crimes against humanity or war crimes. Inadmissibility under these provisions can have wide-ranging consequences under the Act and Regulations. For example, different kinds of criminality provide the basis for harsher forms of removal.[886] Another example is that serious, organized or international criminality may render a foreign national ineligible to apply for refugee status in Canada.[887] A third is that determinations of inadmissibility on these grounds cannot be appealed to the IAD.[888]

524. For all heads of criminal inadmissibility, the standard of proof is reasonable grounds for belief. This follows from section 33 of the Act, which covers inadmissibility under various security and criminality-related grounds:

> 33. The facts that constitute inadmissibility under sections 34 to 37 include facts arising from omissions and, unless otherwise provided, include facts for which there are reasonable grounds to believe that they have occurred, are occurring or may occur.

The Supreme Court of Canada has held that 'reasonable grounds' for belief 'will exist where there is an objective basis for the belief which is based on compelling and credible information'.[889] The 'reasonable grounds' standard is therefore less demanding than the balance of probabilities. It further follows from section 33 that inadmissibility can be based on failures to act and for criminal acts that may be committed in the future.

525. The legitimacy of exclusion on criminal grounds has been recognized by the Supreme Court of Canada in *Chiarelli*, a case dealing with the deportation of a permanent resident for serious criminality under the 1976 Immigration Act:[890]

> One of the conditions Parliament has imposed on a permanent resident's right to remain in Canada is that he or she not be convicted of an offence for which a term of imprisonment of five years or more may be imposed. This condition represents a legitimate, non-arbitrary choice by Parliament of a situation in which it is not in the public interest to allow a non-citizen to remain in the country. ... In such a situation, there is no breach of fundamental justice in

886. Regulations, s. 229(1)(b), (c), (d) and (e).
887. IRPA, s. 101(1)(f).
888. IRPA, s. 64(1) and (2).
889. *Mugesera v. Canada (Minister of Citizenship and Immigration)*, (2005) 2 SCR 100. See also, *Attorney General of Canada v. Jolly*, [1975] FC 216 (CA) (The reasonable grounds standard connotes 'a *bona fide* belief in a serious possibility based on credible evidence'.).
890. *Canada (Minister of Employment and Immigration) v. Chiarelli*, [1992] 1 S.C.R. 711.

> giving practical effect to the termination of [permanent residents'] right to remain in Canada.[891]

The current Act, according to the Supreme Court, aims even more forcefully at criminal inadmissibility: 'Viewed collectively, the objectives of the [Act] and its provisions concerning permanent residents, communicate a strong desire to treat criminals and security threats less leniently than under the former Act.'[892]

I. Criminality

526. Section 36 deals with criminality and serious criminality.[893] The provisions are complex. Section 36(1) renders both foreigners and permanent residents inadmissible on grounds of serious criminality:

> 36.(1) A permanent resident or a foreign national is inadmissible on grounds of serious criminality for
>
> (a) having been convicted in Canada of an offence under an Act of Parliament punishable by a maximum term of imprisonment of at least 10 years, or of an offence under an Act of Parliament for which a term of imprisonment of more than six months has been imposed;
> (b) having been convicted of an offence outside Canada that, if committed in Canada, would constitute an offence under an Act of Parliament punishable by a maximum term of imprisonment of at least 10 years; or
> (c) committing an act outside Canada that is an offence in the place where it was committed and that, if committed in Canada, would constitute an offence under an Act of Parliament punishable by a maximum term of imprisonment of at least 10 years.

527. Section 36(2) makes foreigners inadmissible on grounds of criminality:

> 36. (2) A foreign national is inadmissible on grounds of criminality for
>
> (a) having been convicted in Canada of an offence under an Act of Parliament punishable by way of indictment, or of two offences under any Act of Parliament not arising out of a single occurrence;
> (b) having been convicted outside Canada of an offence that, if committed in Canada, would constitute an indictable offence under an Act of Parliament,

891. *Ibid.* at 27.
892. *Medovarski v. Canada (Minister of Citizenship and Immigration)* [2005] S.C.R 539, para. 10.
893. *The Faster Removal of Foreign Criminals Act S.C. 2013, c16* introduced a number of changes to inadmissibility on grounds of criminality. While it maintains the definition of serious criminality found in s. 36 for the purpose of determining inadmissibility, it includes a new definition of 'serious criminality' for the purpose of restricting access to the Immigration Appeal Division. For details of the new inadmissibility regime, see, Julie Béchard and Sandra Elgersma, 'Bill C-43: An Act to amend the Immigration and Refugee Protection Act, (Faster Removal of Foreign Criminals Act)', Publication No. 41-1-C43-E, Library of Parliament, Revised 3 Jun. 2012.

or of two offences not arising out of a single occurrence that, if committed in Canada, would constitute offences under an Act of Parliament;

(c) committing an act outside Canada that is an offence in the place where it was committed and that, if committed in Canada, would constitute an indictable offence under an Act of Parliament; or

(d) committing, on entering Canada, an offence under an Act of Parliament prescribed by regulations.

528. These provisions are organized around a distinction in the treatment of permanent residents and foreign nationals. The seven classes of criminality covered are also organized according to place and according to whether or not there was a conviction. Hence, the operative categories of criminal offences are convictions in Canada; convictions outside of Canada; criminal acts outside of Canada for which no conviction followed; and, in the case of non-permanent residents, criminal acts committed on entering Canada.

529. Permanent residents must be guilty of a serious offence to be inadmissible. Convictions inside Canada must be for an offence that carries a maximum sentence of at least ten years or for which a six-month sentence was imposed. Convictions outside Canada must be for offences that in Canada would carry a maximum sentence of at least ten years. Criminal acts outside Canada in which no conviction followed must be offences in the country where committed and must have an equivalent Canadian offence that has a maximum sentence of at least ten years.

530. Permanent residents can be found inadmissible for an act committed outside Canada for which they were not convicted only if the commission of the criminal act has been determined based on a balance of probabilities.[894] This is an exception to the usual standard of reasonable grounds for belief, as provided for in section 33.

531. Foreign nationals are covered by the serious criminality provisions. They are also inadmissible for less serious instances of criminal activity. Inadmissibility follows from any conviction in Canada for an indictable criminal offence or any two offences under any federal statute not arising out of a single occurrence. Inadmissibility can result from conviction abroad for any offence that would be indictable in Canada or any two offences not arising out of a single occurrence that would be an offence under a Canadian federal statute. Foreign nationals can also be excluded for committing an act, without a conviction, that is an offence in the place where it was committed and that in Canada would constitute an indictable offence. Finally, foreign nationals are rendered inadmissible if they commit an offence upon entering Canada under one of five prescribed statutes: (1) the Criminal Code;[895] (2) the

894. IRPA, s. 36(3)(d).
895. Criminal Code, R.S.C., 1985, c. C-46.

Immigration and Refugee Protection Act; (3) the Firearms Act;[896] (4) the Customs Act;[897] and (5) the Controlled Drugs and Substances Act.[898]

532. Although technically not a ground of inadmissibility, refugee claimants may be refused protection on criminality grounds. Under Article 1F(b) of the *1951* Convention Relating to the Status of Refugees, refugee protection is not available to persons who have 'committed a serious non-political crime outside the country of refuge prior to his admission to that country as a refugee'.[899] Exclusion suggests a person otherwise considered a refugee does not deserve international protection; therefore the question of serious criminality, as a formal matter, follows the decision on whether an individual qualifies under the Convention refugee definition.

533. The Act incorporates the Convention's exclusion clauses. It also makes serious and organized criminality grounds for ineligibility for applying to the IRB for inland refugee protection in the first place.[900] Under the heading of serious criminality, ineligibility follows if an individual has been convicted in Canada of an offence that carries a maximum sentence of at least ten years and for which an actual sentence of at least two years was imposed. If the individual was convicted outside Canada, the offence must be equivalent to one that carries a maximum sentence of at least ten years in Canada.

534. Section 36(3)(b) of the Act states that a person will not be deemed inadmissible if he or she has received a record suspension for a Canadian offence under this country's Criminal Records Act.[901] However, recent amendments to this statute have rendered individuals who have been convicted of particular offences (primarily sexual offences) ineligible to seek a record suspension Neither the Act nor the Regulations address the effect of a foreign pardon, although courts have said that officers cannot ignore a valid pardon given in a country if the following three conditions are met: (1) the foreign legal system as a whole must be substantially similar to Canada's; (2) the aim, content and effect of the specific foreign law under which the pardon was granted must be similar to and consistent with Canadian law; and (3) there must be no valid reason not to recognize the effect of that law.[902]

535. Under section 36(3)(c) of the Act, individuals otherwise inadmissible for criminality under sections 36(1)(b) and (c) and 36(2)(b) and (c) may apply to the Minister for a determination that they have been rehabilitated after five years, without subsequent conviction, have passed since completion of an imposed sentence or since commission of the original criminal act.[903] Applications to the Minister of

896. Firearms Act, S.C. 1995, c. 39.
897. Customs Act, R.S.C., 1985, c. 1 (2nd Supp.).
898. Controlled Drugs and Substances Act, S.C. 1996, c. 19.
899. Convention, Article 1F(b), incorporated into IRPA, s. 98. See *Febles, supra* n. 703.
900. IRPA, s. 101(1)(f) and (2).
901. R.S., 1985, c. C-47, ss 3–5.
902. *Canada (Minister of Citizenship and Immigration) v. Saini*, (2002) 1 FC 200 (CA).
903. IRPA, s. 36(3)(c) and Regulations,.s. 17.

Public Safety will usually result in an interview, after which an officer will make a recommendation to the Minister of Public Safety or his or her delegate. The Operational Manual states: 'To approve rehabilitation the decision-maker must be satisfied that it is highly unlikely that the person concerned will become involved in any further criminal activities.'[904] Certain applicants will be deemed rehabilitated without Ministerial approval. There are many technicalities but, broadly stated, the rule is that ten years, without subsequent conviction, must have passed since completion of a sentence for or the commission of no more than one non-serious indictable offence (an offence with a maximum sentence of less than ten years); and five years, without subsequent conviction, since the completion of the sentences for two or more convictions for what would be summary offences in Canada.[905] The exclusion of the rehabilitation option for persons covered by sections 36(1)(a) and 36(2)(a) means that persons convicted of serious or non-serious offences in Canada must apply for a record suspension to overcome their inadmissibility. However, section 18.1 of the Regulations creates an exception for foreign nationals inadmissible solely on the basis of having been convicted of two or more summary offences in Canada. Such persons will no longer be inadmissible once five years has passed since completion of the sentence.[906]

536. Equivalence between foreign and Canadian offences is a necessary part of the inadmissibility analysis for those who have been convicted of or who have committed an offence abroad. This is because 'the policy basis [for criminal exclusions] must surely be the perceived gravity, from a Canadian point of view, of the offence the person has been found to have committed and not the actual consequences of that finding as determined under foreign domestic law'.[907] The terms 'equivalent' or 'equivalence' do not appear in the relevant portions of the Act or Regulations, but these are shorthand for the requirement that there exist Canadian offences to match the foreign ones in order to support a finding of inadmissibility. Courts have interpreted equivalence to mean correspondence between the 'essential elements' or 'essential ingredients' of the Canadian and foreign offences, including defences: '"Essential elements" include all "criteria" for establishing that an offence has occurred, whether those criteria are manifested in "elements" (in the narrow sense) or "defences" in the two sets of laws.'[908] If a foreign offence is broader than its Canadian counterpart or if the scope of the foreign offence is unclear, an officer or the ID can look at the facts of the case to determine whether the individual would have been convicted in Canada.[909] It is not necessary, however, to compare all the general principles of criminal responsibility, such as burden of proof, in the two

904. Citizenship and Immigration Canada, Operational Manual ENF2, *Evaluating Inadmissibility*, s. 14.3.
905. Regulations, s. 18.
906. Regulations, s. 18.1(1) and (2).
907. *Canada (Minister of Employment and Immigration) v. Burgon*, [1991] F.C.J. No. 149 (C.A.).
908. *Li v. Canada (Minister of Citizenship and Immigration)*, (1997) 1 FC 235 (CA). See also *Brannson v. Canada (Minister of Employment and Immigration)*, (1981) 2 F.C. 141 at 152-53 (C.A.), cited in Waldman at s. 5.182.
909. *Ibid.*

legal systems.[910] The onus lies on hearings officers to present evidence of foreign law.[911]

II. Organized Criminality

537. Section 37 of the Act renders inadmissible permanent residents or foreign nationals who belong to a group that engages in organized criminal activity or who themselves engage in organized or transnational criminal activity. The section reads as follows:

> 37. (1) a permanent resident or a foreign national is inadmissible on grounds of organized criminality for
>
> (a) being a member of an organization that is believed on reasonable grounds to be or to have been engaged in activity that is part of a pattern of criminal activity planned and organized by a number of persons acting in concert in furtherance of the commission of an offence punishable under an Act of Parliament by way of indictment, or in furtherance of the commission of an offence outside Canada that, if committed in Canada, would constitute such an offence, or engaging in activity that is part of such a pattern; or
>
> (b) engaging, in the context of transnational crime, in activities such as people smuggling, trafficking in persons or money laundering.

538. Section 37(1)(a) includes two grounds of inadmissibility – membership in a criminal organization or engaging in organized criminality, which need not involve membership.[912] 'Membership' may include those who devote themselves full-time to criminal activity but also those only peripherally involved such as, for example, individuals working for a legitimate company that they know is controlled by a criminal organization;[913] it also encompasses past membership.[914] Also, the provision can be used to cover not just persons intending to commit crimes in Canada, but those whose presence in Canada would strengthen or advance the purposes of a criminal organization.[915] Once again, the 'reasonable grounds' standard from section 33 of the Act applies.

---

910. *Ibid.*
911. *Hill v. Canada (Minister of Employment and Immigration)* (1987), 1 Imm. L.R. (2d) 1, 73 N.R. 315 (Fed. C.A.).
912. *Thanaratnam v. Canada (Minister of Citizenship and Immigration)*, (2005) F.C.J. No. 587 (C.A.) at para. 30.
913. Citizenship and Immigration Canada, Operational Manual ENF2, *Evaluating Inadmissibility*, s. 4.5. Further interpretation of the provision can be found in *Chiau v. Canada (Minister of Citizenship and Immigration)*, (2001) 2 FC 297 (CA) and *Chung v. Canada (Minister of Citizenship and Immigration)* (2014) FC 16.
914. *Sittampalam v. Canada (Minister of Citizenship and Immigration)* (2006) F.C.J. No. 1512 (C.A.).
915. *Chiau*, *supra* n. 913, para. 58.

539. In deciding whether a group is a criminal 'organization' the courts will look for certain identifying characteristics, such as identity, leadership, a loose hierarchy and a basic organizational structure. The assessment must be a flexible one:

> Looseness and informality in the structure of a group should not thwart the purpose of IRPA. It is, therefore, necessary to adopt a rather flexible approach in assessing whether the attributes of a particular group meet the requirements of the IRPA given their varied, changing and clandestine character.[916]

540. The Minister of Public Safety has discretion under the Act to determine whether admission of foreign nationals otherwise covered by this ground 'would not be contrary to the national interest'.[917] This discretion cannot be delegated.[918] Finally, no one is to be deemed inadmissible merely for entering Canada with the assistance of someone engaged in organized criminal activity.[919]

III. International Criminality

541. Section 35(1)(a) of the Act provides for the inadmissibility of permanent residents or foreign nationals who, inside or outside Canada, commit genocide, a crime against humanity, or a war crime as these offences are set out in the Crimes Against Humanity and War Crimes Act.[920] These international crimes are defined in that Act as follows:

- 'Crime against humanity' means murder, extermination, enslavement, deportation, imprisonment, torture, sexual violence, persecution or any other inhumane act or omission that is committed against any civilian population or any identifiable group and that, at the time and in the place of its commission, constitutes a crime against humanity according to customary international law or conventional international law or by virtue of its being criminal according to the general principles of law recognized by the community of nations, whether or not it constitutes a contravention of the law in force at the time and in the place of its commission.
- 'Genocide' means an act or omission committed with intent to destroy, in whole or in part, an identifiable group of persons, as such, that at the time and in the place of its commission, constitutes genocide according to customary international law or conventional international law or by virtue of its being criminal according to the general principles of law recognized by the community of nations, whether or not it constitutes a contravention of the law in force at the time and in the place of its commission.

---

916. *Sittampalam v. Canada (Minister of Citizenship and Immigration)*, (2006) F.C.J. No. 1512 (C.A.) at para. 39.
917. IRPA, s. 42.1
918. IRPA, s. 6(3).
919. IRPA, s. 37(2).
920. S.C., 2000, c. 24. This statute provides for the prosecution of any person in Canada for war crimes or crimes against humanity, no matter where they occurred.

- 'War crime' means an act or omission committed during an armed conflict that, at the time and in the place of its commission, constitutes a war crime according to customary international law or conventional international law applicable to armed conflicts, whether or not it constitutes a contravention of the law in force at the time and in the place of its commission.[921]

Persons who conspire or attempt to commit such crimes; accessories after the fact to such crimes; and persons who counsel in relation to such crimes are also covered by section 35(1)(a).[922] The Federal Court of Appeal has also found that the provision includes persons complicit in such crimes, however, complicity cannot be established by mere membership in a brutal organization.[923] Finally, it covers military commanders or non-military superiors if such international crimes are committed on their watch. Such officials must have failed to exercise effective control over those directly committing the international crime; have known, or been criminally negligent in failing to know, that the crime was being or about to be committed; and subsequently failed to prevent, investigate, or prosecute the offence.[924]

542. Also inadmissible, under section 35(1)(b) of the Act, are senior military or civilian officials in a government that, in the opinion of the Minister of Public Safety, engages or has engaged in terrorism, systematic or gross human rights violations, genocide, a war crime or crimes against humanity.[925] Unlike under section 35(1)(a), designated senior officials of such governments do not have to meet any requirements of control or knowledge. Merely being an official in a designated government is enough.

543. Finally, under section 35(1)(c) international sanctions against a country can provide a basis for the inadmissibility of foreign nationals from that country.[926] This provision does not apply to Canadian permanent residents. Note also that section 35(1)(c) provides the lone exception to the general ineligibility for refugee status faced by persons inadmissible for security and serious, organized, and international

921. *Ibid.* at ss 4(3) and 6(3).
922. *Ibid.* at ss 4(1.1) and 6(1.1).
923. *Zazai v. Canada (Minister of Citizenship and Immigration)*, 2005 FCA 303.
924. Crimes Against Humanity and War Crimes Act, ss 5 and 7.
925. Senior officials include heads of state, cabinet members, senior advisers, military and intelligence leaders, ambassadors and other senior diplomats, and members of the judiciary: Regulations, s. 16. Designated governments include: (1) the Bosnian Serb regime between 27 Mar. 1992 until 10 Oct. 1996; (2) the Siad Barré regime in Somalia between 1969 and 1991: (3) the former military governments in Haiti between 1971 and 1986, and between 1991 and 1994 except the period August–December 1993; (4) the former Marxist regimes of Afghanistan between 1978 and 1992; (5) the governments of Ahmed Hassan Al-Bakr and Saddam Hussein in power since 1968; (6) the government of Rwanda under President Habyarimana between October 1990 and April 1994, as well as the interim government in power between April 1994 and July 1994; (7) the governments of the Federal Republic of Yugoslavia and the Republic of Serbia (Milosevic) between 28 Feb. 1998 and 7 Oct. 2000; (8) the Taliban regime in Afghanistan from 27 Sep. 1996; (9) the government of Ethiopia under Megistu Haile Maraiam from 12 Sep. 1974 to 21 May 1991 See Citizenship and Immigration Canada, Operational Manual ENF2, *Evaluating Inadmissibility*, s. 7.4.13.
926. IRPA, s. 35(1).

criminality. That is, foreign nationals otherwise inadmissible because of section 35(1)(c) are still eligible to make a refugee claim in Canada.

544. In cases covered by section 35(1), the standard of proof is the 'reasonable grounds to believe' standard set out in section 33 of the Act. Recall also that by virtue of section 33, section 35(1) also covers acts that are occurring or that may occur in the future.

545. There are no provisions allowing for admission subsequent to a deemed rehabilitation in such cases. Further, the defence of superior orders is not available to individuals challenging inadmissibility under section 35(1). The only defence that has been recognized by the courts is duress.[927] However, except in cases of individual responsibility covered by section 35(1)(a), foreign nationals may be admitted if they satisfy the Minister of Public Safety that their entry would not be contrary to the national interest.[928] In *Esse*, the Federal Court discussed the factors that must be considered when contemplating such an exemption:

> To obtain a Minister's exception, one would have to demonstrate, if indeed it was consistent with the facts, that notwithstanding his or her position as a deemed senior member or official in the service of a government, that there was no complicity in the objectionable acts of that government. While consideration of a person being a danger to the public in Canada might also be included (although there are other provisions dealing specifically with such matters), surely complicity in the acts of the offending government is the most obvious consideration.[929]

This Ministerial power cannot be delegated.[930]

546. The leading case on inadmissibility for crimes against humanity is the Supreme Court of Canada decision in *Mugesera*. Mr Mugesera had spoken at a rally of 1,000 people in Rwanda in 1992 and his words were found to constitute an incitement to murder, genocide and hatred and a crime against humanity – although these had not actually been committed. (The genocide in Rwanda did not occur until April–July 1994.) The speech led the Rwandan government to issue an arrest warrant for Mr Mugesera, who fled to Spain and then Canada, where he became a permanent resident in 1993. Deportation proceedings against Mr Mugesera began in 1995 and eventually made its way to the Supreme Court of Canada.

547. The Supreme Court held that the following four factors must be made out to support a finding of a crime against humanity:

927. ENF18, s. 7.4.
928. IRPA, s. 42.1.
929. *Esse v. Canada (Minister of Citizenship and Immigration),* (1998) F.C.J. No. 46 (T.D.) at para. 11.
930. IRPA, s. 6(3).

(1) an enumerated proscribed act was committed (this involves showing that the accused committed the criminal act and had the requisite guilty state of mind for the underlying act);
(2) the act was committed as part of a widespread or systematic attack;
(3) the attack was directed against any civilian population or any identifiable group of persons; and
(4) the person committing the proscribed act knew of the attack and knew or took the risk that his or her act comprised a part of that attack.

The first three elements describe the physical criminal act, or *actus reus*. The fourth describes the mental element, or *mens rea*. The 'proscribed acts' suggested by the Court are murder, extermination, enslavement, deportation, persecution or 'any other inhumane act or omission'.[931] Both the physical and mental element of the underlying proscribed act must be made out. The second and third elements of the Court's test in *Mugesera* require an interpretation of the context to see whether the underlying crime was committed as part of a widespread or systematic attack directed against a civilian population or identifiable group.[932] The civilian population or identifiable group must be the primary object of the attack; its members must not be mere collateral victims.[933] Finally, the mental element of a crime against humanity requires that an individual know of the widespread or systematic attack and that his or her actions are part of it or take the risk that they will be part of it. Knowledge, and not intention, is all that is required.[934]

§3. Security

548. Section 34(1) of the Act covers inadmissibility for security reasons, which apply to both permanent residents and foreign nationals:

> 34. (1) A permanent resident or a foreign national is inadmissible on security grounds for
>
> (a) engaging in an act of espionage that is against Canada or that is contrary to Canada's interests;
> (b) engaging in or instigating the subversion by force of any government;
> (b.1) engaging in an act of subversion against a democratic government, institution or process as they are understood in Canada;
> (c) engaging in terrorism;
> (d) being a danger to the security of Canada;
> (e) engaging in acts of violence that would or might endanger the lives or safety of persons in Canada; or

931. *Mugesera, supra* n. 889, at para. 129.
932. *Mugesera, ibid.*, at para. 151. Each aspect of this test receives detailed treatment in *Mugesera*.
933. *Mugesera, ibid.*, at paras 161–162.
934. *Mugesera, ibid.*, at paras 171–74.

(f) being a member of an organization that there are reasonable grounds to believe engages, has engaged or will engage in acts referred to in paragraph (a), (b) (b.1) or (c).

549. 'Espionage' and 'subversion' are not intended to be terms of art. In *Qu*, the Federal Court said: '"Espionage" is simply a method of information gathering – by spying, by acting in a covert way.'[935] And further: '"Subversion" connotes accomplishing change by illicit means or for improper purposes related to an organisation.'[936]

550. The Federal Court of Appeal, also in *Qu*, held that the term 'democratic government, institution or process' from section 34(1)(a) is to be interpreted broadly and does not include simply institutions exercising governmental authority:

> a democratic institution for the purpose of subparagraph 19(1)(f)(i) of the Immigration Act [the corresponding provision under the former Act] consists of a structured group of individuals established in accordance with democratic principles with preset goals and objectives who are engaged in lawful activities in Canada of a political, religious, social or economic nature.
>
> In the case of trade unions, professional associations and political parties, it will be easier to ascertain that their structures, their goals and their activities bring them within the definition of a democratic institution for the purpose of the subparagraph.[937]

551. Neither the Act nor the Regulations define 'terrorism'. The Supreme Court of Canada in *Suresh*[938] has accepted the definition of terrorism found in Article 2(1)(b) of the International Convention for the Suppression of the Financing of Terrorism.[939] This definition refers to:

> Any … act intended to cause death or serious bodily injury to a civilian, or to any other person not taking an active part in the hostilities in a situation of armed conflict, when the purpose of such act, by its nature or context, is to intimidate a population, or to compel a government or an international organization to do or to abstain from doing any act.

Officers must provide adequate reasons for finding that an organization falls within this definition – an obligation that is not satisfied by merely stating a conclusion.[940]

935. *Qu v. Canada (Minister of Citizenship and Immigration)*, (2000) F.C.J. No. 518 (T.D.) at para. 48.
936. *Ibid.* at para. 49.
937. *Qu v. Canada (Minister of Citizenship and Immigration)*, (2001) F.C.J. No. 1945 (C.A.) at paras 50–51. Qu had engaged in espionage in Canada, but IRPA does not require inadmissible activity to take place in Canada.
938. *Suresh, supra* n. 721.
939. GA Res. 54/109, 9 Dec. 1999.
940. *Zarrin v. Canada (Minister of Citizenship and Immigration)*, (2004) F.C.J. No. 323 (F.C.). [See also *Ali v. Canada*, (2004) F.C.J. No. 1416 (F.C.); *Mekonen v. Canada (Minister of Citizenship and Immigration)*, (2007) F.C.J. No. 1469 (F.C.)].

Note that section 83.01 of the Criminal Code now includes an extended definition of terrorism that will almost certainly prove influential in immigration cases.[941]

552. Neither the Act nor the Regulations define what it means to be a 'danger to the security of Canada'. Further, there is no jurisprudence on the meaning of this provision. Lorne Waldman, a leading Canadian immigration practitioner, interprets the phrase as follows:

> in order for a person to be considered a danger to the security of Canada, there must be credible evidence to establish the danger and the danger must be serious, i.e. it must be substantial rather than negligible. However, it is not necessary to demonstrate that the danger is directed against Canada. IF the person poses a danger to another country, this may be sufficient to warrant a conclusion that the person poses a threat to the security of Canada, if the danger to the other country implicates Canada either directly or indirectly. Whether or not this will be the case, however, will depend on the particular circumstances of the case.[942]

The Canadian Security Intelligence Service Act also contains an extended definition of 'threats to the security of Canada' that may be relevant.[943]

553. The Minister of Public Safety oversees security-related inadmissibility and, as in the case of organized criminality and international human rights violations, may decide that admission of an otherwise excludable individual would 'not be contrary to the national interest'.[944] This ministerial power cannot be delegated.[945] In the case of terrorism, the Supreme Court of Canada has interpreted this provision as a clause intended to recognize the admissibility of those innocently involved in terrorist groups.[946]

§4. Other

554. In addition to health, criminality and security, migrants may be inadmissible due to financial reasons, misrepresentation, cessation of refugee status, non-compliance with the Act, or because an accompanying or non-accompanying family member is also inadmissible.

941. This section has been analysed in *R. v. Khajawa* (2010) OJ No. 5471 (OCA).
942. Waldman, s. 5.284.1.
943. Canadian Security Intelligence Service Act, 1985, c. C-23, s. 2.
944. IRPA, s. 4(2) and s. 42.1.
945. IRPA, s. 6(3).
946. See *Suresh*, *supra* n. 721, at para. 110, where the Supreme Court of Canada held that 'In such case, the Minister, exercising her discretion constitutionally, would find that the refugee does not fall within the targeted … class of persons eligible for deportation on national security grounds.'

555. All foreign nationals, apart from protected persons,[947] are inadmissible under section 39 of the Act if they are determined to be, on a balance of probabilities, unable or unwilling to support themselves and their dependents without relying on social assistance. Once again, this ground of inadmissibility does not apply to permanent residents. A determination under this section must take into account all of the foreign national's circumstances, including prospects for future legal employment.[948] There is a disjuncture between this provision and the Regulations exempting sponsors of some family class members from minimum necessary income requirements. Generally, a sponsor is required to meet an income standard, in which case section 39 will not bar admission.[949] However, where the sponsored person is a spouse, common-law partner, conjugal partner or a dependent child, the sponsor is exempt and need not meet an income standard.[950] Nevertheless, this sponsored person may still be inadmissible under section 39.

556. The misrepresentation and non-compliance grounds of inadmissibility are intended to safeguard the integrity of Canada's immigration and refugee regime.[951] A permanent resident or foreign national is inadmissible if he or she misrepresents or withholds material facts that could cause an error in the administration of the Act or if he or she is sponsored by someone deemed inadmissible for misrepresentation (this requires ministerial approval);.[952] Except in cases of close family sponsorships, those found inadmissible for misrepresentation have no right of appeal.[953] Inadmissibility for misrepresentation lasts for two years.[954]

557. The misrepresentation provisions do not apply to refugee claimants or to protected persons, except for those who have had their refugee status vacated by the RPD after a finding that refugee protection was obtained due to misrepresentation or the withholding of material facts.[955] Nor can misrepresentation be used as a ground of inadmissibility for the family members abroad of protected persons who have become permanent residents, provided the family members apply for permanent residence less than a year after the protected person was granted status.[956] However, under section 40.1, a foreign national is inadmissible where it has been determined that their refugee protection has ceased.

947. Regulations, ss 21, 139(3).
948. *Libby v. Canada (Minister of Employment and Immigration)*, (1988) F.C.J. No. 287 (T.D.).
949. Regulations, s. 133(1)(j).
950. Regulations, s. 133(4).
951. Citizenship and Immigration Canada, Operational Manual ENF2, *Evaluating Inadmissibility*, ss 9.1 and 10.1.
952. IRPA, s. 40(1).
953. IRPA, s. 64(3).
954. IRPA, s. 40(2).
955. IRPA, ss 40(1)(c) and 109(1).
956. IRPA, s. 21 and Regulations, s. 176. The only grounds of inadmissibility for such family members abroad of protected persons are security, international criminality, serious criminality, organized criminality and some health-related grounds.

558. A foreign national is inadmissible for an act or omission that directly or indirectly contravenes a provision of the Act or Regulations,[957] for example, by remaining beyond their period of authorized stay, by working or studying without a required permit, or by failing to comply with any lawfully imposed condition.[958] A permanent resident may become inadmissible for failing to comply with any condition imposed under the Regulations or for failing to meet residency obligations.[959] There is no requirement that non-compliance be intentional, however, the Operational Manual directs officers to keep in mind 'the person's character, intent, motivation and other equally important factors that led to the person's contravention of the law' when deciding on an enforcement action.[960]

559. Finally, a foreign national, other than a protected person, is inadmissible if he or she has an inadmissible accompanying family member.[961] In addition, a foreign national may be inadmissible if a non-accompanying family member who is a spouse, common-law partner, dependent child or a dependent grandchild is also inadmissible.[962] Also, an individual will be inadmissible if they are the accompanying family member of an inadmissible person.[963]

957. IRPA, s. 41(a). See also s. 2(2), where it says that references to 'the Act' include the Regulations.
958. Citizenship and Immigration Canada, Operational Manual ENF2, *Evaluating Inadmissibility*, Section 11.
959. IRPA, s. 41(b).
960. Citizenship and Immigration Canada, Operational Manual ENF2, *Evaluating Inadmissibility*, s. 11.1.
961. IRPA, s. 42(a).
962. Regulations, s. 23.
963. IRPA, s. 42(b).

Chapter 2. Legal and Administrative Procedures

560. The substantive inadmissibility provisions described in Chapter 1 may come into play at three different points:

- *In determining visa applications from abroad.* Visa applications contain statutory questions aimed at flagging possible inadmissibility concerns. Applicants may then be investigated and examined further by immigration officers. In most cases of applications for PRVs and in some cases of applications for TRVs, the applicant will be subject to medical screening. Visas will be issued only if the officer determines that the person meets the requirements of the Act and is not inadmissible.[964]
- *In reviewing applications for admission to Canada at ports of entry.* Even non-citizens with a valid visa are subject to further examination when they arrive at the port of entry. If the examining officer decides that the non-citizen has complied with the requirements of the Act and is not otherwise inadmissible, the officer must admit the non-citizen to Canada as a temporary or permanent resident.[965] Officers who believe an individual is inadmissible will in most cases prepare an inadmissibility report under section 44(1) of the Act, which is then referred to a delegate of the Minister of Public Safety. The ministerial delegate must decide to pursue the inadmissibility recommendation or not. If the delegate considers the report well-founded, he or she may, in some cases, order removal or, in others, refer the matter to the ID of the IRB for an inadmissibility hearing. Removal orders may be deportation, exclusion or departure orders, each of which carries different consequences. If a person makes a refugee claim at the port of entry, the officer must determine the claim's eligibility within three days. If eligible, the claim will be referred to the RPD of the IRB.
- *In determining whether a permanent resident or foreign national should be removed from Canada.* Foreign nationals or permanent residents in Canada can also be subject to removal on one of the grounds of inadmissibility enumerated in the Act. Removal is initiated by the preparation of a report under section 44(1) of the Act, which is referred to a delegate of the Minister of Public Safety for further action. Once again, the delegate may decide not to act on the report if it is not well-founded. Otherwise, the delegate may order removal or refer the matter to the ID for an inadmissibility hearing. Persons fighting removal may, sometimes appeal such decisions to the IAD of the IRB and may also seek judicial review in Federal Court. They may also pursue alternative means of avoiding removal, such as by seeking one of several forms of equitable relief available under the Act or by making a refugee claim.

§1. Report

561. For permanent residents or foreign nationals at the port of entry or within Canada, an inadmissibility determination normally begins with an immigration

964. Waldman, s. 5.5–5.15.
965. IRPA, ss 21(1) and 22(1).

officer preparing a report under section 44(1) of the Act, setting out the relevant facts and forwarding it to a delegate of the Minister of Public Safety.[966] This report need not be in writing.[967] The Minister of Public Safety has delegated this power both to officers of the Department of CIC and of the CBSA. CBSA officers handle reports dealing with inadmissibility on grounds of organized criminality, international criminality and security. CIC officers deal with all other cases.[968]

562. The report may be referred to the ID of the IRB. An ID member will determine if the person is inadmissible and, if so, will issue a removal order. The ID must provide reasons, orally or in writing. Written reasons are required if requested by the person subject to the hearing.[969] In cases where a person has lawful status in Canada, the burden is on the government to establish inadmissibility. In all other cases, that is, cases of persons who are seeking to enter Canada or who have entered without authorization, the burden lies with the individual.[970]

563. In simpler cases the report need not be referred to the IRB, and the Minister of Public Safety's delegate will issue one of three kinds of removal orders – deportation, exclusion or departure orders.[971] This order also need not be in writing.[972] Such expedited removal orders for foreign nationals are prescribed, for example, in cases of serious or non-serious criminal offences committed in Canada;[973] cases where the IRB has vacated refugee status obtained through misrepresentation;[974] and cases of unauthorized entry by an individual who has previously been ordered removed from Canada.[975] In all these cases, deportation orders – the removal order with the gravest consequences – are mandated. In other cases, exclusion or departure orders are prescribed.[976] For example, exclusion orders are required if an individual is inadmissible for failing to appear for further examination or an admissibility hearing; failing to establish that they hold a visa or other document required under section 20 of the Act; failing to leave Canada at the end of a period of authorized stay; or failing to comply with any condition imposed as a term of temporary admission.[977] Permanent residents inadmissible for failing to

966. IRPA, s. 44.
967. *Malongi v. Canada (Minister of Citizenship and Immigration)*, (2005) F.C.J. No. 1357 (F.C.) at para. 11.
968. Citizenship and Immigration Canada, Operational Manual ENF6, *Review of Reports under A44(1)*, s. 4.
969. IRPA, s. 169(b), (c), and (e).
970. IRPA, s. 45(d). Citizenship and Immigration Canada, Operational Manual ENF3, *Admissibility Hearings and Detention Review Proceedings*, s. 8.2.
971. For example, where a permanent resident has failed to fulfill the residency obligation or (in cases covered by s. 228 of the Regulations.
972. *Malongi, supra* n. 967.
973. IRPA, s. 36(1)(a) and 36(1)(b).
974. In such cases, the removal order is not to be issued until all court challenges to the decision to vacate have been resolved: Citizenship and Immigration Canada, Operational Manual ENF6, s. 3.9.
975. Regulations, s. 228(1)(a), (b), and (c)(ii).
976. Regulations; see also s. 228(2).
977. Regulations, s. 228(1)(c)(i), (c)(iii), (c)(iv), and (d).

meet their residency obligations under section 28 of the Act are subject to departure orders;[978] all other inadmissibility cases against permanent residents must go before the ID. Any removal orders against refugee claimants are conditional upon rejection of their claim.[979] (The different kinds of removal orders and their consequences are discussed below.)

564. Matching removal orders are supposed to be issued to family members. The officer who prepares the initial report must inform family members that they are the subject of a report and of an admissibility hearing where they have a right to be represented and to make submissions. Family members must receive a hearing before the ID to determine their inadmissibility under section 42 of the Act.[980]

565. Sections 44(1) and 44(2) of the Act both contain discretionary language, stating that an officer 'may' prepare a report or that the Minister of Public Safety's delegate 'may' issue a removal order or refer the report for an inadmissibility hearing before the ID. The Operational Manual instructs that officers must 'always consider allowing the person the opportunity to leave Canada voluntarily' before preparing a report. If voluntary departure is presented as an option, the officer must tell the foreign national why they are believed to be inadmissible, the consequences of being made the subject of an inadmissibility report, and that if they leave voluntarily they will be free to seek entry to Canada once the factor causing inadmissibility has been overcome. Further, they must inform the foreign national of the option of seeking entry under a TRP under section 24(1) of the Act.[981]

566. The extent of discretion afforded in preparing and acting on inadmissibility reports appears to be variable. Case law indicates that for more serious grounds of inadmissibility (i.e., in cases of inadmissibility involving security or various types of criminality), reports must be issued and removal proceedings instituted as there is little or no discretion at all in such cases. Discretion also varies depending on the circumstances and status of the individual involved. For instance, there will be greater leeway not to issue and act on a report if a permanent resident is facing removal.

567. In *Cha*, which dealt with a foreign national student deemed inadmissible due to a single indictment for drunk driving, the Federal Court of Appeal held that there is effectively no discretion under sections 44(1) and (2) when faced with criminal inadmissibility:

> [T]he wording of sections 36 [i.e., criminal inadmissibility] and 44 of the Act and of the applicable sections of the Regulations does not allow immigration officers and Minister's delegates … any room to manoeuvre apart from that expressly carved out in the Act and the Regulations. Immigration officers and

978. Regulations, s. 228(2).The residency requirements are set out in IRPA, s. 28.
979. IRPA, s. 49(2).
980. Regulations, s. 227.
981. Citizenship and Immigration Canada, Operational Manual ENF5, *Writing 44(1) Reports*, s. 8.5.

> Minister's delegates are simply on a fact-finding mission, no more, no less. Particular circumstances of the person, the offence, the conviction and the sentence are beyond their reach. It is their respective responsibility, when they find a person to be inadmissible on grounds of serious or simple criminality, to prepare a report and to act on it.[982]

This holding, however, was strictly confined by the Court of Appeal to removal orders against foreign nationals for criminality:

> The scope of the discretion ... may end up varying depending on the grounds alleged, on whether the person concerned is a permanent resident or a foreign national and on whether the report is referred or not to the Immigration Division. There may be a room for discretion in some cases, and none in others.[983]

568. Mindful of *Cha*, the Operational Manual treats the discretion to prepare and act on inadmissibility reports differently in criminal and non-criminal cases. In non-criminal cases, the Manual instructs officers to consider factors such as: whether the individual is a permanent resident or foreign national; the nature or category of inadmissibility; the length of time and existence of relationships of dependency in Canada; whether the person has a record of contravening immigration legislation; whether the person has been cooperative; special circumstances in the country of removal, such as civil war or major natural disasters; the economic viability and independence of a permanent resident; and so on.[984] Officers are to demur from writing reports where it is likely that 'no removal order will be sought' or where 'the objectives of the Act may or will be achieved without the need to write a formal inadmissibility report'.[985]

569. The Manual's interpretation of the grant of discretion under section 44(1) and (2) for criminal cases is narrower than in non-criminal ones, but not as narrow as *Cha* mandates.[986] In cases of criminality, which is treated in the Manual as a broad category involving all types of criminality and security issues covered by the Act, officers are told that their discretion in deciding whether to prepare a report 'will greatly diminish' – though not to a vanishing point, as suggested by *Cha* with respect to criminality. The Manual instructs officers to consider the individual's prior criminal record, the circumstances surrounding the offence, the sentence imposed, whether the offence involved violence or drugs and whether a decision on

---

982. *Canada (Minister of Public Safety and Emergency Preparedness) v. Cha*, 2006 FCA 126 at para. 35.

983. *Ibid.* at para. 22.

984. Citizenship and Immigration Canada, Operational Manual ENF5, *Writing 44(1) Reports*, s. 8.2.

985. *Ibid.* s. 8.1.

986. This interpretation is in line with an earlier decision by the Federal Court, Trial Division: *Hernandez v. Canada (Minister of Citizenship and Immigration)*, 2005 FC 429, esp. para. 42. *Hernandez* dealt with a permanent resident facing removal in a case of serious criminality. (Citizenship and Immigration Canada, Operational Manual ENF5, *Writing 44(1) Reports*, ss 8.1 and 8.3, ENF6, *Review of Reports under A44(1)*, s. 5.1).

rehabilitation is imminent and likely to be favourable.[987] Further, the Manual instructs officers to keep in mind the wide array of considerations taken into account in non-criminal cases as well.[988] These instructions directly contradict *Cha*, which held that it was an error to look at the 'gravity of the offence' and 'the particular circumstances' of the foreign national and the conviction: 'It is simply not open to the Minister's delegate to indirectly or collaterally go beyond the actual conviction. To do so would ignore Parliament's clearly expressed intent that the breaking of the condition of non-criminality be determinative.'[989]

§2. Arrest

570. Arrests of non-citizens believed to be inadmissible may be made, depending on the circumstances, with or without a warrant on several specific grounds. Arrests may be made either by CBSA officers or by national, provincial or municipal police, although the CBSA largely relies on the police to bring individuals subject to warrants to its attention.[990] All immigration warrants are posted on a Canadian Police Information Centre website so that they can be enforced by police across the country.

571. It is difficult to get full information on the number of warrants issued and arrests made under the Act's authority. As of September 2007, there were about 63,000 people with either enforceable removal orders or outstanding immigration warrants for removal. Of these, 41,000 orders or warrants were for individuals whose whereabouts were unknown.[991]

572. Under section 55(1) of the Act an officer may issue a warrant for the detention and arrest of a foreign national or permanent resident who the officer has reasonable grounds to believe is inadmissible and is either: (1) a danger to the public or (2) unlikely to appear for an examination, and admissibility hearing, or removal from Canada.[992] Under section 55(2) of the Act, an officer may, without warrant, arrest and detain a foreign national, other than a protected person, who the officer has reasonable grounds to believe is inadmissible and is either: (1) a danger to the public, (2) unlikely to appear for future proceedings or (3) unable to establish their identity to the satisfaction of the officer.[993] Finally, as discussed below, individuals named in security certificates may also be arrested with a warrant.[994]

---

987. Citizenship and Immigration Canada, Operational Manual ENF5, *Writing 44(1) Reports*, s. 8.3.
988. *Ibid.*
989. *Cha, supra* n. 124, at para. 39.
990. Report of the Auditor General of Canada to the House of Commons, (Office of the Auditor General of Canada, May 2008), Chapter 7, 'Detention and Removal of Individuals – Canada Border Services Agency' at 15–16 (hereinafter 'Auditor General's Report'); online: http://www.oag-bvg.gc.ca/internet/docs/aud_ch_oag_200805_07_e.pdf.
991. *Ibid.* at 14–15.
992. IRPA, s. 55(1).
993. IRPA, s. 55(2).
994. IRPA, s. 81.

573. The above provisions apply to individuals who are in Canada. Under section 55(3) of the Act, an officer may also detain a foreign national, without warrant, upon entry to Canada: (1) if the officer considers it necessary to do so to finish examining the individual[995] or (2) if the officer has reasonable grounds to suspect the foreign national is inadmissible on grounds of security or international criminality.[996]

§3. Detention

574. Section 55 of the Act also gives CBSA officers authority to detain foreign nationals and permanent residents when they are a public safety or flight risk or if their identity cannot be confirmed. In limited circumstances officers are required to detain. Under section 55(3.1), an officer is required to detain individuals who have been designated under section 20.1(1) ('designated foreign nationals') by reason of their mode of arrival. This provision applies to all those who are 16 years of age or older on the day of arrival and also extends to individuals who have been designated after they have entered Canada.[997] Non-citizens detained under the Act may be held at a provincial or municipal correctional facility or at minimum-security detention centres in Montreal or Toronto. There is also a facility for detentions of less than seventy-two hours in Vancouver.[998] Finally, individuals detained under a security certificate are housed in a dedicated facility in Kingston, Ontario.[999] In 2006–2007, 9,261 detainees were held in CBSA detention centres for a total of 80,610 detention days, an average detention of between eight and nine days. That same year, there were 3,563 detainees – typically higher risk detainees – held in provincial or municipal facilities for a total of 144,105 detention days. The average detention in such facilities was between forty and forty-one days.[1000]

575. In most cases the decision to detain is a discretionary one, guided by the Regulations, the Operational Manual, and the IRB's *Guidelines on Detention.* Despite this regulatory and administrative guidance, a 2008 report of Canada's Auditor General found that detention decisions tend to be inconsistent and reflected, more than anything, the availability of beds in nearby holding facilities.

---

995. The Operational Manual states that detention in such cases 'should never be used for administrative convenience': Citizenship and Immigration Canada ENF20, s. 5.4. Alternatives to detention include temporary admission for further examination under s. 23 of the Act and ss 43 and 45 of the Regulations; in the case of migrants coming from the United States, temporary return under s. 51 of the Regulations; or withdrawal of an application, under s. 42(1) of the Regulations.
996. IRPA, s. 55(3)(a) and (b).
997. For discussion of designation under this section see para. 163
998. Canada Border Services Agency, 'Fact Sheet: Arrests and Detentions' (July 2009), available online: http://www.cbsa-asfc.gc.ca/media/facts-faits/007-eng.html. and Fact Sheet: Overview of the CBSA's Immigration Detentioon Programme (October 2012) available online at http://www.cbsa-asfc.gc.ca/media/facts-faits/121-eng.html. See also Delphine Nakache,The Human and Financial Cost of Detention of Asylum Seekers in Canada (UNHCR, December 2011) available online at http://www.refworld.org/docid/4fafc44c2.html.
999. Auditor General's Report at 11.
1000. Auditor General's Report at 10.

576. The Manual provides high-level principles, such as that 'individuals detained under [the Act] are treated with dignity and respect at all times' and 'people who are detained are informed of their legal rights, are given an opportunity to exercise their rights and are informed of the status of their case'.[1001] Officers are instructed to 'exercise sound judgment' in considering 'all reasonable alternatives before ordering detention of an individual' but also 'the impact of release on the safety of Canadian society'.[1002] The Manual instructs officers to detain individuals who are suspected of being a security risk or of violating international or human rights. The detention period is to be used to complete an officer's investigation into the individual's suspected inadmissibility.[1003]

577. The Regulations are more specific and set out several factors to be taken into account for different grounds of detention. The government considers the enumerated factors non-exhaustive, but that is not a self-evident reading of the legislation, which merely states that 'the factors set out in this Part shall be taken into consideration when assessing whether a person' ought to be detained.[1004] In deciding whether an individual is a flight risk, an officer is to consider, among other factors: (1) whether the person is a fugitive from justice in a foreign jurisdiction, (2) previous avoidance of an examination or an escape or attempted escape from custody, and (3) involvement in people smuggling or trafficking.[1005] In deciding whether an individual is a danger to the Canadian public, the officer is to consider, among other things: (1) whether the individual is associated with a criminal organization or engaged in people smuggling or trafficking, (2) whether the individual has been convicted of a sexual offence or an offence involving violence or weapons, (3) whether the individual has been convicted of a serious drug offence.[1006] Another factor listed is whether the individual is the subject of a ministerial danger opinion (danger opinions are discussed below in section 6.2). However, the mere existence of a danger opinion does not automatically mandate detention.[1007] With respect to individuals who may be a danger to the public, the Manual additionally suggests that officers may take into account violent, threatening or mentally unstable behaviour during an examination. It instructs officers to always detain if they conclude an individual is a danger to the public.[1008]

578. If an officer decides that there are grounds for detention, he or she is further to consider when making a decision about detention or release: (1) the reason for detention, (2) the length of time in detention, (3) the likely length of detention, (4) unexplained delays or lack of diligence by the Ministry, and (5) alternatives to detention.[1009] Alternatives include releasing individuals with an order to appear for

1001. Citizenship and Immigration Canada, ENF20, s. 5.1.
1002. *Ibid.* s. 5.2.
1003. *Ibid.* s. 5.6.
1004. Regulations, s. 244.
1005. Regulations, s. 245(a), (e), and (f).
1006. Regulations, s. 246.
1007. Citizenship and Immigration Canada, Operational Manual ENF20, *Detention*, s. 5.6.
1008. *Ibid.*
1009. Regulations, s. 247.

a proceeding or with a posted bond as a performance guarantee.[1010] In 2004–2005, 2,038 cash bonds were posted; of these, 368 were forfeited. The CBSA successfully located 178 of the forfeiters and removed 146 of them. The remaining 190, eighteen of whom had a criminal past, could not be found.[1011]

579. Section 60 of the Act affirms 'as a principle that a minor child shall be detained only as a measure of last resort, taking into account the other applicable grounds and criteria including the best interests of the child'.[1012] The Regulations set out special factors to take into account when the detention of minors is a possibility. These include: (1) the availability of alternative arrangements with local childcare or child protection services agencies, (2) the anticipated length of detention, (3) the continued risk of control of the children by smugglers or traffickers who may have brought the children to Canada, (4) the type of detention facility available, (5) the availability of facilities that segregate children from non-custodial adults, (6) the availability of educational, recreational, and counselling services.[1013] There is no distinction in either the Act or Regulations between accompanied and unaccompanied minors. The same factors apply to both groups. These provisions are meant to meet Canada's obligations under the United Nations Convention on the Rights of the Child.[1014]

580. The Manual further instructs that detention is to be a last resort for other vulnerable groups, such as elderly persons, pregnant women, persons who are ill, persons who are handicapped and persons with behavioural or mental health problems.[1015]

581. The initial decision to detain must be confirmed by a second officer.[1016] Review by the ID of the IRB must then take place within forty-eight hours following the initial detention.[1017] A further review must take place within the following seven days and then during every subsequent thirty-day period. The detainee must be present at the review hearings.[1018] In practice, no evidence is required at such hearings, which proceed by way of submission only.[1019] However, individuals have the right to present evidence and, in case of dispute, witnesses maybe called.[1020]

1010. Other possible alternatives are listed in ENF20, s. 5.11. These factors are a codification of the Federal Court decision in *Sahin v. Canada*, [1995] 1 F.C. 214.
1011. Auditor General's Report at 12.
1012. IRPA, s. 60.
1013. Regulations, s. 249.
1014. Citizenship and Immigration Canada, ENF20, s. 5.10. Nevertheless, all foreign nationals who are designated under s. 20.1(1) of the Act and who are 16 years of age or older, must be detained. IRPA s. 55(3.1).
1015. *Ibid.* s. 5.13.
1016. IRPA, s. 56.
1017. Notice of detention must be provided to the ID without delay: IRPA, s. 55(4).
1018. IRPA, s. 57. Under s. 9 of the Immigration Division Rules, a party with new facts to present may apply for a new review before expiration of either the seven- or thirty-day period.
1019. Waldman, 12.22.
1020. Waldman, 12.23.

582. The Act requires the ID to order release of the detainee unless it is satisfied that: (1) he or she is a danger to the public, (2) he or she is unlikely to appear for future immigration proceedings, (3) the Minister is taking necessary steps to investigate possible inadmissibility on grounds of security or international criminality, or (4) the Minister is of the opinion that the detainee's identity has not been but may be established and either: (a) the detainee is not cooperating, or (b) the Minister is making reasonable investigative efforts to establish identity.[1021] Note this last ground of review does not allow the ID to examine the reasonableness of the officer's underlying opinion that identity has not been but may be established, a gap in judicial oversight criticized by the United Nations Commission of Human Rights.[1022]

583. The ID is to have recourse to the same factors set out in the Regulations discussed above. The ID may continue detention, release the individual with conditions or release the individual without conditions.[1023] It is guided in its decision-making by the IRB *Guidelines on Detention*, published in 2013.[1024]

584. The Guidelines alert adjudicators to the unconstitutionality of ongoing detention under section 7 of the Canadian Charter of Rights and Freedoms, which provides: 'Everyone has the right to life, liberty and security of the person and the right not to be deprived thereof except in accordance with the principles of fundamental justice.' In *Charkaoui*, a case concerning detention under the security certificate regime, the Supreme Court of Canada affirmed that immigration detention engaged section 7 of the Charter and that compliance with the provision required that the 'overarching principle of fundamental justice' that must be complied with is the principle that 'before the state can detain people for significant periods of time, it must accord them a fair judicial process'.[1025] Further:

> This basic principle has a number of facets. It comprises the right to a *hearing*. It requires that the hearing be *before an independent and impartial magistrate*. It demands a *decision by the magistrate on the facts and the law*. And it entails the *right to know the case put against one*, and the *right to answer that case*. Precisely how these requirements are met will vary with the context. But for s. 7 to be satisfied, each of them must be met in substance.[1026]

585. The Guidelines also cite four principles set out in *Sahin*, a 1997 case of the Federal Court, Trial Division. These are: (1) there is a stronger case for continuing a lengthy detention when an individual is considered a danger to the public; (2) the length of time that a person has already spent in detention and the length of time detention will most likely continue, or the fact that the duration of future detention time cannot be ascertained, are factors which should have a bearing on release; (3)

1021. IRPA, s. 58(1).
1022. E/CN.4/2006/7/Add.2 (5 Dec. 2005), paras 74–75.
1023. IRPA, s. 58(2) and (3).
1024. http://www.irb-cisr.gc.ca/Eng/BoaCom/references/pol/GuiDir/Pages/GuideDir02.aspx.
1025. *Charkaoui v. Canada Minister of Citizenship and Immigration)* 2007 SCC 9 at para. 28.
1026. *Ibid.* para. 29.

unexplained delay and even unexplained lack of diligence should count against the offending party; and (4) the availability, effectiveness and appropriateness of alternatives to detention must be considered.[1027]

586. In principle, indefinite detention may also contravene the right against cruel and unusual treatment or punishment enshrined in section 12 of the Charter. In *Charkaoui*, the Supreme Court wrote that, 'while the [Act] in principle imposes detention only pending deportation, it may in fact permit lengthy and indeterminate detention or lengthy periods subject to onerous release conditions'.[1028] Section 12 of the Charter requires that:

> where a person is detained or is subject to onerous conditions of release for an extended period under immigration law, the detention or the conditions must be accompanied by a meaningful process of on-going review that takes into account the context and circumstances of the individual case. Such persons must have meaningful opportunities to challenge their continued detention or the conditions of their release.[1029]

The Court held that the factors that must be considered in reviewing detention include: (1) the reasons for detention ('The more serious the threat, the greater will be the justification for detention.'); (2) the length of detention, with longer detentions favouring release; (3) the reasons for delay in deportation, such that 'an unexplained lack delay or lack of diligence should count against the offending party'; (4) the anticipated future length of detention, such that longer or potentially indefinite detentions will factor in favour of release; (5) the availability of alternatives to incarceration.[1030] These factors incorporate those set out in section 248 of the Regulations as well as the *Sahin* principles, discussed above.[1031]

§4. Removal

587. There are six ways an inadmissible individual who must leave Canada can do so: through voluntary departure if an officer exercises discretion not to prepare an inadmissibility report; through extradition; or under one of four types of removal orders – exclusion orders, departure orders, deportation orders or security certificates determined to be reasonable by the Federal Court. The nature of the order governing departure affects the right of a foreign national to return freely to Canada. Extradition is not discussed in this volume. Voluntary departures are discussed above. Security certificates are discussed below. The other forms of removal are dealt with in this section.

1027. *Sahin v. Canada (Minister of Citizenship and Immigration)*, (1995) 1 F.C. 214.
1028. *Charkaoui, supra* n. 1025, para. 105.
1029. *Ibid.* para. 107.
1030. *Ibid.* at paras 111–117. See also *Sahin, supra* n. 1027.
1031. Regulations, s. 248.

588. The Act gives authority under section 44(2) to a delegate of the Minister of Public Safety to issue removal orders in relatively simple cases following review of an inadmissibility report prepared by a front-line officer. In more involved cases, the removal order, if any, is issued by the ID of the IRB following an admissibility hearing. Removal orders are to be enforced as soon as possible once they come into force.[1032] In non-refugee cases, removal orders come into force either the day it is made or the day a right of appeal expires or a final determination is made on appeal.[1033] Removal orders against refugee claimants generally include a grace period of seven or fifteen days.[1034] The fifteen-day delay (after a negative decision by the RPD or, where an appeal is available, by the RAD) corresponds to the deadline for filing judicial review of a rejected claim.[1035]

I. Circumstances Leading to Removal Orders

See also paragraphs 693–698.

589. 'Deportation orders' are mandated when an individual is deemed inadmissible for reasons of security, international criminality, serious criminality, non-serious criminality committed outside Canada and organized criminality.[1036] Deportation orders are also issued if someone is stripped of their citizenship on account of misrepresentation, fraud or material omission.[1037] Finally, deportation orders are issued, with some exceptions, to individuals subject to a new removal order on the same grounds as a previous order; to individuals who have failed to comply with any condition or obligation imposed under the Act; and if, in addition to the grounds of inadmissibility that led to an initial removal order, an individual has been convicted of an indictable offence or two summary offences.[1038]

590. 'Exclusion orders' are mandated if someone is found inadmissible on health grounds; for financial reasons; on grounds of misrepresentation, except misrepresentation leading to vacation of a refugee claim or loss of citizenship; for failing to appear for an examination by an officer; if applicable, for failing to show they have come to Canada to establish permanent residence; for failing to establish that they will leave Canada at the end of a period of authorized stay; and for any other failure to comply with the Act.[1039]

1032. IRPA, s. 48(2).
1033. IRPA, s. 49.
1034. IRPA, s. 49(2). Refugee claimants deemed ineligible because they transited through a designated safe-third country (i.e., the United States), are removed forthwith: IRPA, s. 49(2)(a). The seven-day lag applies to all other claims determined to be ineligible: IRPA, s. 49(2)(b).
1035. Sasha Jones & Martin Baglay, *Refugee Law* (Irwin Law, 2007), at 325. See IRPA, s. 72(2)(b).
1036. Regulations, s. 229(1)(a) to (e).
1037. Regulations, s. 229(1)(i). See also IRPA, s. 40(1)(d) and the Citizenship Act, R.S. 1985, c. C-29, s. 10(1)(a).
1038. Regulations, s. 229(3).
1039. Regulations, s. 229(1)(f), (g), (h), (j), (l), (m) and (n).

591. 'Departure orders' will be issued in the case of removal of a permanent resident who has failed to comply with the residency obligations or any other conditions imposed by Regulation.[1040] In addition, if an individual has made a refugee claim, a departure order will be issued in most but not all cases where an exclusion order is otherwise stipulated by Regulation.[1041]

592. Should a simple case have been referred to the ID, the tribunal will issue the same kind of removal order as mandated under section 228 of the Regulations in the case of removal orders issued by a ministerial delegate under section 44(2) of the Act, as discussed in paragraph 540.

II. Effect of Removal Orders

593. Being subject to a removal order carries diverse consequences. A removal order that has come into force strips permanent residents of that status.[1042] Persons subject to removal orders may not make refugee claims.[1043] The most obvious effect, however, is that the individual must leave Canada.

594. In ordinary cases, a removal order comes into force the day it is made or, if an appeal is available, the day the appeal period expires or the day of final determination of the appeal.[1044] In cases where a foreign national is a refugee claimant, the removal order comes into force after the bid for protection has failed through rejection for ineligibility, rejection by the RPD, rejection by the RAD where an appeal is available, withdrawal or abandonment. Unless a claim is deemed ineligible, there is a lag of fifteen days before a removal order against a failed refugee claimant comes into force. In cases of ineligibility, the lag is seven days in most instances and none at all if the person is deemed to have come from a designated safe third country (the United States is the only such country).[1045]

595. Once the order has come into force, and so long as it is not stayed, it becomes enforceable. Foreign nationals subject to the order must then leave Canada immediately and the order must be enforced as soon as possible.[1046] No visas shall be issued to foreign nationals who are the subject of an unenforced removal order.[1047]

596. Departure orders require foreign nationals to leave or be removed from Canada within thirty days. To comply, the foreign national must appear before an

1040. Regulations, s. 229(1)(k).
1041. Regulations, s. 229(2).
1042. IRPA, s. 46(1)(c).
1043. IRPA, s. 99(3).
1044. IRPA, s. 49(1)(a) to (c).
1045. IRPA, s. 49(2).
1046. IRPA, s. 48(2).
1047. Regulations, s. 25.

officer at the port of entry, obtain a certificate of departure, and leave Canada.[1048] Departure orders become deportation orders when departure is not confirmed in this manner within thirty days.[1049] The thirty-day period is suspended if the foreign national is detained after the order's issuance.[1050] If the foreign national meets all the requirements for departure orders, he or she will not need written authorization to return to Canada under section 52(1) of the Act.[1051]

597. Where an exclusion order is issued, an individual must leave Canada as soon as is possible either voluntarily or not. Foreign nationals subject to such orders must seek written authorization to return to Canada during the period of one year after its enforcement, unless the order was issued for misrepresentation, in which case the period is five years.[1052] In addition, if an individual is ordered excluded because they are the accompanying family member of an inadmissible person, written authorization will not be required to return to Canada.[1053]

598. Deportation orders must also be enforced as soon as is possible, either voluntarily or not. Written authorization will always be required to return to Canada after enforcement of a deportation order, except in the case where the foreign national is deported as the accompanying family member of an inadmissible person.[1054]

599. An individual may need to reimburse Canada for the costs of removal carried out at government expense (i.e., if the costs were not paid by a transportation company). The amount owing is CAD 750 for removal to the United States or to the French-held islands of St Pierre and Miquelon, south of the province of Newfoundland, or CAD 1,500 for removal to any other country.[1055] Such fees will be levied during the process of granting written authorization to return, if required. In cases where no authorization is required, the fees are supposed to be paid no later than at the time of entry.[1056]

600. Removal orders may be stayed under the Act, the Regulations, through judicial injunction, or through the imposition of discretionary stays by the Minister of Public Safety.

601. Section 50 of IRPA stays removal orders if: (1) a decision has been made in a judicial proceeding, at which the Minister was given the opportunity to make submissions, that would be contravened by removal; (2) if removal would interfere

1048. Regulations, s. 240(1)(a) to (c).
1049. Regulations, s. 224(2).
1050. Regulations, s. 224(3).
1051. Regulations, s. 224(1).
1052. Regulations, s. 225(1) to (3)
1053. Regulations, s. 225(4).
1054. Regulations, s. 226(1) and (2).
1055. Regulations, s. 243.
1056. Sasha Jones & Martin Baglay, *Refugee Law* (Irwin Law, 2007), at 327.

with a term of imprisonment, including a conditional sentence under which a foreign national is not confined to a penitentiary, jail, or prison; (3) if the IAD has issued a stay or if any competent court has imposed a stay; (4) if a stay has been imposed on the removal of an foreign national inadmissible to Canada on grounds of security, serious criminality, international criminality, or organized criminality pursuant to a PRRA by the Ministry of Citizenship and Immigration; or (5) if the Minister of Public Safety has imposed a stay, which may include ministerial undertakings not to remove foreign national during litigation or in other cases considered on an individual basis.

602. The Operational Manual contains extended discussion of when judicial orders will be considered to be contravened by removal, leading to a stay under section 50(a) of the Act. The provision applies to final and interlocutory decisions made in a properly constituted court at which the Minister of Public Safety was given the opportunity to make submissions. To avoid absurdity, section 50(a) has been held by the Federal Court of Appeal not to apply to probation orders, which are designed to ensure social reintegration of dangerous offenders. Application of section 50(a) in such cases would therefore grant greater protection from deportation to more serious criminals. It would also allow them to remain in Canada under an order intended to smooth their reintegration into Canadian society, only to be removed once the probation order was lifted.[1057]

603. The government is further of the view that section 50(a) of the Act does not apply if a foreign national is required to testify in a criminal proceeding but is not subject to a subpoena; if he or she is due to be examined for the purposes of discovery in a civil lawsuit; or if he or she has been summoned to testify in a proceeding before the RPD.[1058] Section 50(a) will apply in cases where there are pending criminal charges or where a foreign national is subject to a summons or subpoena in a criminal or civil proceeding.[1059] Finally, under section 234 of the Regulations, section 50(a) does not apply if there is an agreement between the CBSA and either the Attorney General of Canada or the attorney general of a province to withdraw any criminal charge, subpoena or summons upon the foreign national's removal from Canada.[1060]

604. The Regulations provide for other stays on removal in sections 230–233, to accommodate various protection-related imperatives.

605. Section 230 of the Regulations provides for temporary stays of removal to so-called moratorium countries where circumstances of generalized danger obtain.

1057. See *Cuskic v. Canada (Minister of Citizenship and Immigration)*, (2001) 2 F.C. 3 (F.C.A.) at para. 25. See also Citizenship and Immigration Canada, ENF10, s. 12.8.
1058. *Ibid.* s. 12.5, 12.9, and 12.12.
1059. *Ibid.* s. 12.4, 12.7, and 12.11.
1060. Regulations, s. 234.

Currently the moratorium countries are Afghanistan, the Democratic Republic of Congo, and Iraq.[1061]

606. Section 231 imposes a stay if an individual has filed an application for leave for judicial review of a negative decision by the RAD. Such stays remain in place until the application for leave is refused or the claimant has exhausted all of his or her avenues of appeal to higher courts. The automatic stay is unavailable; if the person is ineligible to appeal to the RAD[1062] if the person is inadmissible on grounds of serious criminality;[1063] if the person sojourns in either the United States or the French-held islands of St Pierre and Miquelon, south of Newfoundland, and is the subject of an inadmissibility report under section 44(1) of the Act;[1064] or if the individual files an application for an extension on the deadline for applying for judicial review.[1065]

607. Section 232 provides for temporary stays when an individual is notified of his or her eligibility to apply for protection under the PRRA process. Such stays remain in effect until the protection needs of the individual have been finally determined. For example, stays expire when a foreign national informs the Ministry that they do not intend to apply for protection through PRRA; if no application is made during the prescribed period; if PRRA protection is granted, but the foreign national fails to apply for permanent residence within 180 days; or once the person has become a permanent resident and, therefore, no longer subject to removal on the old ground of inadmissibility.[1066]

608. Section 233 imposes a stay when the Minister is of the opinion that it is warranted for humanitarian and compassionate reasons under section 25(1) or section 25.1(1) of the Act or for public policy reasons under section 25.2(1) of the Act. Such a stay remains in effect until a decision on the permanent residence of the foreign national is made.

609. Finally, a foreign national may apply for a court-ordered stay on removal if the Act or Regulations do not impose one automatically. This may be necessary, for example, if the decision challenged on review is the rejection of a PRRA application by the Minister; or a decision that the foreign national is ineligible to apply for refugee protection. Such stays must be honoured under section 50(c) of the Act.

610. The criteria for imposing a judicial stay are threefold and follow the test for interlocutory injunctions laid down by the UK House of Lords in *American*

1061. See Government of Canada, *Temporary suspension of removals lifted for Haiti and Zimbabwe* online at http://news.gc.ca/web/article-en.do?nid=910599. See also fact sheet for nationals of moratoria countries, online at http://ccrweb.ca/documents/infosheetmoratoria.pdf.
1062. Regulations, s. 231(2).
1063. Regulations, s. 231(3)(a).
1064. Regulations, s. 231(3)(b).
1065. Regulations, s. 231(4).
1066. Regulations, s. 232.

Cyanamid.[1067] The foreign national must show: (1) that he or she has raised a serious issue to be tried, (2) that he or she would suffer irreparable harm if no order were granted, and (3) that the balance of convenience considering the total situation of both parties, favours the imposition of a stay.[1068] The threshold for the first part of the test is generally held to be low,[1069] though at the very least there must be some outstanding application under the Act or some issue still to be determined in relation to a foreign national's status as an immigrant or refugee.[1070] As to the second part of the test, the irreparable harm must be either personal, non-speculative harm that a foreign national might experience or the harm to his or her legal case. Harm of the first sort must involve 'some prejudice beyond that which is inherent in the notion of deportation itself'.[1071] Harm of the second arises when there is a concern that a legal challenge will be rendered moot by removal; that is, this part of the test will be met if '[d]e facto, refusal of the injunctive relief decides the whole case against him'.[1072] Determination of the second part of the test will usually dictate the outcome with respect to the third. That is, if irreparable harm is found, the balance of convenience will usually favour the claimant unless there are concerns about public safety or past fraudulent behaviour. If no irreparable harm is found, the balance of convenience will never favour a stay.[1073]

§5. Judicial Reviews, Administrative Reviews and Appeals

611. There are several junctures at which a permanent resident or foreign national can fight removal through administrative appeals and through judicial review.

612. For foreign nationals or permanent residents in Canada, the removal process begins with the decision on the part of an officer to prepare an inadmissibility report under section 44(1) of the Act. It is followed by the decision of a delegate of the Minister of Public Safety under section 44(2) of the Act to pursue removal, if he or she is of the opinion that it is well-founded, on an expedited basis or by referring the case to the ID of the IRB. If the case goes before the ID, that body will hold an inadmissibility hearing. If the ID decides a person is inadmissible, that person may file a motion to reopen the case or may, in some cases, appeal the matter to the IAD. The IAD will either allow the appeal, stay a removal order or confirm the removal order. If the latter, the person may file leave for judicial review before the Federal Court and then leave to appeal to the Federal Court of Appeal and, possibly, the

---

1067. *American Cyanamid Co. v. Ethicon Ltd.*, (1975) A.C. 396.
1068. See *Toth v. Canada (Minister of Employment and Immigration)* (1988), 86 N.R. 302 (F.C.A.).
1069. *Copello v. Canada (Minister of Foreign Affairs)*, (1998) F.C.J. No. 1031 (T.D.) at para. 4.
1070. *Okolo v. Canada (Minister of Citizenship and Immigration)*, (2001) F.C.J. No. 23 (T.D.) at para. 4; cited in Sasha Jones & Martin Baglay, *Refugee Law* (Irwin Law, 2007), at 285.
1071. *Melo v. Canada (Minister of Citizenship and Immigration)*, (2000) F.C.J. No. 403 (T.D.) at para. 21; cited in Sasha Jones & Martin Baglay, *Refugee Law* (Irwin Law, 2007), at 285–286.
1072. *Suresh v. Canada,* (1998) O.J. No. 296 (Ct. Jus.) at para. 25; cited in Sasha Jones & Martin Baglay, *Refugee Law* (Irwin Law, 2007), at 286.
1073. Sasha Jones & Martin Baglay, *Refugee Law* (Irwin Law, 2007), at 286–287.

Supreme Court of Canada. Every other decision for which an appeal is not available may also be subject to judicial review.

613. At the same time, there are several avenues of discretionary or non-discretionary protection that may be sought and that, if successful, would prevent removal in most cases. These include applications for TRPs under section 24(1) of the Act; humanitarian and compassionate applications under section 25(1) of the Act; and, for those facing removal, applications for protection following a PRRA. To an extent, applications for refugee protection may serve as a means of curing less serious grounds of inadmissibility. Once again, rejection of such bids for equitable relief may also be subject to judicial review.

614. For those deemed inadmissible to Canada by a visa officer abroad, in most cases the only recourse is judicial review before the Federal Court. If the non-citizen abroad is a sponsored member of the family class, the sponsoring permanent resident or citizen may appeal the decision to the IAD unless the grounds of inadmissibility pertain to security or serious, international or organized criminality and, unless the sponsored person is a spouse, common-law spouse or dependent child, in cases of misrepresentation. In addition an inadmissible person may be issued a TRP.[1074]

I. Forms of Discretionary Relief

615. The Act provides various forms of discretionary relief that may be invoked by those caught up in the removal process. We have already discussed the limited discretion available to officers not to write or act on an inadmissibility report under section 44(1) and (2) of the Act and the discretion not to detain an individual under section 55 of the Act. Apart from these forms of discretion, there are also generally applicable forms of discretionary relief for foreign nationals through temporary residence permits, humanitarian and compassionate relief and PRRA. These are not administrative appeals, since they do not result in the invalidation of inadmissibility decisions. They may, however, negate the effect of such decisions by allowing the foreign national to stay in Canada as a permanent resident or under temporary status notwithstanding inadmissibility. In each case, negative decisions may be the subject of judicial review before the Federal Court.

616. Section 24(1) of the Act allows for the grant of a TRP for persons otherwise inadmissible and who are seeking to come to Canada or in Canada and subject to a section 44(1) report, reportable for a violation of the Act, or otherwise in breach. Such permits may be valid for up to three years and may be extended for two years. They may also be cancelled any time and will be deemed cancelled upon departure from Canada, unless re-entry is authorized on the permit document. The Operational Manual states: 'Officers should issue permits with caution and only in special

1074. IRPA, ss 63(1) and 64.

circumstances.'[1075] They are instructed to weigh the reasons for inadmissibility against the need for admission.[1076] Persons who remain in Canada under a TRP for three or five years, depending on the initial grounds of their inadmissibility, in compliance with all stipulated conditions will be granted permanent residence.

617. Under section 25(1) of the Act, inadmissible foreigners may also apply for permanent resident status or an exemption from any applicable criterion or obligation under the Act if they can persuade the Minister that such relief 'is justified by humanitarian and compassionate considerations relating to them, taking into account the best interests of a child directly affected'. 'H&C' relief is available only to foreign nationals inside or outside Canada, and not to permanent residents. Designated Foreign Nationals may not request 'H&C' consideration for five years after arrival.[1077] The Minister is also authorized to grant exemptions on public policy grounds.[1078] Temporary stays of removal may be granted while humanitarian and compassionate applications are being considered under section 25(1).[1079]

618. Most foreign nationals facing removal, including those who have never sought refugee status, will be notified of their eligibility to apply for protection through a PRRA. PRRA is in most cases a paper-review process through which foreign nationals may establish that they are entitled to protection from removal to a country because once there they would face either persecution for reasons of race, religion, nationality, membership in a particular social group or political opinion; a risk to their life, a risk of cruel and unusual treatment or punishment, or a threat of torture. Applicants may present 'only new evidence that arose after the rejection [of their refugee claim] or was not reasonably available, or that the applicant could not reasonably have been expected in the circumstances to have presented, at the time of the rejection'.[1080] Removals are stayed in most cases once a PRRA application has been filed, unless made at the port of entry.[1081] For most refugees, positive

1075. Citizenship and Immigration Canada, Operational Manual OP20, *Temporary Resident Permits*, s. 5.7.
1076. See *ibid.* at ss 8–11 for discussion of the factors to be considered under various grounds of inadmissibility.
1077. IRPA s. 25(1.01).
1078. IRPA s. 25.2.
1079. Regulations, s. 233. Note that pursuant to amendments implemented in 2012 and with exceptions for cases involving risk to life in the country of origin due to inadequate medical care or where 'removal would have an adverse effect on the best interests of a child directly affected', there are new restrictions in relation to H&C applications. The new provisions stipulate that the Minister may not examine an H&C application if such an application is already made and is pending; or a claim has been made and is pending before the RPD or the RAD; or less than twelve months have passed since the foreign national's claim for protection was last rejected, determined to be abandoned or withdrawn by the RPD or the RAD. In addition, applications for permanent residence on H&C grounds by 'designated foreign nationals' will not be considered for at least five years after designation. Regulations, s. 25 and s. 25.1.
1080. IRPA, s. 113(a).
1081. Regulations, s. 166. Note that pursuant to amendments implemented in 2012 and subject to a limited, ministerial exemption, unsuccessful refugee claimants as well as anyone who has received a negative PRRA decision within the previous twelve months are not eligible for a PRRA for one

decisions result in eligibility to apply for permanent residence within 180 days,[1082] except in cases where a foreign national is inadmissible or excluded on grounds of security, serious criminality, international criminality, or organized criminality. In such cases, the foreign national benefits only from a temporary stay of removal; this may be re-examined and cancelled if the endangering conditions are deemed no longer to exist.

II. Refugee Protection Division

619. The RPD of the IRB is not an avenue of appeal or a vehicle for seeking equitable relief. However, it may in effect be used to overcome removal for grounds of inadmissibility other than those related to security or criminality concerns, such as financial insufficiency, non-compliance with the Act, or past misrepresentation.

620. Refugee claims can be made in Canada by foreign nationals or permanent residents. Such claims must be made to an officer prior to the issuance of a removal order.[1083] Thus, if a person is facing an admissibility hearing but a removal order has not yet been made, he or she would still have a right to make a refugee claim. Indeed, such a claim may be made to an officer in the course of the hearing.[1084] If a removal order is issued after the claim is made, it will be 'conditional' and comes into force only once a final determination has been made on the refugee claim.[1085]

621. A claim will bc incligiblc for inadmissibility rcasons related to security or serious, international or organized criminality or if there are outstanding criminal charges against the claimant punishable by ten or more years of imprisonment.[1086] If a person is facing an inadmissibility hearing on one of these grounds or is the subject of pending criminal charges, an officer may suspend the eligibility determination until the matter is resolved.[1087] Such inadmissibility or criminal proceedings may also lead to the suspension of a refugee hearing that has already commenced.[1088] Finally, if the claim was determined eligible due to a material misrepresentation, the officer can notify the RPD of that fact; such notification will result in termination of the proceedings and provide an additional ground of inadmissibility.[1089] Barring inadmissibility and ineligibility due to security or criminality concerns, or in the case of misrepresentation on an eligibility determination, a

---

year following a negative RPD decision. Further, failed claimants from 'designated countries of origin' are no longer eligible for PRRA until thirty-six months following a negative RPD decision IRPA, ss 112–114.

1082. As discussed in Part III, amendments to IRPA in 2012 imposed a five-year bar on applications for permanent residence by 'designated foreign nationals' (See, Part III, Ch. 4).

1083. IRPA, s. 99(3).

1084. Waldman, s. 9.40.

1085. IRPA, s. 49(2).

1086. IRPA, s. 101(1)(f) and s. 101(2). The constitutionality of these provisions were upheld in *Nguyen v. Canada (Minister of Employment and Immigration)*, (1993) F.C.J. No. 47 (C.A.).

1087. IRPA, s. 100(2).

1088. IRPA, s. 103(1).

1089. IRPA, s. 104(1)(c) and (2)(a).

successful refugee claimant will become a protected person. He or she may then be granted permanent residence despite inadmissibility concerns on grounds unrelated to criminality or security, with the exception of section 38(1)(a) and (b), which renders inadmissible a person who poses a danger to public health or safety,[1090] although any such person will still be protected from refoulement. In all other cases, and so long as he or she is not already a permanent resident, a successful refugee claimant may be granted permanent residence. Any removal order that has not been enforced becomes void if the foreign national becomes a permanent resident.[1091] Unsuccessful refugee claimants may in most circumstances appeal to the RAD.[1092] Where their appeal is rejected they become subject to enforceable removal orders that had been held in abeyance.

III. Immigration Division

622. This section and the next will deal with administrative reviews concerning inadmissibility and detention before the ID and with appeals before the IAD of the IRB. Both the ID and the IAD are meant to deal with cases quickly, informally, but in keeping with the requirements of procedural fairness and natural justice.[1093] Neither division is bound by traditional common-law rules of evidence. The default rule is that hearings are public, but they may be held in private to protect any person's safety, to safeguard public security, or to preserve the proceeding's fairness. Individuals have a right to be represented by counsel at their own expense.[1094] In the case of a foreign national who has not been authorized to enter Canada, the burden of proof lies with the foreign national. In the case of a foreign national authorized to enter Canada or a permanent resident, the government has the burden of proving inadmissibility.[1095] Reasons, oral or written, must be given for all final decisions.[1096]

623. Under section 86 of the Act, the Minister may apply to the ID or IAD to bar disclosure of certain information or evidence considered potentially injurious to national security or to the safety of any person. The decision to withhold such information or evidence, and on the manner of proceeding if information or evidence is withheld, is to made in the same way as that set out in security-certificate proceedings, described below.[1097] Under section 87, the Minister may also apply for non-disclosure on judicial review of the IAD decision before the Federal Court, which

1090. IRPA, s. 21(2).
1091. IRPA, s. 51.
1092. IRPA s. 110(1). Those who may not appeal are identified in s. 110(2). Included within this group qarethose who have come from a designated country of origin, designated foreign nationals and those whose refugee claim has been found by the RPD to be without credible basis or manifestly unfounded.
1093. IRPA, s. 162(2).
1094. IRPA, s. 167.
1095. IRPA, s. 45(d).
1096. IRPA, s. 169.
1097. IRPA, s. 86.

again may be granted in keeping with the provisions governing security certificates. Judicial review of the initial non-disclosure decision would also be available, on a standard of correctness.[1098] In 2004, the Federal Court of Appeal in *Sogi* found that the non-disclosure provisions were constitutional.[1099] Since then, the Act has been amended to give the Federal Court the power to appoint a special advocate to represent the person subject to the proceedings; the special advocate would have access to the secret information in order to challenge its importance to national security or its relevance, reliability or sufficiency.[1100]

624. Well-founded section 44(1) reports may be referred to the ID for an admissibility hearing. Following a hearing, the ID may either: (1) recognize the right of a Canadian citizen, a registered Indian under the Indian Act,[1101] or a permanent resident to enter Canada; (2) grant permanent resident status or temporary resident status to a foreign national if the foreign national meets the Act's requirements; (3) authorize a permanent resident or foreign national, with conditions, to enter Canada for further examination; or (4) make the applicable removal order against the foreign national or permanent resident.[1102]

625. The ID also handles detention review in most cases within forty-eight hours of the start of detention; seven days after that; and then at thirty-day intervals. The ID will order release unless it is satisfied the detainee is a danger to the public, a flight risk, or that the Minister is taking adequate investigative steps. (Detention review by the ID is discussed above.)

IV. Immigration Appeal Division

626. The IAD performs several review functions, including hearing and determining appeals of removal orders made by the ID or by delegates of the Minister of Public Safety under section 44(2) of the Act;[1103] appeals of refusals of sponsorship applications for permanent residence within the family class;[1104] and appeal of decisions made outside Canada to strip a permanent resident of his or her status based on failure to comply with residency obligations.[1105] In this section, we address only IAD appeals of removal orders.

627. The Minister may appeal a decision of the ID from an admissibility hearing.[1106] Further, a right of appeal of removal orders issued by the ID or an officer is

1098. *Sogi v. Canada (Minister of Citizenship and Immigration)*, 2004 FCA 212.
1099. *Ibid.*
1100. IRPA, s. 87.1.
1101. Indian Act, R.S.C., 1985, c. I-5.
1102. IRPA, s. 45.
1103. IRPA, s. 63(2).
1104. IRPA, s. 63(1).
1105. IRPA, s. 63(4).
1106. IRPA, s. 63(5).

granted to: foreign nationals holding a valid PRV;[1107] permanent residents; and protected persons.[1108] When an inadmissibility decision deals with a member of the family class abroad, the sponsoring citizen or permanent resident also has a right of appeal.[1109] Thus, a first question that must be considered by the IAD to ensure it has jurisdiction is the status of the appellant. Foreign nationals who do not hold PRVs, such as temporary students or workers, have no right of appeal.

628. No appeal may be made in cases where a foreign national or permanent resident – including a protected person[1110] – has been found inadmissible on grounds of security or international, serious or organized criminality. For these purposes, serious criminality is defined to include a crime that has been punished in Canada by a term of imprisonment of at least six months. No appeal may be made in cases of inadmissibility for misrepresentation, unless a foreign national is a sponsoring citizen or permanent resident's spouse, common-law partner or child.[1111]

629. IAD hearings are de novo and are not restricted to a review of the evidence that led to the removal order in the first instance.[1112] The IAD may take into account humanitarian and compassionate considerations in cases involving the family class, but only after first affirming that the foreign national is properly a member of the family class with a sponsor.[1113] The Minister may apply for non-disclosure of sensitive information under section 86 of the Act, as described above.

630. The IAD may allow or dismiss the appeal; it may also issue a stay of a removal order.[1114] It may allow appeals if satisfied that the original decision was wrong in law, fact, or mixed fact and law; if a principle of natural (procedural) justice has not been observed; or on equitable grounds if, 'taking into account the best interests of a child directly affected by the decision, sufficient humanitarian and compassionate considerations warrant special relief in light of all the circumstances of the case'.

631. The humanitarian and compassionate ground of appeal has been cast by the Supreme Court of Canada as a 'discretionary privilege'.[1115] The Court elaborated that:

1107. IRPA, s. 63(2). See, *Zhang*, 2007 FC 593 ('Parliament can hardly be said to have intended that foreign nationals would be able to use visas revoked by Canadian officials in an attempt to fraudulently enter the country, and then rely on those revoked visas as a basis for their appeal rights.').
1108. IRPA, s. 63(3).
1109. IRPA, s. 63(1).
1110. See *Tiky v. Canada (Miister of Citizenship & Immigration)* [2005] F.C.J. No. 782 endorsed on appeal at [2005] F.C.J No. 281.
1111. IRPA, s. 64.
1112. See *Kahlon v. Canada (Minister of Employment and Immigration)*, (1989) 7 Imm. L.R. (2d) 91; 97 N.R. 349 (F.C.A.).
1113. IRPA, s. 65.
1114. IRPA, s. 66.
1115. *Prata v. Minister of Manpower & Immigration,* [1976] 1 S.C.R. 376, at p. 380.

> Not only is it left to the IAD to determine what constitute 'humanitarian and compassionate considerations', but the 'sufficiency' of such considerations in a particular case as well. Section 67(1)(c) calls for a fact-dependent and policy-driven assessment by the IAD itself.[1116]

632. In *Chieu*, the Supreme Court of Canada held that the scope of this equitable jurisdiction should be interpreted broadly to include 'the greatest possible number of factors' faced by an individual upon removal, including hardships faced by an individual upon removal from Canada to a given country.[1117] The Court reaffirmed the soundness of the analysis in *Ribic*, a 1985 case. The following passage is from *Ribic*:

> In each case the Board looks to the same general areas to determine if having regard to all the circumstances of the case, the person should not be removed from Canada. These circumstances include the seriousness of the offence or offences leading to the deportation and the possibility of rehabilitation or in the alternative, the circumstances surrounding the failure to meet the conditions of admission which led to the deportation order. The Board looks to the length of time spent in Canada and the degree to which the appellant is established; family in Canada and the dislocation to that family that deportation of the appellant would cause; the support available for the appellant not only within the family but also within the community and the degree of hardship that would be caused to the appellant by his return to his country of nationality. While the general areas of review are similar in each case the facts are rarely, if ever, identical.[1118]

633. If the IAD allows the appeal, it may substitute its own decision or refer the matter back for reconsideration by the ID or the ministerial delegate.[1119] If a Minister's appeal is successful, the IAD must issue a removal order.[1120] Section 71 of the Act empowers the IAD to reopen an appeal 'on application by a foreign national who has not left Canada under a removal order ... if it is satisfied that it failed to observe a principle of natural justice'.

634. Where warranted by 'the best interests of a child directly affected by the decision' and any other humanitarian and compassionate considerations 'in light of

1116. *Canada (Citizenship and Immigration) v. Khosa*, 2009 SCC 12, [2009] 1 SCR 339 at para. 57.
1117. *Chieu v. Canada (Minister of Citizenship and Immigration)*, (2002) 1 SCR 84. Note that Chieu was decided under the previous *Immigration Act*. Despite changes in wording, *Chieu* and *Ribic* continue to be applied under the new Act. See the Operational Manual, Citizenship and Immigration Canada, ENF 19 – Appeals Before the Immigration Appeal Division (IAD) of the Immigration and Refugee Board (IRB)' (30 Dec. 2005) at ss 8–9. (Hereinafter 'ENF19'.) Note that the manual sets out a separate set of factors for humanitarian and compassionate appeals under family class sponsorships, which include whether allowing the application would allow for reunification of close family members. *Ibid.* at 9.
1118. *Ribic v. Canada (Minister of Employment and Immigration)*, (1985) I.A.B.D. No. 4 (QL).
1119. IRPA, s. 67(1) and (2).
1120. IRPA, s. 67(2).

all the circumstances of the case', the IAD may stay a removal order.[1121] Stays may be reconsidered at any time,[1122] so that, for example, a removal order can be reconsidered after a fixed period of time. Any stay issued in a case involving serious or non-serious criminality will be cancelled automatically if the permanent resident or foreign national is convicted of another serious offence.[1123] When a stay is ordered, several conditions are to be imposed, including that the individual not commit any criminal offences.[1124]

V. Motions to Reopen

635. There are two ways to challenge decisions by an administrative decision maker or tribunal, motions to reopen and judicial reviews. If successful, a motion to reopen may result in a new hearing and decision. However, motions to reopen must overcome the doctrine of *functus officio* and are rarely successful. This doctrine states that a decision maker that has reached a final decision cannot revisit its holding simply because it has changed its mind, made an error within its jurisdiction, or because there has been a change of circumstances. Under case law, situations where a decision can be reopened are: (1) when there has been a 'slip in drawing up the formal judgment', (2) 'where there was an error in expressing the manifest intention of the [tribunal]', or (3) where there has been a failure of natural justice. In addition, section 71 of the Act specifies that the IAD may reopen an appeal 'if it is satisfied that it failed to observe a principle of natural justice'; arguably, this eliminates the other two possible grounds for reopening an appeal before the IAD. The failure of natural justice must be one that 'taints the whole proceeding'.[1125] From this it is evident that motions to reopen have only a small chance of success. Where they do succeed, it is most often because it is found that a claimant was denied an opportunity to be heard because of, for example, failure to give notice of a hearing or faulty oral translation.[1126]

VI. Judicial Review

636. Once administrative appeals under the Act are exhausted, or if there are no administrative appeals available, an individual or the Minister can apply for leave for judicial review before Federal Court.[1127] Judicial review is therefore the only recourse for most decisions under the Act, including inadmissibility determinations

1121. IRPA, s. 67(1)(c).
1122. IAD Rule 26.
1123. IRPA, s. 68(4).
1124. Regulations, s. 251.
1125. *Chandler v. Alberta Association of Architects,* (1989) S.C.J. No. 102 at para. 20. (Cited in Sasha Jones & Martin Baglay, *Refugee Law* (Irwin Law, 2007), at 268).
1126. Sasha Jones & Martin Baglay, *Refugee Law* (Irwin Law, 2007), at 268–269. For a recent discussion of the doctrine of *functus officio* see Gil v. Canada (Minister of Citizenship and Immigration) 2014 FC 370.
1127. IRPA, s. 72(1) and (2)(a).

made by visa officers outside Canada. There is no obligation to seek a motion to reopen before applying for judicial review.

637. An application for leave for judicial review must be filed within specified time limits, with more time given to seek leave for review of decisions made outside Canada.[1128] An applicant must establish that the case raises a 'serious issue', i.e., an 'arguable issue that can only be resolved by a full hearing of the judicial review application'.[1129] Decisions on leave are made summarily on paper review, without personal appearance and cannot be appealed.[1130] If leave is granted, the hearing must be held between thirty and ninety days from the date when leave was granted.[1131] As noted above, only a relatively small proportion of leave applications are granted.

638. In most cases, the enforcement measures being challenged may go forward unless an individual applies for and is granted a stay by the Federal Court.[1132] Stays will sometimes be automatic, as for most unsuccessful refugee claimants seeking judicial review of a negative decision by the RAD.[1133] The Court will not normally entertain a stay request unless an application challenging a decision is pending and removal is imminent.[1134] The test for granting a stay consists of three questions: (1) whether there is a serious issue to be decided on judicial review; (2) whether the applicant will suffer irreparable harm if removed; (3) whether the balance of convenience favours granting a stay.[1135] A decision on a stay application is final and cannot be appealed.[1136]

639. The grounds for allowing an application for judicial review are that the decision-maker: (1) acted without jurisdiction, beyond its jurisdiction, or refused to exercise its jurisdiction, (2) failed to observe a principle of natural (procedural) justice, (3) erred in law in making a decision or an order, (4) based its decision or order on an erroneous finding of fact that was made in a perverse or capricious manner, (5) acted or failed to act by reason of fraud or perjured evidence, or (6) acted in any other way contrary to law.[1137]

1128. IRPA, s. 72(2)(b); see also s. 169(f), which specifies when the period for filing a leave application begins to run.
1129. Citizenship and Immigration Canada, Operational Manual ENF9, *Judicial Reviews*, s. 5.11.
1130. IRPA, s. 72(2)(e).
1131. IRPA, s. 74(b).
1132. IRPA, s. 50(a). None of the automatic stay provisions in the Act or Regulations (s. 50 of the Act and ss 230 and 234 of the Regulations) cover applications for judicial review by non-citizens who are not refugee claimants.
1133. Regulations, s. 231 Amendments introduced in 2012 restrict access to the RAD for several categories of claimant, with no automatic stays for judicial review.
1134. Citizenship and Immigration Canada, Operational Manual ENF9, *Judicial Reviews*, s. 5.25.
1135. *Ibid.*
1136. IRPA, s. 72(2)(e).
1137. Federal Courts Act, R.S.C. 1985, c. F-7, s. 18.1(4).

640. Grounds for review differ from standards of review. And so these provisions should be read alongside Canadian case law in which the courts have developed an approach to administrative review that establishes varying levels of scrutiny (i.e., standards of review) for different kinds of decision. This case law is tortured, to put it mildly. Most recently the Supreme Court of Canada has established that there are only two standards for judicial review of administrative action: the exacting standard of 'correctness' and the more deferential standard of 'reasonableness'.[1138] The reasonableness standard extends deference 'not only to facts and policy but to a tribunal's interpretation of its constitutive statute and related enactments'.[1139] The Supreme Court has further elaborated:

> In judicial review, reasonableness is concerned mostly with the existence of justification, transparency and intelligibility within the decision-making process. But it is also concerned with whether the decision falls within a range of possible, acceptable outcomes which are defensible in respect of the facts and law.[1140]

The Supreme Court has held that deference in particular is owed to reviews of IAD decisions under humanitarian and compassionate appeals under section 67(1)(c) of the Act, which are essentially discretionary.[1141] Other forms of judicial review may attract a different standard. For example, in *Pushpanathan*, the Supreme Court held that decisions by the Convention Refugee Determination Division (since replaced by the RPD) as to exclusion from refugee status under Article 1F(c) of the Convention Relating to the Status of Refugees could be reviewed on a standard of correctness. There the Court reasoned that the question at issue was one of law, pertaining to human rights, in which the tribunal had no particular expertise.[1142]

641. Upon judicial review, the Federal Court a may order the officer or tribunal 'to do any act or thing it has unlawfully failed or refused to do or has unreasonably delayed in doing' or it may:

> declare invalid or unlawful, or quash, set aside or set aside and refer back for determination in accordance with such directions as it considers to be appropriate, prohibit or restrain, a decision, order, act or proceeding of a federal board, commission or other tribunal.[1143]

642. Decisions from the Federal Court to the Federal Court of Appeal only if the trial judge 'certifies that a serious question of general importance is involved and

---

1138. *Dunsmuir v. New Brunswick,* [2008] 1 S.C.R. 190, 2008 SCC 9.

1139. *Canada (Minister of Citizenship and Immigration), supra* n. 1116, para. 25; *Dunsmuir, supra* n. 1138, para. 41. See also *Agraira v. Canada (Minister of Public Safety and Emergency Preparedness),* [2013] S.C.C. 36.

1140. *Dunsmuir, supra* n. 1138, para. 47.

1141. *Canada (Minister of Citizenship and Immigration), supra* n. 1116, para. 58.

1142. *Pushpanathan, supra* n. 706.

1143. Federal Courts Act, s. 18.1(3).

states the question'.[1144] Such a question must be one that is 'determinative of the appeal' but which also 'transcends the interests of the immediate parties to the litigation and contemplates issues of broad significance or general application'.[1145] However, once a question has been certified, the Federal Court of Appeal is not restricted to it. The question merely 'triggers' the appeal: 'The object of the appeal is still the judgment itself, not merely the certified question.'[1146] Further appeal lies to the Supreme Court of Canada, either by leave of the Federal Court of Appeal or the Supreme Court.

§6. Security Certificates and Danger Opinions

643. By far the most controversial aspect of Canada's inadmissibility regime has been its provisions aimed at removing non-citizens who pose security and other kinds of threats to Canada, or individuals with a record of violations of international and human rights. The two key regulatory tools aimed at removal of such persons are security certificates, which designate individuals as high-risk, and Ministerial danger opinions, which render them ineligible to claim refugee protection and deprive them of the right against refoulement to a country where they may face persecution or torture. The two mechanisms work in tandem. Security certificates declare individuals security risks and facilitate their detention pending deportation. Danger opinions may remove the last remaining barriers to deportation in cases where an individual faces a real risk of persecution, torture or other serious mistreatment.

I. Security Certificates

644. The Act contains a security certificate procedure aimed at preventing threats by allowing for the expeditious detention and removal certain high-risk non-citizens.

645. The Minister of Citizenship and Immigration and the Minister of Public Safety may sign a certificate designating a permanent resident or foreign national inadmissible on grounds of security, violating human or international rights, or serious or organized criminality.[1147] The certificate is to be referred to the Federal Court for a review of its reasonableness, at which point all other proceedings involving the named individual, other than detention reviews and PRRA applications, can no longer be commenced or continued until the review is concluded.[1148] If found reasonable by a judge of the Federal Court, the certificate is deemed 'conclusive proof

---

1144. IRPA, s. 74(d).
1145. *Canada (Minister of Citizenship and Immigration) v. Liyanagamage, (1994)* F.C.J. No. 1637 (C.A.). at para. 4; cited in Sasha Jones & Martin Baglay, *Refugee Law* (Irwin Law, 2007), at 287.
1146. *Pushpanathan, supra* n. 706, at para. 25; cited in Sasha Jones & Martin Baglay, *Refugee Law* (Irwin Law, 2007).
1147. IRPA, s. 77.
1148. IRPA, s. 77(3).

that the person named in it is inadmissible and is a removal order that is in force without it being necessary to hold or continue an examination or admissibility hearing'.[1149]

646. Individuals named in judicially approved certificates lose permanent resident or protected (i.e., refugee) status as well as eligibility to apply for refugee protection. However, notwithstanding its designation as a removal order, a security certificate does not automatically lead to physical removal from Canada. Individuals named in security certificates may apply for and receive protection, in the form of a stay of a removal order to a particular country or place, from the Minister pursuant to a PRRA application.[1150] If an individual is removed under a certificate, he or she must obtain written authorization to return to Canada at any time.[1151]

647. Named individuals may be detained upon issuance of a warrant, prior to reasonableness review of the certificate. Security detainees have been held in a special holding centre in Kingston, Ontario, although at the time of writing the facility houses only one person, Mohammed Mahjoub, an Egyptian accused of links to al-Qaeda. A Federal Court judge must commence a detention review within forty-eight hours and then at six-month intervals. Detention review is also available every six months once certificates are held to be reasonable. Detention continues if a judge is satisfied that release would compromise national security, endanger the safety of any person, or that the detainee would not appear for later court appearances or removal proceedings.[1152] The judge may also release the individual on bail, subject to conditions. The Minister of Public Safety may at any time order the person's release so that they can be removed from Canada.[1153]

648. Security certification has been part of Canada's immigration law since 1978. However, considerable controversy has surrounded the procedures for security certification and detention review under the Act since 11 September 2001. The two areas of particular concern are the barring disclosure of information to individuals challenging certification and the possibility of prolonged or indefinite detention.

649. The government has sought to ensure information it considers important to national security interests remains confidential. To that end, under an older scheme since ruled unconstitutional by the Supreme Court of Canada in *Charkaoui*, the government could ask that the Federal Court's reasonableness review be conducted in private and without the named individual, his or her counsel, or any other representative. In addition, the named individual had no right to see any sensitive material that provided the basis for the certificate. The reviewing judge was mandated to provide a summary of the case against him or her, but that summary could not disclose

1149. IRPA, s. 80.
1150. See IRPA ss. 112(3)(d) and 114(1)(b).
1151. Regulations, s. 226(3).
1152. IRPA, s. 82(1)–(5).
1153. IRPA, s. 82.4.

any security-sensitive information and was therefore bound to be incomplete in some cases. The judge's determination was final and no appeal was available.[1154]

650. The original statutory regime conferred different rights on permanent residents and foreign nationals with respect to detention. The ministers could issue warrants for the arrest and detention of permanent residents, who had the right to detention review within forty-eight hours. Arrest and detention of foreign nationals, however, was mandatory upon issuance of a certificate, and detention review was not available until 120 days following reasonableness review of the certificate. Both under the old and new regime, lengthy detention was and is a real possibility. First, individuals may remain in detention for years while challenging their removal. Second, if an individual is found both to be a security risk but also to be in need of protection through a PRRA application, there may be no alternative but to keep him or her in detention. In such cases, the only way of getting individuals out of Canada would be to make them the subject of a danger opinion. (Danger opinions are discussed below in section 6.2.)

651. The Supreme Court found in *Charkaoui* that the old procedures relating to certification and detention review both infringed the right granted by the Canadian Charter of Rights and Freedoms to everyone, including non-citizens,[1155] to 'to life, liberty and security of the person and the right not to be deprived thereof except in accordance with the principles of fundamental justice'.[1156] The Supreme Court held that the:

> the secrecy required by the scheme denies the named person the opportunity to know the case put against him or her, and hence to challenge the government's case. This, in turn, undermines the judge's ability to come to a decision based on all the relevant facts and law.[1157]

It further held that this rights violation could not be justified since there were alternatives that were less rights-intrusive available to the government. The Supreme Court specifically referred to the possibility of appointing 'special counsel' for named individuals.[1158]

652. The Supreme Court also held that the 120-day deferral of detention review for foreign nationals violated the Charter's protection for everyone against arbitrary detention. However, the Court found that the detention scheme did not violate the right against cruel and unusual treatment or punishment; nor did the Court find a violation of equal protection for non-citizens.

1154. The former statutory regime is set out in an appendix to *Charkaoui*, *supra* n. 1025.
1155. *Singh*, *supra* n. 181.
1156. Canadian Charter of Rights and Freedoms, s. 7.
1157. *Charkaoui*, *supra* n. 1025, para. 65.
1158. *Charkaoui*, *supra* n. 1025, para. 86.

653. Following *Charkaoui*, in addition to counsel, named individuals may be represented by a special advocate, appointed by the reviewing judge, whose role is to protect the individual's interest in secret proceedings. The special advocate may challenge the Minister of Public Safety's claim that disclosure of purportedly sensitive information would harm Canada's national security. The special advocate may also challenge the relevance, reliability and sufficiency of any other information that is not disclosed to the named individual and his or her counsel. Once sensitive information is disclosed to special advocates, they may communicate about the proceedings with others, including the individual named on the security certificate, only with the reviewing judge's permission. The named individual him or herself still has access to only a summary of the evidence provided by the reviewing judge 'that enables them to be reasonably informed of the case made by the Minister in the proceeding' but that may exclude sensitive information.[1159] The judge may receive into evidence any evidence that he or she considers reliable or appropriate, even if it would not normally be admissible in a court of law.[1160] The Act also now expressly provides that 'reliable and appropriate evidence does not include information that is believed on reasonable grounds to have been obtained as a result of torture … or cruel, inhuman or degrading treatment or punishment … '.[1161]

654. The new scheme allows for appeals from a determination of reasonableness if the judge at first instance certifies that a serious question of general importance is involved.[1162] In addition, the post-*Charkaoui* scheme subjects both permanent residents and foreign nationals the same detention scheme. In both cases, warrants must be issued and an initial review commenced within forty-eight hours.[1163]

655. The new security certificate regime has continued to raise concerns. The main criticisms expressed are fivefold. First, following disclosure of sensitive information, special advocates can communicate with the named individual only with the permission of the judge. No guidance is given in the legislation as to when such permission should be granted or not. Second, while special advocates will see the secret evidence provided by the Minister to the judge, they cannot seek disclosure of other government records that might be relevant, thus hampering their ability to represent the named individual's interests. Third, there have been concerns about the resources and administrative support that would be made available to special advocates. Fourth, critics continue to complain that named individuals may yet be sent to countries where they face persecution, torture or death.[1164] Finally, the new scheme still allows for the possibility of indefinite detention if deportation is not

1159. IRPA, s. 83(1)(e).
1160. IRPA, s. 83(1)(h).
1161. IRPA, s. 83(1.1).
1162. IRPA, s. 79.
1163. IRPA, ss 81 and 82.
1164. These criticisms are summarized in Penny Becklumb, *Legislative Summary – Bill C-3: An Act to Amend the Immigration and Refugee Protection Act (Certificate and Special Advocate) and to Make a Consequential Amendment to Another Act* (Parliamentary Information and Research Service, 9 Jul. 2008) at 22–24.

possible. However, in 2014, the Supreme Court held that the new scheme was constitutional.[1165]

II. Danger Opinions

656. In addition to security certificates under section 77 of the Act, the Minister may issue danger opinions that remove protection from refoulement. Note that, unlike most of the enforcement mechanisms under the Act, danger opinions are not under the jurisdiction of the Minister of Public Safety.

657. An individual's potential danger to Canada comes into play at several points in the Act. Potential danger is taken into account when weighing equitable applications, such as applications for TRPs, humanitarian and compassionate applications, or PRRA protection applications. Danger to Canada can also be a ground for exclusion from refugee protection, under Article 1F of the 1951 Convention Relating to the Status of Refugees, which is incorporated into the Act.[1166] A danger *opinion*, however, may lift the Act's protection against refoulement. The controversy over danger opinions is intimately related to the controversy over security certificates, as generally a danger opinion is required in order to deport named individuals under such certificates.

658. Section 115 of the Act enshrines the principle of non-refoulement to countries where individuals may face persecution, torture or cruel and unusual punishment.[1167] The Act creates two exceptions to the principle, both of which require a danger opinion. The first exception is for any person 'who is inadmissible on grounds of serious criminality and who constitutes, in the opinion of the Minister, a danger to the public in Canada'.[1168] The second is for any person 'who is inadmissible on grounds of security, violating human or international rights or organized criminality if, in the opinion of the Minister, the person should not be allowed to remain in Canada on the basis of the nature and severity of acts committed or of danger to the security of Canada'.[1169] The concern raised by this provision is that individuals may be deported to countries where they face inhumane treatment. Moreover, the prohibition on deportation to torture under the CAT is absolute, unlike the prohibition against deportation to a country where an individual's life or freedom would be threatened.[1170] The possibility of deportation to face torture, than, seems in contravention of Canada's international obligations.

1165. *Canada (Citizenship and Immigration), supra* n. 1116.
1166. IRPA, s. 98 and Schedule.
1167. IRPA, s. 115(1).
1168. IRPA, s. 115(2)(a).
1169. IRPA, s. 115(2)(b).
1170. Convention against Torture and other Cruel, Inhuman or Degrading Treatment or Punishment, Can. T.S. 1987 No. 36, Art. 3(1); and Convention Relating to the Status of Refugees, Can. T.S. 1969 No. 6, Art. 33(1) and (2).

659. Thus danger opinions may involve three different standards: (1) danger to the public in Canada (section 115(2)(a)), (2) 'the nature and severity of acts committed' (section 115(2)(b), and (3) 'danger to the security of Canada' (section 115(2)(b)).

660. The first and third standards have been the subject of discussion by the Supreme Court of Canada in *Suresh*, a case where a Tamil refugee descent faced deportation to Sri Lanka where there was a risk that he would be tortured.

661. The Court held that the phrase 'danger to the public' is 'clearly … intended to address threats to individuals in Canada, but its application is restricted by requiring that any individual who is declared to be a "danger to the public" have been convicted of a serious offence'.

662. The Court held that the phrase 'danger to the security of Canada' must be given a fair, large and liberal interpretation in accordance with international norms. Any determination under this provision will be 'highly fact-based and political in a general sense'. The danger to security need not be to Canada directly:

> [C]ourts may now conclude that the support of terrorism abroad raises a possibility of adverse repercussions on Canada's security. … There must be a real and direct possibility of adverse effect to Canada. But the threat need not be direct; rather it may be grounded in distant events that indirectly have a real possibility of harming Canadian security.

In cases where refoulement of a refugee is at issue, however, the threat must be 'serious'. The Minister must be able to show evidence that 'reasonably supports' a finding of danger to Canadian security.[1171]

663. In summary, the Court stated:

> These considerations lead us to conclude that a person constitutes a 'danger to the security of Canada' if he or she poses a serious threat to the security of Canada, whether direct or indirect, and bearing in mind the fact that the security of one country is often dependent on the security of other nations. The threat must be 'serious', in the sense that it must be grounded on objectively reasonable suspicion based on evidence and in the sense that the threatened harm must be substantial rather than negligible.
> This definition of 'danger to the security of Canada' does not mean that Canada is unable to deport those who pose a risk to individual Canadians, but not the country. A different provision, the 'danger to the public' provision, allows the government to deport those who pose no danger to the security of the country *per se* — those who pose a danger to Canadians, as opposed to a danger to Canada — provided they have committed a serious crime. Moreover, if a refugee is wanted for crimes in a country that will not torture him or

1171. *Suresh, supra* n. 721, at para. 85.

her on return, the government may be free to extradite him or her to face those charges, whether or not he or she has committed crimes in Canada.[1172]

664. Finally, the Court held that there was 'the possibility that in exceptional circumstances, deportation to face torture might be justified' under the Canadian Charter of Rights and Freedoms. However, the Court held that the constitutional balancing required 'will rarely be struck in favour of expulsion where there is a serious risk of torture. However, as the matter is one of balance, precise prediction is elusive. The ambit of an exceptional discretion to deport to torture, if any, must await future cases'.[1173]

1172. *Ibid.* paras 90–91.
1173. *Ibid.* para. 78.

Part V. Sanctions

665. This part outlines a collection of policies and regulatory strategies unified by the collective aim of ensuring the integrity of Canada's immigration and refugee law regime. Chapter 1 discusses Canada's principal interdiction initiative, a safe third country agreement with the United States. Chapter 2 discusses the forms of removal pursued under the *IRPA* and its Regulations, which are discussed at greater length above in Part IV. Chapter 3 discusses sanctions imposed on employers and transportation companies who contravene the Act. Finally, Chapter 4 discusses Canadian measures against the trafficking and smuggling of persons.

Chapter 1. Interdiction

666. Interdiction is a catch-all term that refers to a variety of governance strategies used to prevent non-citizens from reaching a country's territory, inside which they would have greater procedural and other rights in applying for asylum and fighting inadmissibility. Elsewhere in this Encyclopaedia we discuss many common forms of interdiction, such as carrier sanctions, 'direct backs' for further examinations, and visa requirements. Another major interdiction initiative takes the form of a group of fifty-six 'migration integrity officers' stationed in forty-five international locations, where they work with airlines and foreign immigration and law enforcement officials to ferret out document fraud, illegal migration, and inadmissible persons.[1174] By far the most controversial form of interdiction practised by Canada, though, is the Safe Third Country Agreement with the United States.[1175]

667. Safe third country restrictions in national refugee laws seek to deny asylum seekers the opportunity to make a claim on the basis that they should have requested asylum in a country of transit that also complies with international refugee law. Under such agreements, asylum seekers are sent back to the country of transit without being allowed to make a claim. The UNHCR has endorsed such strategies as a means of apportioning responsibility for refugees. The Canada-United States Safe Third Country Agreement was signed December 2002 and implemented two years later. It is Canada's only such agreement. The immediate impact of the Agreement was to significantly diminish the number of refugee claims made at the Canada-US border, from 8,896 in 2004 to 4,033 in 2005. Of these, 3,254 qualified for one of the Agreement's exceptions, as discussed below; a total of 303 claims were deemed ineligible under the Agreement; 337 were US citizens; the results of the remaining 139 are unknown.[1176]

668. The Act and Regulations provide a legislative framework consonant with the Agreement. Section 101(1)(e) of the Act renders individuals who came to Canada directly or indirectly from a designated country, unless the designated country is their country of nationality or habitual residence, ineligible to apply for refugee status.[1177] Removal orders against such ineligible persons take effect immediately.[1178] Such persons may not apply for protection through a PRRA.[1179] The provision does not apply to persons who seek to enter Canada at a location that

1174. *Fact sheet: Keeping Canada Safe*, http://www.cbsa-asfc.gc.ca/media/facts-faits/055-eng.html.
1175. Agreement between the Government of Canada and the Government of the United States of America for cooperation in the examination of refugee status claims from nationals of third countries, 2002, online: http://www.cic.gc.ca/english/department/laws-policy/safe-third.asp.
1176. CIC, 'A Partnership for Protection: Year One Review', Part IV.C – see http://www.cic.gc.ca/english/department/ laws-policy/partnership/chapter4.asp, last accessed 2 Jun. 2013.
1177. See the Agreement, Art. 4. See also Regulations, s. 159.2, which exempts stateless persons who come directly or indirectly from a designated country that is their country of former habitual residence.
1178. IRPA, s. 49(2)(a).
1179. IRPA, s. 112(2)(b).

is not a port of entry,[1180] at a harbour or ferry landing, and, in most cases, to airport arrivals.[1181] That is, the Safe Third Country Agreement applies almost exclusively to arrivals by land.

669. Section 102(1) of the Act authorizes the government to make regulations governing the referral or ineligibility of refugee claims. This includes the power to designate countries as being in compliance with the non-refoulement provisions of the 1951 Convention Relating to the Status of Refugees and its 1967 Protocol (together, the 'Refugee Convention') and the CAT, as well as the power to make further regulations respecting the circumstances and criteria for the ineligibility of claims made by people who arrive directly or indirectly from such countries. The government must consider four factors set out in section 102(2) of the Act when designating a country. These are: (1) whether the country is a party to the Refugee Convention and to the CAT, (2) the country's policies and practices with respect to these conventions, (3) its human rights record, and (4) whether it is party to an agreement with the Government of Canada for the purpose of sharing responsibility with respect to claims for refugee protection. The government can 'not designate a country if it was not satisfied that the country's policies, practices and record indicate compliance' with the two conventions. It is not required, however, to establish that a designated country complies perfectly with the two conventions.[1182] Under section 159.3 of the Regulations, the United States is the only country designated as a safe country.

670. Section 102(3) of the Act requires that the four factors upon which the designation was based be reviewed on a 'continuing basis'. Article 8(3) of the Agreement also formalizes a monitoring role for UNHCR. Section 159.7 of the Regulations allows the government to unilaterally terminate or suspend the Agreement (or any other safe third country agreement) if it feels the country no longer meets the criteria necessary for designation. Canada conducted a review of the Agreement in 2006 that concluded, with the concurrence of UNHCR, that the designation continued to be appropriate and that the Agreement was being implemented in a manner consistent with international refugee law.[1183]

671. In keeping with the Agreement, the Regulations provide for numerous exceptions to the rule of deflection. Section 159.5 of the Regulations exempts from the Safe Third Country Agreement claimants who have a family member in Canada who is a: (1) citizen, (2) a permanent resident, (3) a protected person, (4) a person

1180. Ports of entry are those designated in Sch. 1 of the Regulations. There are seventy-three, including both airports and land crossings. The effect of the Regulations is to restrict the Safe Third Country Agreement to land crossings from the United States into Canada.

1181. Regulations, s. 159.4(2) contains an exemption for individuals transiting through a Canadian airport to another country in the course of the enforcement of a removal order from the United States.

1182. *Canadian Council for Refugees v. Canada*, 2008 FCA 229, [2009] 3 F.C.R. 136, rev'g *Canadian Council for Refugees v. Canada*, 2007 FC 1262, (2008) 3 F.C.R. 606; leave to appeal to the Supreme Court denied, at para. 76.

1183. See 'Year One Review', *supra* n. 1176.

with a pending refugee claim, (5) a holder of a valid work or study permit, or (6) an unaccompanied minor. Also exempted are holders of various valid travel documents authorizing entry into Canada, such as PRVs or TRVs, as well as individuals who do not need a visa to enter Canada. Finally, individuals are exempted if they are Canadian permanent residents ordered removed from the United States or if they are seeking to re-enter Canada after being refused entry by the United States without having their refugee claim adjudicated there. Those who are exempted from the Agreement are not entitled to appeal a negative decision on a refugee claim to the RAD.

672. Section 159.6 of the Regulations provides a public policy exemption for individuals who have been charged with or convicted of an offence punishable by the death penalty either in the United States or some other country. The government explains this last exemption as consonant with a long-standing 'practice' not to return individuals to countries where they may face the death penalty;[1184] however, it may also be required by the Charter of Rights and Freedoms.[1185]

673. Until July 2009, section 159.6 of the Regulations also included a public policy exemption for nationals of so-called moratorium countries, i.e., generally dangerous countries to which individuals cannot be removed. The exception was repealed because of concerns about large influxes from the United States of moratorium-country nationals, purportedly undermining the effectiveness of the safe third country scheme. In 2008, the government said more than 5,000 moratorium-country nationals made claims at the Canada-US border, almost 4,000 of them from Haiti, up from seven Haitian claimants at the border in 2004. The government claims the exception from the Safe Third Country Agreement is not necessary to protect such individuals from refoulement because of individualized risk assessments under the United States asylum regime and because the United States has its own, albeit different, list of moratorium countries.[1186] The government may be correct that the repeal does not violate its obligations not to refoule under the Refugee Convention or the CAT; one's views on that question depend on one's views of the US asylum regime. The government's rationale for the repeal nonetheless seems at odds with the goals of Canada's moratorium programme. Moratorium countries are so designated because of generalized danger faced by all individuals, even those who do not qualify for refugee status or do not face torture or cruel and unusual treatment or punishment. Following the repeal of the moratorium-country exemption, individuals will face return to countries where Canada has decided they face such a generalized risk. A more consistent course of action would have seen the government lift the moratorium designation for countries that they believed do not pose sufficient generalized risks. Otherwise, the government could have lifted the exemption from the Safe Third Country Agreement for countries that the United States has also placed on its moratorium list. Currently there are two such countries, El Salvador and the Sudan.

1184. Canada Gazette, http://publications.gc.ca/gazette/archives/p2/2004-11-03/pdf/g2-13822.pdf.
1185. See, *United States, supra* n. 645.
1186. Canada Gazette, http://gazette.gc.ca/rp-pr/p2/2009/2009-08-05/html/sor-dors210-eng.html.

674. The Agreement has been subject to extensive criticism in Canada. The issues that have been highlighted as problematic are: (1) the alleged US propensity to allow foreign policy considerations to influence decisions on asylum cases; (2) the US system of expedited removals, which permits the removal of foreign nationals without proper travel documents; (3) the potential for long-term detention of asylum seekers in the United States; (4) the one-year time limitation for filing asylum claims in the United States; (5) the significant differences between the two countries in their interpretation of the refugee definition, particularly with respect to gender-based claims for refugee status; and (6) the lack of appeal mechanism for denials of entry into Canada under the Agreement.[1187]

675. The Agreement has survived a legal challenge directed to the question of whether the government had acted within its jurisdiction in designating the United States as a safe country. The Federal Court of Appeal decided that it had.[1188] In the majority opinion, the Court of Appeal expressly declined to decide a constitutional challenge, having found the challengers had no standing to proceed without a claimant who had actually come to Canada and been turned away.[1189] However, a concurrence suggested that the Canadian Charter of Rights and Freedoms may require a risk assessment, not currently provided, for individual claimants before returning them to the United States:

> Article 33 of [the Refugee Convention] and Article 3 of the CAT proscribe indirect as well as direct *refoulement*. Hence, refugee claimants at the Canadian land border may not be turned back to the United States pursuant to the [Safe Third Country Agreement] Regulations if they can establish that, if returned, they would face a real risk of their removal by the United States to a country where they have a well founded fear of torture, or persecution on a Convention ground. Such a risk assessment must be made in respect of individual claimants, in light of the United States' law and practice at that time as it pertains to them. A denial of access to Canada's refugee determination system would be subject to an application for leave and for judicial review. These propositions would seem to flow inexorably from *Singh v. Minister of Employment and Immigration*, [1985] 1 S.C.R. 177.
>
> Claimants for refugee status at the Canadian land border must already be examined to determine if they are eligible for access to Canada's refugee determination system as falling within one of the categories excluded from the [Agreement]: the presence of a close relative in Canada, for example. … This process could equally well be used to determine whether a person was eligible for a refugee determination in Canada, on the ground that, as a person facing a real risk of *refoulement* if returned to the United States, the Regulations may not validly be applied to her.

1187. Carasco, Emily et al., *Immigration and Refugee Law, Cases, Materials and Commentary* (Emond Montgomery, 2007) at 488.
1188. *Canadian Council for Refugees v. Canada. supra* n. 1182.
1189. *Ibid.* at paras 98–104.

> Of course, adding a risk assessment in some cases may increase the time and resources needed to make a decision on eligibility, even though, until a risk of *refoulement* was established, a full refugee determination would not be required. Nor could a claimant be returned to the United States pending an eligibility determination, unless the United States' authorities provided an assurance that the claimant would not be removed until the eligibility decision had been made. However, I see no viable alternative if refugee claimants are not to be subject to indirect *refoulement* in violation of their Charter rights and IRPA. No doubt guidelines will be developed to assist officers in making these eligibility determinations.[1190]

Thus far, no such guidelines appear to have been put in place.

1190. *Canadian Council for Refugees v. Canada* at paras 123–125. Justice Evans cites the House of Lords decision regarding the Dublin Convention: *Reg. v. Secretary of State for the Home Department, ex. p. Yogathas*, (2002) UKHL 36.

Chapter 2. Expulsion

See also paragraphs 592–610.

676. Expulsion from Canada is carried out by removal order. These are discussed at greater length above. There are three kinds of removal order: departure orders, exclusion orders and deportation orders. All three carry diverse consequences, the most obvious being the requirement that a foreign national leave Canada. In addition, under section 52(1) of the Act, foreign nationals subject to exclusion or deportation orders must obtain written authorization to return to Canada.

677. Removal orders may be issued in simpler cases by a delegate of the Minister of Public Safety and, in more involved cases, by the ID of the IRB. Ordinarily, a removal order comes into force the day it is made or, if an appeal is available, the day the appeal period expires or the day of final determination of the appeal.[1191] Where a foreign national is a refugee claimant, the removal order comes into force after the bid for protection has failed through rejection for ineligibility, rejection by the RPD, withdrawal or abandonment. Unless a claim is deemed ineligible, there is a lag of fifteen days before a removal order against a failed refugee claimant comes into force. In cases of ineligibility, the lag is seven days in most instances and none at all if the person is deemed to have come from a designated safe third country (the United States is the only such country).[1192] Stays may also be imposed to prevent removal temporarily, as when the Federal Court orders a stay during judicial review.

678. Once the order has come into force, and so long as it is not stayed, it becomes enforceable. Except in the case of departure orders, foreign nationals subject to the order must leave Canada immediately and the order must be enforced as soon as practicable.[1193] Visas shall not be issued to foreign nationals who are the subject of an unenforced removal order,[1194] nor can persons subject to removal orders make a refugee claim.[1195]

§1. Departure

679. 'Departure orders' will be issued in the case of removal of a permanent resident who has failed to comply with residency obligations or any other conditions imposed by Regulation.[1196] If an individual has made a refugee claim, a departure order will be issued in most but not all cases where an exclusion order is otherwise

1191. IRPA, s. 49(1)(a) to (c).
1192. IRPA, s. 49(2).
1193. IRPA, s. 48(2).
1194. Regulations, s. 25.
1195. IRPA, s. 99(3).
1196. Regulations, s. 229(1)(k).

stipulated by Regulation.[1197] Departure orders require foreign nationals to leave or be removed from Canada within thirty days. To comply, the foreign national must appear before an officer at a port of entry, obtain a certificate of departure, and leave Canada.[1198] Departure orders become deportation orders when departure is not confirmed in this manner within thirty days.[1199] The thirty-day period is suspended if the foreign national is detained after the order's issuance.[1200] If the foreign national meets all the requirements for departure orders, he or she will not need written authorization to return to Canada under section 52(1) of the Act.[1201]

§2. Exclusion

680. 'Exclusion orders' are mandated if someone is found inadmissible on health grounds; for financial reasons; on grounds of misrepresentation, except misrepresentation leading to vacation of a refugee claim or loss of citizenship (in which case a deportation order will be issued); for failing to appear for an examination by an officer; if applicable, for failing to show they have come to Canada to establish permanent residence; for failing to establish that they will leave Canada at the end of a period of authorized stay; and for any other failure to comply with the Act.[1202] Where an exclusion order is issued, an individual must leave Canada as soon as is reasonably practicable, either voluntarily or not. Foreign nationals subject to such orders must seek written authorization to return to Canada for one year after its enforcement, unless the order was issued for misrepresentation, in which case the period is two years.[1203] If an individual is ordered excluded because they are the accompanying family member of an inadmissible person, written authorization will not be required to return to Canada.[1204]

§3. Deportation

681. 'Deportation orders' are mandated when an individual is deemed inadmissible for reasons of security, international criminality, organized criminality, serious criminality and non-serious criminal offences committed outside Canada or for former refugees whose status was vacated account of misrepresentation.[1205] Deportation orders are also issued if someone is stripped of their citizenship on account of misrepresentation, fraud or material omission.[1206] Finally, deportation orders are

1197. Regulations, s. 229(2).
1198. Regulations, s. 240(1)(a) to (c).
1199. Regulations, s. 224(2).
1200. Regulations, s. 224(3).
1201. Regulations, s. 224(1).
1202. Regulations, s. 229(1)(f), (g), (h), (j), (l), (m) and (n).
1203. Regulations, s. 225(1) to (3).
1204. Regulations, s. 225(4).
1205. Regulations, ss 228(a) and (b); 229(1)(a) to (e).
1206. Regulations, s. 229(1)(i). See also the Act, s. 40(1)(d) and the Citizenship Act, R.S. 1985, c. C-29, s. 10(1)(a).

issued, with some exceptions, to individuals subject to a new removal order on the same grounds as a previous order; to individuals who have failed to comply with any condition or obligation imposed under the Act; and if, in addition to the grounds of inadmissibility that led to an initial removal order, an individual has been convicted of an indictable offence or two summary offences.[1207] Deportation orders must also be enforced as soon as practicable, either voluntarily or not. Written authorization from an officer will always be required to return to Canada after enforcement of a deportation order, except in the case where the foreign national is deported as the accompanying family member of an inadmissible person.[1208]

1207. Regulations, s. 229(3).
1208. Regulations, s. 226(1) and (2).

Chapter 3. Fines and Imprisonment

682. This chapter discusses sanctions imposed on transportation companies and employers who contravene their obligations under the Act, as well as general criminal offences created under the Act.

§1. Carrier Sanctions

683. Under the Act, commercial transportation companies have several obligations, such as ensuring passengers have the correct documentation and refusing to carry them if not.[1209] Prescribed documents include passports and other travel documents, any visa that are required, permanent resident cards, single-journey travel documents issued to refugees selected abroad for resettlement, or travel documents issued to other protected persons.[1210] Where a transport company has reasonable grounds to believe a passenger's identity documents may not be available for inspection upon arrival in Canada, it is authorized by the Act to hold the documents until examination at the port of entry.[1211] This provision is evidently directed at the practice by smugglers of providing individuals with identity documents to board a transport vehicle and then reclaiming them en route, prior to arrival in Canada.

684. Transport companies are also required to: (1) carry from Canada persons who have been directed to leave, ordered removed or allowed to withdraw their application for entry;[1212] (2) provide facilities at ports of entry for examination and holding individuals until they have been examined by CBSA officers;[1213] (3) provide prescribed passenger information, including documentation and reports upon request.[1214] Passenger information is electronically assessed at the National Risk Assessment Centre, which looks at several factors to identify high-risk passengers including past seizures, intelligence information, improper reporting of goods imported, the extent of criminality, and the point of origin of the traveller or goods. Individuals who are electronically flagged are subject for further examination on arrival.

1209. IRPA, s. 148(1)(a). The Act also says that a transporter cannot carry to Canada any person who an officer has directed not be carried. The Operational Manual, however, expressly authorizes officers not to use this power: 'CBSA maintains an advisory role and the decision to deny boarding is the carrier's, and the carrier's alone.' See ENF15 s. 7.2.

1210. Regulations, s. 259.

1211. IRPA, s. 148(1)(b) and Regulations, s. 260.

1212. IRPA, s. 148(1)(f) and Regulations, s. 272.

1213. IRPA, s. 148(1)(e) and Regulations, ss 37, 261, 271 and 272. Operators of airports or an international bridge or tunnel must provide physical facilities in the form of office space, laboratories, etc. Other transporters (such as cargo ships) must provide facilities on board their vessels.

1214. IRPA, s. 148(1)(d) and Regulations, ss 264 (information required upon arrival) and 269 (advanced required in advance). The provision of passenger information is also regulated by the Customs Act and the Passenger Information (Customs) Regulations, SOR/2003-219. Note that transporters can also be required to provide security: Act, s. 148(1)(h) and Regulations, s. 283.

685. Failure to comply with the requirements of the Act can lead to the imposition of fees and, in some cases, to prosecution. Administration fees may be charged if the transport company has carried any of several categories of inadmissible foreign nationals to Canada. No fees are to be charged for the transport of foreign nationals, other than crew members, authorized to enter and remain in Canada on a temporary basis; foreign nationals who leave Canada immediately, voluntarily or pursuant to a removal order; foreign nationals who have refugee travel papers issued by the Minister of Foreign Affairs; and others.[1215] The fee will be CAD 3,200 per foreign national unless a memorandum of understanding between the transport company and the CBSA is in place, in which case fees can range from CAD 3,200 to nothing, depending on past compliance with the memorandum, other administrative costs incurred by the company, and the level of the company's interdiction success.[1216]

686. Transport companies are also liable for removal costs for foreign nationals. This includes all foreign nationals subject to removal orders and some who are not, including those who cannot be examined, those who are directed back to the United States pending completion of a decision on admissibility, and individuals who withdraw their application to enter Canada. It does not include foreign nationals authorized to enter Canada on a temporary basis or those in possession of PRVs or TRVs at the time of their examination.[1217] If an officer has to make other arrangements to remove an individual, the transport company will be charged. Removal costs in all cases include: (1) expenses within or outside Canada for the foreign national's accommodation and transport; (2) accommodation and travel expenses of escorts; (3) applicable fees; (4) cost of meals and incidental expenses; (5) regular and overtime wages for escorts and other accompanying personnel; and (6) costs and expense for interpreters, medical personnel, and other personnel assisting removal.[1218] There is no time limit on liability for removing individuals subject to removal orders.[1219]

687. Transport companies are liable for the medical examination and treatment of foreign nationals who are inadmissible or who are crew members. The company can avoid such costs by establishing that the foreign national holds PRVs or TRVs and that their health condition is not the result of the company's negligence. Also, companies will not have to pay if the foreign national's medical costs are otherwise covered. In all other cases, any medical costs incurred by the foreign national are payable by the company. Further, upon request the company may be required to arrange for medical examination and treatment.[1220] Such liability also continues for as long as the foreign national requires medical care and has not been authorized to enter Canada.[1221]

1215. Regulations, s. 279(2).
1216. Regulations, s. 280, read together with ENF15 at 9 (s. 9.4).
1217. Regulations, s. 277.
1218. Regulations, s. 278.
1219. ENF15, s. 11.2.1.
1220. IRPA, s. 148(1)(c) and Regulations, s. 263.
1221. ENF15, s. 12.2.

688. Transport companies may be required to post security. Security may relate to specific foreign nationals or may be a general deposit from which required fees may be deducted. Deposits for ship owners, operators and agents in specific cases are CAD 25,000 per foreign national, which covers the administration fee and estimated costs of removal. Smaller or larger amounts can be required depending on the circumstances of individual cases. Most airlines are required to deposit general security under the terms of a memorandum of understanding with the CBSA. The minimum amount of general security is CAD 30,000, but it may be higher, depending on such factors as the frequency of the carrier's arrivals in Canada, the number of passengers with each transport, whether the carrier has brought inadmissible foreign nationals to Canada before, and the anticipated risk of it doing so again.[1222] Overland transportation companies may be required to post security in individual cases.[1223]

689. If a transport company fails to provide security when ordered to do so or fails to pay any other fees or costs for which it is liable, it is subject to two possible enforcement actions. First, the company's vehicles or other assets (other than land, a building or a transportation facility) may be subject to seizure, detention, or forfeiture.[1224] Vehicle detention is the preferred enforcement mode. It is enforced by notifying the Canadian Coast Guard, local port authorities or airport control towers of the order.[1225] Second, if the company has no vehicles or assets in Canada that can be seized, detained, or forfeited, the CBSA can file a certificate in Federal Court, at which point the debt becomes recoverable in the same manner as any court judgment. In practice, this usually means seizure of the amount payable from the company's bank account.[1226]

§2. Employer Sanctions

690. The Act provides for a fine of up to CAD 50,000 or imprisonment for up to two years for anyone that 'employs a foreign national in a capacity in which the foreign national is not authorized ... to be employed'. Under this provision, a person who fails to exercise due diligence to determine whether employment is authorized is deemed to know that it is not.[1227] It is unclear how many prosecutions there have been under these provisions, if any. A 2009 report by the Auditor General of Canada concluded: '[T]here has been no systematic follow-up by either [CIC] or [Human Resources and Skills Development Canada] to verify that employers are complying with the terms and conditions under which the LMO [labour market

1222. ENF15, s. 13.2; Regulations, s. 283(1).
1223. ENF15, s. 13.3.
1224. IRPA, s. 148(2); Regulations, s. 284; ENF15, s. 14.
1225. ENF15, s. 14.1.
1226. IRPA, s. 146; ENF15, s. 14.5.
1227. IRPA, ss 124(1)(c) and (2) and 125.

opinion] application was approved, such as wages to be paid and accommodations to be provided.'[1228]

691. The Regulations set out a list of factors to be considered by officers when deciding, if a job offer is genuine.[1229] These factors include: (1) whether the employer is actively engaged in the business in respect of which the offer is made, (2) whether the offer is consistent with the reasonable employment needs of the employer, (3) whether the offer's terms can be reasonably fulfilled by the employer, and (4) the past compliance of the employer or of the employer's recruiter with legislation regulating employment and the recruitment of employees. An offer will be deemed not genuine if an employer in the two years previous has provided a foreign national with wages or working conditions significantly different from those offered; has employed a foreign national in a significantly different occupation than offered; or has, in the past two years, had an offer deemed not genuine for either of the first two reasons.

692. In response to widely reported employer abuse of temporary foreign workers and the TFW programme in 2013 and 2014, the government introduced additional investigation and enforcement measures. These include the following:

- increase in size of corps of inspectors monitoring employer compliance;
- undertaking to inspect one quarter of TFW program employers annually;
- increased scope of investigations and powers of inspectors to enter, search, compel document production etc.
- anonymous 'tip' line for people to phone in to report abuse of the TFW programme;
- intention to increase criminal investigations;
- increase in fines to $100,000;
- Blacklisting of employers who violate TFW Programme, including publication of names, revocation of existing LMIA, and potential ban on acquisition of future LMIAs.[1230]

§3. Criminal Penalties

693. In addition to the specific regimes covering employer and carrier sanctions, the Act creates several general criminal offences. Immigration may also be enforced

1228. Report of the Auditor General of Canada to the House of Commons, Ch. 2, 'Selecting Foreign Workers under the Immigration Program' (Office of the Auditor General of Canada, Fall 2009) at 33 (hereinafter '2009 Auditor General's Report], online: http://www.oag-bvg.gc.ca/internet/english/parl_oag_200911_02_33203.html.
1229. Regulations, ss 200(1)(c)(iii) and 203(1).
1230. 'Reforming the Temporary Foreign Worker Program; Stronger Enforcement and Tougher Penalties', http://www.esdc.gc.ca/eng/jobs/foreign_workers/reform/enforce.shtml (accessed 1 Feb. 2015). See also, Employment and Social Development Canada, 'Discussion Paper: Regulatory proposals to enhance the Temporary Foreign Worker Program'http://www.esdc.gc.ca/eng/jobs/foreign_workers/consultations/tfwp_discussion_paper.pdf, (accessed 1 Feb. 2015). See also paras. 266–288.

using several general criminal offences set out in the Criminal Code of Canada,[1231] though these are not dealt with in the Encyclopaedia. The Act gives authorized immigration officers police powers to enforce its regulatory offences.[1232] It also provides for search and seizure powers.[1233] It is unclear, however, to what extent the regulatory offences created in the Act are prosecuted as statistics are not readily available.

694. Section 122(1) of the Act creates various criminal offences relating to documentation fraud. It is an offence to: (1) possess a passport, visa or other document, Canadian or not, in order to contravene the Act; (2) use any such document in order to contravene the Act, including for the purpose of entering or remaining in Canada; or (3) import, export, or deal in such a document in contravention of the Act. Possession is an indictable offence punishable by imprisonment of up to five years. Use and dealing in such documents are indictable offences punishable by imprisonment of up to fourteen years.[1234] Contravention in association with a criminal organization or for profit, even if no profit was realized, will be considered aggravating factors in sentencing.[1235] Asylum seekers who come to Canada directly or indirectly from the country where they claim to face danger may not be charged under this provision pending resolution of their claim or if refugee protection is granted.[1236] That means that asylum seekers who do not come from the country where they face danger and those whose claims are refused are liable to prosecution.

695. Section 124(1) creates several general offences for non-compliance with the Act. It is an offence: (1) to contravene any provision of the Act for which a penalty is not specifically provided or to fail to comply with any condition or obligation imposed under the Act,[1237] (2) to escape or attempt to escape from lawful custody or detention under the Act, and (3) to employ a foreign national in a capacity not authorized under the Act; in this last case, a person who fails to exercise due diligence will be deemed to know that employment is not authorized.[1238] These offences are punishable on indictment by a fine of not more than CAD 50,000 or imprisonment of not more than two years, or both; and, on summary conviction, by a fine of not more than CAD 10,000 or to imprisonment of not more than six months, or both.[1239] Again, asylum seekers who come to Canada directly or indirectly from the country where they claim to face danger may not be charged for

1231. These include: Sections 340 (fraudulent destruction of documents); 354 (possession of property obtained by crime); 366 (forgery); 368 (uttering a forged document); and 403 (fraudulent impersonation). This list is obviously not exhaustive.
1232. IRPA, s. 138(1).
1233. IRPA, ss 139 and 140.
1234. IRPA, s. 123(1).
1235. IRPA, s. 123(2).
1236. IRPA, s. 133.
1237. Transportation companies will not be liable under this heading if they can show they exercised due diligence: see IRPA, s. 124(3).
1238. IRPA, s. 124(2).
1239. IRPA, s. 125.

general contraventions of the Act pending resolution of their claim or if refugee protection is granted.[1240]

696. Sections 126 and 127 create offences related to misrepresentation. Section 126 makes it an offence to (or attempt to) counsel, induce, aid or abet any person to directly or indirectly misrepresent or withhold material facts relating to a relevant matter that could induce an error in the administration of the Act. Section 127 makes it an offence to: (1) make a direct or indirect material misrepresentation that could induce an error in the administration of the Act; (2) communicate false or misleading information with the intent to induce or deter immigration to Canada; and (3) refuse to be sworn or to affirm or declare, or to answer a question put to a person at an examination or proceeding convoked under the Act. These offences are punishable on indictment to a fine of not more than CAD 100,000 or to imprisonment of not more than five years, or both; on summary conviction, to a fine of not more than CAD 50,000 or to imprisonment for not more than two years, or both.[1241] Refugee claimants who come to Canada directly or indirectly from the country where they face danger are exempt from prosecutions under section 127 while their claims are being determined or if refugee protection is granted.[1242]

697. Section 129(1) creates a series of offences meant to address potential corruption among immigration and other officers charged with the administration of the Act. The provision makes it an offence, if one is an officer or other government employee, to knowingly make or issue any false document or statement, to accept a bribe or other benefit, or to knowingly fail to perform any duty under the Act. It also makes it an offence to seek to bribe an officer; to falsely impersonate an officer; or to obstruct an officer in the performance of his or her duties under the Act. These offences are punishable on indictment by a fine of up to CAD 50,000 or imprisonment of up to five years, or both; or, on summary conviction, by a fine of up to CAD 10,000 or imprisonment of up to six months, or both.[1243]

1240. IRPA, s. 133.
1241. IRPA, s. 128.
1242. IRPA, s. 133.
1243. IRPA, s. 129(2).

Chapter 4. Sanctions against Trafficking and Smuggling

698. Section 3(1)(i) stipulates that one of the objectives of the Act is to promote international justice and security by fostering respect for human rights. Section 3(3)(f) further states that the Act is to be construed in a manner that complies with Canada's commitments to international human rights instruments. One of Canada's express commitments is to the international effort to combat trafficking and smuggling. In May 2002, Canada signed and ratified the UN Convention Against Transnational Organized Crime and the protocols under the Convention aimed at trafficking and smuggling. Canada signed all three instruments in December 2000 and ratified them in May 2002. Pursuant to its obligations under these protocols, Canada established criminal prohibitions against trafficking and smuggling in the Act. It has also used the Criminal Code to prosecute both offences.

§1. Human Trafficking

699. The RCMP has estimated that approximately 600 women and children are trafficked into Canada each year for sexual exploitation; at least 800 are trafficked into Canada for other markets such as the drug trade, domestic work, and the garment industry. The RCMP estimates between 1,500 and 2,200 people are trafficked from Canada into the United States each year. The government reported that at least twenty-five trafficking convictions in 2013.[1244] Asian countries, countries of the former Soviet Union, and parts of Africa are the primary sources of trafficked persons into Canada. There is also a growing awareness of trafficking within Canada of vulnerable groups, such as immigrants and Aboriginal people.[1245]

700. The *Protocol to Prevent, Suppress and Punish Trafficking in Persons* defines trafficking as:

> the recruitment, transportation, transfer, harbouring or receipt of persons, by means of the threat or use of force or other forms of coercion, of abduction, of fraud, of deception, of the abuse of power or of a position of vulnerability or of the giving or receiving of payments or benefits to achieve the consent of a person having control over another person, for the purpose of exploitation. Exploitation shall include, at a minimum, the exploitation of the prostitution of others or other forms of sexual exploitation, forced labour or services, slavery or practices similar to slavery, servitude or the removal of organs.

1244. US Department of State, *Trafficking in Persons Report* (2014) at 125, online: http://www.state.gov/documents/organization/226845.pdf.
1245. Jacqueline Oxman-Martinez et al., Victims of Trafficking in Persons: Perspectives from the Canadian Community Sector (Department of Justice, Research and Statistics Division, August 2005) at 2, online: http://www.justice.gc.ca/eng/rp-pr/cj-jp/tp/rr06_3/rr06_3.pdf. See, also, Royal Canadian Mounted Police, 'Human Trafficking in Canada' (Ottawa: March 2010), online: http://publications.gc.ca/collections/collection_2011/grc-rcmp/PS64-78-2010-eng.pdf; and United Nations Office on Drugs and Crime, 'Global Report on Trafficking of Persons', February 2009, online: http://www.unodc.org/documents/Global_Report_on_TIP.pdf.

The Protocol further provides that consent is irrelevant if obtained through any of the exploitative means listed in the main definition. Recruitment, transportation, transfer, harbouring or receipt of anyone under 18 years for the purpose of exploitation will count as trafficking even if none of the exploitative means are employed.[1246]

701. The Protocol's definition can be divided into three parts. First are the activities prohibited, that is the transportation, etc. of persons; second is a description of the various prohibited means of carrying out that activity, which might be described as various degrees of coercion, in that each means listed is a way of supplanting the will of the individual being moved; third is a prohibited aim, namely exploitation. The definition is clearly not restricted to international trafficking.

702. Canada added the offence of trafficking both to the Act when enacted in 2001 and to the Criminal Code in November 2005, in language that differs from the Protocol. Section 118(1) of the Act provides:

> No person shall knowingly organize the coming into Canada of one or more persons by means of abduction, fraud, deception or use or threat of force or coercion.

This provision is obviously much shorter than the definition of trafficking in the Protocol. It is expanded somewhat by the definition of 'organize' in section 118(2):

> 'organize', with respect to persons, includes their recruitment or transportation and, after their entry into Canada, the receipt or harbouring of those persons.

Section 118 is narrower than the Protocol definition in some ways. Obviously it is limited to international trafficking. Further, absent from section 118 are references to subtler means of coercion, like abuse of power, abuse of positions of vulnerability, or payments to someone with control over another person. In one important respect it is broader than the Protocol definition, since it is not limited to trafficking for exploitative purposes. This may not be a definitional virtue, however, since it makes it more difficult to distinguish the offence of trafficking from that of smuggling. The only difference between the two lies in the sometimes hazy distinction between freely given and coerced consent.[1247]

1246. UN Convention against Transnational Organized Crime and its Protocol to Prevent, Suppress and Punish Trafficking in Persons, especially women and children, G.A. res. 55/25, annex II, 55 UN GAOR Supp. (No. 49) at 60, UN Doc. A/45/49 (Vol. I) (2001).

1247. See IP1, s. 16.2: 'Both smuggling and TIP may present similarly and are often only distinguished after further inquiry. Smuggled persons may become (victims of trafficking in persons at any point in the smuggling process. Some may consent, for example, to being smuggled across a border, but find on arrival in the country of destination that debt bondage, or other forms of coercion, have been imposed. If this occurs, they become [victims of trafficking in persons], regardless of whether they consented to being smuggled in the first place.'

703. Under the Act, persons convicted of contravening section 118 are liable to fines of up to CAD 1,000,000 or to life in prison.[1248] In determining the penalty to impose, the convicting court is to consider whether the trafficking resulted in bodily harm or death; whether it was committed for the benefit of or in association with a criminal organization; whether the trafficking activity aimed at profit; or whether the trafficking resulted in a person being 'subjected to humiliating or degrading treatment, including with respect to work or health conditions or sexual exploitation as a result of the commission of the offence'.[1249] Amendments in 2012 added 'endangering the life or safety of any person as a result of the trafficking of persons' as an aggravating factor to be considered by the court.[1250] It is unclear if there have been any prosecutions under section 118, although the provision has survived constitutional challenge in a lower court.[1251] In addition, trafficking may render an individual inadmissible on grounds of serious and non-serious criminality, organized criminality, international criminality, misrepresentation or non-compliance with the Act.[1252] It also potentially renders them ineligible for or excludable from refugee status on one of these grounds.

704. The trafficking offence in Canada's Criminal Code tracks the Protocol more closely, though with a less severe penalty:

> 279.01(1) Every person who recruits, transports, transfers, receives, holds, conceals or harbours a person, or exercises control, direction or influence over the movements of a person, for the purpose of exploiting them or facilitating their exploitation is guilty of an indictable offence and liable
>
> (a) to imprisonment for life if they kidnap, commit an aggravated assault or aggravated sexual assault against, or cause death to, the victim during the commission of the offence; or
> (b) to imprisonment for a term of not more than fourteen years in any other case.
>
> (2) No consent to the activity that forms the subject-matter of a charge under subsection (1) is valid.
>
> Section 279.04 stipulates that a person 'exploits' another if they:
>
> (a) cause them to provide, or offer to provide, labour or a service by engaging in conduct that, in all the circumstances, could reasonably be expected to cause the other person to believe that their safety or the safety of a person known to them would be threatened if they failed to provide, or offer to provide, the labour or service; or
> (b) cause them, by means of deception or the use or threat of force or of any other form of coercion, to have an organ or tissue removed.

1248. IRPA, s. 120.
1249. IRPA, s. 121(1).
1250. IRPA, s. 121.(1)(a).
1251. See *R. v. Ng*, (2006) B.C.J. No. 774, 2006 BCPC 111. Mr Ng was convicted of human smuggling but not trafficking: see *R. v. Ng*, (2008) B.C.J. No. 2576, 2008 BCCA 535 (sentence appeal).
1252. IRPA, ss 35 (international criminality), 36 (criminality), (37 (organized criminality), 40 (misrepresentation), 41 (non-compliance).

The Code differs from the Protocol in that, except for the reference to coercive organ removal, there is a greater emphasis on the threat to the individual's safety as a means of procuring the offered service. The Code is thus less explicitly directed at trafficking for purposes of sexual exploitation, forced labour and slavery. The Code also creates two other trafficking-related offences: it is an offence to knowingly receive financial or other benefit that results from trafficking; and also to conceal, remove, withhold or destroy any travel or identity document belonging to another person in order to commit or facilitate trafficking.[1253] Finally, other Criminal Code offences have been used to prosecute trafficking, including the offences of kidnapping, forcible confinement, extortion, keeping a common bawdy house and child abduction.[1254]

705. The Protocol mandates not only that states criminalize trafficking,[1255] but also that they provide assistance and protection to its victims.[1256] The Ministry has accordingly issued guidelines for the treatment of victims of trafficking.

706. The main regulatory tool used by the Ministry to assist trafficking victims is the issuance of temporary residence permits under section 24(1) of the Act. Under the authority of section 24(3) of the Act, Ministerial instructions have been issued to guide the issuance of temporary residence permits to trafficking victims.[1257] According to the Ministry's 2008 Annual Report, in 2013, fourteen permits were issued under the instructions.[1258]

707. Under the instructions, officers may provide a TRP for 180 days to an individual who it appears, on preliminary assessment, may be a victim of trafficking. Short-term permits are issued because of the complexity of trafficking cases and because it may not be appropriate immediately to conduct a thorough examination of a traumatized and fearful victim. The six-month period is intended, among other goals, to provide victims with a period of reflection and recovery, to allow him or her to consider their options, and to assist in the related criminal investigation. Officers are directed to assist victims in contacting their country's embassy or high commission and appropriate non-governmental organizations or municipal or provincial agencies for social and other kinds of assistance. Medical and social counselling assistance may be granted under the IFHP.[1259] Officers are also instructed to inform the victim of his or her right to apply for a work permit under section 199 of the Regulations.[1260]

1253. Criminal Code, s. 279.02 and 279.03.
1254. IP1, Appendix F.
1255. Protocol, Art. 5.
1256. Protocol, Art. 6.
1257. The instructions are found at CIC Operational Manuals, Inland Processing, Temporary Resident Permits, IP1, Appendix G.
1258. CIC, Annual Report to Parliament on Immigration, 2014, s. 3, online: http://www.cic.gc.ca/english/resources/publications/annual-report2014/index.asp.
1259. IP1, s. 16.3.
1260. IP1, s. 16.3.

708. Longer-term TRPs may also be issued, but the ministerial instructions and Operational Manual call for a more exacting examination of the victim's case. Officers are instructed to consider whether it would be reasonably safe for the person to re-establish a life in their country of origin; whether they are needed and willing to assist in the investigation and prosecution of the traffickers in their case; and 'any other reason the officer may judge relevant'. The Manual instructs officers not to consider certain standard factors – such as illiteracy, a lack of legitimately marketable skills or a lack of social support networks – when deciding on the permit. TRPs may be issued for the time necessary to qualify for permanent residence. Victims may also apply for refugee status.

709. Victims may choose to return home. If they are subject to an enforceable removal order, their case will simply be processed by the CBSA. Subject to restrictions recently imposed pursuant to Bill C-31 (discussed in Parts III and IV), victims subject to removal orders may also obviously avail themselves of the various options available to avoid removal, such as refugee claims, humanitarian and compassionate consideration and PRRA.

§2. Human Smuggling

710. Most smuggled migrants are thought to reach Canada by land, often in the trunks of cars. In one tragic case, a mother and son tried to enter Canada by Jet Ski across the Detroit River; on the way, the son fell into the river and drowned. Migrants are also smuggled from Canada into the United States by truck, train or boat.[1261] Considering the 'moral panic' engendered by illegal immigration in many countries, and despite occasional flare-ups in Canada on the issue, there is surprisingly little available data or research about migrant smuggling into and from Canada. While there have been several convictions under the Act, there is no data source that compiles these. Most discussion of the problem of smuggling into Canada can therefore be characterized as impressionistic.

711. Article 3 of the Protocol Against the Smuggling of Migrants by Land, Sea and Air defines the smuggling of migrants to mean:

> the procurement, in order to obtain, directly or indirectly, a financial or other material benefit, of the illegal entry of a person into a State Party of which the person is not a national or a permanent resident.

Each state party to the Protocol is required to make smuggling a criminal offence.[1262] Parties are further obligated not to make migrants smuggled into the country liable to prosecution for smuggling-related offences.[1263] Canada does not do

1261. See *R. v. Alzehrani,* (2008) O.J. No. 4422 (Sup. Ct.) at para. 3.
1262. Article 5.
1263. Article 6.

so. Further, no one is to be deemed inadmissible merely for entering Canada with the assistance of someone engaged in organized criminal activity.[1264]

712. Unlike the case of trafficking, which is dealt with in the Act and the Criminal Code, the criminalization of migrant smuggling has been undertaken only in the Act. Section 117(1) of the Act makes it a criminal offence to smuggle migrants into Canada:

> No person shall organize, induce, aid or abet the coming into Canada of one or more persons knowing that, or being reckless as to whether, their coming into Canada is or would be in contravention of this Act.[1265]

The severity of the penalty imposed depends on the number of people being smuggled. If fewer than ten, the offence may be punished on indictment for a first offence with a fine of up to CAD 500,000 and/or term of imprisonment of up to ten years; for subsequent offences, the maximum penalties rise to CAD 1,000,000 and fourteen years. On summary conviction, the offender may be fined up to CAD 100,000 or imprisoned for up to two years.[1266] If more than ten persons are smuggled, an offender faces a fine of up to CAD 1,000,000 and/or life imprisonment.[1267] Pursuant to amendments implemented in 2012, mandatory minimum sentences are imposed in circumstances where the person, in committing the offence, (i) 'endangered the life or safety of, or caused bodily harm or death to, any of the persons with respect to whom the offence was committed'; or (ii) 'the commission of the offence was for profit, or was for the benefit of, at the direction of or in association with a criminal organization or terrorist group'.[1268] The penalty imposed depends on whether one or the other or both of these two conditions apply.

713. In *R. v. Alzehrani*, Justice Molloy wrote:

> [T]o establish a breach of this section, the Crown must prove that: (i) the person being smuggled did not have the required documents to enter Canada; (ii) the person was coming into Canada; (iii) the accused was organizing, inducing, aiding or abetting the person to enter Canada; and (iv) the accused had knowledge of the lack of required documents. Both the lack of documents and the accused's knowledge of that are essential elements of the substantive offence under s. 117 of IRPA.[1269]

1264. IRPA, s. 37(2)(b).
1265. IRPA, s. 117(1).
1266. IRPA, s. 117(2).
1267. IRPA, s. 117(3).
1268. IRPA, s. 117(3.1) and (3.2). See also Béchard and Elgersma Legislative Summary: Bin 6.31 at 17.
1269. *R. v. Alzehrani*, (2008) O.J. No. 4422 (Sup. Ct.) at para. 11. Internal citations omitted. After this decision, the Section was amended to its current form with the inclusion of the term reckless. See also *R. c. Savaresse-Belapatino*, (2007) J.Q. no 1448 (Cour du Québec) at para. 49.

Since *Alezhrani*, a constitutional challenge to section 117 of the Act has been brought to the courts. The British Columbia Court of Appeal in *R v. Appulonappa*[1270] ruled that section 117 was overly broad and therefore inconsistent with the guarantee to life, liberty and security of the person entrenched by the Charter. According to the BCCA, the section is meant to protect against human smuggling for profit but wrongfully includes family members and humanitarians who altruistically help others across the border. The government's appeal was heard by the Supreme Court of Canada in February 2015.

714. Other offences in the Act address smuggling less directly. Section 119 makes it an offence to 'disembark a person or group of persons at sea for the purpose of inducing, aiding or abetting them to come into Canada in contravention of this Act'. Section 123 of the Act makes it an offence to possess, use or deal in travel and identity documents to contravene Canadian immigration law:

(1) No person shall, in order to contravene this Act:
  (a) possess a passport, visa or other document, of Canadian or foreign origin, that purports to establish or that could be used to establish a person's identity;
  (b) use such a document, including for the purpose of entering or remaining in Canada; or
  (c) import, export or deal in such a document.
(2) Proof of the matters referred to in subsection (1) in relation to a forged document or a document that is blank, incomplete, altered or not genuine is, in the absence of evidence to the contrary, proof that the person intends to contravene this Act.[1271]

Conviction for these offences can result in imprisonment of up to five years (for possession) or fourteen years (for use or dealing).[1272]

715. Smuggling offences are sometimes prosecuted in tandem with the offence of conspiracy, which is contained in the Criminal Code.[1273] It is also through conspiracy that individuals can be charged with smuggling or attempting to smuggle persons into the United States or other countries.[1274]

716. Even smugglers whose guilt cannot be proven beyond a reasonable doubt can be deemed inadmissible on grounds of serious and non-serious criminality,

1270. *R v. Appulonappa*, 2014 BCCA 163, 239 A.C.W.S. (3d) 719. Section 37 of the Act adds 'people smuggling' as a ground of inadmissibility. The scope of people smuggling under s. 37 has also been interpreted by the Federal Court of Appeal in *Canada v. J.P. et al*, 2013 FCA 262 and *Canada v. B010*, 2013 FCA 87.
1271. IRPA, s. 122.
1272. IRPA, s. 123.
1273. Criminal Code, s. 465(1)(c) and (d) and 465(4).
1274. Criminal Code, s. 465(3).

organized criminality, international criminality, misrepresentation or non-compliance with the Act.[1275] (These grounds of inadmissibility are discussed in Part IV, Chapter 1.) Smuggling may also be a ground for ineligibility for and exclusion from refugee status. (See Part III, Chapter 4.)

In addition to the criminal penalties imposed for people smuggling, if a non-citizen who is smuggled also worked as a crew member aboard a smuggling vessel, he or she can be found guilty of aiding and abetting human smuggling and therefore inadmissible to Canada and ineligible to apply for refugee status.[1276] Smuggling does not have to be for a financial or material benefit. In *P. (J.) v. Canada,*[1277] and in *B010 v. Canada,*[1278] the appellants submitted that smuggling must be for a material or financial benefit as outlined in the *Protocol Against the Smuggling of Migrants by Land, Sea or Air*—an international treaty to which Canada was a signatory. The Board stated that to require a financial or material benefit would lead to absurd results. The Federal Court of Appeal found no compelling reason to require a financial benefit to qualify an act as people smuggling. The Supreme Court of Canada granted leave to appeal in 17 April 2014 and will make the final decision on the matter.

1275. IRPA, ss 35 (international criminality), 36 (criminality), (37 (organized criminality), 40 (misrepresentation), 41 (non-compliance).

1276. See *Hernandez v. Canada (Minister of Public Safety and Emergency Preparedness),* 2012 FC 1417, 45 Admin. L.R. (5th) 267. and *B306 v. Canada (Minister of Public Safety and Emergency Preparedness),* 2012 FC 1282, 222 A.C.W.S. (3d) 772.

1277. *P. (J.) v. Canada (Minister of Public Safety and Emergency Preparedness),* 2013 FCA 262, 20 Imm. L.R. (4th) 199.

1278. *B010 v. Canada,* 2013 FCA 87.

Part VI. Legal Remedies and Procedural Safeguards

Chapter 1. Legal Remedies in Case of Refusal of Right to Enter, Stay or Reside

§1. Introduction: Appeals, Applications for Discretionary Treatment and Judicial Review of Immigration Decisions

I. Appeals

717. Since late 2012, subject to specified exceptions (see Part III, Chapter 4), a refugee claimant whose claim is rejected by the RPD may appeal to the RAD of the IRB. Appeals to the RAD are submitted in writing and determined by a single decision maker, unless the RAD decides to hold and oral hearing and/or empanel three members to determine the appeal. The ability to introduce new evidence before the RAD is limited to evidence that was not available or could not reasonably have been obtained at the initial hearing before the RPD. The scope of the RAD's mandate as administrative appellate body is the subject of ongoing litigation.[1279]

718. Appeals are not available in relation to most other decisions concerning the grant of a visa or permit, the acquisition or loss of status, detention, or entry into or residence in Canada. In fact, the IRPA makes available an appeal to the IAD of the IRB only in six narrowly prescribed situations.

719. First, where a Canadian citizen or permanent resident seeks to sponsor a foreign national as a member of the family class of permanent resident, but the foreign national's application has been denied, the sponsor may appeal the decision to the IAD. It is the sponsor rather than the foreign national who has the right of appeal. Subsection 63(1) of the IRPA provides:

> a person who has filed in the prescribed manner an application to sponsor a member of the family class may appeal to the Immigration Appeal Division

1279. See, e.g. *Huruglica, supra* n. 776. The case has been appealed by the Minister to the Federal Court of Appeal.

against the decision to not issue the foreign national a permanent resident visa.[1280]

720. Second, an appeal is available to a foreign national who holds a PRV in relation to a decision to issue a removal order against them.[1281]

721. Third, a permanent resident may appeal a decision to issue a removal order against them.[1282]

722. Fourth, a protected person may also appeal against the issuance of a removal order.[1283]

723. Fifth, a permanent resident has a right to appeal a decision made outside Canada that they have failed to comply with the residency requirement.[1284]

724. Sixth, the Minister may appeal against an admissibility decision made by the ID.[1285]

725. The grant of an appeal in each of these situations is restricted by a set of qualifications found in section 64(1) of the IRPA, a poorly worded section that leaves open some serious interpretive issues. It provides:

> (1) No appeal may be made to the Immigration Appeal Division by a foreign national or their sponsor or by a permanent resident if the foreign national or permanent resident has been found to be inadmissible on grounds of security, violating human or international rights, serious criminality or organized criminality.

726. On its face, the section implies that foreign nationals who are being sponsored may launch an appeal, where a specified ground of inadmissibility has not been found to exist. However, this runs counter to the terms of section 63. It also implies that a sponsor or a protected person may launch an appeal even if they were inadmissible on one of the specified grounds. While both these implications seem to flow from the English version of the Act, the equally authoritative French version is worded differently. It provides:

> 64.(1) L'appel ne peut être interjeté par le résident permanent ou l'étranger qui est interdit de territoire pour raison de sécurité ou pour atteinte aux droits humains ou internationaux, grande criminalité ou criminalité organisée, ni par dans le cas de l'étranger, son répondant.

1280. The inclusion of the requirement that the application be filed in the prescribed manner may entail that no appeal will be available should the application be incomplete.
1281. IRPA, s. 63.
1282. *Ibid.*
1283. *Ibid.*
1284. IRPA, s. 63 (4).
1285. IRPA, s. 63 (5).

This version makes it clearer that every individual who could otherwise appeal will be disqualified by the listed grounds of inadmissibility.

727. An appeal before the IAD is a hearing de novo in the broadest sense. Not only may the IAD reconsider the evidence that was before the original decision-maker, it may consider new evidence that was not introduced earlier.

728. However, the Federal Court has determined that the IAD may not consider the question whether an individual was inadmissible under section 64(1) of the IRPA. The determination by a previous decision-maker that a person falls within the terms of section 64(1) is unappealable. The individual concerned has no right to appeal to the IAD. In *Kang v. Canada (Minister of Citizenship and Immigration),* it was held that a different interpretation would render section 64(1) meaningless. The Court stated:

> Requiring that the Board revisit the question of admissibility would essentially confer a right of appeal on the very individuals who have been denied such a right by virtue of the section.[1286]

729. Where an appeal is properly before the IAD, it has the authority to uphold it on a number of grounds. First, it may determine that the decision appealed 'is wrong in law or fact or mixed law and fact'.[1287] It may also allow the appeal because of procedural irregularities that amount to a breach of the principles of natural justice.[1288] It may also determine that 'taking into account the best interests of a child directly affected by the decision, sufficient humanitarian and compassionate considerations warrant special relief in light of all the circumstances of the case'.[1289]

730. The decision to uphold an appeal on humanitarian and compassionate grounds is referred to as an exercise of the Division's 'equitable jurisdiction'. It may be exercised only in limited circumstances. Thus, the IAD may not take into account humanitarian and compassionate considerations where it is the Minister who has launched the appeal.[1290] Moreover, in a sponsorship appeal it may only take into account humanitarian and compassionate considerations after it has decided that the sponsoree is a member of the family class and the sponsor meets the definition of a sponsor found in the regulations. Thus where a person is ineligible to be sponsored because they fall outside the definition of a member of the family class, the sponsor may appeal the decision but the appeal will be limited to questions of fact, questions of law, or mixed questions of fact and law.

1286. 2005 FC 297 at para. 42.
1287. IRPA, s. 67 (1) (a).
1288. IRPA, s. 67 (1) (b).
1289. IRPA, s. 67 (1) (c).
1290. *Ibid.*

731. One important consequence of the grant of equitable jurisdiction to decide appeals on humanitarian and compassionate grounds, is that the IAD may order that a visa be provided to individuals who would otherwise be inadmissible. This power is particularly important for individuals who are attempting to sponsor family members who are *eligible* to be sponsored but who are *inadmissible.* Thus, for example, where a sponsorship of a parent is denied because the parent is found to be inadmissible for medical reasons, the denial may be appealed to the IAD.

732. The IAD has held that the seriousness of the medical impediment may be taken into account when weighing the case for humanitarian and compassionate relief. In *Jugpall,*[1291] the following analysis was offered:

> The Appeal Division has long held that the exercise of its statutory discretion is a function of the context created by a determination of inadmissibility … . The facts and the law which give rise to an applicant's inadmissibility form the context in which compassionate or humanitarian circumstances are considered … .
>
> A simple example illustrates the point: if one applicant is inadmissible to Canada because he has a relatively minor, treatable medical condition and another applicant is inadmissible because he has chronic kidney disease, has experienced renal failure and requires dialysis for the rest of his life, then both applicants are equally inadmissible. From the point of view of the law, they are similarly inadmissible. However, when the potential burden on health services of allowing the first applicant into Canada is compared with the potential burden of allowing the second applicant to enter Canada, it is evident that the two applicants are not in the same position. In order to succeed on appeal, both applicants need to show that there are compassionate and humanitarian grounds that warrant the granting of special relief, but the second applicant needs to bring forward a considerably more compelling case than the first applicant, given the nature of his condition.

733. The Court in *Jugpall* went on to consider cases where a person's medical condition may change between the time of the original decision and the appeal:

> The Appeal Division has consistently applied an approach which requires the degree of compelling circumstances to be commensurate with the legal obstacle to admissibility in order to justify granting discretionary relief. Thus, in cases where changes in the circumstances of the case by the time it gets to appeal are such that the original basis for a finding of inadmissibility has been overcome, a mildly compelling case may be sufficient to warrant granting discretionary relief. For example, in medical inadmissibility cases the jurisprudence holds that a medical refusal is valid in law if it was reasonable at the time that it was made. Thus in a medical inadmissibility case where, by the date of the appeal, the applicant has undergone successful treatment and cured

1291. *Jugpall v. Canada (Minister of Citizenship and Immigration)* (1999), 2 Imm. L. R. (3d) 222.

the condition which gave rise to inadmissibility, the initial refusal is nonetheless valid in law. However, a complete surmounting of the substance of the original ground of inadmissibility weighs very heavily in the Appeal Division's assessment of the compassionate or humanitarian circumstances of the case.

734. Similar reasoning has been used in cases of criminal inadmissibility. The IAD (and its predecessor, the Immigration Appeal Board) have developed a series of factors, known as 'the *Ribic* factors' (after the case in which they were originally conceived) which govern the exercise of its equitable jurisdiction in appeals of removal orders based on criminality. These factors have received the approval of the Supreme Court of Canada. In *Chieu*, the issue before the Supreme Court was whether it was appropriate for the IAD to take into account the hardship that would be faced by an appellant who was removed to his country of nationality. The Court decided that it would, and cited the following excerpt from *Ribic*:

> In each case the Board looks to the same general areas to determine if having regard to all the circumstances of the case, the person should not be removed from Canada. These circumstances include the seriousness of the offence or offences leading to the deportation and the possibility of rehabilitation or in the alternative, the circumstances surrounding the failure to meet the conditions of admission which led to the deportation order. The Board looks to the length of time spent in Canada and the degree to which the appellant is established; family in Canada and the dislocation to that family that deportation of the appellant would cause; the support available for the appellant not only within the family but also within the community and the degree of hardship that would be caused to the appellant by his return to his country of nationality. While the general areas of review are similar in each case the facts are rarely, if ever, identical ...[1292]

735. Where an appeal is allowed, the IAD may set aside the original decision and substitute the decision that in its opinion should have been made or it may refer the matter back for reconsideration.[1293]

736. Where the appeal relates to a removal order, the IAD may stay the order. Section 68 of the IRPA provides:

(1) to stay a removal order, the IAD must be satisfied, taking into account the best interests of a child directly affected by the decision, that sufficient humanitarian and compassionate considerations warrant special relief in light of all the circumstances of the case.
(2) where the IAD stays the removal order
  (a) it shall impose any condition that is prescribed and may impose any condition that it considers necessary;

1292. *Chieu, supra* n. 1117.
1293. IRPA, s. 67(2).

(b) all conditions imposed by the ID are cancelled;
(c) it may vary or cancel any non-prescribed condition imposed under paragraph (*a*); and
(d) it may cancel the stay, on application or on its own initiative.

(3) If the IAD has stayed a removal order, it may at any time, on application or on its own initiative, reconsider the appeal under this Division.

(4) If the IAD has stayed a removal order against a permanent resident or a foreign national who was found inadmissible on grounds of serious criminality or criminality, and they are convicted of another offence referred to in subsection 36(1), the stay is cancelled by operation of law and the appeal is terminated.

737. Decisions of the IAD may be judicially reviewed by the Federal Court with leave.

II. Applications for Discretionary Treatment

738. As noted previously, an individual may apply to the Minister for exemption from the relevant rules that determine the right to enter or remain in Canada basing the application on the particular circumstances of the case. This relief granted under this H&C is: (1) permanent resident status, or (2) an exemption from any applicable criteria or obligation of the Act.

739. Section 25(1) of the IRPA provides that:

> The Minister shall, upon request of a foreign national in Canada who is inadmissible or who does not meet the requirements of this Act, and may, on the Minister's own initiative or on request of a foreign national outside Canada, examine the circumstances concerning the foreign national and may grant the foreign national permanent resident status or an exemption from any applicable criteria or obligation of this Act if the Minister is of the opinion that it is justified by humanitarian and compassionate considerations relating to them, taking into account the best interests of a child directly affected, or by public policy considerations.

This sweeping provision potentially applies to every aspect of the Act or Regulations, including the formal and substantive criteria for admission as short- or long-term residents, grounds of inadmissibility, certain sanctions, administrative fees, and so on.[1294] The power to exempt a person from the operation of the statute is viewed as a concession to the fact that no system of migration rules could possibly account for all the variables, exigencies, and mitigating circumstances that would render the operation of the rules harsh, unjust or contrary to Canada's own interests.[1295]

1294. An interesting question is whether it applies to the criminal penalties under IRPA.
1295. Carasco et al., p. 177.

740. Despite the apparent capaciousness of section 25(1), various statutory provisions, regulations and Ministerial instructions enacted since 2011 restrict eligibility to apply for H&C discretion.[1296] Nonetheless, the Operational Manual makes clear that certain grounds of inadmissibility – such as being out of status under section 41 of the Act – should not be a bar to permanent residence on H&C grounds.[1297] All officers have the authority to grant exemptions for inadmissibility on grounds of non-serious criminality, financial sufficiency, misrepresentation, non-compliance with the Act and the inadmissibility of a family member. H&C considerations will not be available to those who are found inadmissible pursuant to sections 34 (security grounds), 35 (violating human an international rights), and 37 (organized criminality) of the IRPA.[1298] Cases involving health must be referred to national headquarters. In some cases, officers may grant exemptions from the grounds for inadmissibility on their own initiative.[1299]

741. A foreign national outside Canada who is inadmissible may apply for H&C consideration. Subject to the specified exceptions in Bill C-31 (see Part III, Chapter 4) a foreign national in Canada may make request permission under H&C to apply for permanent resident status from within Canada. And further, a person who has been issued a removal order may make an application that they should be allowed to remain in the country. In each case, the Minister (or his or her delegate) may determine that ulterior factors justify overriding the applicable rules and standards. Where the individual is in Canada, the Minister's delegate has a duty to consider the application. Outside, Canada, the delegate has the discretion not to consider the application.

742. Section 25(1) should be read in conjunction with section 87.3(4) of the Act, under which the Minister may issue instructions for officers tasked with considering section 25(1) applications:

> Officers and persons authorized to exercise the powers of the Minister under section 25 shall comply with any instructions before processing an application or request or when processing one. If an application or request is not processed, it may be retained, returned or otherwise disposed of in accordance with the instructions of the Minister.

Here the Minister is explicitly authorized to issue instructions restricting the exercise of discretion by officers.[1300]

1296. See, e.g., Regulations, ss 67–69.
1297. Citizenship and Immigration Canada, Operational Manual IP5, *Immigrant Applications Made in Canada on Humanitarian or Compassionate Grounds*, s. 5.12. Bill C-43 has imposed further eligibility restrictions. See, Béchard and Elgersma, 'Bill C-43: An Act to amend the Immigration and Refugee Protection Act, (Faster Removal of Foreign Criminals Act)', p. 4.
1298. *Bill C-43: An Act to amend the Immigration and Refugee Protection Act, (Faster Removal of Foreign Criminals Act),* S.C. 2013 c. 16, s. 9.
1299. For interim instructions to CIC officers concerning the examination of H&C applications (in Canada) see: http://www.cic.gc.ca/english/resources/manuals/bulletins/2006/ob021.asp.
1300. IRPA, s. 87(3.1) seems to preclude Ministerial instructions regarding H&C applications by foreign nationals outside Canada, but in fact that Minister has since instructed officers not to consider

743. The courts have provided some guidance as to the nature of the discretionary decision made under section 25(1). In *Baker*, a case dealing with a similar provision from the former Act, the Supreme Court said 'discretion must still be exercised in a manner that is within a reasonable interpretation of the margin of manoeuvre contemplated by the legislature, in accordance with the principles of the rule of law'.[1301] It also held that the words 'humanitarian' and 'compassionate' must be central to the analysis.[1302] What is required is a weighing of 'the compassionate and humanitarian aspects of an individual's case' against 'the legal obstacles to admissibility'. Where the latter are minor, less compelling circumstances are required. Where the legal obstacles are significant, so too must be the circumstances.[1303]

744. A further important development in *Baker* was the articulation of the requirement that in humanitarian and compassionate cases, the best interests of the child is an important factor that must be given substantial weight.[1304] Decision-makers must pay 'close attention to the interests and needs of children. Children's rights, and attention to their interests, are central humanitarian and compassionate values in Canadian society'.[1305] The Supreme Court of Canada observed that protecting the best interests of the child is a norm expressed in the Convention on the Rights of the Child, Canadian family law. Even the Ministerial guidelines (Operational Manual) that guides officers in interpreting and applying the IRPA and the Regulations, expressly mentioned the importance of family relationships and the interests of family members as relevant factors in an H&C application.

745. In H&C cases, 'the best interests of the child' is an important factor that must be given substantial weight.[1306] However, children's best interests are not to be given preponderance:

> For all practical purposes, the officer's task is to determine, in the circumstances of each case, the likely degree of hardship to the child caused by the removal of the parent and to weigh this degree of hardship together with other factors, including public policy considerations, that militate in favour of or against removal of the parent.[1307]

---

certain applications for H&C by economic class applicants from outside Canada, in apparent contradiction of s. 87(3.1) of IRPA. See OP6, at 10.

1301. *Baker v. Canada (Minister of Citizenship and Immigration)* [1999] 2 SCR 817, at para. 53.
1302. See also the discussion of humanitarian and compassionate grounds of appeal to the Immigration Appeal Board, predecessor to the current Immigration Appeal Division, in *Chieu* at paras 36–41; *Chiarelli* at p. 737.
1303. *Jugpall, Sukhjeewan Singh v. Minister of Citizenship and Immigration* (IAD T98-00716), Aterman, Goodman, Townshend, 12 Apr. 1999, at 9–11; 17–18., cited in IRB, Sponsorship Appeals, Ch. 10, pp 3–4.
1304. *Baker, supra* n. 1305, at para. 75.
1305. *Baker, supra* n. 1305, at para. 67.
1306. *Hawthorne* at para. 2.
1307. *Hawthorne* at para. 6.

The Court's finding is now reflected directly in the reference to the best interests of the child in the wording of section 25(1). The Operational Manual lists the following factors, among others, in making best interest determinations: the age of the child; the level of dependency upon the principal applicant or sponsor; the degree of the child's establishment in Canada; the child's link to the country in which he or she would live if the application were refused, as well as the conditions of that country; medical issues related to the child; the impact of the decision on the child's education; matters relating to gender; and whether the decision might place the child in a situation of risk.[1308]

746. The best interests of the child are included in a non-exhaustive list in the Operational Manual that identifies factors that should be taken into account in an H&C application. This list is meant to exclude factors which were or could have been taken into account in an unsuccessful application for refugee protection. The relevant H&C factors include:

- establishment in Canada;
- ties to Canada;
- the best interests of any children affected by their application;
- factors in their country of origin (this includes but is not limited to:
  (a) economic opportunities or climate in cases of medical conditions);
  (b) health considerations;
  (c) family violence considerations;
  (d) consequences of the separation of relatives;
  (e) inability to leave Canada has led to establishment; and
- any other factor they wish to have considered.

747. Section 25(1) has been used to make occasional blanket public policy orders. For example, the government relied on its authority in establishing a special set of procedures for admitting a small group of Vietnamese living in the Philippines without permanent residence and who are the siblings or adult children of Canadian citizens or permanent residents.[1309] This community originated with the exodus from Vietnam following the fall of Saigon in 1975.[1310] The Ministry has also cited section 25(1) as authority when granting fee waivers for applicants affected by some natural disasters, such as the Tsunami of 26 December 2004 and an October 2005 earthquake in Pakistan.[1311] Section 25(1) has also been used to exempt victims of human trafficking from administrative fees when applying for TRPs, temporary

1308. IP5, *supra* n. 1301, s. 5.12.

1309. Other close family members can be sponsored through the family class.

1310. Citizenship and Immigration Canada, News Release – 'Canada's new government to facilitate the immigration of stateless Vietnamese living in the Philippines', 22 May 2007, CIC: http://www.ccnc.ca/content/pr.php?entry=125.

1311. *Toussaint v. Canada (Minister of Citizenship and Immigration)*, 2009 FC 873, [2010] 3 FCR 452 at para. 29; 2011 FCA 146; Leave to Appeal to Supreme Court of Canada denied [2011] SCCA. No. 295.

work permits, and other applicable fees.[1312] While not objectionable, such broad policy orders are nonetheless not obviously authorized by the provision, which on its face seems to contemplate equitable relief on a case-by-case basis. Moreover, section 87.3 does not seem available as a source of future authorization for some of these policy orders unless amended, since the provision only applies to ministerial instructions concerning section 25(1) applications from within Canada.

748. Putting these concerns aside, section 25(1) is largely used as a means of achieving permanent residence by applicants who do not meet the formal or substantive criteria for a given class. For this reason, humanitarian and compassionate applications relating to family members are often accompanied by sponsorship undertakings. These are not mandatory, but they may be considered among the humanitarian and compassionate reasons for admission. Failure to live up to their obligations under the sponsorship undertaking could result in the sponsor being found in default, as with family class sponsorships.[1313]

749. Sections 66 through 69 of the Regulations put in place formal and procedural requirements for applying for humanitarian and compassionate leave and imposing general conditions on foreign nationals granted leave.

750. Where the H&C application is rejected, the applicant may seek judicial review by the Federal Court. There is no automatic stay of removal associated with a humanitarian and compassionate application, but applicants may apply to the courts for a judicial stay pending the outcome of the application. There is also no right of appeal to the IAD from humanitarian and compassionate cases, though judicial review is available, with leave.[1314] On judicial review, the courts will seek to ensure that the exercise of discretion was reasonable and that no 'implied limitations and/or patently relevant factors' were ignored.[1315]

III. Judicial Review

A. Powers of the Federal Court

751. Judicial review of a decision is available only to an applicant who has exhausted all available appeals.[1316] The aim of judicial review is to ensure the legality, reasonableness and fairness of the administrative process and its outcomes.[1317] Subsection 18.1(3) of the Federal Courts Act (FCA) identifies the relevant powers of the Federal Court and the grounds for granting judicial review of

1312. 'Public Policy concerning payment of application fees for initial temporary resident permits and initial work permits for victims of trafficking in persons,' included as Appendix I to IP1, at s. 53.
1313. Citizenship and Immigration Canada, Operational Manual IP2, *Processing Applications to Sponsor Members of the Family Class*, s. 5.5.
1314. Carasco et al., at p. 542.
1315. *Suresh*, *supra* n. 721, at para. 37.
1316. IRPA, s. 72(2)(a).
1317. *Dunsmuir*, *supra* n. 1138, at para. 28.

an administrative decision. It provides that on an application for judicial review, the Federal Court may:

(a) order a federal board, commission or other tribunal to do any act or thing it has unlawfully failed or refused to do or has unreasonably delayed in doing; or
(b) declare invalid or unlawful, or quash, set aside or set aside and refer back for determination in accordance with such directions as it considers to be appropriate, prohibit or restrain, a decision, order, act or proceeding of a federal board, commission or other tribunal.

752. Section 2 of the FCA defines the phrase 'federal board, commission or other tribunal' sufficiently broadly to include all officers and decision-makers who are part of the immigration regime. It provides that the phrase embraces 'persons having, exercising, or purporting to exercise jurisdiction or powers conferred by or under an Act of Parliament … '. It does not distinguish between decisions made within Canada and decisions made outside the country, and thus both the decisions of visa officers as well as decisions of those officers and tribunals operating in Canada are equally subject to the provisions of the Act.

753. The FCA does not directly authorize the Court, when quashing a decision, to substitute its views for those of the original decision-maker. However, by permitting it to attach directions as it considers appropriate, it may allow the Court to do so indirectly. In *Xin v. Canada*,[1318] it was determined that a Court may order a decision-maker to reach a specific determination only after it addressed the following questions: Is there evidence on record that is so clearly conclusive that there is only one possible conclusion? Is the sole issue to be decided a pure question of law which will be dispositive of the case? Is the legal issue based on uncontroverted evidence and accepted facts? Is there a factual issue which involves conflicting evidence which is central to the claim? Only when a single legal conclusion is possible and there are no factual disagreements should the Court direct the decision-maker to make a specific determination.

754. It should be noted that under the FCA, monetary damages cannot be awarded on an application for judicial review.[1319] However, section 17 of the FCA does allow the Federal Court to hear actions for damages brought against the Crown under the Crown Liability and Proceedings Act. Such actions may also be launched in the provincial superior courts.

755. The powers identified in section 18.1 (3) overlap with those associated with the common law prerogative writs of *certiorari*, *prohibition* and *mandamus*. These along with the power to issue an *injunction* and offer *declaratory relief* are mentioned explicitly in section 18(1) of the FCA which provides:

1318. (2007) FCJ. No. 1769.
1319. See *Canada (Minister of Citizenship and Immigration) v. Hinton*, 2008 FCA 215.

18. (1) Subject to section 28, the Federal Court has exclusive original jurisdiction

(a) to issue an injunction, writ of *certiorari*, writ of prohibition, writ of *mandamus* or writ of *quo warranto*, or grant declaratory relief, against any federal board, commission or other tribunal; and
(b) to hear and determine any application or other proceeding for relief in the nature of relief contemplated by paragraph (*a*), including any proceeding brought against the Attorney General of Canada, to obtain relief against a federal board, commission or other tribunal.

756. A party seeking *certiorari* is applying to have a previously made decision quashed by the court. The person seeking *prohibition* seeks an order proscribing a future action or decision that is beyond the decision-maker's jurisdiction. Many of the restrictions that originally attached to these powers have since disappeared.

757. The order of *mandamus* requires the decision-maker to positively perform a duty.[1320] As explained in *Vaziri*,[1321] *mandamus* will be granted only if certain conditions are met:

> The equitable remedy of *mandamus* lies to compel the performance of a public legal duty that a public authority refuses or neglects to carry out when called upon to do so. *Mandamus* can be used to control procedural delays ... .The test for *mandamus* is set out in *Apotex Inc. v. Canada (Attorney General),*[1994] 1 F.C. 742 (C.A.), aff'd[1994] 3 S.C.R. 1100 (and, more recently, discussed in the immigration context in *Dragan v. Canada (Minister of Citizenship and Immigration)*, [2003] 4 F.C. 189 (T.D.), aff'd[2003] F.C.J. No. 813, 2003 FCA 233). The eight factors are:
>
> (i) There must be a public legal duty to act;
> (ii) The duty must be owed to the Applicants;
> (iii) There must be a clear right to the performance of that duty, meaning that:
> a. the Applicants have satisfied all conditions precedent; and
> b. there must have been:
> I. a prior demand for performance;
> II. a reasonable time to comply with the demand, unless there was outright refusal; and
> III. an express refusal, or an implied refusal through unreasonable delay;
> (iv) no other adequate remedy is available to the Applicants;
> (v) the Order sought must be of some practical value or effect;
> (vi) there is no equitable bar to the relief sought;
> (vii) on a balance of convenience, *mandamus* should lie.

1320. The rarely used writ of *quo warranto* requires an official to identify the legal authority that justifies their actions.
1321. [2006] FC 1159.

758. In determining whether a delay is sufficiently unreasonable to warrant the granting of *mandamus*, three criteria must be met:

(1) The delay in question must have been longer than the nature of the process required;
(2) The applicant or his or her counsel must not be responsible for the delay;
(3) The authority responsible for the delay must not have provided satisfactory justification for the delay.[1322]

759. A permanent injunction may be sought where the applicant is challenging the authority of the decision-maker to proceed. The order may be issued where for example the applicant alleges that the execution of a removal order infringes his constitutional rights.

760. A party may also seek declaratory relief when challenging the legality of a decision. This remedy would be appropriate where, for example, a proposed course of conduct is found to be unconstitutional.

B. The Requirement of an Application for Leave

761. There is no automatic right to judicial review after a negative decision has been made by an immigration officer or tribunal. Under section 72(1) of the IRPA:

> Judicial review by the Federal Court with respect to any matter … under this Act is commenced by making an application for leave.

762. Only if leave is granted will the Federal Court hear the application for judicial review of a decision made by an officer or tribunal. No reasons are provided for denying leave nor may the decision to deny leave be appealed.[1323]

763. The test for determining whether leave should be granted has been stated as follows:

> [O]n an application for leave one should grant such a request unless it is plain and obvious that the applicant would have no reasonable chance of succeeding.[1324]

764. Approximately 14.44% of leave applications are granted.[1325]

1322. *Hamalipoor v. Canada (Minister of Citizenship and Immigration),* 2005 FC 803.
1323. IRPA, s. 72(2)(e).
1324. *Saleh v. Canada (Minister of Employment and Immigration)*(1989) FCJ. No. 825.
1325. Sean Rehaag, 'Luck of the Draw? Judicial Review of Refugee Determinations in the Federal Court of Canada (2005 – 2010)', Research Paper Series No. 9/2012, Osgoode Hall Law School, SSRN: http://papers.ssrn.com/sol3/papers.cfm?abstract_id=2027517, at p. 14.

765. Under section 74 of the IRPA, the judge who grants leave must fix the time and place for the hearing of the application for judicial review. It must be held within ninety days of the grant of leave.

C. The Grounds for Review and the Standard of Review

766. Subsection 18.1(4) of the FCA lists the grounds for granting relief in an application for judicial review of a decision. It provides:

> (4) The Federal Court may grant relief under subsection (3) if it is satisfied that the federal board, commission or other tribunal
>
> (a) acted without jurisdiction, acted beyond its jurisdiction or refused to exercise its jurisdiction;
> (b) failed to observe a principle of natural justice, procedural fairness or other procedure that it was required by law to observe;
> (c) erred in law in making a decision or an order, whether or not the error appears on the face of the record;
> (d) based its decision or order on an erroneous finding of fact that it made in a perverse or capricious manner or without regard for the material before it;
> (e) acted, or failed to act, by reason of fraud or perjured evidence; or
> (f) acted in any other way that was contrary to law.

767. The terms of section 18.1(4) have been supplemented by recent jurisprudence. The Supreme Court of Canada has developed a 'standard of review' test to determine when a court should exercise its supervisory jurisdiction over inferior tribunals or government officials and when it should defer. The test is an attempt to resolve the tension created by two opposing considerations. On the one hand, it is incumbent on courts to ensure that decision-makers respect the legal limits of their powers. On the other, it is important for the courts to respect the expertise of officials to perform specific tasks – expertise which the judiciary may not share and which is the very reason behind the officials' appointment by the legislature. Lax supervision by the courts will allow decision-makers to extend their powers beyond what was intended. Excessive supervisory zeal, on the other hand, risks uninformed interference within a province entrusted to the experts.

768. According to the 'standard of review' test developed by the Supreme Court, it will sometimes be appropriate for a reviewing court to determine that a decision-maker reach the correct decision, as defined by the court. In other cases, the court must defer to decisions that have been made as long as they are reasonable.

769. In *Dunsmuir,* the Supreme Court explained the standard of reasonableness in the following terms:

> Reasonableness is a deferential standard animated by the [following] principle … : certain questions that come before administrative tribunals do not lend themselves to one specific, particular result. Instead, they may give rise to a number of possible, reasonable conclusions. Tribunals have a margin of appreciation within the range of acceptable and rational solutions. A court conducting a review for reasonableness inquires into the qualities that make a decision reasonable, referring both to the process of articulating the reasons and to outcomes. In judicial review, reasonableness is concerned mostly with the existence of justification, transparency and intelligibility within the decision-making process. But it is also concerned with whether the decision falls within a range of possible, acceptable outcomes which are defensible in respect of the facts and law.

770. The Court went on to explain the notion of 'deference':

> Deference in the context of the reasonableness standard therefore implies that courts will give due consideration to the determinations of decision makers. As Mullan explains, a policy of deference 'recognizes the reality that, in many instances, those working day to day in the implementation of frequently complex administrative schemes have or will develop a considerable degree of expertise or field sensitivity to the imperatives and nuances of the legislative regime': D. J. Mullan, 'Establishing the Standard of Review: The Struggle for Complexity?' (2004), 17 *C.J.A.L.P.*59, at p. 93. In short, deference requires respect for the legislative choices to leave some matters in the hands of administrative decision makers, for the processes and determinations that draw on particular expertise and experiences, and for the different roles of the courts and administrative bodies within the Canadian constitutional system.

771. In *Dunsmuir*, the Supreme Court noted that 'where the question is one of fact, discretion or policy, deference will usually apply automatically'.[1326] However, *Dunsmuir* is more ambiguous about questions of law. Where the issue is characterized as jurisdictional, or raises an issue of constitutionality, or concerns a question of 'central importance to the legal system as a whole and beyond the expertise of the decision-maker', the standard of review will be correctness.[1327]

772. Further, the Court in *Dunsmuir* draws a hard and fast distinction between review on substantive grounds (which may be based either on the correctness or reasonableness standard) and review on procedural grounds. Yet it is frequently difficult to distinguish between a procedural aspect and a substantive aspect of a decision. For example, the Federal Court has determined that the failure to provide adequate reasons is a procedural deficiency, yet it will also focus on the inadequacy of reasons to determine that a decision-maker failed to take into account relevant factors.

1326. *Dunsmuir, supra* n. 1138, para. 53.
1327. *Ibid.*, para. 60.

773. The Court also held that it is unnecessary to engage in a full standard of review analysis where the appropriate standard of review is already settled by previous jurisprudence.[1328]

774. In *Khosa,*[1329] the Supreme Court considered the refusal of the IAD to allow an appeal of a deportation order against a permanent resident convicted of a crime. The Court viewed the decision by the IAD as one that involved the exercise of discretion and a high degree of fact finding and inference. It concluded that it ought to defer to the IAD decision, and that the decision met the standard of reasonableness. The Court in *Khosa* also noted that the legislature indicated that a high level of deference should be shown in relation to fact finding by prescribing that the court only has the power to quash a finding of fact where 'erroneous it made in a perverse or capricious manner or without regard for the material before it'.[1330]

In *Agraira v. Canada,*[1331] the Supreme Court reiterated that reasonableness is the standard of review for decisions by the IAD. In this case, an alleged member of a terrorist organization sought judicial review after he was denied permanent residence status on the grounds that the Minister did not expressly define the term 'national interest'. The Court held that reasonableness would be the standard of review for IAD decisions. While the Minister did not actually interpret the term 'national interest', the Court provided an interpretation that would justify the Minister's outcome, imputed it to the Minister, and found it reasonable.

D. Mootness

775. Where a dispute between an individual and the government has become moot, the Federal Court may nevertheless continue to hear and determine the case. In *Borowski v. Canada,*[1332] the Supreme Court determined that there is a two-part approach to the question of mootness. First, the court must determine whether the tangible and concrete dispute between the parties has disappeared. If it has, the court must decide whether to exercise its discretion to hear and determine the case. In deciding whether or not to exercise its discretion the Court must consider three basic principles: that an adversarial context guarantees that issues are fully argued; that there is a need to ration scarce judicial resources; and there is the need to avoid intruding into the legislative role.

E. Appeals to the Federal Court of Appeal and the Supreme Court of Canada

776. A decision of the Federal Court may be appealed to the Federal Court of Appeal only when the judge who heard the original application has certified that a

1328. *Ibid.* at para. 57.
1329. *Canada (Citizenship and Immigration), supra* n. 1116.
1330. Federal Courts Act, s. 18.1(4(d)).
1331. *Agraira, supra* n. 139.
1332. [1989] 1 SCR 342.

serious question of general importance is raised and only after stating that question. According to the Federal Court Immigration and Refugee Protection Rules, a judge hearing an application for judicial review must provide the parties with the opportunity to request that the judge certify that a question of general importance is raised. A party making the request must specify the precise question but the judge decides the final formulation.

777. The certified question is only a device to filter cases that may heard by the Federal Court of Appeal. In the actual appeal, the Court is not limited to hearing arguments relating to that question. It may consider and base its decision on other issues.

778. A decision of the Federal Court of Appeal may be appealed to the Supreme Court of Canada with the leave of the latter court.

§2. Remedies Where Permission to Enter Canada Has Been Denied

I. Foreign Nationals Seeking to Enter Canada on a Temporary Basis

779. Where a TRV has been denied to an applicant, he or she may try to persuade the officer to reconsider the decision. However, the Operational Manual advises officers not to re-open a decision for re-consideration. It states:

> Applicants or their representatives often submit information after a refusal. Officers should not acknowledge receipt and consideration of this information when responding … Applicants or their representatives should be invited to submit new information with a new application.[1333]

780. Some decisions of the Federal Court suggest that visa officers do not have jurisdiction to reconsider the original decision.[1334] However, the issue is a contested one.[1335]

781. As noted above, foreign nationals who have been denied temporary entry into Canada do not have access to an appeal of the decision. Thus, no appeal is available in relation to a decision to refuse a TRV, nor in relation to a decision to refuse a TRP, nor in relation to a decision to deny entry and issue a removal order at a port of entry. Where a TRV or a TRP has been denied to a foreign national, he or she may re-apply and in the re-application may address the reasons for the

1333. Citizenship and Immigration Canada, Operational Manual OP1, *Procedures* at s. 17.

1334. See *Dumbrava v. Canada (Minister of Citizenship and Immigration)* (1995) 31 Imm LR (2d) 76, 101 FTR 230 (T.D.).

1335. For the opposing view, see *Nouranidoust v. Canada (Minister of Citizenship and Immigration)* [2000] I FC 123 (T.D.).

original denial. Similarly, where a foreign national has been issued a departure order, he or she may seek re-entry.

782. Similarly, where the inadmissibility of a person seeking entry as a temporary resident has been referred to the ID of the IRB, the applicant may also apply for leave to seek judicial review of any decision made by that body also.

783. By way of example, it is instructive to consider applications for judicial review of the decision of a visa officer to refuse to issue a TRV. One of the most frequent grounds for seeking judicial review is to challenge a decision that a visa should not be granted on the ground that the visa officer was not satisfied that the applicant would depart from Canada after the authorized period has elapsed. The Federal Court has held that the standard of review in such cases is reasonableness. The focus of the review will be on whether the visa officer misapprehended the evidence that was introduced to show that the applicant would return, whether the decision-maker considered all the evidence that was introduced, and whether the officer drew a reasonable inference from the evidence.

784. The standard of review in such cases has been explained as follows:

> The officer's decision is an administrative decision made in the exercise of her discretionary power, having in mind the obligation imposed on her by the Law and its regulations. Such a discretionary decision is for the most part a question of fact, and as such, a decision entitled to considerable deference in view of the officer's special expertise, and that certain questions she has to decide call on her experience and do not lend themselves to one specific, particular result but instead give rise to a number of possible and reasonable conclusions. When the decision at issue falls within that spectrum, the Court should not interfere.[1336]

785. In *Sempertegui*, it was held to be a reviewable error to deny a visa on this ground for the sole reason that the applicant was an unmarried woman in her twenties. The matter was sent back for re-determination.[1337]

786. In other cases also, the Federal Court has also shown that it is unwilling to accept stereotypical inferences in the reasons of visa officers. For example, in *Groohi*, Russell J states:

> the visa officer states that her spouse 'doesn't appear well-established financially in Iran' but offers no explanation as to how this fact is relevant. Is the officer of the view that the applicant wife may choose not to return to him after her visit because he is not financially well-off? If so, it is a finding made

1336. *Obeng*, *supra* n. 45, 2008 FC 754 at para. 21.
1337. *Sempertegui v. Canada (Minister of Citizenship and Immigration)*, [2009] FCJ. 1475; 2009 FC 1176.

> without evidence and is a stereotypical view of marriage between those not well-off.[1338]

The applicants' applications for a TRV was remitted to a visa officer who had no previous role in the applications for determination, 'to be made as soon as possible after giving the applicants an opportunity to provide such further information as they think appropriate'.

787. However, in *Dhillon* the decision to dismiss the application for judicial review was based on the following reasons:

> Considering Mr. Dhillon's lack of proof of income, combined with his allegations that the majority of his children reside in Canada and his lack of travel history, there was a serious possibility that he would, in fact, not leave Canada at the end of the period authorized for his stay.[1339]

788. In *Rudder*, it was held to be a reviewable error to fail to consider the factors listed in the Operational Manual as relevant to the decision whether a person is likely to depart from Canada.[1340] The decision of the officer refusing to issue a TRV to the Applicant was set aside and the matter was referred to a different visa officer with directions that a TRV for the period of one month be issued forthwith to the Applicant.

789. The Federal Court has also been willing to entertain applications for judicial review of refusals to issue a TRP. In *Dhandal,* the applicants had applied for a TRV but it had been denied on grounds of misrepresentation.[1341] They then submitted an application for a TRP but the visa officer replied that there would be no further consideration because their file had been closed. The Federal Court held this to be an error of law since there was no legal requirement to submit an application for a TRP at the same time as an application for a TRV. It referred the matter back to a different visa officer for a determination as to whether the applicants should be granted temporary residence.

790. In most circumstances, an individual seeking judicial review will seek an order that the original decision be quashed and the matter be sent back for re-determination. As noted, according to section 18.1(3)(b) of the Federal Courts Act, the Court may attach any directions it considers appropriate to an order referring the matter back for re-determination.

1338. *Groohi v. Canada (Minister of Citizenship and Immigration)*, [2009] FCJ. 988; 2009 FC 837 at para. 19.
1339. *Dhillon v. Canada (Minister of Citizenship and Immigration)*, [2009] FCJ. No. 794; 2009 FC 614 at para. 33.
1340. *Rudder v. Canada (Minister of Citizenship and Immigration)*, [2009] FCJ No. 852; 2009 FC 689.
1341. *Dhandal v. Canada (Minister of Citizenship and Immigration)*, [2009] FCJ No. 1029; 2009 FC 865.

II. Foreign Nationals Seeking to Enter Canada on a Permanent Basis

791. A similarly broad range of approaches to the standard of review has been expressed in relation to the decisions of visa officers to deny applications for a PRV. An application for a PRV may be denied on the ground that the individual does not meet the selection criteria. It may also be denied on the ground that the applicant is inadmissible. Moreover, these two separate reasons may overlap.

792. For example, in *Hilewitz*, the Supreme Court considered the case of an individual applying as an investor who, along with his family members, was denied a PRV because it was determined that his son might reasonably be expected to cause excessive demand on social services. The visa officer determined that his ability and intent to privately take care of his son's needs had no bearing on the issue of inadmissibility. This was held to be an error of law. It was noted that it is 'incongruous to interpret the legislation in such a way that the very assets that qualify investors and self-employed individuals for admission to Canada can simultaneously be ignored in determining the admissibility of their disabled children'.[1342]

793. Where a visa officer has denied a PRV on the basis that an applicant has not met prerequisites of eligibility or has not met the selection criteria or is not admissible, one may base an application for judicial review on the ground that the officer has misinterpreted the law, has failed to take into account relevant facts, has improperly taken into account irrelevant facts, or has exercised discretion unreasonably.

794. As with cases dealing with the denial of a TRV, in most circumstances where an individual is seeking judicial review of a denial of a PRV, the remedy sought will be an order quashing the original decision and sending the matter back for re-determination.

795. Where a foreign national who holds a PRV is denied status at a port of entry or by the ID of the IRB, the decision to issue a removal order may, in most circumstances, be appealed to the IAD. As discussed above, where a serious ground of inadmissibility is the reason for issuing a removal order, the IAD lacks jurisdiction to hear an appeal. Applicants who have exhausted available appeals may seek leave to apply for judicial review from the Federal Court.

796. Where an officer at a port of entry concludes that a Permanent Resident seeking entry into Canada has lost his status by failing to comply with the residency requirement, the resident will be issued a removal order. This decision may be appealed to the IAD.

797. Where the officer determines that there is another ground for concluding that the permanent resident has lost his status, the issue will be referred to the ID of

---

1342. *Hilewitz, supra* n. 876, at para. 40.

the IRB. Again the decision of that body may be appealed to the IAD, unless it is based on a serious ground of inadmissibility.

§3. Legal Remedies in Case of Administrative Decisions on the Right to Reside

798. Where a foreign national in Canada applies for an extension of their authorization to remain in Canada and it is refused, they may seek judicial review of the decision. Where the individual is successful, the decision will be quashed and sent back for re-determination.

799. Moreover, there are some circumstances where a foreign national may apply for permanent resident status from within Canada. The decision to reject such an application may be judicially reviewed on the grounds listed in the Federal Court Act.

800. As explained above, and subject to some exceptions, foreign nationals may also apply for Humanitarian and Compassionate relief under section 25 of the IRPA.

801. Where an application for judicial review of a humanitarian and compassionate decision is successful, the matter will normally be sent back for re-determination.

§4. Legal Remedies against Expulsion Measures

802. Where a removal order has been issued against a foreign national or a permanent resident, the immediate remedial concern is to get the order stayed while legal action against the order can be launched. The IRPA makes available statutory stays in a limited set of circumstances. For example, where the subject has been imprisoned the removal order will be stayed until the sentence is completed. However, there is no general statutory stay available to allow the person to challenge a removal order after it comes into force.

803. However, the Federal Court will grant an interim stay where a three-part test is met. To obtain a stay pending determination of a case on its merits, an applicant must establish all of the following three requirements:

(1) that there is a serious question to be tried;
(2) that he/she would suffer irreparable harm if the Court refused relief; and
(3) that the balance of convenience favours the applicant because he/she will suffer the greater harm from the refusal of the stay.[1343]

1343. See *RJR-MacDonald Inc. v. Canada (Attorney General)*, [1994] 1 SCR 311, [1994] SCJ No. 17; and *Omar v. Canada* (2009) FCJ No. 129.

804. In very limited circumstances, an individual may be able to argue successfully that a removal order infringes their constitutional rights. Although there is strong authority that the rights to life, liberty and security of the person, guaranteed by section 7 of the Charter are not normally engaged by removal, if the person faces persecution or the risk of torture after removal, the decision to deport them may be open to constitutional challenge. The Supreme Court of Canada has decided that the legal provision which permits the minister to deport an individual to face a risk of torture is not necessarily unconstitutional. Each exercise of the power must be examined on its own merits to determine whether the harm of torture to the individual is outweighed by the benefit to national security by deporting him.[1344]

805. In the absence of a constitutional challenge, an individual may seek legal redress in an appeal of a decision where such is available, or a judicial review of a decision relating to removal. In the special circumstance where a security certificate has been issued by the Minister of Citizenship and immigration and the Minister of Public Security and Emergency Preparedness, a Federal Court judge must determine whether or not the issuance of the certificate was reasonable.

806. An application for judicial review may relate to: (a) the decision to issue the removal order, (b) a decision that the person is ineligible to seek Canada's protection (including a decision by the Minister to issue an opinion that the individual is a danger to the public), (c) a decision of the RPD not to grant protection, (d) a decision of a PRRA officer not to grant protection or stay the removal order, (e) a decision not to grant an exemption on Humanitarian and Compassionate grounds, (f) a decision of the IAD where it had jurisdiction to consider an appeal, and (g) a decision of an enforcement officer relating to the reasonable practicability of enforcing the removal order.

807. Where a removal order has been issued, a successful application for judicial review will generally lead to the order being quashed.

§5. Procedural Safeguards

808. Canadian law offers two sources of procedural protection for individuals who are subject to government decisions relating to entry, residence and removal. First, section 7 of the Canadian Charter of Rights and Freedoms guarantees the right not to be deprived of the right to life, liberty and security of the person except in accordance with the principles of fundamental justice. Where a court accepts that the substantive rights of an individual are engaged by a legal decision, then it will examine and evaluate the legal procedures that were followed. Second, the Federal Court Act authorizes the Federal Court to grant relief where a decision-maker 'failed to observe a principle of natural justice, procedural fairness or other procedure that it was required by law to observe'. In applying this section the Federal Court relies on the common law doctrines of procedural fairness that have been

1344. *Suresh, supra* n. 721.

developed by the judiciary. Although there is a clear overlap between the constitutional standards of fundamental justice and the common law standards of procedural fairness, each will be examined in turn.

I. Constitutional Protections

809. In *Charkaoui,* the Supreme Court determined that the principles of fundamental justice to which reference is made in section 7 of the Charter[1345] are context dependent, and that their content will depend on the matters that are at stake.[1346] Thus, where, in a judicial proceeding evidence is kept confidential by the government, the fact that the underlying reason is national security is relevant to the determination whether the resulting procedure is fundamentally just. Nevertheless, the court determined that in the particular instance the failure to devise a process that would allow more extensive access to the information rendered the process unconstitutional. It stated:

> Yet, the secrecy required by the scheme denies the named person the opportunity to know the case put against him or her, and hence to challenge the government's case. This, in turn, undermines the judge's ability to come to a decision based on all the relevant facts and law.[1347]

In response to *Charkaoui*, the government enacted a regime whereby a security-cleared 'special advocate' was entitled to meet the named person, and then view and test the secret evidence in a closed hearing before the court. This process was upheld by the Supreme Court in *Harkat* as compliant with constitutional principles of fundamental justice.[1348]

810. The Supreme Court has also determined that the principles of fundamental justice apply to administrative decisions, including a Ministerial decision about whether to remove a person from Canada and expose them to the risk of torture. The Court noted the parallels between the constitutional standards of fundamental justice and the common law principles of fairness. In deciding the ambit of these principles it followed the leading case of *Baker*[1349] stating:

> More specifically, deciding what procedural protections must be provided involves a consideration of the following factors: (1) the nature of the decision made and the procedures followed in making it, that is, 'the closeness of the administrative process to the judicial process', (2) the role of the particular decision within the statutory scheme, (3) the importance of the decision to the individual affected, (4) the legitimate expectations of the person challenging

1345. Canadian Charter of Rights and Freedoms, Part I of the Constitution Act, 1982.
1346. *Charkaoui v. Canada (Minister of Citizenship and Immigration)* [2007] 1 SCR 350.
1347. *Ibid.* at para. 65.
1348. *Re: Harkat,* 2014 SCC 37.
1349. *Baker, supra* n. 1305.

> the decision where undertakings were made concerning the procedure to be followed, and (5) the choice of procedure made by the agency itself: ... . This is not to say that other factors or considerations may not be involved. This list of factors is non-exhaustive in determining the common law duty of fairness: ... It must necessarily be so in determining the procedures demanded by the principles of fundamental justice.[1350]

II. Procedural Fairness

811. Decided in 1999, *Baker* is a seminal case in which the Supreme Court fine-tuned an approach to administrative due process that it had been developing for over twenty years. The Court determined that, where legislation does not specify particular procedures to be followed by a decision-maker, when making a determination relating to the interests or rights of a party, it is appropriate to apply common law standards of procedural fairness. As the Court explained:

> The values underlying the duty of procedural fairness relate to the principle that the individual or individuals affected should have the opportunity to present their case fully and fairly, and have decisions affecting their rights, interests, or privileges made using a fair, impartial, and open process, appropriate to the statutory, institutional, and social context of the decision.[1351]

812. As noted above, the court specified a non-exhaustive list of five factors that should be considered when deciding the level of procedural protection that should be accorded.

813. First, one must consider the nature of the decision, and its resemblance to a judicial decision. The closer the resemblance, the more the procedural safeguards should resemble those accorded in a formal trial. Second, one must consider the nature of the statutory scheme and in particular the scope for an appeal. Where no appeal is available, the concern for procedural safeguards may be greater, although where an appeal is available it may be more important for the individual to receive reasons for the original decision. Third, the Court emphasized that the importance of the decision to the individuals affected should have a bearing on the procedures. The more important, the more stringent the procedures required. Fourth, the Court noted there was reason to accord particular protections to an individual where there had been created a legitimate expectation that they would be made available. Lastly, the Court noted that the choice of procedures made by the agency itself should be accorded a level of deference.

814. In *Baker*, the appellant had argued that she had been treated unfairly by the officer who had considered her application on Humanitarian and Compassionate grounds to be allowed to apply for permanent resident status from within Canada.

1350. *Suresh, supra* n. 721, at para. 115.
1351. *Baker supra* n. 1305, at para. 28.

She based her argument on the fact that she had Canadian children who would be affected by the result of her application and advocated that she was entitled to an oral interview before the decision-maker, notice to her children and their other parent of that interview, a right for the children and the other parent to make submissions at that interview, and notice to the other parent of the interview and of that person's right to have counsel present. She also alleged that procedural fairness required the provision of reasons by the decision-maker, and that comments in the notes of the officer give rise to a reasonable apprehension of bias.

815. In response, the court concluded that she was not entitled to an oral hearing, and that a procedure that allowed for written submissions was sufficient in the circumstances:

The Court stated:

> An interview is not essential for the information relevant to an H&C application to be put before an immigration officer, so that the humanitarian and compassionate considerations presented may be considered in their entirety and in a fair manner. In this case, the appellant had the opportunity to put forward, in written form through her lawyer, information about her situation, her children and their emotional dependence on her, and documentation in support of her application from a social worker at the Children's Aid Society and from her psychiatrist. These documents were before the decision-makers, and they contained the information relevant to making this decision. Taking all the factors relevant to determining the content of the duty of fairness into account, the lack of an oral hearing or notice of such a hearing did not, in my opinion, constitute a violation of the requirements of procedural fairness to which Ms. Baker was entitled in the circumstances, particularly given the fact that several of the factors point toward a more relaxed standard. The opportunity, which was accorded, for the appellant or her children to produce full and complete written documentation in relation to all aspects of her application satisfied the requirements of the participatory rights required by the duty of fairness in this case.[1352]

816. The appellant had also argued that she was entitled to detailed written reasons for the decision. The Court agreed that written reasons were an important component of procedural fairness. It stated:

> Reasons, it has been argued, foster better decision making by ensuring that issues and reasoning are well articulated and, therefore, more carefully thought out. The process of writing reasons for decision by itself may be a guarantee of a better decision. Reasons also allow parties to see that the applicable issues have been carefully considered, and are invaluable if a decision is to be appealed, questioned, or considered on judicial review. … In my opinion, it is

1352. *Ibid.* at para. 34.

> now appropriate to recognize that, in certain circumstances, the duty of procedural fairness will require the provision of a written explanation for a decision. The strong arguments demonstrating the advantages of written reasons suggest that, in cases such as this where the decision has important significance for the individual, when there is a statutory right of appeal, or in other circumstances, some form of reasons should be required. This requirement has been developing in the common law elsewhere. The circumstances of the case at bar, in my opinion, constitute one of the situations where reasons are necessary. The profound importance of an H&C decision to those affected, … militates in favour of a requirement that reasons be provided. It would be unfair for a person subject to a decision such as this one which is so critical to their future not to be told why the result was reached.[1353]

However, the Court concluded that Baker had actually received adequate reasons in the form of notes by the immigration officer who reviewed her file.

817. The Court did however conclude that comments made by the officer about Baker and her circumstances had given rise to a reasonable apprehension of bias. It stated:

> Procedural fairness also requires that decisions be made free from a reasonable apprehension of bias by an impartial decision-maker … The context here is one where immigration officers must regularly make decisions that have great importance to the individuals affected by them, but are also often critical to the interests of Canada as a country. They are individualized, rather than decisions of a general nature. They also require special sensitivity. … Because they necessarily relate to people of diverse backgrounds, from different cultures, races, and continents, immigration decisions demand sensitivity and understanding by those making them. They require a recognition of diversity, an understanding of others, and an openness to difference.
>
> In my opinion, the well-informed member of the community would perceive bias when reading Officer Lorenz's comments. His notes, and the manner in which they are written, do not disclose the existence of an open mind or a weighing of the particular circumstances of the case free from stereotypes. Most unfortunate is the fact that they seem to make a link between Ms. Baker's mental illness, her training as a domestic worker, the fact that she has several children, and the conclusion that she would therefore be a strain on our social welfare system for the rest of her life. In addition, the conclusion drawn was contrary to the psychiatrist's letter, which stated that, with treatment, Ms. Baker could remain well and return to being a productive member of society.[1354]

818. The impact of the *Baker* decision has been significant. The decisions of officers at every point in the immigration process from visa officer to enforcement

1353. *Ibid.* at paras 39–43.
1354. *Ibid.* at paras 45, 47, 48.

officers charged with removing individuals from the country have been challenged for failing to accord procedural fairness.

819. In general, cases have revolved around a number of central issues. The first is whether the individual has been given adequate notice of the issue to be decided or the concerns of the decision-maker. The general principle has stated effectively by Kelen J. in *Yuan:*

> While the duty of fairness does not necessarily require an oral hearing, there is a requirement that the visa officer provide the applicant with an opportunity to address a major concern, in other words, respond. The fact that the visa officer is of the opinion that there are many visa applicants from this location in China who apply for refugee status upon receiving the visa is not a fair or reasonable basis to dismiss all applicants from that region without providing a fair opportunity for the applicant to respond to this concern.[1355]

He also notes:

> While visa officers are legally entitled to apply their own experience toward a decision … a visa officer cannot stereotype an applicant based on that experience. …
> If officers wish to take into account outside information, particularly where that information leads to concerns/doubts about the applicant's bona-fides, they must be able to show that the applicant was made aware of the information taken into account and/or the concerns and was given an opportunity to address those concerns.[1356]

820. Similar themes are developed in *Bonilla*,[1357] where the applicant, a Colombian, had applied to attend high school in Canada. Her application for a TRV included additional family information, the acceptance letter from the school board, a copy of the applicant's birth certificate and passport, a notarized letter of authorization from her parents, an affidavit from her guardian indicating that he had accepted guardianship, and an affidavit from her guardian indicating that he was married to her sister, employed, earning over CAD 80,000 a year and would pay the applicant's tuition and living expenses. The affidavit also indicated that the applicant would leave Canada when her student status expired. Included with the affidavit were: a marriage certificate; proof of residence of the applicant's sister; employment and reference letters. The applicant was not interviewed by the visa officer who considered her application. The refusal letter indicated that visa officer found that attending high school in Canada would have a detrimental impact upon her ability to function in Colombia and that her separation from her culture during these formative years would motivate her to remain in Canada The applicant was

1355. *Yuan v. Canada (Minister of Citizenship and Immigration)*, 2001 FCT 1356, (2001) FCJ 1852 at para. 12.
1356. *Ibid.* at para. 13.
1357. (2007) FCJ 14.

therefore unable to establish that she would return to her home country where she was to be given a visa. O'Keefe J. determined that the visa officer's decision was based on stereotyping:

> This is not a case in which the applicant's application itself was incomplete, but a situation where the officer subjectively formed an opinion that the applicant would not return to Colombia following the completion of her studies. In my view, the officer in this situation should have allowed the applicant an opportunity to respond to his concerns. The applicant had no way of knowing that the visa officer would act upon his view that those in their 'formative years' may not study in Canada for a four year period, since they would be unlikely to leave the country. The visa officer's failure to give the applicant an opportunity to respond to his concerns, on the facts of this case, amounted to a breach of the rules of natural justice.[1358]

821. These cases reveal an important underlying distinction between, on the one hand, an incomplete application, where the applicant has failed to introduce sufficient evidence to show that he or she will leave Canada when required, and, on the other hand, a complete application which does not persuade the visa officer because the latter has concerns that the applicant has not addressed. In many circumstances, the distinction between these two will be difficult to draw and may depend on the reasonableness of the officer's concerns.

822. Recent jurisprudence has emphasized the lack of clarity in this area. For example, in *Ogunfowora,* Lagacé J. states:

> When no extrinsic evidence is relied on, it is unclear when it is necessary to afford an applicant an interview or a right to respond. However, the jurisprudence suggests that there will be right to respond under certain circumstances. In ... *Hassani v. Canada (M.C.I.),*[2006] F.C.J. No. 1597, 2006 FC 1283, the Court reviews the case law and highlights the uncertainty in the jurisprudence. In some cases, the officer was not required to put before the applicant any tentative conclusions he might be drawing from the material. Other cases have concluded that sometimes an applicant must have an opportunity to respond to concerns even where it arises out of the evidence tendered by the applicant.[1359]

On the other hand, in *Azali*, 2008 FC 517 where the officer refused a visa based on contradictions between the application and previous applications, Beaudry J. states:

> This is not a case where the Officer failed to confront the applicants with extrinsic evidence; rather, he relied on information which was not only known to the applicants, but supplied by them. Their duty of fairness does not require

1358. *Ibid.* at para. 27.
1359. *Ogunfowora v. Canada (Minister of Citizenship and Immigration),* [2007] FCJ No 637; 2007 FC 471 at para. 52.

that the applicants be confronted with information which they themselves supplied.[1360]

823. Decisions requiring that the individual be aware of the factors that influence a decision have had an impact on the practices of officers within the immigration bureaucracies. For example, where a medical officer after a medical examination has concerns about a visa applicant's health, the applicant is now entitled to a 'fairness letter' disclosing the nature of the concerns.

824. A related issue is whether the individual has had sufficient opportunity to present his or her case and to respond to the case against him or her? In *Chiau*,[1361] the Federal Court of Appeal considered the applicability of principles of procedural fairness where a visa application is being assessed. The appellant had been found to be inadmissible on the basis of confidential information that was not disclosed for reasons of security.

Evans J.A begins his analysis by noting that:

> It is trite law that the content of the duty of procedural fairness varies according to context: the concept of fairness is situational, not abstract or absolute. The Supreme Court of Canada [in *Baker*] has identified a number of factors to be taken into consideration in determining the content of the duty of fairness in any given situation.[1362]
>
> In relation to the first of these factors – the importance of the decision to the individual – Evans J.A. notes that the appellant did not have a right to a visa, nor did the appellant have any close connection with Canada that would render a refusal a hardship. He also takes into account the fact that the appellant could always apply again, and in that sense the decision was not final. In relation to the second factor – the resemblance of the process to that of adjudication, Evans J.A. states:
>
> visa officers do not hold adjudicative-type hearings before reaching their decisions: visa application interviews ... could not be mistaken for the kind of hearing conducted by most independent administrative tribunals. Officers' decisions are based in large part on the content of the file, supplemented by the interview.[1363]

Evans J.A. also held that considerations of the public interest counted against the appellant in the circumstances. In relation to the factual context, Evans J.A. made the following comments:

> Mr. Chiau was relatively well informed. He knew the legal basis on which the officer was minded to base his decision; he knew the organization of which he

---

1360. *Azali v.Canada (Minister of Citizenship and Immigration),* [2008] FCJ No 6742008 FC 517 at para. 26.

1361. *Chiau v. Canada (Minister of Citizenship and Immigration),* [2000] FCJ No 2043; [2001] 2 FC 297; Leave to appeal to SCC dismissed [2001] SCCA No 71.

1362. *Ibid.* at para. 36.

1363. *Ibid.* at para. 43.

> was suspected of being a member; he knew that the basis of this suspicion included his relationship with allegedly triad-controlled studios and their heads, and with another member of the triad. He was thus far from being in the dark about the officer's concerns, and could have attempted to assuage them ...[1364]

825. There has also been a significant amount of case law about the adequacy of reasons. For example, the *Leahy v. Canada,* the Federal Court of Appeal stated:

> If the reasons for decision are non-existent, opaque or otherwise indiscernible, and if the record before the administrative decision-maker does not shed light on the reasons why the administrative decision-maker decided or could have decided in the way it did, the requirement that administrative decisions be transparent and intelligible is not met.[1365]

826. Other factors that define procedural fairness include whether the individual has been accorded the opportunity to be represented by counsel; whether the individual has been provided with the services of a competent interpreter and whether the individual has been prejudiced by delay.

827. The Supreme Court has determined that the standard of review for issues relating to procedural fairness is correctness.[1366]

828. Where the Court finds that there has been a breach of procedural fairness the proper remedy is an order quashing the decision, with the matter being sent back for re-determination.

1364. *Ibid.* at paras 48–49.
1365. *Leahy v. Canada (Minister of Citizenship and Immigration),* 2012 FCA 227 at para 121.
1366. *Dunsmuir, supra* n. 1138, para. 129 per Binnie J.

Chapter 2. Legal Remedies in Case of Detention

829. See Part IV, Chapter 2

Part VII. Employment Rights

Chapter 1. Overview of Applicable Legislation

830. Non-citizens may apply to come as permanent residents under the category of family class, economic class or humanitarian-class. The general rules for admission under these classes are discussed above. Once admitted, permanent residents generally have the same employment rights as Canadians, except for those who must meet conditions imposed in accordance with their entry class. For example, business class immigrants who qualify as entrepreneurs must spend one of their first three years in Canada running a business that will create at least one full-time position in that business for a Canadian citizen or permanent resident, other than a family member.[1367] The emphasis in this part, however, will be on foreign nationals who come to Canada temporarily to work.

831. Non-citizens may come as temporary residents, who may be visitors, students or foreign workers. In general, temporary residents do not have the right to work in Canada unless authorized to do so. Foreign students have limited employment rights, for instance allowing them to work on-campus while studying.[1368] In most cases, foreign temporary workers must obtain work permits that tie them to specific employers.[1369] In recent years, the number of temporary foreign workers coming to Canada has shot up dramatically. The stock of temporary workers in Canada has risen from 125,010 in 2004 to 388,221 in 2012. The numbers of initial entries has risen from 112,228 in 2004 to 213,441 in 2012.[1370] Since 2008, the numbers of migrant workers entering on temporary permits has exceeded the numbers admitted as permanent residents. It has been widely alleged that the Temporary Foreign Worker programme was modified in recent years in ways that enabled employers to use it as a substitute for the backlog-ridden Federal Skilled Worker

1367. Regulations, s. 98. The full-time job requirement can be satisfied by several part-time positions, provided the total hours of paid work amounts to 1,950 hours per year Regulations, s. 98(1)(c).
1368. Regulations, s. 186(f).
1369. Regulations, ss 8(1), 186, 196; see also generally Part 11 of the Regulations.
1370. Citizenship and Immigration Canada, 'Facts and Figures 2012 – Immigration overview': online: http://www.cic.gc.ca/english/resources/statistics/facts2012/index.asp. See also, Alboim, Naomi, and Maytree 'Adjusting the Balance: Fixing Canada's Economic Immigration Policies' (Maytree Foundation, July 2009); online: http://www.maytree.com/wp-content/uploads/2009/07/adjustingthebalance-final.pdf.

Programme, and as a means for filling low-wage positions designated as 'low skill'. For example, the number of TFWs admitted in the food services, accommodation and retail trade sectors increased tenfold between 2005 and 2012.[1371]

1371. Employment and Social Development Canada, 'Labour Market Opinions – Annual Statistics', online: http://www.edsc.gc.ca/eng/jobs/foreign_workers/lmo_statistics/annual-industry.shtml.

Chapter 2. Conditions for Entitlement to Work

§1. General Conditions

832. Foreign nationals who 'work' in Canada in jobs that are normally compensated in general must be authorized by issuance of a permit or must fall into one of twenty-one exempted categories of workers. If a permit and visa are required, these usually must be obtained prior to entry into Canada after receiving a job offer from a Canadian employer.[1372] Some categories of persons may apply for a work permit from within Canada, such as foreign nationals applying for an extension; study-permit holders; and professionals, intra-company transferees, or traders or investors covered by the NAFTA.[1373]

833. An officer 'shall' – i.e., is required to – issue a work permit if it has been properly applied for; if satisfied the foreign national will leave Canada at the end of his or her authorized stay; if the foreign national needs to be and has been screened medically; and if the foreign national has been offered employment and the officer has determined that the 'offer is genuine and that the employment is likely to result in a neutral or positive effect on the labour market in Canada'.[1374] This last condition applies in most cases, but various exceptions exist for certain humanitarian-class foreign nationals and certain kinds of work, such as work covered by an international agreement or that advances Canadian interests.[1375]

834. An officer shall refuse to authorize an otherwise qualified application for a work or study permit if, according to instructions issued by the Minister, the applicant is 'at risk of being subjected to humiliating or degrading treatment, including sexual exploitation'.[1376] The intent of this provision is to prevent the admission of women otherwise eligible to enter as temporary foreign workers under the category of 'exotic dancer'.

835. A work permit will not be issued if there are reasonable grounds to believe the foreign national is unable to perform the work; if, in the case of employment in Québec, no *Certificat d'acceptation du Québec* has been issued; if employment of the foreign national is likely to disrupt an ongoing labour dispute or the employment of a permanent resident or Canadian national involved in that dispute; if the foreign national has failed to comply with the conditions of a previous work or study permit and less than six months have passed since the unauthorized work or

1372. Regulations, s. 8(1). Section 198 of the Regulations states foreign nationals may apply for a work permit at a point of entry if they come from a visa-exempt country. This exemption, however, only applies if no LMO is needed, and so will in general not apply.
1373. Regulations, s. 199.
1374. Regulations, s. 200(1).
1375. Regulations, ss 200(1)(c)(ii) and 204, 205. For the exemption from LMO, see Regulations, s. 203(1).
1376. IRPA, s. 30 1.1–1.6.

study has stopped;[1377] if the business is a strip club, escort service or massage parlour;[1378] or if the foreign national wants to enter Canada under the live-in-caregiver programme but has not met that programme's requirements.[1379] In addition, under new regulations implemented in 2011 and subject to limited exceptions, a work permit will not be issued to a foreign national who has worked temporarily in Canada for a cumulative period of four years.[1380] The 'four-in four-out' rule means that a temporary foreign worker is required to depart after four years and may not return for at least four years. However, employers are not subject to the same constraint, and so may replace temporary foreign workers who have departed with new temporary foreign workers indefinitely into the future.[1381]

§2. Administrative Rules and Procedures

836. The general rule is that a foreign national must apply for a TRV and work permit at a Canadian diplomatic office abroad before coming to Canada.[1382] To issue a work permit, an officer must determine whether the job offer is 'genuine' and whether the employment of the foreign national is likely to have a neutral or positive economic effect on the labour market in Canada on the basis of a LMO/LMIA provided by HRSDC/EDSC.[1383]

837. The LMO (now LMIA) is the most cumbersome step of the work permit application process. LMIAs provided by HRSDC (now ESDC) on the effect of a job on the Canadian labour market are to be based on six factors: (1) whether employment of the foreign national is likely to result in job creation or job retention for Canadian citizens or permanent residents, (2) whether employment of the foreign national is likely to lead to the creation or transfer of skills or knowledge for the benefit of Canadian citizens or permanent residents, (3) whether employment of the foreign national is likely to fill a labour shortage, (4) whether wages offered to the foreign national match prevailing wage rates and whether conditions at the proposed workplace meet generally accepted Canadian standards, (5) whether the employer has made or agreed to make reasonable efforts to hire or train Canadian

1377. There are exemptions to this requirement. For example, work permits will be issued to foreign nationals provided they only breach conditions specifically imposed by an officer when admitting them for temporary residence; in the case of refugee claimants or foreign nationals subject to an unenforceable removal order; or in the case of foreign nationals subsequently issued a temporary resident permit under s. 24(1) of IRPA: Regulations, s. 200(3)(e)(ii), (iii), and (iv).

1378. See CIC, 'Temporary Foreign Worker Program and International Mobility Program: Protecting workers from abuse and exploitation', http://www.cic.gc.ca/english/resources/tools/temp/work/vulnerable.asp (accessed 1 Feb. 2015).

1379. Regulations, s. 200(3).

1380. Regulations, s. 200(3)(g).

1381. See also, Regulations Amending the Immigration and Refugee Protection Regulations (Temporary Foreign Workers), Canada Gazette, Vol. 144, no. 17, 18 Aug. 2010, online: http://gazette.gc.ca/rp-pr/p2/2010/2010-08-18/html/sor-dors172-eng.html; and, Citizenship and Immigration Canada, 'Backgrounder – Four-year limit for foreign nationals working in Canada', online: http://www.cic.gc.ca/english/department/media/backgrounders/2011/2011-03-24.asp.

1382. Regulations, ss 8(1), 197.

1383. Regulations, ss 200, 203.

citizens or permanent residents, and (6) whether employment of the foreign national is likely to adversely affect settlement of labour dispute in progress or the employment of any person involved in a dispute.[1384] As part of its efforts to prevent exploitation of foreign workers, the government in April 2009 stopped granting LMO extensions. Employers must now apply for a new LMIA when the previous one has expired. Further, under the new regulations implemented in October 2011, LMO/ LMIAs issued by HRSDC will indicate whether an employer has failed to comply with any terms of employment offered to foreign workers in the past two years and include an expiration date after which the opinion will no longer be valid.[1385]

838. There are several exceptions to the LMIA requirement. No LMIA is required: (1) if the job would create or maintain significant social, cultural, or economic benefits or opportunities for Canadian citizens or permanent residents; (2) if it would create or maintain reciprocal employment for Canadian citizens or permanent residents abroad; (3) if the permit is sought by a refugee claimant or protected person or if certain other humanitarian concerns are present; (4) if the Minister has designated the job as related to a research, educational or training programme for which 'limited access to Canadian labour market is necessary for reasons of public policy relating to the competitiveness of Canada's academic institutions or economy'; or (5) if the job is of a religious or charitable nature.[1386] International reciprocal employment arrangements falling under ministerial designation range from high-level trade agreements such as the NAFTA or the GATS to such narrowly tailored endeavours as the International Pacific Halibut Commission, a Malaysian accounting trainee programme, and the North American Cooperative Waterfowl Survey and Banding Programme.[1387] If no LMO is required, in some cases an individual may be issued an open work permit. Open permits may be unrestricted or restricted to a particular occupation or occupations.[1388]

839. In practice, an employer will generally receive a favourable LMIA and work permit for the foreign national if it has advertised in a manner consistent with industry practices for jobs of similar skill levels and posted its opening for at least fourteen days in an online national job bank maintained by the government.[1389] LMIAs may be unfavourable if it is determined that temporary employment of a foreign national will disrupt an ongoing strike or lockout. The Regulations also state that work permits can be refused if:

> the specific work that the foreign national intends to perform is likely to adversely affect the settlement of any labour dispute in progress or the employment of any person involved in the dispute, unless all or almost all of the workers involved in the labour dispute are not Canadian citizens or permanent

1384. Regulations, s. 203(3).
1385. Regulations, ss 203 (2), (2.1) and (3.1).
1386. Regulations, s. 205.
1387. For a listing of international agreements under which LMOs are not required, see Citizenship and Immigration Canada, Operational Manual FWI, at ss 5.26–5.27.
1388. *Ibid.* s. 10.1.
1389. Service Canada Job Bank, available online at: http://www.jobbank.gc.ca/.

> residents and the hiring of workers to replace the workers involved in the labour dispute is not prohibited by the Canadian law applicable in the province where the workers involved in the labour dispute are employed ...[1390]

Another situation that can occur involves authorized temporary foreign workers caught up in a strike at their place of employment. In such cases, the Ministry allows temporary foreign workers to remain in Canada on strike pay for the length of their permit, or seek other employment and apply for a new work permit.[1391] A temporary foreign worker who cannot or does not want to change jobs but is worried about falling out of status must apply for an extension. Filing of the application provides the temporary foreign worker with implied status for at least four months until a decision is made on their application.[1392]

840. In 2011, the government implemented new regulations to govern the assessment of when a job offer would be considered genuine. These factors include: (1) whether the employer is actively engaged in the business in respect of which the offer is made, (2) whether the offer is consistent with the reasonable employment needs of the employer, (3) whether the offer's terms can be reasonably fulfilled by the employer, and (4) past compliance of the employer or of the employer's recruiter with legislation regulating employment and the recruitment of employees. An offer will not be deemed genuine if an employer in the two years previous has provided a foreign national with wages or working conditions significantly different from those offered; has employed a foreign national in an occupation significantly different than that which was offered. Also, any offer made by an employer who has had a previous offer deemed not genuine for either of the first two reasons will also be deemed not genuine. The Ministry is to maintain a list on its website of employers whose offers have been deemed not genuine. The effect of these amendments will be to suspend an employer from eligibility to hire temporary foreign workers for two years following a violation of the terms of employment offered to a temporary foreign worker.[1393]

841. All temporary residents are required to leave Canada by the end of their authorized stay and are not permitted to work or study unless they hold valid permits.[1394] The default period for temporary resident authorization is six months, although an officer at a port of entry can stipulate a different duration based, among other things, on the applicant's means of support or length of programme of study.[1395] Officers may impose other conditions, such as limits on travel within

1390. Regulations, s. 200(3).
1391. Citizenship and Immigration Canada, Operational Manual FWI, *Temporary Foreign Worker Guidelines*, s. 8.2.
1392. See, Citizenship and Immigration Canada, Operational Manual OP11, *Temporary Resident*, *Ibid.* s. 24.
1393. Regulations, ss 200(1)(c), 200(5), 203(5) and (6).
1394. For these conditions, see IRPA, ss 29(2) and 30(1); Regulations, s. 183.
1395. Regulations, s. 183(2).

Canada.[1396] In practice, many temporary residents extend their status, transfer to another temporary status or become permanent residents.

§3. Conditions for Special Categories of Workers

842. In July 2002, the government launched a pilot project for hiring lower-skilled foreign workers temporarily. These were workers in jobs that need at most a high school diploma or two years' training. Work permits can be issued in such cases for a maximum of twenty-four months. Initially, foreign nationals then had to return home for a minimum of four months 'to ensure that [temporary foreign workers] maintained a connection with their home country'.[1397] Under changes that came into effect in May 2009, however, foreign workers were allowed to apply for new permits from within Canada so long as their employer procures a new LMO, a new employment contract is signed, the original work permit has not expired (and the cumulative four-year cap, if applicable, has not been reached).[1398] Employers seeking to take advantage of the low-skilled foreign worker programme in a unionized workplace must offer wages comparable to those provided in the collective agreement. They must also extend the same benefits to the foreign workers as to Canadian or permanent resident employees. Employers must help foreign workers find suitable accommodation and provide medical coverage until they become eligible for coverage under provincial health plans. Finally, they must cover transportation costs.[1399]

843. The 'four-in four-out' rule limits the length of a temporary foreign worker's sojourn in Canada to four years. This is a means of ensuring that individual workers remain in Canada temporarily, even if demand for their work is indeterminate 'low skill' temporary foreign workers do not enjoy labour mobility. They are tied to a single employer and not permitted to seek the same job with a different employer or move into a different occupational sector.

844. Beginning in 2013, the TFW programme sparked significant public controversy. Media reports revealed that some Canadian employers were not hiring, or even firing, Canadian and permanent resident employees in favour of using the TFW programme to secure cheaper and more compliant temporary foreign workers.[1400] The government responded by announcing several changes to the

1396. Regulations, s. 185.
1397. Citizenship and Immigration Canada, Operational Bulletin 113 (12 May 2009), online: http://www.cic.gc.ca/english/resources/manuals/bulletins/2009/ob113.asp.
1398. *Ibid.* and 'Changes to the Temporary Foreign Worker Program- Pilot for Occupations Requiring Lower Levels of Formal Training', online: http://www.cic.gc.ca/english/work/low-skill.asp.
1399. Employment and Social Development Canada, *Stream for Lower-skilled Occupations*, (23 Jun. 2014), available online at: http://www.esdc.gc.ca/eng/jobs/foreign_workers/lower_skilled/index.shtml.
1400. See, e.g., CBC News, 'McDonald's Accused of Favouring Foreign Workers', 14 Apr. 2014, online: http://www.cbc.ca/news/canada/british-columbia/mcdonald-s-accused-of-favouring-foreign-workers-1.2598684; 'Foreign Worker Reports Death Threats, Coercion', 4 May 2014, online: http:

programme, mainly in relation to those in 'low wage' occupations. The reforms, which go into effect at various times, include the following: First, the LMO was renamed as LMIA and made more rigorous. Second, the proportion of low-wage temporary foreign workers that an employer may hire will be capped. Third, no 'low skill' work permits in the food, accommodation or retail sectors will be issued in regions with more than 6% unemployment. Fourth, fees for LMIAs will be increased. Fifth, the length of a single work permit will be reduced to one year (from two). Fifth, the government proposes to improve enforcement of applicable rules, including by increasing inspections and penalties for employers who violate the rules. [1401]

845. Since 1966, the government has also operated a targeted programme for recruitment of agricultural workers for seasonal work. In the first year, 263 farm workers first came over from Jamaica. Under long-standing international memoranda of understanding, agricultural workers from Mexico and eleven Caribbean countries may be hired to work in British Columbia, Alberta, Saskatchewan, Manitoba, Ontario, Québec, New Brunswick, Nova Scotia and Prince Edward Island (the excluded province – Newfoundland – and the territories have limited agriculture.) In 2012, there were almost 30,000 seasonal agricultural worker programme permit holders.[1402] Foreign workers can only be hired if Canadian recruiting has been unsuccessful. The job offer must be for at least 240 hours of work over six weeks or less, for a maximum duration of eight months between 1 January and 15 December, by which date every worker must be repatriated. The workers must receive free housing with a usable kitchen[1403] and must be paid prevailing wages or the rate being paid by the employer to Canadians doing the same work. An LMO is required under the programme.

//www.cbc.ca/news/canada/british-columbia/foreign-worker-reports-death-threats-coercion-1.2630278; See also Fay Faraday, 'Made in Canada: How the Law Constructs Migrant Workers' Insecurity', September 2012, online: http://metcalffoundation.com/wp-content/uploads/2012/09/Made-in-Canada-Full-Report.pdf; 'Profiting from the Precarious: How Recruitment Practices Exploit Migrant Workers', April 2014, online: http://metcalffoundation.com/wp-content/uploads/2014/04/Profiting-from-the-Precarious.pdf.

1401. Employment and Social Development Canada, 'New Reforms for the Temporary Foreign Worker Program', 11 Jul. 2014, online: http://www.esdc.gc.ca/eng/jobs/foreign_workers/reform/highlights.shtml.

1402. Employment and Social Development Canada, 'Labour Market Opinions –Annual Statistics: Number of temporary foreign worker positions on positive labour market opinions under the Agricultural. Occupations, by location of employment', 24 Jan. 2014, online: http://www.esdc.gc.ca/eng/jobs/foreign_workers/lmo_statistics/annual-agriculture.shtml

1403. Except in British Columbia: see Employment and Social Development Canada, *Hiring Seasonal Agricultural Workers* (20 Jun. 2014), online at: http://www.esdc.gc.ca/eng/jobs/foreign_workers/agriculture/seasonal/index.shtml.

Chapter 3. Sanctions against Illegal Labour Market Participation

§1. Sanctions against Employers

846. The IRPA provides for a fine of up to CAD 50,000 or imprisonment for up to two years for anyone that 'employs a foreign national in a capacity in which the foreign national is not authorized ... to be employed'. Under this provision, a person who fails to exercise due diligence to determine whether employment is authorized is deemed to know that it is not.[1404] It is unclear how many prosecutions there have been under these provisions, if any. A recent report by the Auditor General of Canada concluded: '[T]here has been no systematic follow-up by either [CIC] or [Human Resources and Skills Development Canada] to verify that employers are complying with the terms and conditions under which the LMO application was approved, such as wages to be paid and accommodations to be provided.'[1405] (The exception to this was a pilot project in Alberta and British Columbia for the issuance of LMOs electronically. Employers who sign on to the pilot project must consent to compliance reviews demonstrating adherence to wages, working conditions standards, recruitment efforts and other requirements.[1406])

847. The Ministry's position is that neither the Act nor the Regulations provide authority for compliance reviews of employers who have not consented.[1407] It has also generally failed to provide formal evaluations of programmes where abuse is foreseeable, such as the Live-in Caregiver Programme or the Low-Skilled Temporary Worker Pilot Project.[1408]

848. The government has been criticized for failing to ensure that employers are not exploiting or abusing temporary foreign workers by violating commitments made to workers or in the LMO process.[1409] Regulations address concerns about employers who fail to abide by their commitments to foreign temporary workers, for instance, by paying them less than promised, providing substandard working conditions or allowing third-party agents to charge fees to workers in contravention of provincial or territorial legislation.

849. In the past, assessments of the genuineness of a job offer rarely occurred.[1410] The proposed measures set out a list of factors to be considered by

1404. IRPA, ss 124(1)(c) and (2) and 125.
1405. Office of the Auditor General of Canada, Report of the Auditor General of Canada to the House of Commons, Ch. 2, 'Selecting Foreign Workers under the Immigration Program' (Fall 2009) at p. 33.
1406. *Ibid.* at p. 33.
1407. *Ibid.* at p. 34.
1408. *Ibid.* at p. 34.
1409. See, e.g., Report of the Standing Committee on Citizenship and Immigration, Temporary Foreign Workers and Non-Status Workers (May 2009 – 40th Parliament, 2nd Session), Ch. 4; see also Alberta Federation of Labour, Entrenching Exploitation (April 2009) at 6.
1410. Report of the Auditor General of Canada to the House of Commons (Fall 2009) at p. 32.

officers when deciding, as required in the Regulations,[1411] if a job offer is genuine. These factors include: (1) whether the employer is actively engaged in the business in respect of which the offer is made, (2) whether the offer is consistent with the reasonable employment needs of the employer, (3) whether the offer's terms can be reasonably fulfilled by the employer, and (4) the past compliance of the employer or of the employer's recruiter with legislation regulating employment and the recruitment of employees.

850. In addition, an offer will be deemed not genuine if an employer in the two years previous has provided a foreign national with wages or working conditions significantly different from those offered; has employed a foreign national in a significantly different occupation than offered; or has, in the past two years, had an offer deemed not genuine for either of the first two reasons. LMO/LMIAs issued by ESDC are supposed to reflect whether the employer has failed to comply with the terms of employment offered in the past two years. They will also expire in six months. Finally, the Ministry is to maintain a list on its website of employers whose offers have been deemed not genuine. The effect of these amendments will be to suspend an employer from eligibility to hire temporary foreign workers for two years following a violation of the terms of employment offered to a temporary foreign worker. As a result of the controversy that erupted in early 2014 regarding abuse of the Temporary Foreign Worker programme, the government announced administrative measures to enhance detection, enforcement and punishment of offending employers.[1412]

851. Section 124(1)(c) makes it an offence to employ a foreign national in a capacity not authorized under the Act; in this last case, a person who fails to exercise due diligence will be deemed to know that employment is not authorized.[1413] It is punishable on indictment by a fine of not more than CAD 50,000 or imprisonment of not more than two years, or both; and, on summary conviction, by a fine of not more than CAD 10,000 or to imprisonment of not more than six months, or both.[1414]

§2. Sanctions against Workers

852. Foreign nationals working without authorization may be inadmissible for non-compliance with the Act or Regulations.[1415] There is no requirement that non-compliance be intentional, however the Operational Manual directs officers to keep

1411. Regulations, ss 200(1)(c)(iii) and 203(1), entered into force January 2013.
1412. Employment and Social Development Canada, 'Reforming the Temporary Foreign Worker Program: Tougher Enforcement and Penalties', 26 Jun. 2014, online: http://www.esdc.gc.ca/eng/jobs/foreign_workers/reform/enforce.shtml.
1413. IRPA, s. 124(2).
1414. IRPA, s. 125.
1415. IRPA, s. 41(a). See also, Citizenship and Immigration Canada, Operational Manual ENF2, s. 10.1.

in mind 'the person's character, intent, motivation and other equally important factors that led to the person's contravention of the law' when deciding on an enforcement action.[1416] Workers found inadmissible for non-compliance may be subject in most cases to exclusion orders for failing to comply with the Act.[1417] Under exclusion orders, foreign nationals must obtain written authorization to return to Canada for one year following departure.[1418] Deportation orders, under which authorization will always be required to return to Canada, will be imposed under certain circumstances, for example, if a removal order has previously been issued on the same ground[1419] or if a foreign national has returned to Canada without the required written authorization.[1420] Removals are processed by immigration officers and either ordered on an expedited basis by a delegate of the Minister of Public Safety or, in more complex cases, by the ID of the IRB.

853. Section 122(1) of the Act creates various criminal offences relating to documentation fraud. It is an offence to: (1) possess a passport, visa or other document, Canadian or not, in order to contravene the Act; (2) use any such document in order to contravene the Act, including for the purpose of entering or remaining in Canada; or (3) import, export, or deal in such a document in contravention of the Act. Possession is an indictable offence punishable by imprisonment of up to five years. Use and dealing in such documents are indictable offences punishable by imprisonment of up to fourteen years.[1421] Contravention in association with a criminal organization or for profit, even if no profit was realized, will be considered aggravating factors in sentencing.[1422] Asylum seekers who come to Canada directly or indirectly from the country where they claim to face danger may not be charged under this provision pending resolution of their claim or if refugee protection is granted.[1423] That means that asylum seekers who do not come from the country where they face danger and those whose claims are refused are liable to prosecution.

854. Section 124(1) creates several general offences for non-compliance with the Act that may apply to foreign nationals who work illegally in Canada. It is an offence under section 124(1)(a) to contravene any provision of the Act for which a penalty is not specifically provided or to fail to comply with any condition or obligation imposed under the Act.[1424] Section 124(1)(b) makes it an offence to escape or attempt to escape from lawful custody or detention under the Act. These offences are punishable on indictment by a fine of not more than CAD 50,000 or imprisonment of not more than two years, or both; and, on summary conviction, by a fine of not more than CAD 10,000 or to imprisonment of not more than six months, or

1416. ENF2 at s. 10.1.
1417. Regulations, ss 228(1)(c) and 229(1)(n).
1418. Regulations, s. 225(1).
1419. Regulations, s. 229(3)(a).
1420. Regulations, s. 228(1)(c)(ii).
1421. IRPA, s. 123(1).
1422. IRPA, s. 123(2).
1423. IRPA, s. 133.
1424. Transportation companies will not be liable under this heading if they can show they exercised due diligence: see IRPA, s. 124(3).

both.[1425] Again, asylum seekers who come to Canada directly or indirectly from the country where they claim to face danger may not be charged for general contraventions of the Act pending resolution of their claim or if refugee protection is granted.[1426]

1425. IRPA, s. 125.
1426. IRPA, s. 133.

Chapter 4. Legal Remedies and Procedural Safeguards

855. Foreign nationals fighting removal will have recourse to certain forms of appeal, judicial review, and equitable relief, described above in detail. Inadmissibility decisions may be appealed to the IAD of the IRB. Negative decisions by the IAD may, with leave, be the subject of judicial review applications before the Federal Court, and thereafter of appeals to the Federal Court of Appeal and the Supreme Court of Canada. Foreign nationals may also apply for equitable relief in the form of TRPs under section 24(1) of the Act; humanitarian and compassionate applications under section 25(1) of the Act; and, for those facing removal, applications for protection following a PRRA. To an extent, applications for refugee protection may serve as a means of curing less serious grounds of inadmissibility.

Selected Bibliography

Adelman, Howard. 'Refugees and Border Security Post-September 11'. *Refuge* 20, no. 4 (2002): 5–14. Online: <http://www.yorku.ca/crs/Refuge/back%20issues%20online.htm>.

Alboim, Naomi & Karen Cohl. 'Shaping the Future: Canada's Rapidly Changing Immigration Policies'. Toronto: Maytree, 2012. Online: <http://maytree.com/wp-content/uploads/2012/10/shaping-the-future.pdf>.

Alboim, Naomi, Ross Finne & Ronald Meng. 'The Discounting of Immigrants' Skills in Canada: Evidence and Policy Recommendations'. *IRPP Choices*, 11, no. 2 (2005). Online: <http://www.irpp.org/indexe.htm>.

Avery, Donald. *Dangerous Foreigners*. Toronto: McClelland and Stewart, 1979.

Basok, Tanya. *Tortillas and Tomatoes: Transmigrant Mexican Harvesters in Canada*. Montreal and Kingston: McGill-Queen's University Press, 2002.

Beach, Charles M., Alan G. Green & Jeffrey G. Reitz, (eds). *Canadian Immigration Policy for the 21st Century*. Montreal and Kingston: McGill-Queen's University Press, 2003.

Bossin, Michael & Laila Demirdache, 'A Canadian Perspective on the Subjective Component of the Bipartite test for "Persecution": Time for Re-evaluation'. *Refuge* 22, no. 1 (2004): 108–118. Online: <http://pi.library.yorku.ca/ojs/index.php/refuge/article/viewFile/21322/19993>.

Brem, Max. *Migrant Workers in Canada: A Review of the Canadian Seasonal Agricultural Workers Program*. Policy Brief, Ottawa: North – South Institute, 2006. Online: <http://www.nsi-ins.ca/content/download/MigrantWorkers_Eng_Web.pdf>.

Carasco, Emily and Sharryn Aiken, Donald Galloway & Audrey Macklin. *Immigration and Refugee Law: Cases, Materials and Commentary*. Toronto: Emond Montgomery Publications, 2007.

Collacott, Martin. 'Canada's Immigration Policy: The Need for Major Reform'. *Public Policy Sources* No. 64. 2nd ed. Vancouver: The Fraser Institute, 2003. Online: <http://www.fraserinstitute.ca/admin/books/files/immigration-2ndEdition.pdf>.

Côté, Andrée, MichèleKérisit & Marie-Louise Côté. Part III: Sponsorship and the Equality Rights of Immigrant Women; 'Sponsorship… For Better or For Worse: The Impact of Sponsorship on the Equality Rights of Immigrant Women' (March 2001), Online: Status of Women Canada: <http://www.swc-cfc.gc.ca/pubs/0662296427/200103_0662296427_15_e.html>.

Crépeau, François. 'Anti-Terrorism Measures and Refugee Law Challenges in Canada'. *Refugee Survey Quarterly* 29, no. 4 (2010): 31–44.

Crépeau, François & Nakache, Delphine, 'Controlling Irregular Migration in Canada: Reconciling Security Concerns with Human Rights Protection'. *IRPP Choices* 12 (2006): 1–44.

Dauvergne, Catherine. *Humanitarianism, Identity and Nation: Migration Laws of Australia and Canada*. Vancouver: UBC Press, 2005.

Dyzenhaus, David & Mayo Moran, eds. *Calling Power to Account: Law, Reparations, and the Chinese Canadian Head Tax Case*. Toronto: University of Toronto Press, 2005.

Dyzenhaus, David ed. *The Unity of Public Law*. Portland Oregon: Hart Publishing, 2004.

Eliadis, Pearl F. 'The Swing from Singh: The Narrowing Application of the Charter in Immigration Law'. *Imm. L.R.* (2d) 26 (1995): 130.

Galloway, Donald *Immigration Law* Toronto: Irwin Law, 1997.

Harvard Law Student Advocates for Human Rights *et al*. 'Bordering on Failure: The US-Canada Safe Third Country Agreement Fifteen Months After Implementation', 2006 Online: <http://www.law.harvard.edu/academics/clinical/asylum_law/Harvard_STCA_ Report.pdf>.

Hawkins, Freda. *Critical Years in Immigration: Canada and Australia Compared*. Kingston: McGill-Queen's University Press, 1991.

Heckman, Gerald. 'Canada's Refugee Determination System and the International Norm of Independence'. *Refuge* 25, no. 2 (2008): 79–102. Online: <http://pi.library.yorku.ca/ojs/index.php/refuge/article/viewFile/26033/24066>.

House of Commons, Standing Committee on Citizenship and Immigration. Report 4 – 'Competing for Immigrants' June, 2002. Online: <http://cmte.parl.gc.ca/cmte/CommitteePublication.aspx?COM=212&Lang=1&SourceId=37302>.

Hrick, Pamela. 'A Dangerous Step Backwards: The Implications of Conditional Permanent Resident Status for Sponsored Immigrant Women in Abusive Relationships'. *Dalhousie Journal of Legal Studies* (Forthcoming 2012): 21.

Immigration Legislative Review Advisory Group. *Not Just Numbers: A Canadian Framework for Future Immigration*. Ottawa: Minister of Public Works, 1997. Online: <http://www.chba.ca/uploads/Policy%20Archive/1998/1998-02-28.pdf>.

Jones, Martin & Sasha Baglay. *Refugee Law*. Toronto: Irwin Law, 2007.

Kelley, Ninette & Michael J. Trebilcock. *The Making of the Mosaic: A History of Canadian Immigration Policy* (2nd ed.). Toronto: University of Toronto Press, 2010.

Knowles, Valerie. *Strangers at Our Gates: Canadian Immigration and Immigration Policy, 1540-2006*. Toronto: Dundurn Press, 2008.

Li WaiSuen, Rachel. 'You sure Know How to Pick 'Em: Human Rights and Migrant Farm Workers in Canada'. *Geo. Immigr. L.J.* 15 (Fall 2000): 199.

Li, Peter S. *Destination Canada, Immigration Debates and Issues*. Don Mills, ON: Oxford University Press, 2003.

Macklin, Audrey. '*Ward v. Canada*: A Review Essay'. *International Journal of Refugee Law* 6 (1994): 362–381.

Macklin, Audrey. 'Foreign Domestic Worker: Surrogate Housewife or Mail Order Servant?' *McGill Law Journal* 37 (1992): 681–760.

Madsen, Lene. 'Second Class: Law Meets Family in the Immigration Context'. *Canadian Family Law Quarterly* 21 (2003): 103.

Powell, John. *Encyclopedia of North American Immigration*. New York: Facts On File, 2005.

Rehaag, Sean. 'The Luck of the Draw? Judicial Review of Refugee Determinations in the Federal Court of Canada'. (2005-2010) (forthcoming) *Queen's Law Journal.*

Reitz, Jeffrey G. 'Pro-immigration Canada: Social and Economic Roots of Popular Views'. (2011) 20 IRPP Study, Montreal: Institute for Research on Public Policy. Online: <http://www.irpp.org/pubs/IRPPstudy/IRPP_Study_no20.pdf>.

Sharma. Nandita. *Home Economics: Nationalism and the Making of 'Migrant Workers' in Canada*. Toronto: University of Toronto Press, 2006.

Showler, Peter. *Refugee Sandwich: Stories of Exile and Asylum*. Montreal and Kingston: McGill-Queen's University Press, 2006.

Stoffman, Daniel. *Who Gets In: What's Wrong with Canada's Immigration Program and How to Fix It.*Toronto: Macfarlane, Walter and Ross, 2002.

Verma, Veena. 'The Mexican and Caribbean Seasonal Agricultural Workers Program: Regulatory and Policy Framework, Farm Industry Level Employment Practices, and the Future of the Program under Unionization'. Ottawa: North-South Institute, 2003.

Waldman, Lorne. *Immigration and Refugee Law Practice.* Markham ON: LexisNexis Canada, 2012.

Walker, Barrington. *The History of Immigration and Racism in Canada: Essential Readings*. Toronto: Canadian Scholars' Press, 2008.

Zambelli, Pia. 'Problematic Trends in the Analysis of State Protection and Article 1F(a) Exclusion in Canadian Refugee Law'. *International Journal of Refugee Law* (2011): 252–270.

Zambelli, Pia. *Immigration Law and Practice.* 2nd edn. LexisNexis Canada, 2005.

Selected Bibliography

Index

The numbers here refer to paragraph numbers.

www.ingramcontent.com/pod-product-compliance
Lightning Source LLC
Chambersburg PA
CBHW071426230926
51846CB00001B/136
* 9 7 8 9 0 4 1 1 6 0 1 3 3 *